ESSENTIAL WOODWORKING HAND TOOLS

Paul Sellers

ROKESMITH LIMITED

ESSENTIAL WOODWORKING HAND TOOLS

Published by Rokesmith Limited.

A CIP Catalogue record for this publication is available from the British Library.

ISBN for this publication: 978-0-9934423-0-8

This book was printed for Rokesmith Limited in the United Kingdom by the Pureprint Group. The printing facility has most operations under one roof and employs mainly local people. It is certified to ISO 9001 and produces carbon neutral publications. The ink used for this book is 100% vegetable-based and the paper is Essential Velvet FSC, which is produced from 100% Elemental Chlorine Free (ECF) pulp that is fully recyclable. The paper has a Forest Stewardship Council (FSC) accreditation and is produced by a mill that supports well-managed forestry schemes.

This book is dedicated to the memory of my father,
Joseph Eric Sellers (1925–2012).

SAFETY NOTICE

Woodworking can be dangerous if you do not take appropriate care. You should adopt the following precautions to ensure your safety and the safety of others:

- Ensure that you have sufficient skills and experience to use the tools and equipment before commencing any task.
- Have and use a safe and suitable place to work, with adequate space to carry out the task.
- Have and use appropriate safety wear and devices for the task.
- Have all due regard for the safety of others.
- Do not leave tools or equipment unattended.
- Carry out tasks away from unsupervised children and vulnerable adults.
- If you involve children or vulnerable adults in woodworking tasks only allow them to work with tools that are safe and appropriate for the task and which are matched to the ability of the user.

Contents

ACKNOWLEDGEMENTS

In a written work such as this, where many creative talents merge into a single volume, the work of many artists often lies hidden behind the text and images that are developed to express the content. This is my opportunity to thank everyone who helped me in the ambition I had to write about and draw the tools I have used for a lifetime.

In February 1965 my mentoring craftsman, George Mycock, took me under his wing for five years to guide me through my apprenticeship. In my journeyman years Derek Pott continued the work and he and I are still friends. Now, 50 years on, the heart of those years has become the work surrounding this volume and much more beyond. I would like to thank my son, Joseph, for the insight and sensitivity he brought in diligently editing each page, as no other editor could. He and I have worked together most days since he could barely stand at a bench vise. He is the only person I know who understands my feelings on the significance of hand tools, hand skills, and what hand work can mean to our wellbeing. My wife, Liz, deserves my greatest thanks for her unending support, over many decades, knowing my dedication to woodworking.

This book has relied on many behind-the-scenes people, who became friends through the work. They came to form a dependable team of highly gifted people, unswerving in the task of pulling together the missing pieces to compliment everything I have striven for. Phil Adams has worked alongside me every day throughout the process. He helped with the photo needs at the drop of a hat and listened to endless sentences and phrases to see if I had made any sense of things at all. The top-notch photography in the full-page images and banner images at the beginning of each chapter is self evident and easily picked out from the rest. These, as well as the images on the dust jacket, came from the critical eye and skilled photography composed by Ryan Cowan, who captured the detail I wanted to make the book an all-inclusive resource for woodworkers around the world. For the graphics layout I thank Michael Ward, who understood the inner workings that brought the book to life. He has captured the theme behind everything Joseph and I worked through to produce the pages we wanted. Writing any book ultimately makes you a writer, whether this comes naturally or not. Emily Bacon might tell you that my gift is working with wood and not writing, as she has spent many hours refining the pages. She did this with great sympathy and care to ensure that what I wanted to say was carried through with the accuracy such a work demands. There are others, too many to mention, that helped me in my work. Thousands of students have stood around my workbench, in clustered circles of 10 to 20, over two decades. They have taught me as much, if not more, about crafting lives as I ever taught them about woodworking, as I struggled to answer questions to help them become the best woodworkers they could be.

Introduction

Why Did I Write This Book?

Stood at the bench, an apprentice asks a question; and an exchange of questions and answers goes back and forth over several years, and the training is ongoing. The knowledge of one generation is transferred to another through this exchange and a young artisan emerges. So it was for me. No one recorded what was said but this wisdom passed seamlessly from the older generation to those teaching me and then from them to me, without hindrance, through a culture that sustained craftsmanship for centuries. The words and the demonstrations of techniques, in day to day work, gradually energised my life with an undeniable richness surrounding the workings of hand tools. Such priceless lessons should always be written down.

This is my reason for wanting a book like this. It is not a rigid list of do's and don'ts but what I have always given to my apprentices and my own children, as we worked alongside one another in the workshop and at the workbench. Some of it is the information passed to me in an exchange of words some five decades or more ago. What I have written here is not a complex, scholarly work but answers for a new generation of emerging woodworkers, who may never know the relationship of master and apprentice. In my case, it was a boy's hunger for understanding how the man he worked with did what seemed so very impossible. Now I have worked with my hands, day in and day out, throughout my working life, using the tools and equipment you see in this book. I have written down here what I learned, for the missing generations yet to follow, who may never have the benefit of learning from someone as closely as I did.

This Book Is About Essentials

We boast that our present age provides easy access to information and I think that, in some measure, that is true but our freedom to access information is often not the issue. The daunting task of sifting through such a mass of information, to find what is needed, has become ever more time consuming. It takes a great deal of effort, thought, and care to distill something down to its essentials. This is especially the case with woodworking hand tools, where there is such a rich variety of choice. This book is not meant as a comprehensive guide to a limitless range of tools but rather to bring focus, as a practical starting point, to the tools I consider essential.

In mastering the techniques of my craft, I followed a path that went full circle, only to end where I began in the adventure; but with increased knowledge and the skills in my hands. I discovered that the few hand tools I began working with were the same ones I would still be using at the end of my journey. Though I worked with them in the everyday

of my life, the simplicity in this conclusion surprised me greatly. Aside from a few small changes, perhaps a new steel alloy, a little more advanced engineering here and there, the best chisels are still steel and wood and the saws push and pull the same way, with the human hand, coordinated by the eye, directing them as perfectly as humanly possible. The planes of steel and wood may have developed some eccentricities yet they too seem destined to follow what was given centuries or even millennia ago. For those of us who want to do the work ourselves, these tools equip us to create whatever perfections we want. As it was in the beginning of my apprenticeship so it is now. The tools must be well cared for and sharp – loved if you will. The use of them never depends on harshness and rigid control but sensitivity, often lightness of hand, with the added firmness to meet all resistance challenging our will. The end product is the reflection of who we are as crafting artisans, striving, striving, striving with every stroke of the pencil and knife, plane, saw, and whatever other cutting edge we choose for the task. We indeed live in a world of ever-shifting cultures. The tools I own are many hundreds but, in the following pages, I separate the preferences from the essentials that I reach for at my bench every day.

A Great Deal Can Be Accomplished With Relatively Few Hand Tools

30 years ago I began to understand how some woodworkers were adopting mass manufacturing processes to perform even the simplest of woodworking tasks. Living in the US, I saw many people set up dedicated machine shops paralleling commercial workshops to work just for an hour or two at weekends and evenings. What seemed obvious to me then was that the hand work I relied on so much and could never live without was missing for many people. However, I also saw how, after even small demonstrations and explanations, there was a real desire to apprehend the development of hand skills. Hand tool methods seemed an obvious step to complement the machine work they already knew. When I saw how willing the audience was to learn, I began to demonstrate my work at craft events and then woodworking shows, with an intent to help woodworkers integrate additional hand skills. Using a handful of very common but fundamentally essential hand tools seemed somehow to dismantle any preconceptions they had as to their own inabilities. I felt equipped to infuse them with inspiration as they watched from around the bench. At last I was able to bridge the gap between the generations by simply cutting dovetails, inlaying picture frames, and then showing how simple it was to develop sharp edges to tools in seconds and minutes. The people watching wanted to be included in my world, where they could master the same skills I proved worked so effectively. By telling them that they too could do this with the right instruction and some dedication and patience, they felt truly empowered to take those first steps. Back then I was not selling a thing, just telling them about my woodworking life as a crafting artisan.

What Tools Are Really Essential?

The tools I have included in my 'essential woodworking hand tools' are not at all rare but they may not be so common as those generally found around the garden shed or garage. Screwdrivers, claw hammers, dividers, scale rules for technical drawing, and so on are, of course, tools we rely on but they are not dedicated woodworking tools. Though a woodworker, I often use additional tools like metalworking hammers, pliers, and hacksaws, which are essential to metalworking but, again, I have restrained this book to exactly what I need for working my wood. This book is focussed on tools that are essential specifically to woodworking. Were I to include all of the diverse range of tools ancillary to my work and then the thousands of other woodworking tools available, I would be adding to the confusion rather than helping to bring clarity and focus. Over my five decades of working wood and doing much of it with hand tools, I have discovered the freedoms in the few rather than the many and, whereas the right tool for the job is often important, most of the time we can achieve extraordinary things by simply adapting and using the ordinary.

I chose to follow the same paths as those who made and adapted tools to make them work in ways beyond what was intended by their original design. I suppose I wanted to somehow defy specificity in the sense that, just as the constructs of our human bodies constantly adapt to both the special and ordinary use of hand tools, so too the tools are adapted to perform tasks they were often never designed for. I often slice the two walls of short rebates with tenon saws and use wire nails as perfectly sized drill bits to bore holes in wood. In some ways it is a form of minimalism and, economically, it fits my quest to use my time well. Whereas so many expect only the best for everything, I prefer not to follow an advocacy of owning planes that sit waiting to be used on a shelf for six months. Just using the knifewall will render some tools almost obsolete and an upturned chisel flush-cuts protruding nubs perfectly. Most work, when skills have become fully honed, requires fewer tools and not more. While skill does take time to develop, once you master it you have it for life. It has always been natural for me to adapt tools and when we stop and reach only for specialisation we lose the ability to adopt and adapt other methods and techniques and the freedom to explore other options too. It is not just a question of not buying into the excesses so much as becoming skilfully competent with what we have to work with. It is more important to understand sharpening and be able to alter cutting edges according to task, wood, and tool than to buy tools and equipment as substitutions for skill. My book gives you the start you need but you must work the wood with the tools to gain your own insights into woodworking.

In Respect for the Surviving Modern Makers

In the time that I have been woodworking I have seen many changes, with tool manufacturers appearing and then leaving the market. It has been important to me not to tie this book in with specific brands and models but rather focus on the attributes of the tools that I rely on. It would be wrong however not to acknowledge today's tool makers who entered the field when others abandoned it; who raised the bar and produced outstanding hand tools that we can rely on in the future. Most of them will not be included in the following pages, though some are. Many of the tools made by passionate modern makers are truly fine tools, well engineered using the finest materials. You must consider which ones you add to your collection of usable hand tools. On the one hand, new tools may (though will not always) be ready to use from the box and have guarantees should they fail. This may give you the initial positive feeling of using a tool successfully. On the other hand, the tools in the following pages are mostly secondhand and may need remedial work before they can be used. Whether you postpone remedial work by buying new or buy older models secondhand, you will inevitably come to the place where, new or old, the tools will need sharpening, filing, adjusting or setting. Most likely you will, like me, own some tools that are a century old and others that were made more recently. Each will often compliment the other and you will know you can rely on them the more you use them. It is impressive to own a perfected hand tool, whether you inherited it from an aging parent or grandparent or you bought it brand new from a modern maker making the best. In some cases, you will have no choice. Some tools are no longer made and must be bought secondhand, while others never existed before recent years.

Who Is This Book For?

When I started teaching it was with the intention of training aspiring woodworkers to become producing artisans. Many people I met said they would love to make a living working with their hands. I anticipated people leaving what they said was uninspiring work to pursue becoming furniture makers. Yet I have rarely seen anyone take this last step. After the first two years I changed my goals. I knew then that people were often looking for something different from what I had looked for three decades before them; that many were contented in their occupations but did still aspire to become skilled artisans and nothing less would suit them. Today I find myself better understanding that different people have varied interests and that their lives can depend on the craft just as much as for the person being paid for the work. Whether you are paid or not, wellbeing often results from simply working creatively with your hands and that can be done skillfully or unskillfully. Woodworking is not age specific in the same way it is not gender specific - although there is an ideal age range, when young people can capitalise on developing their spatial awareness, working in a three-dimensional environment that is equipped for them to gain hands-on experience and knowledge in the craft. I believe that young people should ideally be trained in hand skills between the ages of 14 and 20 years old. For most people, this exposure becomes postponed by educational systems that have changed culturally in favour of academics; and arts and crafts, as always, take second place. My gut feeling tells me that more focus should be given to teaching people to grow food and raise chickens for eggs and meat; that they would enjoy real cooking and real gardening and real craft that supports these things and gives the craft meaning. Such is the need for hand work with hand tools.

My hope for this book is that people will get off the conveyor belt of 'do it yourself' woodworking, using mass manufacturing, and that they will discover what hand tool woodworking has to offer. The footprint and finances involved are much smaller and the benefits far greater. The health and safety risks are far less and the sense of accomplishment is immeasurable.

Sharpening & Sharpening Equipment

It soon becomes clear to every new woodworker that the tools they use must always be sharp. There are tools used for working the wood and there is equipment needed for developing and maintaining the cutting edges of the tools themselves. Sharpness is essential. This sharpening equipment takes the bevels and angles, points, tips and so on and abrades them to specific shapes. It is then used to polish out the two surfaces forming the cutting edge so that it cuts wood with effective sharpness.

Many of the edge tools used by woodworkers are edges formed with single-sided bevels. Sharpening such tools predates our modern-day internet era by millennia. There are examples of ancient woodwork ranging from simple, carved effigies to complex carvings and inlays. These demonstrate seams that have no gaps along entire lengths, with no air or glue lines. This takes great skill. It is also true that such work is not possible without creating sharp edges to work with. It takes a particular level of skill and sensitivity to achieve the sharpness needed to cut wood this flawlessly. Abrasives and their cutting qualities may have changed through the ages but the methods for creating a sharp edge remain the same.

For the main part, sharpening involves the use of abrasive material either in the form of stone, abrasive coated paper, film, or one kind of file or another. It is a strange anomaly that we use a rough surface, be that by degrees of roughness, to make another smooth. Whether abrasive or file, both methods are available in varying degrees of fineness depending on the materials used and the manufacturer. I will discuss this in detail shortly.

Sharpening most cutting tools and cutting blade edges is not particularly complex once we work through the confusion of mass information. It takes a modest amount of practice to establish the rhythms and patterns of freehand sharpening. A little determination will make you expertly fast and effective, and once you have established these modest skills you will have them for life. Anyone can sharpen any edge tool with any abrasive they choose but some abrasives work better than others.

Sharpening Issues

Before I outline my recommendations for specific sharpening equipment, I would like to discuss a few of the issues that often arise when I teach and demonstrate sharpening.

HONING GUIDES AND HONING ANGLES

In my experience there is nothing at all wrong with honing guides in principle. I use one from time to time for different reasons and especially when experimenting and researching. Freehand sharpening however gives me much greater speed and economy of movement. I find it totally freeing to sharpen in this way. Use of a honing guide often arises from a desire to sharpen to an exact angle. A cutting edge however can be sharpened to somewhere between 25-35 degrees, according to task or indeed preference. Whereas you may aim to sharpen to 30 degrees, often sharpening within 25-35 degrees

GLASS
CLEANER

is a good and practical range, and rigid enforcement is not at all necessary. On plane irons however you should avoid too high an angle as the heel of the blade may contact the surface of the wood, preventing the cutting edge from making contact. For plane blades you should aim for 25-30 degrees. For chisels, choosing where in the 25-35 degrees range you are aiming really depends on whether you are paring wood or chopping into it. A lower angle allows less resistance to paring, and the steeper angle provides greater strength on the cutting edge. Freehand sharpening gives you total flexibility as well as control. Honing guides do have their place but they can be a little too mechanical. This can prevent me from honing specifically to task or for a particular preference I have in mind as I work. Losing this total versatility diminishes my flexibility for the work I am doing at a particular time. The problem is usually that people do not feel comfortable with freehand sharpening, especially in the beginning, and they often reach for the honing guide first. You might want to buy one of the less expensive guides when starting out. They are simple, quick, and easy enough to set up as well as reliable for lifelong use. Use a protractor to set the distance from the wheel on the guide to the cutting edge and you are away.

As an apprentice I went straight to freehand sharpening at 15 and have stayed with it for over 50 years. It took me a few hours over several weeks to master the skill and now I have it for life. Although I can see that honing guides are sometimes useful, I certainly do not consider them essential tools. Of course, if you just cannot get it without one then I suggest you just use a guide. Most people I have known can quickly, and fairly easily learn to sharpen without one.

One of the simplest, least expensive, and easy to understand honing guides to use.

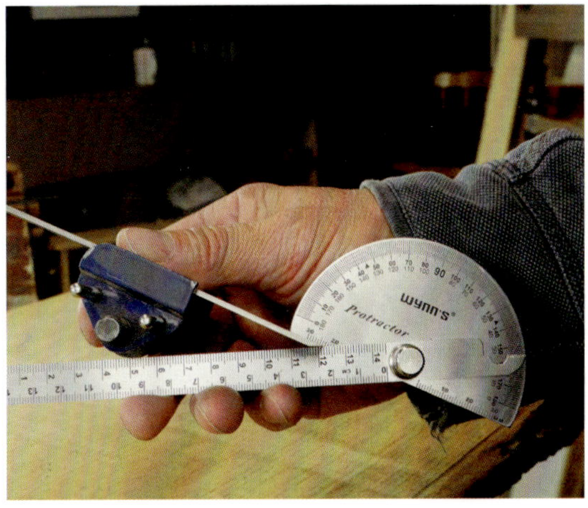

Though you can use a protractor initially, once you have the distance established, it is quicker to mark a fixed distance somewhere and set the edge of the blade to that distance.

SUPERHARD STEELS

New steel alloys give us ever harder steels and new names that describe either the processes of hardening or the steel alloys used. At first glance, harder steels may seem beneficial if they reduce the time we spend grinding and honing our edge tools. Harder steels however need more aggressive methods to cut the steel to the correct bevel. On the other hand, softer steels need more regular sharpening. At the bench, we are always looking for practical results that give balance to our efforts. I want a steel that takes and holds a good edge and that can be readily sharpened without using machines. Some steels touted for hardness are often prohibitive because they are designed more for machine grinding than honing using hand methods. So remember when selecting your tools that a tool advertised as having a superhard blade will often require much more effort to sharpen.

SUPERTHICK IRONS

Retrofitting planes with thick irons to counter any unwanted aberrations (reportedly resulting from the use of standard cutting irons) is an issue that comes up quite regularly. Misinformation like this results from manufacturers and dealers declaring that the thicker irons reduce chatter, which they associate with the standard, thinner irons that come with the plane. In my experience the issue is rarely, if ever, anything to do with the iron thickness and is more likely caused by the uncertainty associated with anyone new to using a hand plane. It takes a certain amount and type of energy to start the plane and continue through to the exit of the stroke. Most people new to woodworking do not get this exactly right when they begin their woodworking journey so this lack of confidence is mirrored in their work. With practice, new confidence comes and the more you plane, the less surface marring you get because you are better able to gauge the energy it takes to effect the cut. Almost any and every wood type can be planed to perfection with the standard iron that came with the plane; any surface texturing left by the plane is not usually the quite rare phenomenon called chatter. The cause is more likely skudding causing the plane to skip and jump in the cut and not chatter at all. Thick irons do not resolve such issues.

Thick plane irons can be over one third thicker than regular cutting irons. It stands to reason then that, with these thick irons, it takes much greater effort to remove the extra steel during the sharpening process. Combining this extra thickness with steels that are harder often means the cutting edges are much more difficult to sharpen because the whole bevel must be reduced to 25-30 degrees. This, again, requires considerably more effort, which often forces the use of machine grinding in what is otherwise a truly simple process.

Thick irons may, at first glance, seem to be an advancement in woodworking but the advantage, if indeed there is any, is soon countered by the extra work that it takes to sharpen them.

MACHINE GRINDING

I rarely advocate the use of machines for sharpening hand tools because, for the main part, they are not essential. At some point in any woodworker's life the question of machine grinding will inevitably come up. The question mostly occurs when speed seems to somehow become paramount or perhaps there is an understanding that an exact angle is critical to the sharpness or usability of an edge. Generally machines work well for mass manufacturers to obtain both consistent repeatability for angles to bevels and, in some cases, sharpness in one or two steps and in massive volumes. Woodworking craftspeople, on the other hand, need only a keen edge on a single chisel or plane from time to time during the workday; two very different mandates altogether. For us, it takes less than a minute provided we do not use a machine or a jig to guide us.

At first it seems to make sense that if we damage an edge on a nail or by dropping the chisel on concrete we would use a grinder to establish a continuous edge. The question for me then is how essential is such a machine to the average hand tool woodworker? Whereas using a grinder does remove steel quickly, for the rare occasion such a need arises, say once a year at most, the chisel can be reground on coarse sandpaper fairly quickly.

There is no doubt that severe damage to an edge can take a long time to grind out using hand methods only. Only you can decide whether buying and using a machine is a valid option.

Obsessive Sharpening or Necessity?

Sharpness is critical to the work we do in hand tool woodworking. However, it seems to me that, at some point, some woodworkers cross a line between what is a basic and important task undertaken several times in a workday to this becoming more of a fascination. When I first learned to sharpen my edge tools, the men I worked with sharpened on one grit to about 600, stropped on the palm of their hand to break the wire edge, and went back to planing or chiselling. While I recommend using a leather strop and not the hand, this was a simple process that barely interrupted the flow of work. In recent decades, as the role of workmen has declined, craft knowledge and the skills surrounding different methods of working have been gradually transferred to the amateur private sector. The old methods have been reshaped without real regard for how craftsmen worked in the past. Whereas I do advocate a more in-depth sharpening process to establish a pristine, even surgically sharp, edge, I encourage everyone to consider sharpening in the same way our forebears did; keep it integral to the work flow and not so much an academic or scientific consideration. It is not at all necessary to separate sharpening from the main body of woodworking as though it is somehow a more specialised level. For centuries sharp tools have been the fundamental to good work, with sharpening playing a key part in the process. For me it is this that keeps things balanced and efficient so that I can enjoy the whole as a continuing process of work and not so much in isolated parts.

Essential Sharpening Tools & Equipment

The tools and equipment I consider essential to sharpening hand tools are listed below, along with the page number of the section where I discuss them in more depth:

Sharpening Stones

Sharpening most of the edge tools we use in woodworking relies on abrasive of one kind or another. The size of the grit determines the fineness of the surface polish you achieve on the two faces forming the cutting edge. It is the level of grit fineness that then determines the sharpness of the cutting edge itself. Most of the commercially available abrasive stones, papers, and plates will work and work well, so it is a matter of choice for you to establish the stone or abrasive type you choose to work with for sharpening. I will, however, be making my recommendation for the stones I think work best later in this section.

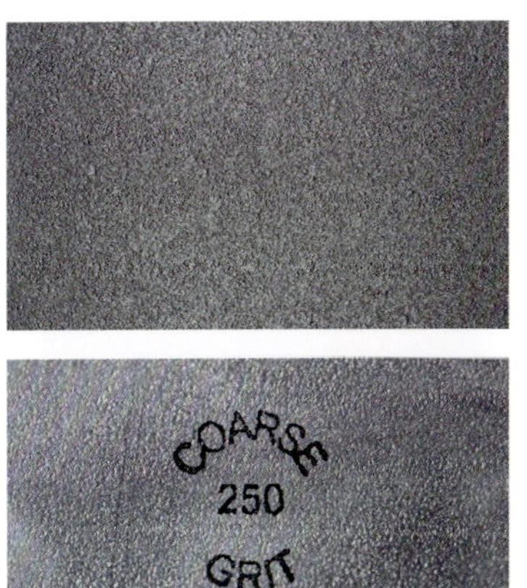

Today we tend to name each stone with its place of origin, maker's name, or particulate type, depending on a variety of considerations. In times past, oilstone, sharpening stone, and whetstone were the three most common generic terms used to describe any type of stone used for sharpening. That is because, in the western world, oilstones were the common stone used by craftsmen and the term 'whet' means to sharpen. So, whetstone can be applied to any and all sharpening stones. Even though we tend not to use this term today, I think it is still a valid term to describe sharpening stones including diamond plates. Whether the stones are flooded with oil, water, specially prepared honing fluids, or auto glass cleaner it is still quite proper to refer to them as whetstones or sharpening stones.

Oilstones

Oilstones range in hardness and particulate size depending on the type or composition of the stone. Coarse stones, comprising large abrasive particles, abrade steel quickly to establish the primary surface to the bevel. Subsequent abrading with ever finer grits polishes the bevelled edge of tools to develop a more refined cutting edge. Oilstones originated as naturally occurring stones hewn from a diverse range of rock formations around the world. As demand grew, consistent particle sizing in a wide range of grits became more essential for the ever-widening industrial world. As such, industrial manufacturers developed man-made stones well suited to both oil and water. Whether man-made or natural, the stones work in exactly the same way but the abrasive qualities of the various stones may vary markedly.

To keep the oilstones in good and clean condition you should flood a small area of the surface with light machine oil. As you sharpen the bevel, the cutting edge moves the oil over the surface of the oilstone. The abraded steel and stone particulate that is created floats in the oil and so prevents the stone from glazing over with a residue of these particles, which always occurs if no oil is used. Because we use oil with oilstones, the stones are best housed in some type of wooden holder to contain them and to keep the work area, stowage and workbench clean and oil free.

Waterstones

Waterstones are often associated with Asia but have become a widespread option. There are a wide range of waterstones available both as naturally occurring stone and man-made composites. These work in the same way as each other and, in presentation of the iron to the stones, are the same as oilstones. That said, the abrasive qualities of the various stones can and do vary greatly. So, to find out the difference takes a little experimentation on your part. Like oilstones, waterstones range in hardness and particulate size depending on the regions they come from and, if natural stones, the type of rock. Unlike oilstones, where oil alone prevents the stones from glazing, waterstones rely on the constant application of sprayed water to keep the stones wet and also float off particles of steel. Additionally a second stone called a nagura stone is applied to the surface of the main waterstone to prevent the surface from developing a glaze from a build-up of particles and to create a fine slurry for further polishing the steel bevel. Further abrading with finer grit stones polishes the tool's edge to create a more refined cutting edge.

Waterstones may initially seem like an excellent option because they cut steel relatively quickly, but these stones work through continuous surface fracture and so wear quickly with use and must generally be flattened frequently. Special stones are used to do this and the process is messy and awkward at best. For the different stones to work effectively a suitable waterproof tray must be used throughout the stone preparation, use, and flattening process.

Abrasive & Glass/Granite

Using abrasive papers and abrasive films should be seen mostly as just an initial option for sharpening edge tools. This enables a new woodworker to sharpen their first tools without making a commitment to the more expensive stones, which are used by woodworkers who have the budget or who have had longer to research their options. This method becomes the most expensive method when used long term but it does work to get started. For new woodworkers evaluating their options but needing to develop their viably sharp edges as they learn, it is a good first step to better understand the tools they are working with and it works as an entry-level sharpening system.

Abrasives like these need a solid and hard support surface such as thick plate glass or granite. Ceramic tiles will work too as long as they are as near to flat as possible, as will steel and other metal plates of at least ¼" (6mm) thick. This support base keeps the abrasive firm and also keeps it flat for sharpening. I use a granite block 2" (50mm) thick and 10" (250mm) by 12" (300mm) long. It is a proven block, finished to within near perfect flatness, and I use this for some of my flattening work for chisels, planes, and plane irons. It may be something of a luxury but, because I have so many tools to take care of, it works well for me, especially given that many of the tools are used in teaching. Plate glass on the other hand is relatively inexpensive and a piece 10" (250mm) by 12" (300mm) will cost very little. Most glass suppliers will even give you some scrap for the asking when you tell them what it is for.

The most widely available type of abrasive paper or film is 'wet and dry.' It is the type of abrasive used for car body repair work before spraying the finish. As the name suggests, wet and dry can be used both wet or dry. That said, it works best wet because the liquid floats off particles of steel and abrasive, which stops the surface from clogging and glazing over. A light misting of spray adhesive on the back of the sheet gives enough light tackiness to hold the abrasive to the surface of the support block or plate. This abrasive works in much the same way as whetstones and diamond plates where you work from coarse to fine until you are ready for final polishing on the bevel and the flat face with the strop. The strop is a simple piece of wood topped with leather, which is 'charged' with buffing compound. The strop is discussed further on page 31.

Initially, paper and film cuts steel fast and it works well for getting your edges in good shape when you are starting out. Unfortunately the main difference between paper or film abrasives and abrasive stones or plates, such as diamond plates, is that the papers and films are easily damaged and quickly rendered useless. Because you are working with sharp edges and corners, this can happen in the first few minutes of starting to sharpen. Even when great care is taken, the papers and films lose their abrasive qualities very quickly with normal use. It is this then that makes paper and film expensive long term, but it should not be dismissed out of hand as an option for the beginner woodworker. Sometimes a roll of coarse 120-grit abrasive paper is useful for quickly abrading bevels of tools or plane soles and also it is useful if you have multiple tools that have surfaces that need flattening.

Diamond Stones

Diamonds are the hardest wearing surfaces available for abrading edge tools. Until relatively recently, they were available only to industrial users for abrading glass and metal as a commercial process. Today they have become a practical solution for every user regardless of whether they are commercial users or home workers. Some makers use monocrystalline diamonds and others use polycrystalline diamonds. Both makers make claims with regards to longevity and cutting quality. Despite strong opinion, one over the other, I have not found the difference between the two types to be significant. Both types offer the same basic abrasive choices with regards to coarseness and fineness. The abrasive choices are limited to half a dozen or so but the level of choice is more than sufficient.

My Preferred Stones

I introduced diamond sharpening plates to my students in 1998 because, when so many people are frequently sharpening, maintenance and mess becomes an issue. I found that the other sharpening stones were too messy and the surfaces of the stones wore down unacceptably quickly. We needed fast cutting abrasive that was both hard wearing and that stayed flat. Diamond plates provide all three qualities in a single type.

Other sharpening stones, cut from a naturally occurring mass of stone as well as composite man-made stones, still offer a more traditional choice for woodworkers. I suggest that diamond plates offer the best long-term solution to sharpening edge tools. That said, these more traditional options are still valid and more than adequate for rapidly achieving keen edges. Someone who has the option should purchase diamond sharpening plates, like the ones shown here, as early as possible in their woodworking. However, I in no way advocate that people discard other, perfectly good, sharpening stones without seriously considering that they too work well. I and hundreds of thousands of tradesmen before me, who used these for millennia before diamond plates became available, found them to be perfectly adequate.

Natural sharpening stones have worked well for millennia...

...but I believe diamond stones work best for today's woodworker.

Stone Sizes

Most stones and plates used by woodworkers are between 2-3" (50-75mm) wide and 8-10" (200-250mm) long, but larger stones and plates are available and may be useful in certain circumstances. I use 3" (75mm) by 8" (200mm) diamond plates. Most bench plane irons are between 1 ¾-2 ⅜" (45mm and 60mm) wide so the 3" (75mm) wide plate gives room to maneuver. A non-essential additional plate I use is an 8x8" (200x200mm) coarse diamond plate. I keep this mostly for the more aggressive flattening and restoration processes I need from time to time. The larger surface is handy for flattening, as long as it is truly flat so you must check for this with a straightedge and winding sticks.

"Most stones and plates used by woodworkers are between 2-3" (50-75mm) wide and 8-10" (200-250mm) long, but larger stones and plates are available and may be useful in certain circumstances"

I generally recommend the use of three grits but I could actually manage with two (the 600 and 1200 grit) at a pinch. I use coarse (250 grit), medium to fine (600 to 800 grit) and superfine (1200 grit). Lined up in that order from left to right and mounted in my plate holder they are convenient, orderly, and clean to use. I use a spray bottle with auto glass cleaner (not window cleaner) to keep them flooded during sharpening and this keeps everything moving quickly throughout the sharpening process.

Suggested Grit Levels of Abrading

It is important to choose the right grit size for the different stages of abrading and so you must select the appropriate stone according to purpose. This guide will help you choose:

1. For coarse work - reestablishing original bevels and grinding out nicked and damaged edges, or working on neglected or abused tools with extremely dull edges - use a 120-400 grit abrasive. The coarser stones remove steel fast to establish a good bevel and flatten the backs of tools if that has become necessary.

2. For second-level abrading the most suitable grit abrasive will be between 600-1000 grit.

3. For entering the pre polishing phase but before using the strop charged with buffing compound, we then use a 1200-1500 grit stone. At this level any tool will be generally sharp enough to work well and give good results in the wood, whichever work you do or tool you use. Taking it to the higher level on the strop (discussed further on page 31), however, takes only a few seconds more and often woodworkers like that extra fineness in their sharpening.

The grit ranges you see above may seem wide-ranging within the three levels, but I have found that levels within these ranges work and, in some cases, the aggressiveness of the particles changes as the stones and plates become smoother through use.

The stone should generally be flat unless you choose to use a hollow or curved stone. A stone that is worn to a concave surface will only be capable of producing a curved face or bevel. Some crafting artisans prefer working with curved or cambered bevels to their tool edges while others prefer dead flat. Waterstones are renowned for high fracture surface wear and developing into a hollow surface; it is generally accepted that they need constant flattening if you want flat abrading stones. It is possible to keep the stones close to flat during the abrading process by using the full surface of the stone during sharpening. Some companies also sell specific flattening stones for this purpose however the abrading by the stones on the flattening stone has a reciprocal effect, which can leave both stones out of flat.

Using the Stones

Sharpening must become so habitually integrated into the work that you slide seamlessly from the work into sharpening and back to the work again with scarcely a hiccup. It is an aspect that should never be neglected and therefore nothing should obstruct it. Because of this I keep my diamond stones within arm's reach at the business end of my workbench and close to my work position near the vise. Here I have customised a shelf to keep them close to hand, otherwise they take up space on my benchtop and make my life more awkward. Sharpening occurs many times in a given day so I do not want to chase them around elsewhere. They need to be kept away from the work surfaces when not in use and of course there is always the dirt factor associated with all sharpening too.

I keep a couple of strops right by them too. That way, immediately after using the sharpening stones, I pull the strop out and put it straight into the vise, polish out the bevel and get back to the work in hand as an integral part of my work flow. Fast, clean and tidy, convenient, and highly effective.

Whichever stone type you choose to use, they need protecting from damage and generally they are kept in some kind of convenient box or holder. Oilstones traditionally have a base and a lid that lifts off to access the stone. I keep my diamond plates in a special holder I designed to hold the plates in three recesses as shown here. The diamond plates are, of course, thick steel and thick enough for recessing this way. They need this level of solidity and retention but do not necessarily need covering if kept in a shelf close to hand as are mine.

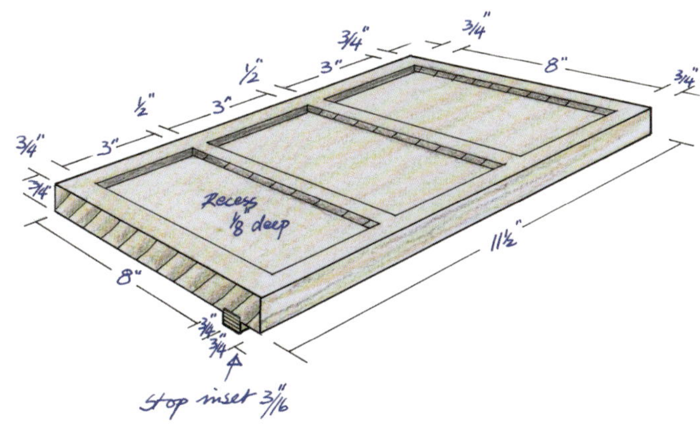

Setting up the Plates

I have designated the stones according to my being right-hand dominant. What works best for me is housing the coarsest plate to my left and the finest to my right with the medium plate between the two, as I face the bench and the plate holder. The recesses being exactly the same depth means the surfaces of the plates are at the same level. The coarse plate being on my left gives me the opportunity to flatten larger faces with the excess of the blade overhanging to my left.

The middle plate for honing is still accessible for the bevel but less so for the larger flat face. This is not usually a problem as this level of abrading on the flat surfaces is less common and is minimal after the first sharpening. The right hand plate is as accessible as the coarse plate and again the excess of the blade overhangs the edge. I use a thin squiggle of clear bathroom sealant to bed the plates into the recesses. This is not to seal the plates but to support them and secure them to stop any rocking.

To make the plate holder I actually prefer a better grade of plywood to solid wood as this is more stable under the wet conditions of sharpening; using solid wood can be a problem in that excess water can gather and cause the wood to bow. This can then cause the plates to rock.

The Sharpening Strop

Strops are very basic pieces of equipment used for final polishing of cutting edges and for removing burrs formed during sharpening on the stones. They are highly effective and as relevant for today's hand tool woodworker as they ever were in times past. Compared to mechanical methods they give high levels of polish, while being much safer and without overheating or burning the steel. I use the strop many times throughout every day to keep my chisels ultra sharp and I would be lost without it. My strops are simple to use and can be made easily in a matter of minutes. Depending on how it is used, a strop can last for years if not decades.

The strop comprises two elements adhered to one another to create a firm foundation for pressing the tool against. The base can be wood or just about any smooth, flat composite board such as plywood or MDF. This is then skinned with leather. To date, I have never found any other material that will hold a charge of buffing compound as well and as evenly as leather. The effectiveness in this, the final stage of the sharpening and polishing process, is truly astounding.

For sharpening chisels, plane irons, and spokeshaves I have found the most practical size for a strop is about ¾" (18mm) thick by 3" (75mm) wide and 10" (250mm) long. This takes care of all my needs with straight-edged edge tools. For curved edges, say gouges and so on, it is best to make the curved hollows and rounds to suit the gouges being sharpened. This is covered on page 35.

Using the Strop

The strop must be securely held, either screwed to the sharpening station or held in the vise. The vise works best for me. I keep my sharpening stones and strop side by side on a shelf at the end of my workbench. That way they are easily and readily accessible throughout my workday. Sharpness is key to good work and the strop gives me the edge I need.

With the strop tightly held in the vise, I charge the strop with buffing compound, which is a fine abrasive suspended in a waxy substance. The wax holds the particulate on the surface of the strop and ensures the abrasive is equally distributed across the full length and width of the strop. Once charged, the tool is applied to the strop and pulled in long strokes along the strop repeatedly until the bevel becomes fully polished.

Stropping always follows honing on the sharpening stones. Generally, the idea of stropping and polishing out the tool is to return the whole bevel back to its fully polished condition and, though we do this to the whole bevel, it is actually the last 1⁄16" (2mm) or so along the cutting edge that truly matters. Polishing the whole bevel simplifies the procedure because it would be near impossible to polish just the very edge. Throughout the sharpening process, through every grit, we work the angle to 25-30 degrees (or in some cases 35 degrees) across the full bevel. The same is true when polishing out the bevel on the strop. This is both quick and effective.

Buffing compound only needs to be applied occasionally after the strop is initially charged. Once every half a dozen, or so, times you sharpen is sufficient.

With the dominant hand holding the tool or blade as shown, place the heel of the non-dominant hand on the flat face of the tool or blade above but near to the cutting edge. Wrap your fingers around the tool and press firmly with the heel of your hand, applying as much pressure as you feel comfortable with while ensuring that you have total control. Now, trailing the cutting edge along the strop, move the bevel, at the same angle as you did for honing, along the strop with about 30-40 successive strokes. You should use almost the full length of the strop but without going off the end. You must lift the tool off the strop at the end of each pull-stroke and replace it at the start each time you strop; otherwise the cutting edge gouges and cuts into the leather surface and makes stropping more difficult. The movement should be rhythmic, not jerky or awkward. It soon becomes second nature.

Buffing Compound

Buffing compound can come in many forms but the simplest and cleanest, with the least added fuss, comes in the form of a block. This block can be powdery or waxy depending on the maker and both work fine. However, the waxy is best as this adheres to the leather strop and means fewer fragments on the bench top. It can be difficult to determine exactly what the particulate size is because many makers shoot for a maximum sized particle that then contains many finer levels too. We are generally looking for something around 5 micron in size but, for our work, the main thing we are concerned with is finding and using something that will polish the bevel to a mirror finish. This mirror finish is actually far more than we need because as soon as the tool hits the wood the edge deteriorates to a much lesser level of sharpness no matter the steel or the maker. In our work we are shooting for anywhere between 8,000 to 10,000 grit but often we go to 15,000 without really knowing - unless we find a guaranteed product stating the particle size is indeed 15,000 or higher. My suggestion is not to take this too far. Most makers do not actually give such details on their product labels and, to find out what the size is, you must ask for the safety data sheets that give the details of the exact product and its content. Most often makers and sellers sell the product as being suitable for polishing certain resistant materials and metal types like glass, plastics, and ferrous and non-ferrous metals of different types. For sharpening steels we look for buffing compounds that polish stainless steel and steel. These usually take care of our needs. The buffing compounds we use are generally, but not always, made up of one or both of two commonly available abrasive types called chromium oxide and aluminium oxide. These abrasives cut steel exceptionally fast and can be used for mechanical polishing using a polishing wheel made of sisal, cloth, or leather or on a leather strop. We turn to the buffing compound for final polishing only after exhausting the finest level on the whetstones or diamond plates. The bevel will still have fine striations that we polish out further to develop the higher level of sharpness we need. To use the compound simply apply the bar to the surface of the strop and draw it several times from one end to the other and across the whole width. The leather will hold its charge for many sharpenings and, even though it will turn black with abraded steel, the strop will continue to polish the cutting bevels. It is important not to change the presentation angle of the tool too much, if at all, from the abrading angle as this tends to dull the edge. Remember that the leather, under compression as you draw the cutting bevel across it, mushrooms up behind and can dull the edge. If anything, keep it even lower than the abrading angle and the whole bevel soon becomes polished out.

Making the Strop

I make my strop using double-sided mounting tape to secure the leather to the wood. I find that plywood works best for the board but have often used solid wood with equal success. However, in this instance, plywood works very well because it stays flat while, depending on the species used, solid wood tends to belly or cup.

First I cut and plane the edges of the plywood to 3" (75mm) by 10" (250mm) and remove the arris to the corners of the underside face. I cut my leather oversized by about half an inch (12 mm) or so in length and width. Cutting oversized enables me to pinch and stretch the leather as I apply it. The suede side of the hide will work well for general sharpening so it is the smooth side that goes to the board. I have used everything from old handbags to upholstery hides and leather jackets, leather cushions and so on. Almost any secondhand or new leather works well for this. I am sure that harder, less stretchy, and new leathers, such as tooling leather, might give a more durable surface, but all strops do get get gouged, even with careful use.

First I apply the two-sided tape to the plywood and remove the backer paper. It is best to do this using the vise to hold the board. Apply the leather, stretching it as you do so.

Stretch it in its length and width and then apply pressure by placing it in the vise. Trim off the excess leather and the strop is ready for use.

This strop type can be used for just about all edge tools and this includes knives and carving chisels of different types too.

Shaped Strops

It is necessary to create strops shaped to suit gouges. Many wood carvers use mechanical means to sharpen their edges for ease, effectiveness, and speed. They often do not realise that shop-made strops can work equally well and can be custom shaped to match every shape of gouge or paring tool they use.

To make a practical strop for gouges, use the gouge itself to give you a profile near to the shape you need. You can use the gouge edge to mark the exact shape onto each end of an 8" (200mm) section of wood by placing it on the end and giving it a light tap. Then it only takes a few minutes to shape the profile, using a smoothing plane. It does not have to be exact, just close and with a slightly tighter radius. The wood can be under-width and certainly need not be any wider. I suggest using a fairly soft-grained wood such as spruce, soft maple, or pine.

Using the gouge bevel down, work along the length of the wood on the opposite side to create the hollow side. Start at one end first with the gouge bevel down to establish the first shape. Work backwards in short stages towards to opposite end, and then use forward strokes to smooth out the shape and establish the hollow along the length. Often one strop of this type will work for several gouges of similar radii and sizes. Gouge the hollow along the length as evenly as you can. The surface need not be perfect at all. You can then apply the leather to the hollow and round surfaces using the double-sided tape. You could also keep the leather separate and clamp both leather and support in the vise to use the same leather with other strop shapes if preferred.

Temporary/Quick Gouge Strop

In many circumstances you can strop the outside of a gouge on a flat strop and then wrap some suitably sized dowel with leather for the inside hollow. I have often used a broom handle for my larger spoon and bowl gouges. This is very effective.

Sharpening Files

In daily use, the cutting edges of all edge tools fracture under the pressure of being forced into the wood. This happens quite soon after sharpening, when the tools first come into contact with the wood, and the edge continues to wear away as cuts are made throughout the work. Hard knots and changes in grain density, leveraging out waste and so on all cause these tool edges to become fractured and ineffective. Files smooth and level the rough edges of one or both of the flat faces either side of the damaged cutting edges until a new and keen edge is formed between the two faces. For some tools the file is enough but with other tools the edge is further refined and polished by abrading on stones and strops. We use files to restore cutting edges to tools such as saws, scrapers, shears and scissors, axes, splitting knives, froes, and other tools that require strength rather than hardness. This works where the steel has been hardened but not left so hard that it cannot be filed, which would generally be the case with say chisels and plane irons. These tools are too hard for effective filing and the file glides off the tool's bevel edge when it is offered to the face for sharpening. When a steel edge is too hard, the steel will permanently damage the teeth of the file by leaving them either turned or fractured to the point that the file no longer cuts effectively at all.

There are different types of files with various tooth patterns, lengths, widths, and shapes that cut into the surface faces of hard and resistant materials such as wood, metal, and hard plastics. We call the face of the file the working face. The teeth of files are cut to a consistent surface level so that all the teeth presented to any surface engage in the cutting action as we pass the file over the material. The best files are made from premium high-carbon steel and heat treated through a steel hardening process. When made to tight tolerances, a file will last a long time if stored, used, and cared for properly. Because the file teeth are so hard they are also brittle and so should be prevented from clashing and rubbing against one another in trays. I keep my files and rasps separated from one another in a narrow shelf space.

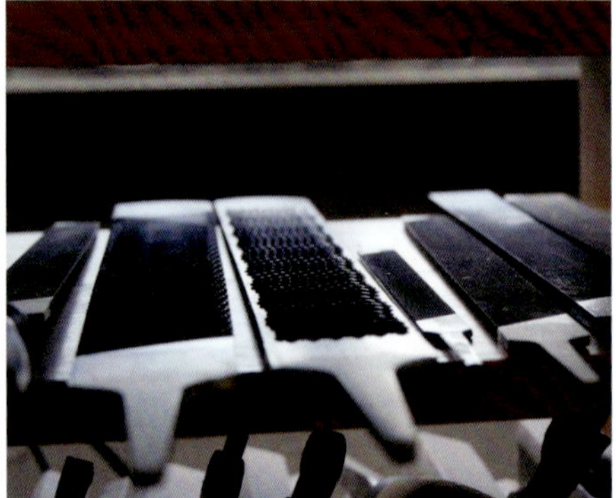

Good files have become increasingly difficult to locate, with fewer and fewer domestic makers to each country and continent. Lower cost goods increase profit margins but the result is less accountability, reduced quality, and fewer choices. Inferior goods have gradually displaced the quality we once knew because company buyers know little of the goods being made or the standards required. Therefore, unfortunately, modern files tend to wear down and wear out much more readily unless you find a good maker maintaining quality standards. Because standards constantly shift, it is a question of finding a maker and testing out their files. For as long as they work well and cut steel to your satisfaction, stay with them. I was loyal to one US maker for decades but then found that the quality of their files dropped drastically and they did not last anywhere near long enough. At first I could not work out what was happening but the files just stopped cutting. This made saw sharpening very expensive. It was only when I magnified the file's cutting edges and found that they were fracturing straight away that I knew I had to find another maker.

It is important to buy as good a quality file as you can get and this is especially so with the three-square type saw files we use for filing saw teeth. Saw files are the files most commonly used by hand tool woodworkers for sharpening, firstly, saw teeth and also the auger bits we use for boring larger sized holes, where twist drills no longer work for us. At first glance, saw files look to have three equally sized faces, but actually they have six faces; three large and obvious faces and three minute faces forming the intersecting corners of the file. There are good makers producing files that last and cut well but there is definitely space in this market for improvement, especially amongst some of the biggest file manufacturers.

File Levels or Grades

Files are manufactured in varying widths according to the desired size. They are also made in different lengths, which can also influence the tooth sizing depending on the maker. The number of teeth cut into the surface over a given distance of the file then determines the file's level of fineness. For sharpening I rely on only a handful of files; three or four triangular files for filing my panel saws and tenon saws, including smaller-toothed dovetail saws; and then a 10-12" (250-300mm) single-cut flat file for other sharpening and saw topping needs. I also keep a similar file, which I reserve for working directly on wood; see page 398.

Single-cut Files

For sharpening, we rely mostly on single-cut files for the finer surfaces, which we need to form a cutting edge. Double-cut files do remove material more quickly but do not leave a sufficiently refined surface for the types of tools we use at the workbench. There are three standard grades generally used to grade our single-cut files: 'bastard' or 'rough cut' files are the coarsest cut, 'second cut' files are medium grade, and 'smooth cut' files are generally the finest in this file type. Bastard cut has the fewest number of teeth to the centimetre or inch. At the opposite end the smooth cut file has the greatest number of teeth to the inch. The second cut file falls in between these numbers with a medium number of teeth.

The degree of fineness is only comparable if you compare files of the same length because often the coarseness of a file increases according to the length of the file. A file's length is measured from the base of the heel, just below the tang, to the end or point of the file (see 'Parts to the File' on page 51). The tang and file handle are not considered in the sizing of files. So then, a file 6" (150mm) long, whether single-cut or double-cut, will likely have more teeth to the centimetre than the 10" (250mm) long file.

The depth of the 'gullet' or 'gulley' is determined by the distance between the teeth; hence the bastard file, with the larger, coarser teeth also has the deeper gullet. It therefore has the capacity to cut deeper and more aggressively, if needed, than the smooth cut file, which has a shallower gullet between the teeth.

“*For sharpening, we rely mostly on single-cut files for the finer surfaces, which we need to form a cutting edge*”

Single-cut files are the simplest files. They have a single set of teeth cut in diagonal rows, parallel to one another, across the working faces of the file. Tooth sizes are governed by spacing so the smaller the distance between the teeth, the smaller the teeth and the shallower the depth of cut. The wider the spacing, the larger the tooth and the deeper the cut. These teeth are cut full-width from edge to edge, usually at 60-65 degrees, across both wide working faces of the file. Usually, but not always, teeth are also cut on the narrow edges of the file. In this case the teeth on the narrow edges are cut square to the length of the file and not at an angle.

Most of the woodworker's sharpening needs require only the single-cut file. We also use this file type for finishing other metal parts, draw-filing, arris removal, fine fitting, trimming and so on.

Double-cut Files

Another file we use is the double-cut file. This file type has two sets of diagonal rows resulting in a diamond pattern to form the cutting or abrading surface of the file. We generally use this file for roughing work because it abrades the steel away more rapidly but does not produce as clean an edge or surface. Usually we follow up with finer cuts from the single-cut files.

I have included this short description and these images (next page) of the double-cut files more to help you to understand and differentiate between the files. Double-cut files are not part of my essential tools but rather are secondary tools, which work great for specific and less common uses.

Second cut and double-cut should not be confused as one and the same. Second cut files are single-cut files of a certain level of fineness; double-cut files are files which have diamond shaped teeth. Knowing the correct terminology will help you as you grow in your understanding of files.

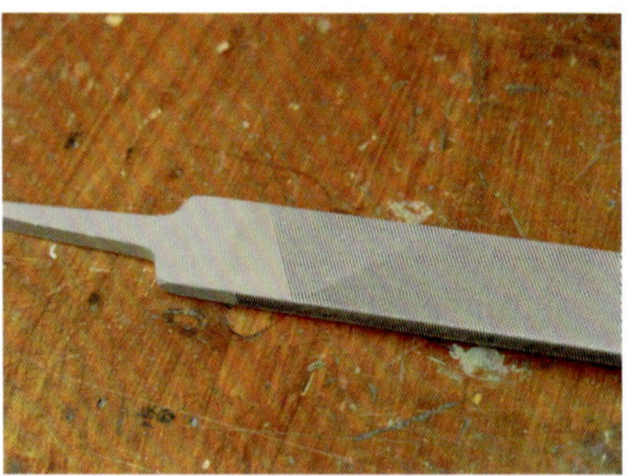

Shapes and Sizes

Regardless of the file type and shape, files used for sharpening woodworking edge tools are generally manufactured in one of the patterns discussed. That being so, it is really a question of knowing three or four things when you choose a file - the aggression of the cut, which is governed by the size of the file teeth, the file tooth pattern and the shape and size of the file itself. Though there are many file shapes to choose from, we in woodworking need only two shapes for our general sharpening work; a flat file and a triangular file.

Flat Files

We generally use a 10-12" (250-300mm) flat bastard (coarse) file and the finer file known as a second (medium) cut file for our different needs. We use these for filing and shaping cabinet scrapers and for topping, or jointing, saw teeth. We also use the same file for filing edge tools such as axes, draw-knives, scissors, awls and other tools.

Three-square or Triangular Saw Files - Sizing

Selecting the correct saw file requires an understanding of the teeth that they will sharpen. This is especially important when choosing the correct size of the saw file in relation to the saw teeth that it will be used on. Saw teeth sizes are generally identified by the number of teeth there are to the inch followed by an abbreviation. Two systems exist; TPI, meaning the number of teeth per inch of saw length; and PPI, meaning the number of points per inch. This was established before the acceptance of the more internationally accepted use of the metric measurement system and has generally been retained.

PPI equals the number of points per inch (25mm) of saw length whilst TPI equals the number of teeth per inch of saw length. The reference PPI is the abbreviation showing the frequency of tooth points on a saw blade. The measurement is taken by setting the point of one tooth at the zero mark on a ruler and counting the number of points between that start point and the one-inch mark, including both the start point itself and any point that lines up precisely with the one-inch mark. There is always one more point per inch than there are teeth per inch, so a saw with 11 PPI has 10 TPI.

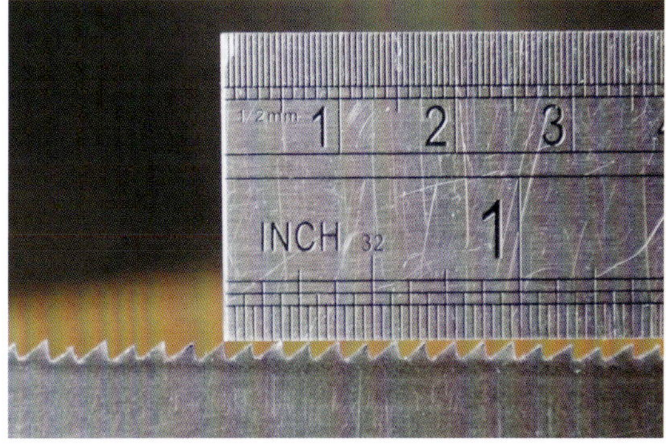

For filing the individual teeth of saws we use triangular files with single-cut teeth. Three sizes of triangular saw file will take care of most saw sharpening needs. However, extra large saws and then very small saws - both with teeth sized proportionally to the saws - need additional, appropriately sized, files commensurate to the different tooth sizes. The saw files I use are generally marked as slim taper, extra slim taper, or double extra slim taper. This refers to the width of the file faces, not necessarily the file length. These sizes correspond to the size of the saw teeth established and are governed by the number of teeth or points per inch of saw length. Although there are various levels of fineness for each size of file, for saw files almost any grade available will work fine. In almost all cases we use single-cut, smooth or second cut saw files for saw filing. One important thing to remember is that the face width should be wider than double the height of the teeth being sharpened. This allows the file to be used from all three sides and to still have a fresh cutting surface when rotated. For saws, my recommended file ranges are these:

SAW FILES

7" (175mm) Slim taper file for handsaws (6-7 PPI)

6" (150mm) X Slim taper file for handsaws and larger tenon saws (8-11 PPI)

6" (150mm) XX Slim taper file for tenon saws, dovetail saws and some gent's-saws (12-16 PPI)

5" (125mm) XX Slim taper file for finer dovetail and gent's-saws (16 PPI and smaller)

FLAT FILES

10" (250mm) Bastard (coarse) single-cut flat file

10" (250mm) Smooth cut (fine) single-cut flat file

12" (300mm) Second cut (medium) single-cut flat file

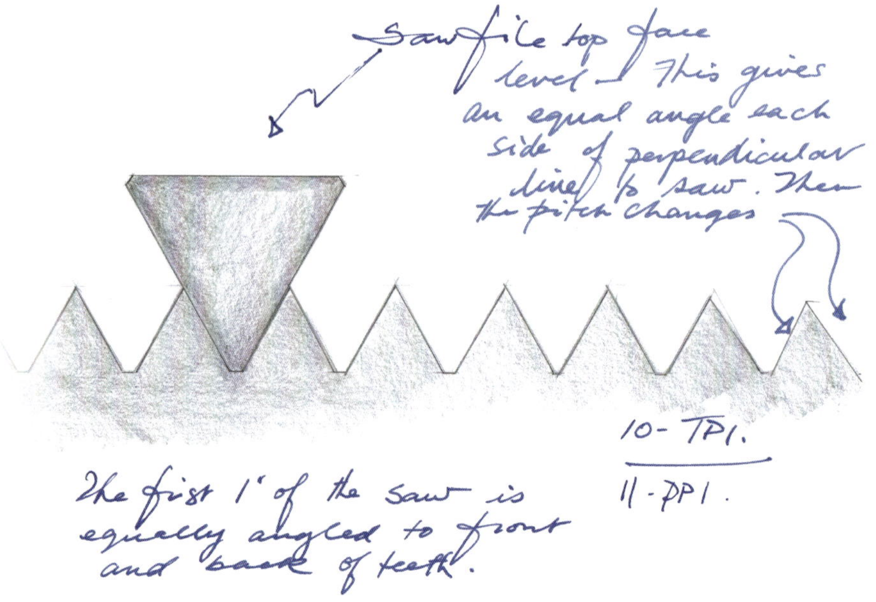

Care in Using Files

Learning to file metal is an art in itself. It demands sensitivity and care yet many see the work as being more coarse and abrasive. Basic principles governing the work should always be considered before the work actually begins. It is important to hold the work in as vibration-free a securement as possible. You also need to consider the filing type, direction of filing movement, body stance, file grip, filing motion and filing pressure. All of these affect the work and have a direct bearing on the quality of the filing cuts. You develop technique only by experimentation at the bench but the techniques can be learned quite quickly. The results depend very much on your ability to respond to how the file feels in the work and through your hands. Any slight directional change can determine the quality and consistency of the work, which then determines the levels of sharpness you can achieve straight from the file itself. You can practise on the actual tool without losing much steel or harming the tool itself. This is ideal because you are managing a real material with the exact hardness you are likely to encounter in the day to day of your work.

Holding and Securing the Work

Generally the work is held in a vise of some type, be that a woodworking or metalworking vise, some type of wooden saw holder, or with some other type of clamp adapted for the task. Sometimes the work can, or must, be held either in the hand or some other way. Whichever method is used, it must be as firm as possible otherwise the metal being filed vibrates and flexes under force, which results in chatter marks in the surface of the work. Chatter is caused by momentary loss of connection between the file teeth and the work. This intermittent movement results in varying levels of staggered interruptions on the surface being filed.

Although not always possible, metalworking vises should be positioned higher than the woodworking workbench. This is simply because most of the work relies on direct pressure from the upper shoulder down through the bent elbow and onto the hands. Heavy filing work is generally lower but the type of filing we use for sharpening is usually light but firm and rarely ever heavy or aggressive. It also places the work nearer to the eyes for observation during the different filing processes.

Two Types of Filing

In woodworking, to sharpen our different tools, we use two filing techniques; forward (or straight) filing, where the file width is thrust forward in a straight line, square across the material; and draw filing, where, instead of using the handle, we grab the file like a bike handle, between two hands, and, holding it perpendicular to the long axis of the blade being sharpened, we push it along the length of the blade, with firm even pressure.

FORWARD FILING

First we must look at body stance in relation to the work and the workbench, and then we will look at hand positioning. Start by facing the work, left foot forward, right foot back and braced (for right-hand dominant or vice versa if you are left-handed). For straight filing we hold the file with the dominant hand on the handle, and the tip, or toe, of the file between the thumb and the side of the forefinger of the other hand. The filing movement is generally square across and away from the body as we feel for the most effective angle to push the file into the work. This is usually slightly angled from the body. The file is lifted from the surface of the work for a return stroke as the teeth cut on the forward stroke only. It damages the file teeth to drag it back across the surface under pressure.

It is important to ensure an equal application of contact pressure across the surface as this prevents rounding and vibration chatter. It is important to keep the file level in the final strokes to establish the squareness needed if square edges are indeed the goal.

When filing, the initial pressure on the file begins at the toe end with the non-dominant hand applying the pressure. As the file moves forward, the pressure becomes equal between the two hands and, towards the end of the stroke, the pressure has been transferred to the dominant hand, which is holding the handle.

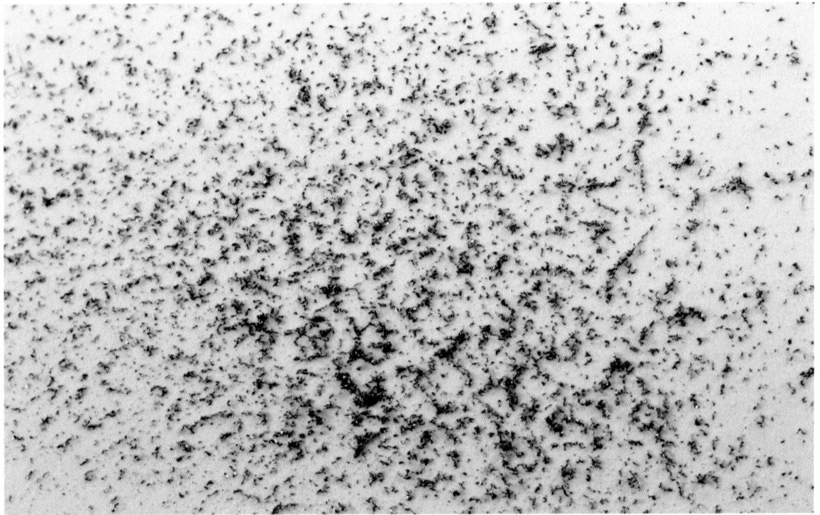

Swarf resulting from forward filing into the steel.

DRAW FILING

In draw filing we pull or push the file perpendicular to the edge of the metal being filed to create a flat, smoothly cut edge or surface. To do this we grasp the file with both hands; one hand at either end of the file. We then push or pull the file along the edge, using even pressure as much as possible, in a continuous motion from one end to the other. The direction depends on which hand holds the handle end; push in the wrong direction and the file glides instead of cutting. Pushing the right way cuts into the steel and you can feel that some effort is needed to push into and through the cut. Otherwise you can be pushing or pulling the back of the teeth against the metal which does not cut and can fracture the teeth of the file.

The draw filing motion cuts the steel in ribbons that twist in spirals as if peeled from the surface. This results in a continuous surface to the steel with zero or minor surface chatter and undulation. This method of filing also prevents the file teeth from scoring and scratching the surface as is the case with through filing. Instead we get long spirals of metal that peel away from beneath the file to form a continuous cut along the edge or face being filed. This method produces the clearest, cleanest, and smoothest surface, with minimum scudding and chatter, which causes unevenness. With this method, only a few file teeth engage the material. These slice-cut the steel, resulting in a continuous slicing action along the edge. This engagement cuts and lifts the material into the groove between the file teeth. The steel shavings then turn long-ways into a spiral and exit at the side of the material being filed; hence the long spirals and the smoother surface.

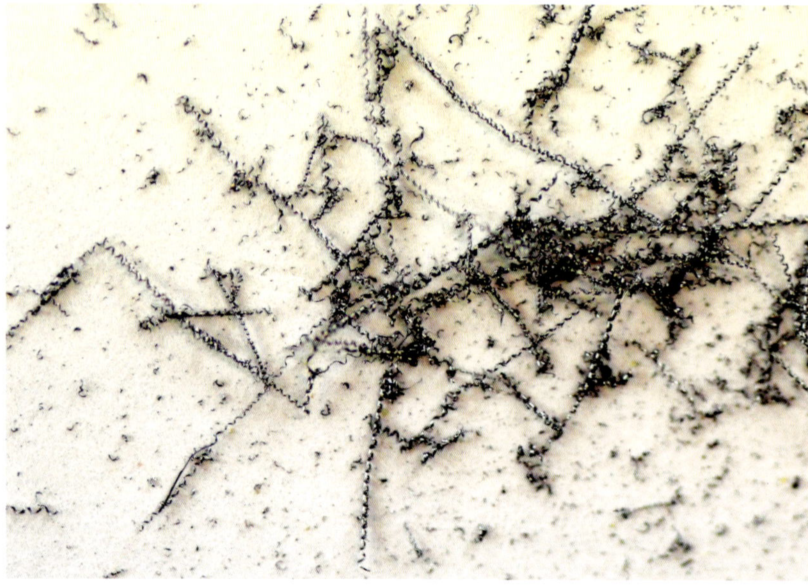

Spiral waste is the result of draw filing, which cuts the steel in a continuous and unbroken manner, leaving the edge or surface of thin metal smooth.

File Holding

Though the hand positions given are generally good for most work, they may well vary with different tasks. As you work all the more with files you will develop a knowledge for the worth of other hand positions. The file handle can be cupped inside the palm of the dominant hand and gripped by the other fingers except the fore finger, which rests in the upper part of the file handle in a relaxed pointing position.

Stroke and Pressure

Due to the shape and nature of the file teeth, the file cuts on the forward stroke only and not when the file is pulled on the reverse stroke. Therefore, to prevent damage and unnecessary wear to the file teeth along the cutting edge, lift the file from the work after each forward thrust and relocate for subsequent forward thrusts. This may not seem obvious but it really saves the file.

Remember it is all too easy to consider filing as an aggressive work of forcing steel into steel. That is far from the case. The work demands the same sensitivity we use to plane wood.

Files clog when too much pressure is applied wrongly and swarf jams in the teeth. This prevents the teeth from reaching the material to cut cleanly and effectively. A special stiffly-wired brush called a file card is purposely made to disgorge the swarf but, in most cases, a wire brush works fine. Brush the waste from the teeth of the file by running the brush along or with the teeth. It is important to work parallel to the teeth and into the grooves between them, not into the edges of the teeth. This is because the hardened spring steel of the file card or wire brush can quickly damage the file's cutting edges.

Never use a file without a well-fitted handle except for topping saw teeth, where the hands straddle the file and the saw teeth (see page 307). Common hand and arm injuries occur when the unhandled tang of the file penetrates the inner wrist, forearm, and palm.

Parts to the File:

Point (toe), length, side–working face, heel, tang, teeth, edge

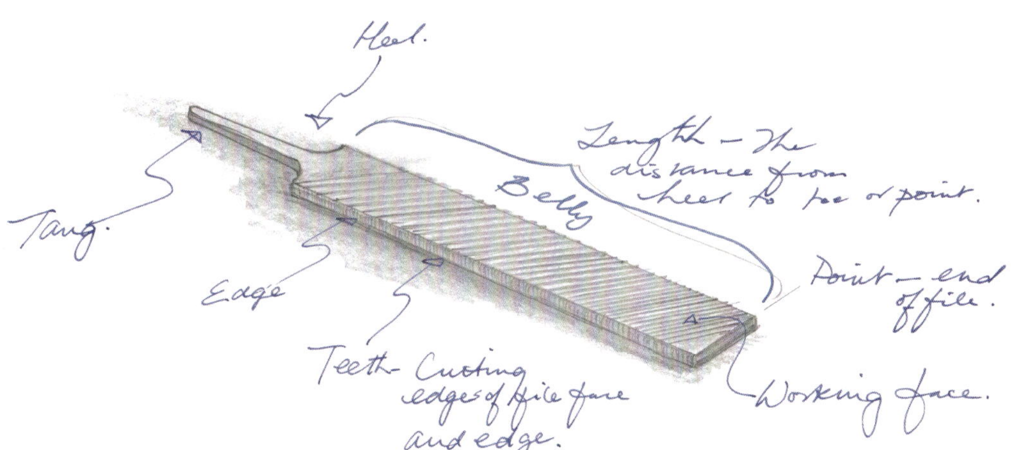

The Sawset

How sawsets work and what they do may not be obvious from looking at the sawset alone but they are simple to use once you understand them. For a saw to work effectively it must create a cut that is wider than the thickness of the saw blade. Otherwise the saw will bind in the cut and become difficult or impossible to use. A sawset is a device used by woodworkers to slightly bend the teeth on the different saws used throughout the various woodworking crafts and trades. Sawsets make the task very direct and accurate. We use the mechanism to bend each alternate saw tooth in the opposite direction so that the teeth create a passage into the wood that allows the saw cut to deepen without binding in the cut. This bend in the tooth is generally slight and uniform, and once the tooth is bent it is set and fixed at the exact angle needed. These alternate bends create what we call 'saw kerf.' As well as creating the passage for the body of the saw, saw kerf also allows realignment if the saw drifts slightly from its course and minor redirection is needed. Sometimes, as the saw progresses into and through the cut, it loses perfect alignment for different reasons. Without this slight margin for correction the saw would be governed by the rigidity of the stiff plate. This drawing shows how the saw kerf relieves the side pressures as the teeth-points slice the wood regardless of whether the cuts are cross-grain or rip-grain cuts.

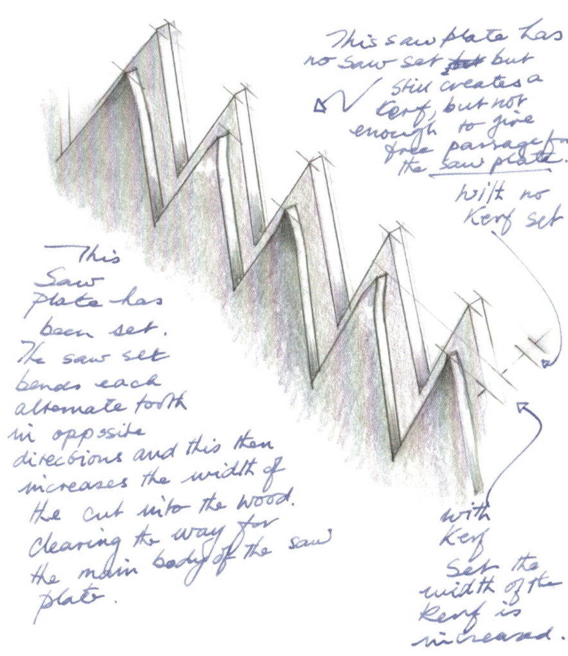

Different types of sawsets have evolved throughout the last century or so but the one remaining in daily use is the one we commonly know as the Eclipse 77 sawset. Originating in Sheffield, England, this sawset has proven to be the most popular but the originals are only available secondhand today as the UK maker is no longer manufacturing them. Fortunately though, this tool has retained an unparalleled international popularity and other brands, with the same design, are available. Secondhand ones are rarely worn out or worn beyond functionality and can be bought fairly cheaply.

This sawset, like almost all sawsets, is a plier-type set; one moveable arm squeezes and secures the saw plate between two support points and allows a plunger to force the chosen tooth against an opposing disc. The outer edge of the disc has a shallow bevel and, when the handles are squeezed, a second part we call the hammer or tooth setter emerges from the center of the plunger and bends the tooth away from the user. Following the existing tooth-set pattern along the length of the saw shows us that we set only every alternate tooth. We generally keep track of the teeth we have set by starting at one end or the other and setting the teeth leaning away from us. Often we discover secondhand saws with no set at all and this is usually due to wear. In this case it makes no difference which teeth you set. Simply start with the first one and press the handle to set the first tooth. From here on you miss every other tooth until you reach the other end. At this point, turn the saw end for end and set the other teeth in the opposite direction. Keep the same setting to both sides. Uneven saw setting causes the saw to curve as it progresses into the cut.

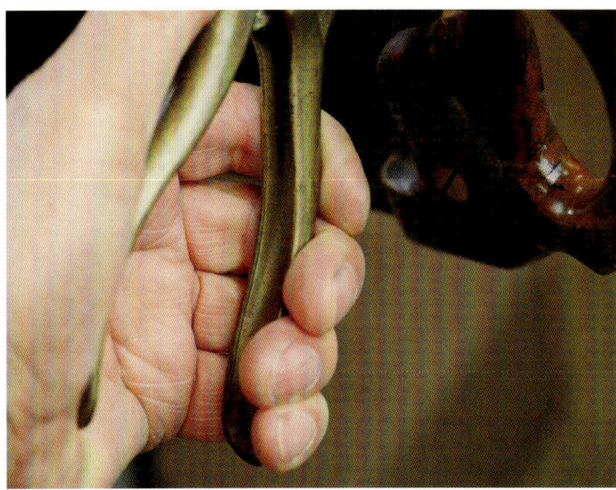

Sawsets allow us to select different depths of set to the teeth. This is controlled by setting the depth corresponding to numbers on the edge of the anvil. The numbers around the edge of the disc enable you to set the teeth according to a predetermined set. These numbers provide a reference point; a guide to help establish a preferred set for particular saw types and tooth sizes. Generally, it is best to minimize the amount of set you apply. It stands to reason however that the larger saws need greater set. But remember that the more set you have, the more wood you must remove; and the more energy the subsequent sawing work takes to push each stroke into and through the wood. This is a fact seldom recognised by woodworkers today, and most new saws I come across have more set than is generally needed. To check the depth of saw set, cut into, say, a ¾" (20mm) thick board of pine. As you progress into the cut and the cut deepens, look at the sides of the plate on both sides to see how much of a gap you have between the face of the plate and the wood. If the gap is too big it allows wobble from side to side. We discuss removing the depth of set, if needed, later.

The amount of set we need on any saw is often determined by different conditions, mostly the nature and type of wood, and also the amount of moisture in the wood. Wet softwoods tend to bind the saws when the set is too small. We often add extra set when the wood has higher levels of internal moisture content or if the wood has been resaturated by being stacked, unprotected, outdoors for an extended time. When extra set is needed temporarily or situationally, we can set to task and then remove the set after the work is concluded by tapping the teeth between two hammers, see page 57. This is less common these days because most wood purchased will be kiln dried.

Adjusting the Set

Setting the distance of kerf is an easy thing. The rotary anvil that governs the depth of set comprises a diminishing bevel to the face of the wheel. When the wheel is rotated, the angle the teeth are pressed to changes according to the setting. On the rim of the wheel are reference numbers to set the wheel to different positions in relation to the plunger or hammer. To change the setting, slacken the knurled knob a little, sufficient to turn the anvil wheel with the numbers on. Then turn the wheel to the desired setting and retighten the knurled knob. The higher the number on the anvil, the least set or bend to the teeth and the lower the number, the most. We therefore set the anvil at 12 for a minimal set and then use the other numbered reference points for other preferred settings, with the heaviest set being 4. Tooth size determines the number of teeth or points there are per running inch of saw length. I generally set all of my saws with the minimum set and only increase it if the saw binds in the cut due to either moisture in the wood or if a particular wood type requires it. That said, most saws, including tenon and dovetail saws, are almost always set between 10-12 depending on the wood type and the work in hand. Larger handsaws can be set between 8-10. If the wood is wet, and this generally pertains to handsaws only as we would not generally use finer backsaws with wet wood, it is easily changed to perhaps 6-8, but only if needed after a test cut.

Alternate Methods

You may find that the smaller-toothed saws can be more awkward to set. Also occasionally there are slight differences between even seemingly identical sawsets made by the same company, and that might raise issues too. Sometimes the plunger (hammer) protrudes past the top of the teeth on the saw and also slightly above the rim corner of the wheel (anvil). This then bends the tooth more over the edge of the anvil and creates a more aggressive tooth set. The thinness of the saw plate can also affect set too. Where I find it useful, I use a nail punch and a small hammer to set the teeth. I find this method more precise if placing the nail punch dead centre on the tooth and, provided you use the same light tap for each tooth, the set is surprisingly accurate too. After the teeth have been set, using the same alternate tooth pattern on both sides that we used for the sawset, we then secure a second hammer in the vise with the flat or slightly domed face of the hammer facing uppermost. Moving the saw along the upturned hammer face, we then tap, tap, tap the teeth with constant light tapping as we pull the saw plate from one end to the other between the two hammer faces. First we tap from one side of the plate and then flip the saw and do the other with the same small taps. This then sets the teeth to an exact depth because there is enough memory in the steel to return the teeth to a uniform set according to the pressure of the tapping. Once done, the saw is set. As an added measure, tape masking tape on each side of the plate next to the saw teeth to create a precise depth and use a diamond file or other whetstone to refine the teeth with a couple of strokes to each side of the plate. You can add a second layer of tape if you want to retain more set.

Using the Sawset

The body position used when setting saws varies according to the saw type, size and so on. The saw can be clamped between wooden holders in the vise. Alternatively, you can use a specially devised holder like the one I am using (below left). This is usually the most commonly practised and the quickest means to get started. When setting small saws like gent's and dovetail saws, the device used to hold the saw can impair the sawset from reaching the teeth squarely and adequately. In such cases we hold the saw in a braced position between the non-dominant hand and the body or the non-dominant hand and, say, a bench top. This may seem awkward at first but sometimes it is necessary.

I like to bring the saw up to a working height, where I can work the sawset comfortably and see the work too. You must align the sawset against the exact tooth. Particularly when working with small teeth, you can easily skip one too many or not skip at all and end up mis-setting any remaining teeth. This negates the set and you end up with all the remaining teeth set to one side. You may want to mark the teeth with a marker pen, especially when eyesight is an issue. Marking both sides along the teeth means that when the plunger or nail punch strikes the teeth it marks the individual teeth by removing traces of the marker. Then you can see which ones you have set and which you have not.

Using the sawset is simply a question of setting the plunger, centered on the tip or point of the tooth and then squeezing the handles, plier-fashion, with the dominant hand. Keep the sawset firm and tight to the plate throughout each press and watch to make sure that each tooth moves to the anvil disc. Sometimes, without the right pressure, the plunger or hammer can slip off the tooth and end up in the gullet between the teeth points, and no tooth is set at all. A magnifying headpiece helps if eyesight is diminished. Often, light is the main problem and it is good to find a well lit position for sharpening and setting saws. We rely greatly on tell-tale reflection throughout the process when we both sharpen and set saws.

Refining Saw Sets

Sawsets, like the Eclipse ones shown, are often inexpensive finds at garage sales, flea markets, and car boot sales; mostly because they look like some kind of plier and no one knows what they are or indeed what they do. Even if someone did know what they do, the chances are that they have never used one and do not need one so they go for very little money. For some reason, on the earlier models of the Eclipse, the hammer - the little plunger that bends the teeth - is generally about half the thickness of that on the post 50's models. The finer hammer is more practical on fine-toothed saws with teeth smaller than, say, 10 TPI and they are just as effective on larger teeth too.

The problem is that the heavier or thicker hammer can be too wide for the small teeth; it often does not fit between the teeth to reach an individual tooth. When this happens, the set ripples the saw plate, along with the tooth, instead of simply setting the individual teeth. If necessary, it is simple enough to remove the hammer from the barrel and grind the sides of the plunger to the fineness you need for setting your saw. The hammer can then be reinstalled in the barrel of the set. That does not mean you must have more than one sawset. If you are purchasing a new sawset and have a choice between a thicker and finer hammer, go for the finer. The finer sawset will set all saws.

The Burnisher

The burnisher is a specialised tool we use to consolidate the steel into itself to create a highly refined cutting edge. Made from hardened steel and held in a wooden handle, the burnisher is simple enough yet most people would not know what the tool is or how it is used. The burnisher itself, though non-abrasive and non-cutting, is a sharpening tool that creates a cutting edge for shaving the surface of wood. We need to understand that the type of blade the burnisher sharpens is not a plane blade or a part of a plane but, in fact, a scraper. Just as the burnisher is unique to sharpening scrapers, the scraper itself is not a plane at all, although it does rely on a sharpened edge. The sharpened edge is truly uniquely formed and the tool blade is used in a very unique way too; whether held only in the hands or held in a two-handled holder as in the #80 scraper or similar (see the section starting on page 365 for more information on scrapers and how they are used). The steel used to make the burnisher is usually round, oval, or triangular with all of the corners rounded so that there are no sharp edges. There are other shapes too. If you have the opportunity you should try different shapes and see which ones you prefer. These burnishers all work and work well, so it is usually a matter of preference as to which one you choose.

Burnishers create a highly refined and sophisticated cutting edge to what is otherwise simply the square edge on a sheet of plate carbon tool steel. The resulting work creates a unique cutting tool that slices through the surface of wood in wide bands. The width of cut is generally between 1-3" (25-75mm) wide. Scrapers, especially the card scraper, present the cutting edge at the lowest possible angle of any of the woodworking tool types.

Some makers of burnishers extend the steel several inches from the handle. However, in use, we do not need a long steel burnisher as we generally apply pressure to the tool near the handle. This minimises leverage and increases power and accuracy throughout use. The men I worked with used a well-worn and worn down chisel that did the same remedial work as the burnisher in developing the edges needed; no such special tool existed for most craftsmen. When I was starting out, I was taught to use the back of a bevel-edged chisel and it worked just fine. In my ignorance, I did not know burnishers existed until I had been burnishing with a chisel or a gouge for over a decade. I was in my early thirties when I picked up my first dedicated burnisher, which worked better and was much safer to use.

As I said, there are several designs in burnishers on the market for you to try and consider, and some are well designed and practical. Take a look in most tool boxes though and you will most likely own several options in tools that will turn an edge to a scraper. Make sure you consider your safety in using tools with sharp edges or points but anything from a simple nail punch to a screwdriver will burnish, consolidate, and turn an edge easily. That said, it is nice to own a dedicated tool like the one I designed for my own use (below). Mine is made from O1 hardened steel and has a turned hardwood handle; it is slightly curved and is oval shaped in section. The length of metal is ideal at 3" (75mm) and the handle too is 3" (75mm) long and 1 ⅛" (28mm) in diameter. The steel was made from ⅜" (10mm) diameter round stock.

The first time I used a nail punch was in an emergency when I had no other tool to burnish with. My expectation then was that such a poor-man's burnisher would drag because of the small diameter size but that was not the case at all. It burnished just as well as the nice, wooden-handled type. It feels fairly safe in the hand and takes up no room in the tool chest till. The nail punch will be one of the most inexpensive burnishers you can buy to get started if money is an issue and if traveling light to a job is a consideration.

Choosing a Burnisher

The burnisher we use for much of our work at the woodworking school is one used mostly by engineers for removing wire edges and burrs from the edges of their milled and machined parts. These are made from tool steel and are hardened for purpose and longevity. However, for scraper blades they really prove the reality that iron can indeed sharpen iron. Being harder than the scraper blades they are burnishing and because they are generally used by woodworkers to consolidate steel into itself, they just last indefinitely and have no reductive wear influence from the scraper edges being burnished.

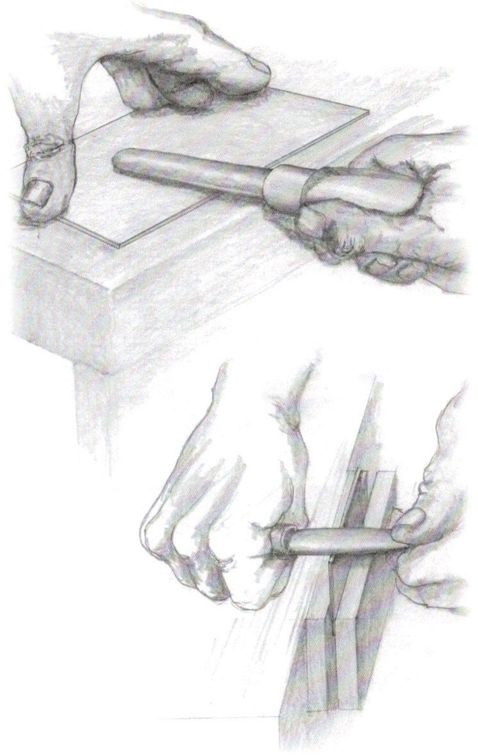

Burnishers developed for woodworkers by engineers have taken on a life of their own over recent decades. A range of dedicated burnishers have now replaced the adapted and serendipitous ones. I generally like a larger radius over a small one and I like an oval rather than a basic round. That does not mean that the others do not work equally as well too. It is just that a bigger radius gives a wider distribution of pressure and the pressure is more even over the surface of the narrow edges. This then reduces the tendency of uneven impressing causing indentation to the worked edge. I think this is why the back face of a gouge and a bevel-edged chisel worked so well too. I think it is worth mentioning that oval burnishers can be more versatile because they allow the use of the tighter radius along their narrower edges. This is useful for sharpening shaped scrapers that might not be accessible to round burnishers with larger radii.

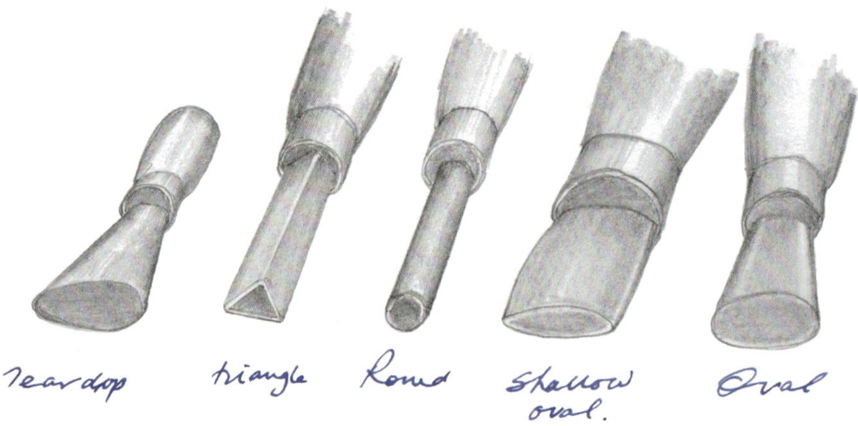

Holding the Burnisher

I will discuss using the burnisher further in the section on scrapers (page 371) but here I want to show a few of the positions for using the burnisher. The burnisher comprises hardened steel held in a wooden handle, which allows you to use good pressure.

In single-handed use the handle is gripped firmly and forcefully. In this application the burnisher is held in a full-handed grip by the dominant hand which allows a series of successive upward pulls from the bench to the top corner.

Two-handed use relies on the same dominant-hand grip plus the side of the forefinger and thumb of the other hand to hold the tip of the burnisher. In two-handed use the scraper is anchored in the vise; the hands hold the burnisher across the edge and pull or push or both to burnish and turn the edge.

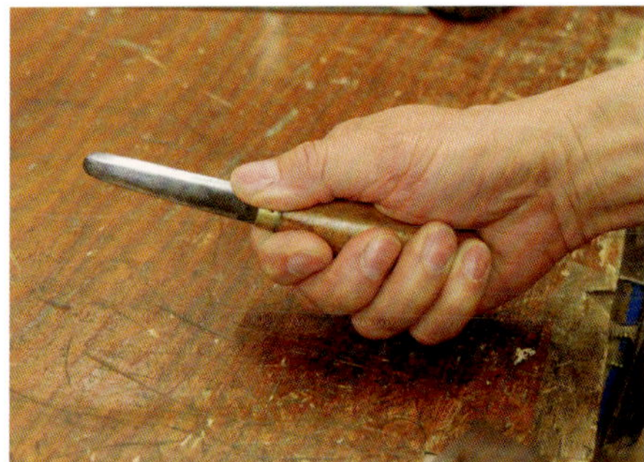

Layout Tools

The Importance of Layout Tools

In most cases, the tools we use for laying out are the less noticed tools. They are mostly simple and they may initially seem less interesting than other groups of tools. This is true of just about all of the layout tools because they seem more ancillary to the real or 'doing' work. At one time I had less regard for them myself but then one day it struck me that without them my work would always be second rate. It was at that point that I started to esteem them more highly and searched out the ones I knew would keep me honest. I wanted layout tools that would last me a lifetime and ones I would take care of. The pursuit of fine woodworking demands uncompromised accuracy and uncompromised accuracy relies totally on good layout tools. Every layout tool then became critically important to both me and my work. The wood, the steel, and the brass they are made of, and even the plastics too, should be of a quality that means they guarantee accurate lines. High quality, accurate layout tools help to ensure accuracy in the markings that they make or those made by the tools that run up against them. They are also used, in some cases, directly against the wood to check that the wood itself is square and true or that projects with multiple pieces are configured correctly.

Layout is a Time-tested Methodology

Layout tools are a small and unique group of tools. We use them to map out the lines that later guide the tools used to make cuts into the wood. The lines we make follow a well-developed and systematic approach to layout, which was established by time-served craftsmen in an era when skilled workmanship reached its pinnacle. The demands on craftsmen led to the development of layout procedures that we still rely on today; procedures which guarantee economy of movement, efficiency, and accuracy. Nothing has ever replaced the traditional methods of layout with something new or better. I think it is amazing that we still use the same basic layout tools and simple layout procedures that have been used by woodworkers for centuries.

> *The pursuit of fine woodworking demands uncompromised accuracy and uncompromised accuracy relies totally on good layout tools*

The Art of Layout

The layout methods and techniques are the starting point for building a wide range of structural frames, cases, cabinets, and boxes. It is through this process that we create the lines needed to work the flat faces of wood sections and boards to create our three-dimensional works of art. Laying out the work means we trace the positions of cuts onto adjacent faces to show where material needs to be removed to create joints. During layout we rotate each section of squared-off wood to align each of the faces for marking out the lines for working into joinery, rabbeting, and grooving. The forethought layout requires means thinking three-dimensionally. We create lines that we then work to, using cutting tools such as chisels, saws, planes, and spokeshaves. Using squares, rulers, tape measures, marking and mortise gauges, and knives, we place markings which define where we are to make permanent marks and cuts. Laying out the parts is critical to our preparation work. Without the order of laying out, accuracy is impossible.

Essential Layout Tools

The tools we use for laying out rarely, if ever, actually remove any material from the wood we work. We mostly mark the surfaces, part the fibres, and slice or cut the grain. The tools are the square, pencil, marking, mortise or combination gauges, the knife, tape measure, sliding bevel, and compasses.

Before going into further detail on the other layout tools, I want to highlight two that can often be taken for granted but nevertheless are essential to layout. They are the pencil and the compasses.

THE PENCIL

There was an age when pencils, as we know them today, did not exist for woodworking and when they first came in they were expensive. That is no longer the case and, throughout my lifetime, I have relied on them for one reason; pencils lay down the initial guidelines for the permanent guide and cut lines with gauges and knives. They do this without damaging the wood. This then shows where to start and stop such lines so that they are never seen after they have been placed and indeed used. I can lay out the position of the width of a mortise in pencil and then run the mortise gauge lines between the pencil lines. These gauge lines start and stop right on the pencil lines. Then I can use the knife or chisel for a knifewall or chop-cut delineating the extreme width of the tenon exactly. Had I not had the pencil, telltale lines from a scribe point would have been permanent and visible. Often we take such things for granted but dovetail lines and marking around the dovetails, as templates for the corresponding pins, is another good example of where a pencil can help provide temporary marks that guide permanent cuts. Marking material with the face and face-edge markings is clearly practicable too, durable yet easily removed when done with.

As a general-use pencil, I use an imported, US-made, #2 pencil, which generally, but not always, equates to the UK's HB grade. There are different grades and colours of pencil but, for work on woodworking as well as taking notes and drawing, this is my essential pencil.

When I arrived to live and work in the USA I liked the way they attached erasers to the ends of their pencils. We do now have them more commonly in the UK, but only on a fifty-fifty basis so far. I like attached pencil erasers but it is also important to realise

that not all erasers are created equal and some erasers do not work well; they leave behind a deposit of the eraser, damaging paper and leaving unsightly marks on wood. I have found that there are several better quality pencils available that have consistent graphite values, cedar wood casings, and a top-notch eraser. My experience tells me that, in no way, are all pencils of the same quality and you should test a variety of pencils to find one that works for you. The flat rectangular carpenter's pencil associated with general carpentry is less suited to fine woodworking, furniture making, and bench work so I do not use them myself and do not generally recommend them.

Ultimately, pencil choice depends on your particular use. Though I prefer to use a #2 or HB pencil for almost all of my benchwork layout and general marking, there are other types available and you might prefer something softer and darker or harder and lighter.

THE COMPASSES

I use my compasses frequently enough to say they are important and essential. In any given day, I embark upon at least one task or project that requires geometric layout, stepping off repeatable distances, describing arcs to work to and a myriad other uses. My favourite types are the old brass ones from the days when a 1 ½" (38mm) point was not considered an offensive weapon in school. The pair

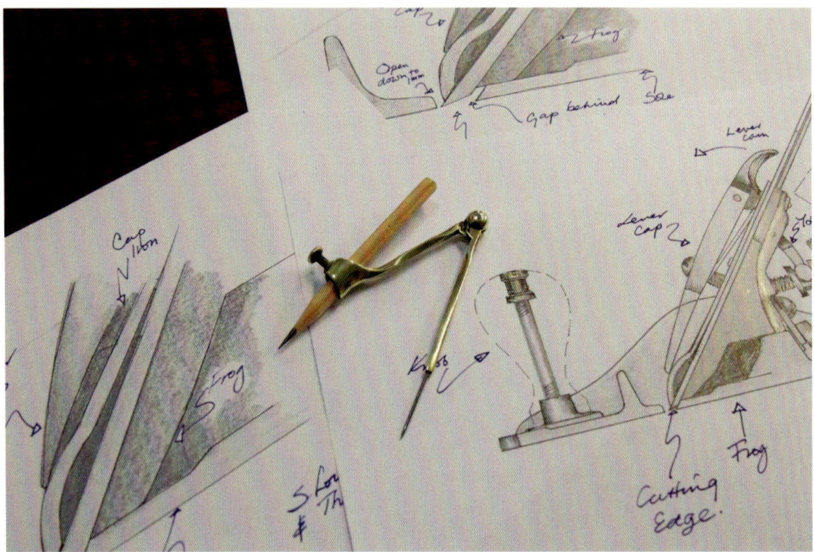

of compasses you see here is about 100 years old. They need to be stiff in opening and must retain the distance, once opened, to unwavering exactness. That is what to look for when you buy them secondhand. If they are loose and move after distance setting, the setscrew usually tightens enough to take up the slack. If not, you can peen over the end of the brass setscrew just enough to tighten the two legs, as you would a rivet. The main feature I like is that they receive the standard pencil into the holder. This is both functional and convenient.

The rest of the tools I consider essential to layout are listed here, along with the page number of the page where I discuss them in more depth:

The Square p. 71
The Tape Measure p. 87
The Layout Knife p. 93
The Marking Gauge p. 105
The Sliding Bevel p. 119

The Square

There is more information about almost every other woodworking tool type than there is about the square. It is not a frequent topic of conversation among woodworkers and yet squares feature very highly in the minute-by-minute of any woodworker's day. I can talk about squares all day long, as much as I can about planes and saws. I want to use this section to show you what to look for in a good square and how to use this tool that we woodworkers can barely function without.

Experience has taught me to never take the square for granted and to fully respect it even though it is likely one of the most humble and least noticed tools that woodworkers rely on. Squares do indeed rule just about all of the other tools we use in woodworking. Working at the bench, I have learned that the square is the means by which we control almost every aspect of our work. All of the projects we make begin with the preparation of stock and the subsequent layout of joints and joinery components. Just about all the other tools take their reference from the square.

I have collected many squares of different types and sizes over the years although, for the main part, I rely on just one. The combination square is not merely a useful tool but it is also versatile, well balanced in the hand, and designed to give total control in my work. New woodworkers often underestimate how essential it is to own a square that is well made and accurate. I have made it a policy not to allow any square in my workshop that is not dead square and of a lasting quality. Any deviation from this demand for dead-on accuracy always risks the possibility of inaccurate work.

Whenever I lead the work on an important piece of furniture, I must ensure that every square used in the project is perfectly accurate. This is because I know that every component will be critically fitted, square and mitred, one to the other. Therefore, I check every person's square against my own tested and proven square. This guarantees each person's work with the square equals the standards of all the others'.

The square is always used for initial marking and layout prior to any and all joint making and the opening cuts. Though machines often rely on an accurate square for setup, this is never more significant than in the use of hand tools and the traditions of hand work. In hand tool woodworking, these are the main areas that the square is used for:

- Laying out the shoulder lines in joinery
- Checking accuracy when planing wood square and planing stock foursquare
- Guiding knifewall cuts
- Checking general accuracy in cuts and configuration of parts
- Checking each phase and the finished work before and after glue-up

Squares Come in All Shapes and Sizes

Choosing a square from the many available types of squares can be challenging. While I will make a recommendation for the ideal first square, as time goes on, you may want to own additional squares for certain work, depending mostly on the size of the work in hand. This chapter should remove some of the confusion and help you determine which square to buy first.

The square is used throughout almost all the various woodworking crafts. A try (also tri) square derives its name from trying or testing a material part and its accuracy in any 90-degree configuration. Though a maker might name a square according to some function or use, almost all squares could be referred to simply as a square. For instance, a 'speed square' is designed for use in building construction; it works well with dimensional lumber and guides power tools, such as skill-saws, for crosscutting wood to length. It is still perfectly acceptable to refer to a speed square just as a square.

Parts of the Square

A square is a simple tool used to lay out projects and project parts at right angles to an edge as well as to check that one surface is 90 degrees to another. Though different types of squares are available, most squares comprise two basic elements; the beam (also called the blade) and the stock (sometimes called the head). The heavier section, whether steel or wood, is the stock. Some stocks are moveable along the beam and some are fixed.

THE STOCK

The heavier aspect of the square, known as the stock, is usually the shorter part of the square that you register against a proven straight edge. Once the stock is anchored in place by hand pressure, the beam then projects at exactly 90 degrees to the edge. This provides a square line for marking and cutting with a pencil, steel scribe or knife. We can also use the stock of the square up against the adjacent parts of work in progress, or completed work to check that one part is 90 degrees to another. A moveable stock is especially useful when checking internal and external corners as it adds versatility.

THE BEAM

The beam is the thinner blade of steel (or wood in the case of all-wood squares) extending from the stock at 90 degrees. Depending on the square type, this beam is either made from hardened or tempered steel or, depending on the thickness of the steel plate used, may also be made from flexible spring steel. The joiner's try square usually uses this thinner plate with a wooden stock and brass wear insert running along the inner edge of the stock.

Wooden stock with brass insert and steel plate as beam.

The combination square has a moveable stock. You might think that introducing a moving part leads to inaccuracies where fixed components allow no such movement. My experience is different. I have used the same engineer's combination square six days a week for the past half-century and there is no discernible difference in terms of wear and accuracy since the first day I bought it.

The Combination Square

The original engineer's combination squares are fine examples of accuracy and the designs are exceptionally well thought through. In terms of functionality and application they seem, in my view, to be unsurpassed. Cast-iron, weighty stocks and hardened steel beams lock solidly to one another and allow adjustment along the beam. This helps to balance the square throughout the many diverse variables in the work in hand. The adaptable versatility permitted by a single combination square replaced multiple sized squares in one tool and gradually rendered the try square more or less obsolete.

The engineer's combination square has been adopted by woodworkers despite the fact that, as the name implies, this square was designed for engineering. The term 'combination' relates to the inclusion of both a 90-degree square and a 45-degree angle in the stock. This combination enables the tool to be used for both square and mitred marks and cuts. Marks are usually established by running the pencil or knife along the beam. Furthermore, the combination part of the name also refers to the fact that these squares are often available with an optional centre-finder and protractor.

Engineer's squares are generally more highly engineered than carpentry squares, which are often stamped-out and low quality. Carpentry squares are often used for rough marking and use with hand-held power tools. That said, no matter the craft, there can be no allowance for any square to be less than accurate; they must always be square. Any minor discrepancy, even in more crudely made carpenter's roofing squares, will always translate into major inaccuracy; no matter the tools used subsequent to marking and laying out with the square, there will generally be a knock-on effect that escalates as the work progresses. This is why a tool designed for engineers, who are perceived to have a greater need for accuracy than woodworkers, is actually better than many other square types.

The Combination Square has a sliding beam. This allows the beam to move into different places. adjustability!

Pull or push stroke

The Combination Square.
I think a real advantage the moveable beam has is to mark parallel lines using the stock of the square against the edge of board or billet and setting the distance needed to keep the pencil parallel to the edge. You can also use a knife for dead accuracy for work such as hinge recessing or inlay lines.
I drew this drawing from my head; in my mind's eye, not from an image or drawing. It worked but this is rare for me.

The Try Square

At one time the try square would have been the most commonly used of any square ever made. During the 1800s try squares were manufactured by toolmakers using a variety of materials known for hardness, durability and resistance to wear. Brass, steel, ebony, and rosewood fitted these criteria and also resisted changes in humidity.

Try squares often comprise a wooden stock, a brass wear insert or plate along the inside face of the wooden stock and a steel beam made from plate steel. The sizes do vary but common sizes along the beam are 4" (100mm), 6" (150mm), 8" (200mm), 10" (250mm), and 12" (300mm). The most commonly used and convenient size for most work at the workbench is around 12" (300mm).

The largest all-wooden try squares were generally made from dimensionally stable woods such as oak and mahogany. I frequently came across these in my youth when sent to retrieve a tool for one of the joiners from their tool chests. We used these for laying out and checking frames during construction and found them especially useful for sheet materials such as plywood and engineered boards. These were almost always craftsman-made tools, but I have occasionally come across try squares made by known makers.

"These squares have a proven track-record and, when they are well-maintained and proven to be accurate, they are a great tool to own"

Unfortunately, long term use takes its toll on tools like these and I have generally found them, especially those made with wooden components, to be less accurate than would be acceptable. It has been difficult to find a modern-day manufacturer producing consistent accuracy in these tools and yet we, as crafting artisans, can accept nothing less than dead-on squareness.

That said, if you do find a try square in good condition and it is accurate then it will work very well. These squares have a proven track-record and, when they are well-maintained and proven to be accurate, they are a great tool to own.

Choosing Your First Square

I believe the best choice of square for working wood is the 12" (300mm) engineer's combination square. You may want additional squares as you grow in your craft and develop different interest areas such as boat building and timber-framing, instrument making or miniature work. The main advantages to the combination square are its adjustability, ergonomic comfort, and its functionality. Ridges, rims, and pierced castings facilitate clutching and squeezing the stock to the work, which is essential throughout every aspect of use.

Combination squares are also available with 6" (150mm), 9" (225mm), 12" (300mm), and 18" (450mm) beams. These can be bought as complete units with stocks or the beams can be bought independently for use as needed. I own larger try squares that generally work well for larger expanses, and I also like having a 6" (150mm) combination square for small work and working in more confined areas. The 12" (300mm) combination square, however, is generally my recommended first choice and takes care of 99% of my daily furniture making and woodworking needs.

Features of the engineer's combination square comprise:

Cast iron stock.

Hardened steel beam.

Marking pin (scribe).

Easy hand holding.

Imperial and metric markings.

Adjustable beam and lockable mechanism.

Use for distance marking.

Use as depth gauge.

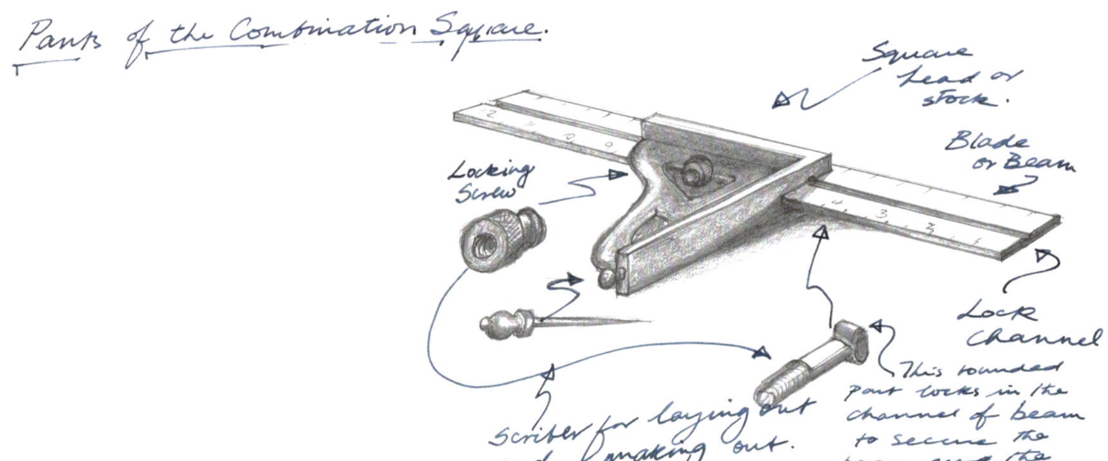

Checking the Accuracy of a Square

Because almost every cut made using hand tools takes its reference from the square, the squares we use must be as dead-on accurate as possible before any work such as joinery can commence. Even the smallest infraction, which some might consider inconsequential, leads to inaccuracy that then telegraphs throughout every aspect of the work. For this reason it is essential we choose a reliably accurate square right from the outset. Without it, we build problems into the work and we have no way of reconciling the problems that occur as a result.

It is always good to question the accuracy of a square and I am frequently asked how you check squares for squareness. Even if you own a good quality square, testing it out at intervals gives you confidence and takes away any niggling doubts. Over the long term, squares can and do lose their accuracy, especially if they are damaged through droppage or misuse. They also go out of square through wear itself - it is a good thing to check them periodically if only for your own reassurance.

The easiest and quickest way to check any square for accuracy is against an existing square. Provided you do indeed have access to a guaranteed square, it is simple enough to align one beam against the stock or beam of the other to see how the parts align. Most people starting out, however, may not have that luxury.

The alternative method for checking a square for accuracy is to develop a straightedge. To do this you need two flat boards about 9-10" (225-250mm) wide. You can use narrower boards, say 6-8" (150-200mm), but the wider the board, the greater the length to test against, making the testing more accurate. Any wood will work but a softwood like pine works just fine. This method is also workable with plywood and MDF too but, if they need planing straight, they do not plane as easily as real wood. That said, sometimes high-quality MDF is machined to high standards and starts out with a perfectly machined edge.

Here are the steps to developing dead-straight edges on solid wood for testing squares:

1. I edge-joint two meeting edges of the boards as if edge-jointing two boards for making a jointed panel. If you have a jack plane it works well for this but a number 4 smoothing plane works just fine too. My pieces are about 24" (600mm) long, which is long enough for this.

   The reason for truing two boards is that one checks the other. This works because planing the two edges side by side means that if you plane a belly it will be exaggerated and show gaps at each end when the

edges are aligned in opposition to one another. If hollowed, the gap in the centre will show as twice the actual discrepancy of each individual board. Once there are no gaps, both must be straight because they were planed simultaneously side by side. It sounds complicated but it is not.

Start planing in the usual manner from one end to the other, just to eliminate any disparity in levels. Then move to a central point in the length of the two boards and begin planing with short strokes working from either side of the centre with longer and longer strokes until you get a continuous stroke from one end to the other. Provided the plane's sole is straight and the plane is sharp, you should have two straight edges when they meet. If the board is bellied, and you check this by sighting along the edge corner, you must correct it and take care not to simply follow a bellied edge and so retain the belly or make it worse.

2. Bring the two edges together and if the two meet seamlessly then the edges can be nothing else but truly straight because, as long as they are planed simultaneously in the vise, side by side, it is impossible to plane one straight or hollow and the other the opposite.

3. You can use either a very sharp pencil or a sharp knife for this step. I prefer to use a knife. Square a line across the board from one side to the other with the stock of the square registered firmly against the planed edge of the board as shown (top right). Use a light pass for this.

4. Flip the square over with the stock along the same edge and test it against the same knife line. If the points meet across the width exactly then the square must be square. Also, check along the whole length of the knife line made with the square after the flipover. This will highlight any deviation if the edge of the square's beam is not straight too.

You must check both sides of the beam by sliding the stock along to check the inner edge of the square too as we use both sides of the beam.

If you are checking a try square, with a wooden or metal stock, you must also check the outer edge of the stock of the square. This is simply a measurement check to see if it is dead parallel to the inner face. If it is, and if the stock is parallel, it will also be square to the beam.

An alternative source for a guaranteed straight edge to work from is all the simpler and just as accurate for checking and that is using card stock. Card stock and thick paper have extremely precise and straight and squared edges because of their manufacturing processes. This is to our advantage. Place the card on a flat surface such as a square-edged table or board and then the longer edge of the card can be used for registering the square to check its squareness. The method is then the same as before; place the stock of the square against that long edge of the card, make two knife marks either end of the beam, flip over and look to see if the marks still align to the beam. Any discrepancy reflects an inaccuracy in the square.

Restoring Squareness to Try Squares

Squares made from quality materials that have properly hardened and well-engineered components generally are made to retain their accuracy. Because of the more complex engineering methods used to make combination squares it would be extremely difficult to repair them using hand methods. Older squares however, are often made from softer steel, brass, or wood. Restoring these to accuracy is not so complicated and can be accomplished with a sharp 10-12" (250-300mm) single-cut flat file provided all of the components are in good condition, solidly fixed and with no movement in the riveting connecting the beam to the stock of the square. If there is movement, however, this too can be fixed by peening existing rivets or adding additional rivets. Filing and draw-filing the steel plate takes only a few minutes, using careful freehand application of the file. Subsequent checking with a square or a straightedge ensures accuracy and usually the square stays square once restored.

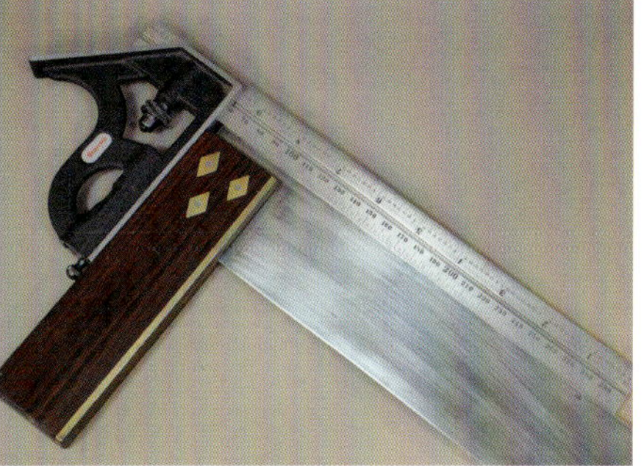

Using the Square

Squaring pencil lines and using a sharp knife with the square means we must learn to hold the square to the wood firmly with no slippage and at the same time keep the beam of the square flat against the face of the wood as lines are drawn or cut. Holding the stock of the square cradled in the fingers is often awkward initially. I talk further in the next pages about the best hand positions for handling the combination square for different applications and situations in woodworking.

We generally need the wood being marked to be secure. Sometimes the weight of the wood is enough to resist the pressures we apply when the square is offered to the wood. However, at other times, it would be best to hold the wood securely against the bench or in the vise. Here, on a square or rectangular section, it is not really an issue using a pencil and square simultaneously. Wood resting on the bench top allows us to press downwards against the wood and, at the same time, hold the square against the wood to effect cut lines and pencil marks. Wider boards are even easier to work with on the benchtop and also for making our marks and initial cut lines.

Hand Dominance and the Square in Use

Often we naturally want to use our dominant hand, or at least we feel we should, when in fact the dominant hand is in demand to use another tool alongside it such as a pencil or knife. At other times we need to hold the wood itself and so it might be more convenient or feel more natural to use our dominant hand for greater accuracy. In time it becomes more natural to know which position and which hand will work best purely by our experience. What is written is not law, but generally the stock of the square is placed against the long, straight edge of a section of wood and the beam placed across the adjacent face. For new users this is often a fumbling point for a minute or two. When it comes to checking the end of a board, it is common to see students register the stock of the square against the end grain cut and not the long proven face or edge. Generally you will register the stock of the square against the originally proven face or edge and this is not usually the end of the board.

When holding a square the important issue is that of registration. Keeping the square level and parallel is mostly about the application of pressures; pressing the stock against the wood and then, at the same time, pressing down on the beam to keep it flat to surface. This corresponding alignment on two planes sometimes causes unequal pressure by necessity and it takes a little practice to know where and when differing pressures are appropriate. It is also not inconsequential that sometimes we must hold wood up to the light to sight the square to the wood. It will vary which hand you use in these circumstances according to your preference and the position, size, and weight of the wood. Most often we apply the square to the wood with the non-dominant hand. Yes, on rarer occasions it might be necessary to use the non-dominant hand to make the marks or knifewalls, but generally I find I get the best results using my non-dominant hand to hold the square and hold all other tools, especially the knife, with my dominant right.

Hand Positions and the Square

The stock is the part of the square usually held in the hand and we only rarely hold the beam. It is the stock that we always register to the wood for subsequent work such as laying out and marking with pencil lines, making knifewalls, and cross referencing throughout any project. It is best to always pick up the square by the stock regardless of which hand you use to actually hold it. The stock is always where the weight is and this immediately brings balance to usage and immediacy to applying the square to the work.

Hand positions will vary as you apply different pressures and also because the placement of the wood being worked differs dramatically too. Hand application relies constantly on an opposing force to hold both the wood and the square and then apply the marking or cutting tool. Sometimes it is sufficient to use the bench to bear down on the square against the wood. At other times it is best to have the wood secured in the vise to free the hands from having to hold the wood and the square securely at the same time. The nature of the work may well determine this; knife work inevitably demands higher levels of pressure on the square (both the stock and the beam) and using the vise facilitates this best. Securing in the vise brings ever-important additional safety and also generally results in higher levels of accuracy. This is especially true when squaring across wider boards where the hand span is not large enough to both apply the square to the wood and squeeze the stock to the wood between the fingers and the opposing thumb. With the wood in the vise, the stock of the square can be pushed securely and safely against the wood, which can then be marked with a pencil or knifewall, depending on the work in hand. The vise itself is, of course, an effective 'third hand' and so we rely on it in much of our work. The vise also holds multiple pieces for ganging-up parts before making marks and cut lines that might be inaccurate or unsafe any other way. Sometimes we use clamps for this too. Often it is a weight-to-strength issue; the wood may be heavy enough to press against or small enough to squeeze the square and wood together. Eventually such decisions become patently obvious every time although sometimes it just feels plain awkward whatever you choose to do.

The Tape Measure

Another hand tool that is possibly hard for people to get too excited about is the ubiquitous retractable tape measure. We may take this tool for granted but it is truly one of those very marvellous inventions we have come to rely on in the everyday of woodworking. It is a tool that has never really stood still in its development and I have personally watched its evolution come to greater levels of functionality. Makers have invented new ways to improve them to maximise extension lengths, stiffness, resistance to kinking, full retractability, and yet allow clear visibility without compromise. The slight hollow channelling gave the tape its rigidity and the neat, yet simple, locking mechanism transformed the tape to hold its own. Those who used them soon laid down their wooden types in favour of using the more convenient measuring instrument for maximised efficiency. I think that, as long as they are accurate and lightweight, they fit my criteria for a simple and efficient measuring device.

In times past, the humble tape measure was a coiled, semi-flat tape that had no mechanical spring retraction nor even a nib at the end to hook onto the work being measured. The spring steel tape fitted into a low profile canister with a wide, rimmed opening that retained the tape as a coil. The spring in the tape held it inside and it could be pulled out partially, through the large opening, to get the measurement. This allowed part, or all, of the tape to be pulled into action and was then manually fed back into the hole. Most tapes now have somewhat standard features and even inexpensive, plastic-

Rabone
Chesterman

cased tapes are usually very accurate and long lasting. You need not spend too much for a decent working model. Many notable manufacturers create a range of measuring tapes that vary in size and length giving you a choice of sizes. Most of the tapes offered are made more for general carpentry work on construction sites where long measurements, e.g. 25 feet (7.5m) long, are more typically needed. On the workbench you might find these tapes too cumbersome for small work and furniture making, general woodworking and woodturning. It is quite rare to work with measurements longer than say 10 feet (3m), with most work at the bench being around two or three feet (600-900mm) and almost all work is under 8 feet (2.5m) long. I keep tape measures that slip into my pocket easily and this works well for me. In the well of my workbench I have a small box to stow half a dozen in. When I work elsewhere in the shop throughout the week I can leave a tape wherever I have need and always be ready for measuring.

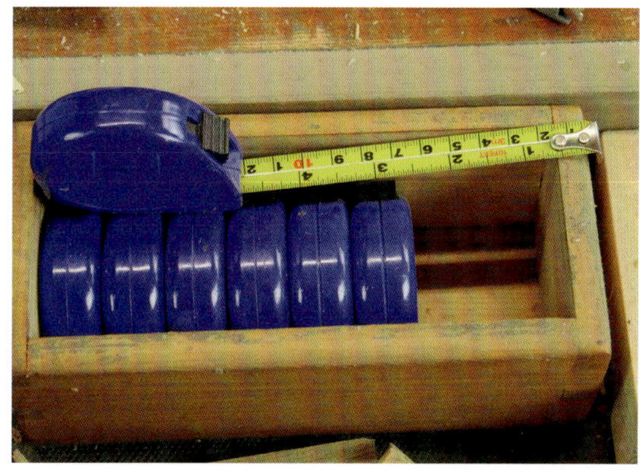

“*When I work elsewhere in the shop throughout the week I can leave a tape wherever I have need and always be ready for measuring*”

Choosing a Tape Measure

I can recall the early days, when tape measures were made without the self-adjusting ‘hook’ or tip at the start-end of the measurements. By self-adjusting I mean that the hook on the end moves to compensate for the metal thickness of the actual hook or tip itself. It is surprising how many people think that they bought a flawed tape when they discover slight movement at this critical point and look for one that is rigidly fixed without movement. This clever addition came early on in the evolution of measuring tape development and separated the better quality manufacturers from the cheap imports of the day. The two small rivets holding the hook are secure but loose enough to allow movement so that when the hook catches on an end at a start point, it extends the length by the thickness of the hook. When taking measurements with the hook butted up against an inside surface, for example, the inside of a box or up against a skirting board, the hook then slides back up against the tape end and so lines up with the zero start point. A movable tip on a tape measure is a positive feature and one you should look for when you purchase one.

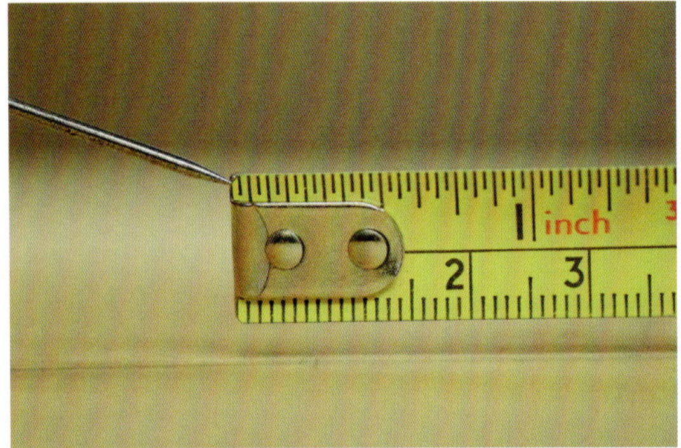

Here the hook-on end is shortened into the tape tip for butting up to take an inside measurement...

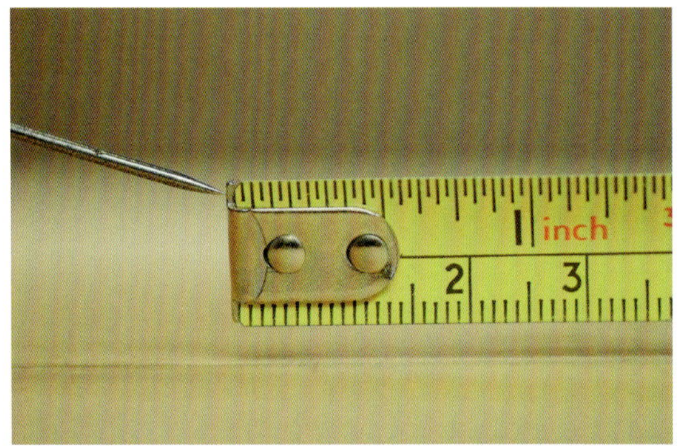

... and here the hook is extended for pull-measuring.

The early tapes had no sliding tape lock to hold the tape out in the extended position in use. We were used to them then but when the lockable tapes came out it was a great solution and everyone embraced them. Simple improvements made a big difference and eventually the measuring tape replaced all of the wooden folding rules we were used to. It has been a worldwide development and a positive one.

The tape on the left has no locking mechanism for keeping the tape extended whereas the tape on the right does.

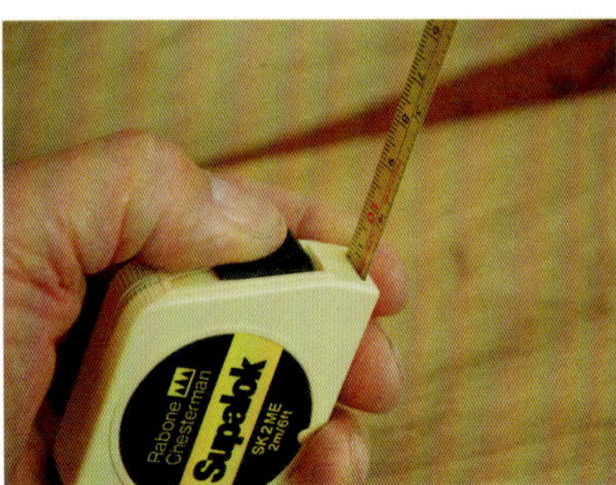

Tape locked open.

Tape released and closed.

Something else I look for is the inclusion of both imperial and metric measuring systems in one tape. I use both systems because, although Britain converted from imperial to metric in the 60s, here in the UK, there is still a remnant of people who have continued to use the system they are used to. The US still uses imperial measurements but Britain's interrelationship with Europe and other continents necessitated a change. My working between the US and UK means that both systems are very much alivc to mc. In mainland Europe you will find dedicated metric tapes with no hint of a reference to imperial measuring. In the US it can be the other way around. I find having both to be useful.

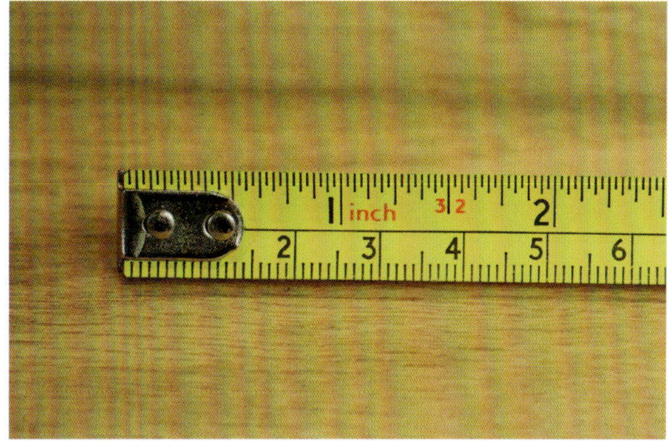

I look for tapes with both metric and imperial measurements.

Wooden Four-fold Rules

As an apprentice of 15 years old, I started out, just as every man I worked with did, using a Rabone Chesterman three-foot four-fold rule. I would most likely still use it were it not for the fact that I retired it, in favour of the tape measure, before it wore out. Rigid rules like the ones shown do have some advantages over tapes not the least of which is the rigidity during some layout procedures and when taking measurements etc. I am glad that I had those two decades when I used the three-foot folding rule. It is nice to have that as part of my history. That said, tapes do take some beating in the day-to-day of working wood and I like them very much. So the tape measure has more than adequately replaced the wooden rule as my essential measuring device.

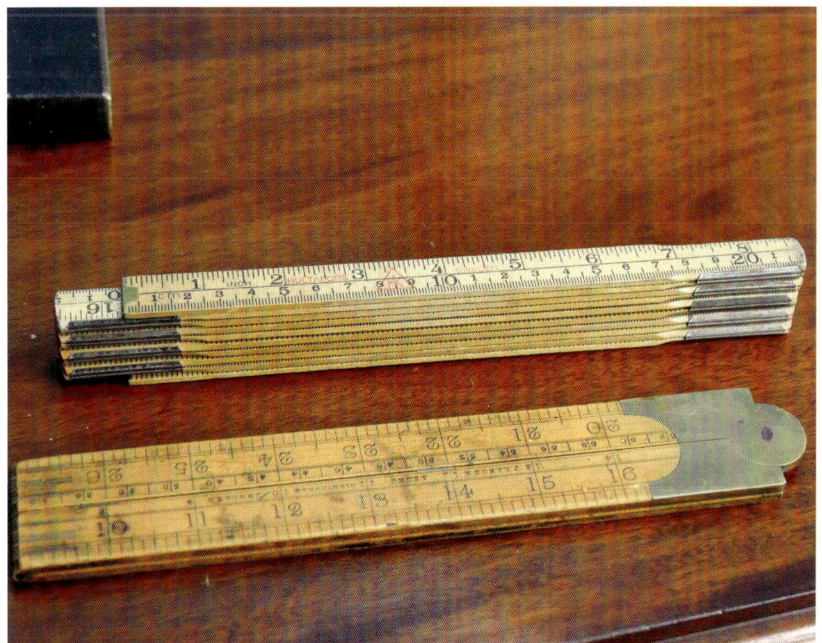

“*So the tape measure has more than adequately replaced the wooden rule as my essential measuring device*”

Steel Rules

In addition to the retractable tape measure, for more general measuring, I also rely very much on a 12" (300mm) steel rule especially for close measuring. I find these rigid measuring aids handy for setting the different marking and cutting gauges, measuring small items like hinges, locks and other hardware, and also when sizing things such as chisel sizes, depths of recesses and so on. I also reach for them for tighter tolerances in layout, say, for the actual joints like dovetails and mortise and tenons. Look for one with fine, machine-cut or engraved markings rather than surface-printed markings. You can often start your knife in one of the cut marks and so get dead-on positioning for markings. Again, look for steel rules with both imperial and metric measurements in one rule if you are working within the US and Britain where imperial measuring either dominates or lingers.

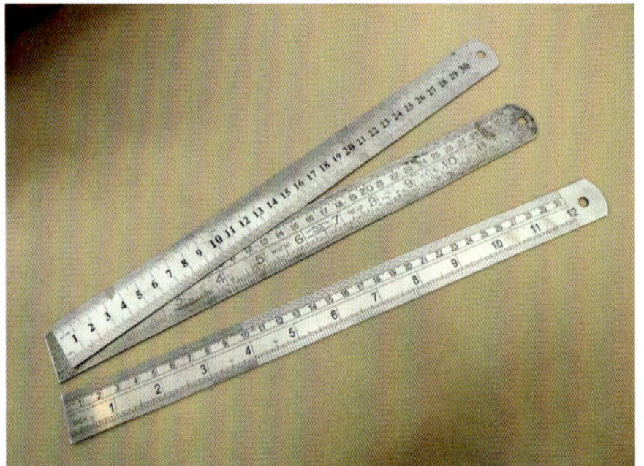

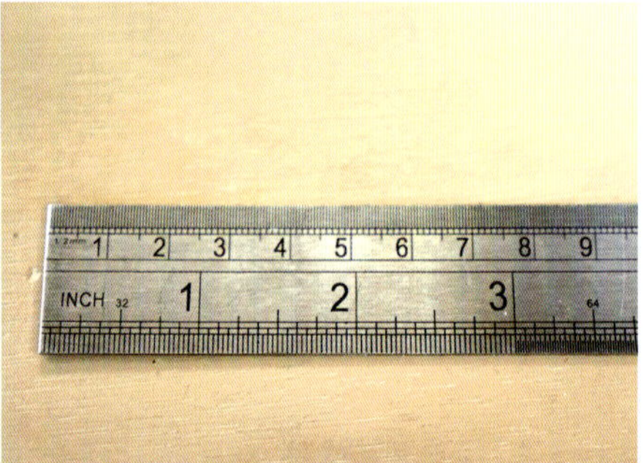

The Layout Knife

A woodworker's knife should be a thin but strong, flat-bladed cutting tool made of tool-grade steel and supported on both sides of the blade by a wooden, metal, or plastic handle to give firmness, grip, and rigidity to the blade as well as comfort to the hand.

The knife is as critically important as all the other tools and, for fine working at least, quickly follows the square in order of importance. Whereas most cuts in general carpentry usually come directly from the tools, fine woodworking, especially the work surrounding joinery, relies on preparatory knifewalls that initiate more progressive cuts with other cutting tools. Manmade panel boarding has wood strata, building up its thickness and providing an inner core that is often veneered to create wider sheets as boards. Even though the structure of these manmade boards is different to solid wood, it can still benefit from knifewalls if the boards require clean cuts to the edges of the panels being cut. A sharp knife and a straightedge creates a perfect edge on the outcut side of any panel.

Knifewalls to both faces of plywood reduce the risk of splintering to the veneered surfaces when cut with handsaws.

All hand-sawn cuts, as well as machine cuts, even on MDF, benefit from knife-cut knifewalls.

Knife Types

Within woodworking there are a broad range of tasks and specialities. This has led to a rich choice of tools but also a confusion of terminology. When you are looking for a knife to use in woodworking you may come across a great number of terms used to describe them. The terms scoring knife, striking knife, marking knife, and layout knife all refer to knives used in woodworking to mark wood for identification or in preparation for subsequent cuts. It must be remembered that encased pencils are a relatively recent development in woodworking and that metal implements were used

extensively to mark wood before pencils were an option. When I refer to a knife used in woodworking I mean the highly refined cutting knife that is used to create knifewalls. I rarely use the knife for initially marking my wood or for the identification of parts and so I have little use for a traditional marking knife, which scored the surface of the wood rather than slicing the fibres. Despite the reduced demand for the less refined traditional marking implements, the terminology is still around and there is often some confusion around the way that they are labelled and marketed. My favourite knife is marketed as a 'folding pocket knife' but if you go looking for knives that match that description you will certainly find many that would be unsuitable for refined joinery layout. I will continue to refer to the knives I use in woodworking as layout knives or simply knives but you should bear in mind the potential for confused terminology when searching for a knife. You should look at the attributes of the knife and keep in mind its intended use rather than rely on the way that it is labelled or marketed.

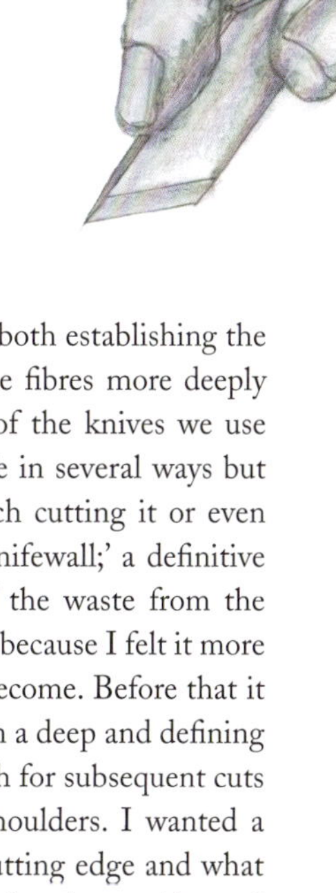

Many woodworkers now rely on more sharply pointed knives for both establishing the position of cross-grain cut lines and also cutting through surface fibres more deeply to develop an actual wall. This then changes the functionality of the knives we use markedly. The layout knife is quite different to the striking knife in several ways but mainly because one marks or scores the surface without so much cutting it or even intending to and the other creates what I decided to call the 'knifewall;' a definitive separation with the knife delineating the exact demarcation of the waste from the wanted. Twenty or so years ago I named this cut line the knifewall because I felt it more accurately described exactly what I was creating my cut lines to become. Before that it was a mere knife-line that was simply a marked surface rather than a deep and defining cut. These, more accurate, knifewall cuts bring exactness and depth for subsequent cuts to follow in the development of shoulder lines to form joint shoulders. I wanted a term that described more fully what actually takes place at the cutting edge and what it does for finer work in creating and deepening a definitive wall that then guides and guarantees accuracy in the next cuts made with planes, chisels, and saws. The striking knives I knew of in my early woodworking and apprenticeship were used in joinery and carpentry and would not generally be described as sharp knives; they just scored the surfaces for markings to position the joints.

“*I have little use for a traditional marking knife, which scored the surface of the wood rather than slicing the fibres*”

There are many knife types to choose from including specialised knives designed for joinery and those designed for carving wood, such as hook-bladed knives and chip carving knives. Although these are not specifically designed for layout work, they do work well. Carpenters in construction work often carry the thin-bladed knives with retractable and replaceable blades known as utility or Stanley knives. These knives generally work well for the tasks they were designed for but they tend to be heavy and clunky for the finer hand work relating to furniture making and other fine woodworking.

I have a dozen or more knives of different types (above), mostly ones I have custom made for my own use but also some I have bought to test out for woodworking at different times. Today I mostly rely on a thin-bladed folding knife. This is the perfect knife for every type of joinery and though, in appearance, perhaps it looks a little utilitarian and lightweight, the knife handles really well; it fits inside the cup of my hand and suits just about every cutting purpose I need in joinery layout. Also, though the blades are designed as disposable or replaceable, they are sufficiently robust to be sharpened dozens of times before replacement is needed. A single blade will generally last me for a year or two even with very regular use.

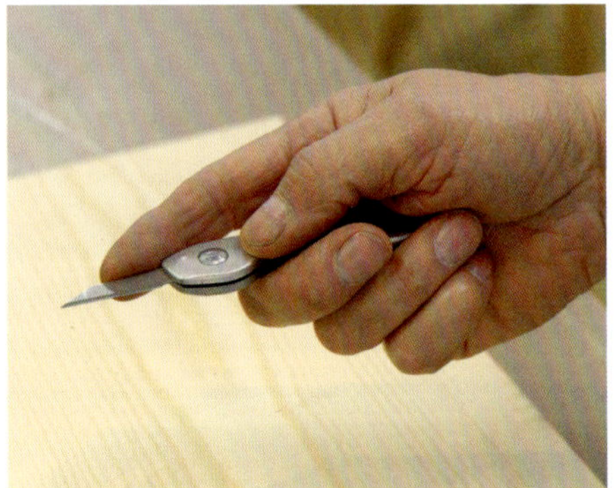

What to Look for in a Layout Knife

In an ideal world perhaps, a knife would be wafer-thin to give the thinnest line possible. In reality though, the problems would be numerous; edge fracture, unclear visibility, fibre reclosure and so on. So, although thickness should be minimised, it should never be so thin as to compromise the cutting edge. Remember here that the bevelled sides, forming the cutting edge, compress the fibres and show the visible line we need to work to. Passing the knife across the grain does not actually remove any wood at all. The reason we can indeed see a knife line is because the wood compresses on each side of the cutting edge. So it is actually the compressed wood, uniformly bruised, that gives us the visible line.

This picture shows the compression of the wood to the waste side of the cut. The other side is vertical because this was guided by the straight edge of the square as the knife followed the straightedge.

I look for thin-bladed knives with long points like the one shown here. It is not so much the longer cutting edge of the knife that is needed in layout and knifewall work but rather the first ⅜" to ⅝" (10-15mm) or so of the blade from the point itself. This is the business end for most woodworking and especially joinery work, which involves reaching into tight corners and following straightedges for establishing cut lines. So we need the extra length in the blade more for added reach rather than for actual cutting. The blade on this knife extends from the handle about 1 ¼" to 1 ½" (30-40mm). Thin, simply refined blades really work best for fine woodworking and can be readily adapted, shaped and further reshaped to suit your particular needs. We use the same type of knife for many other areas in woodworking too, incised carving, inlaying, veneering, repair work and so on.

The blade in this knife is 1 ½" (38mm) long by just under 1⁄32" (1mm) thick and 7⁄16" (10mm) wide at the widest point. Even though the blade is thin, it is robust enough for me to apply as much pressure as is needed for all laying out work and for cutting knifewalls in any wood too. With reasonable care the blade lasts for a year or two yet costs only a small amount. For general daily work I redefine the point, albeit slightly, by snapping off the first 1⁄16" (2mm) of the tip with needlenose pliers and then further shape it to a slight curve from the top, sloped edge of the blade to the bottom cutting edge. This strengthens the working point and prevents the tip from breaking accidently in use. Without this I have found that the original, ultra-fine tip can break unpredictably anyway.

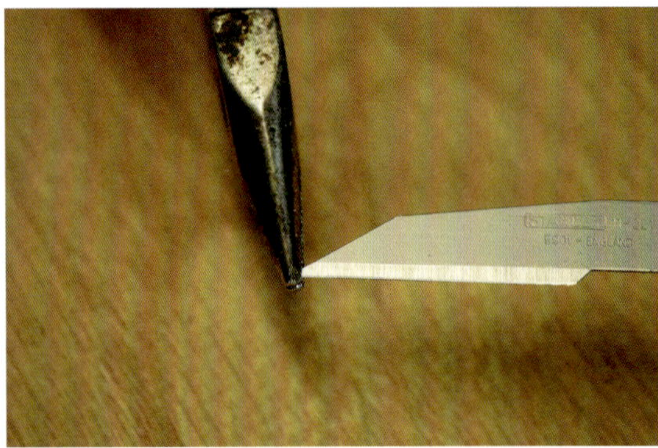

Upcycling Knives

If cost or convenience is an issue, just about any kitchen knife can be reground for benchwork. Stainless steel does take and hold a good enough cutting edge and I have found that these knives work very well for woodworking in general. I have two or three of these from when I did different tests in functionality, edge retention, and sharpness. They are more than equal to all layout tasks and often superior to more specialised layout knives, including knives such as spear- or diamond-point knives. You may prefer a more dedicated knife but that is usually an aesthetic choice based on personal preferences. One thing I like about these upcycled butter-knives is the wide and shallow tapered grind that goes from a thicker back edge to a thinner cutting edge like pocket

The lambfoot folding knife.

knives. This feature means the blade edge is very close to the beam of the square when creating straightedge cuts. Thinness matters to me as much as anything.

I keep another folding pocket knife, called a lambfoot knife, ready and sharp for marking out and it is one I always have in my pocket. It opens to a rigid lock but it is not a lock knife as such, just tight at the knuckle of the knife.

Holding and Using the Knife

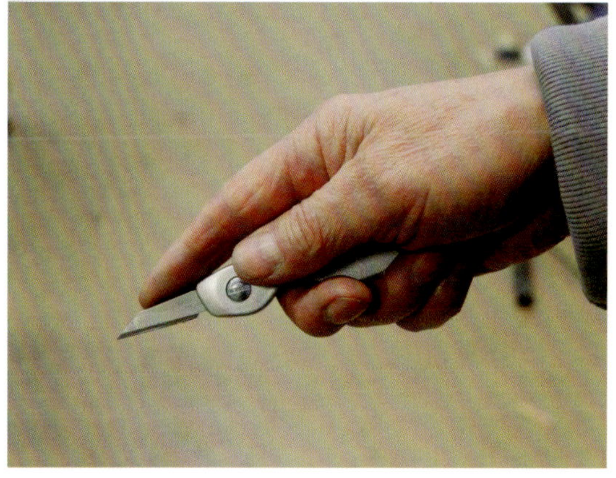

Most people know how to hold knives and, of course, generally it is readily apparent. It is surprising though just how many people use a layout knife like a bread knife or a machete with a full-fisted wrap-around grip rather than with the forefinger pointing along the top edge. Shorter knives, used for laying out and such, are cupped within the palm as shown. I prefer this for most of my general knifewall working and so I usually choose knives with shorter rather than longer handles. That way my three fingers wrap around the handle, my thumb presses the side, and my forefinger presses in a pointing position over the top of the blade. This pointing forefinger helps to give balance, correction, and precision to the tip of the knife. Whereas the hand takes the main strain, the forefinger applies pressure directly behind the tip and, at the same time, directs the course of the knife in its delivery of cut. For convenience, strength, and body alignment, I prefer double-bevel knives; these are knives with an equal bevel on both sides, which form a single cutting edge. To compensate for the small bevel, I angle the knife very slightly out of perpendicular so that the face of the bevel is up against the straightedge of my square and is perpendicular to the wood. This actually makes more sense than a flat blade because our shoulders are wide; using the knife and square brings the hands into triangular positioning as the non-dominant hand holds the square and the dominant hand the knife. For woodworking, I find this to be a natural body-alignment.

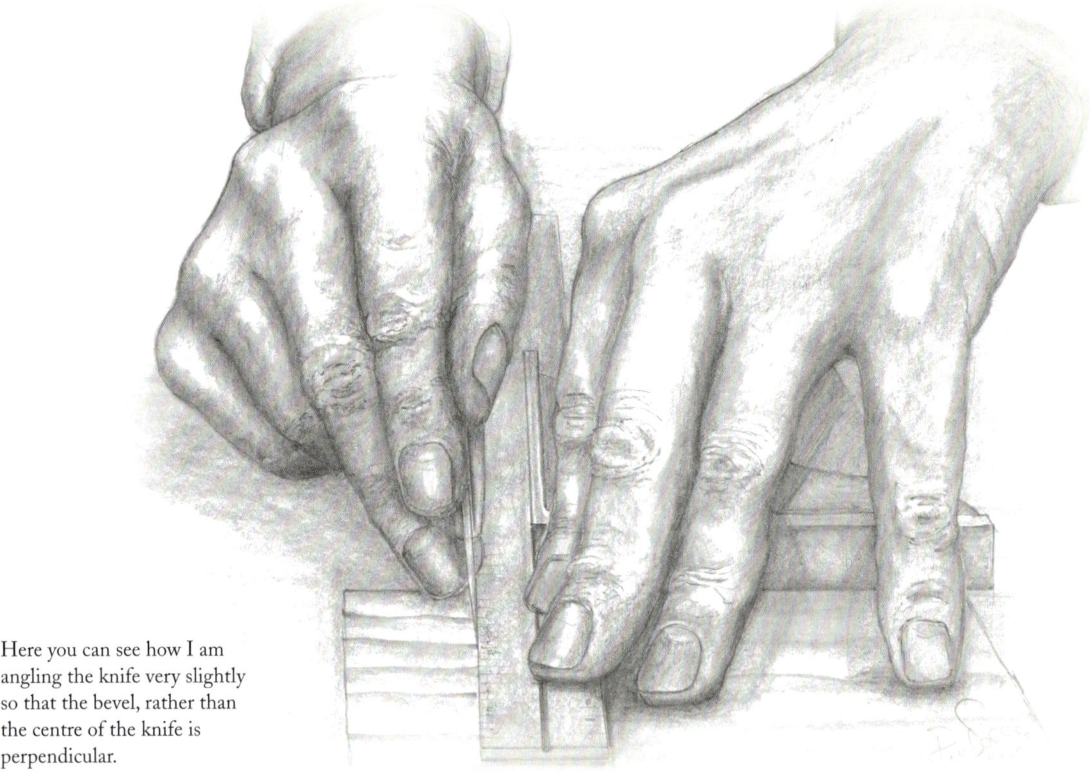

Here you can see how I am angling the knife very slightly so that the bevel, rather than the centre of the knife is perpendicular.

It is quite unusual to use the knife without some additional guide, such as the square or a straightedge of some kind, be that wood or steel. In woodworking we generally use the square because it is used most for joinery where almost all cuts are 90 degrees to an adjacent edge. The combination square also has a 45-degree angle for laying out cut lines, say, for mitres and such. When we need other angled cuts we rely on the sliding bevel. The blade on this tool adjusts to any desired angle and the stock of the bevel registers and aligns with an edge in the same manner as the standard square does. Pressing the stock against the trued edge of the material being worked and, at the same, time pressing the blade of the sliding bevel flat with a finger or two ensures clean, straight cuts. In any case, we rely on the square, sliding bevel, or straightedge to guarantee straightness, security and safety. The knife and straightedge work in unison with one another for the predominance of our work.

On Diamond-point or Spear-point Knives

Knives with a spear point that projects a double-edge bevel on a single face of the knife have become popular. This creates a left- and right-handed knife in a single tool. This is supposed to aid vertical cutting in woodworking because you can hold the flat face of the blade vertically so that it is perpendicular to the material as the line is made. In theory that seems to make sense but, in practice, that is not altogether what functionally happens.

In my experience it is somewhat rare that someone can use both hands with equal dexterity and exactness; that is, most left- or right-handed people cannot work using both hands capably, with the same measure of accuracy, power, and deliberation. I believe it is actually far less problematic to adjust the knife in the cut, as you have to with a knife with bevels on both sides, rather than use a knife with less accuracy and efficiency. You may still use your non-dominant hand with all knife types but this is fairly unusual except with these spear-point knives.

The spear-point knife can be flipped to work both sides of the beam of a square or other straightedge.

As I said previously, spear-point knives may seem to make logical sense and they have been around for centuries. Ultimately it comes down to personal preference but there are a couple of considerations that occurred to me along the way and made me really rethink my decision making on what made a good knife for me. In practice, of the ones I used, be they single-piece flat bar stock or shaped and handled, spear-point knives always felt more awkward and I found that most other users seemed to find them awkward too. This was especially so when they tried using them with their 'wrong' hand, which supposedly is the purpose of the design. I felt they were also awkward because they are quite wide at the end, which obscures visibility too.

Another issue that I have is that spear-point knives tend to lose the tip or angled point of the knife because this point is weak and fractures away when pressure is applied. The point then has to be reworked and the same thing happens again. Inevitably the answer came by rounding the point to a continuous bevelled edge following around the missing point to more of a bullnose round. This works fine actually but the very corner is missing. A combination of this and the awkwardness in use has influenced me away from them.

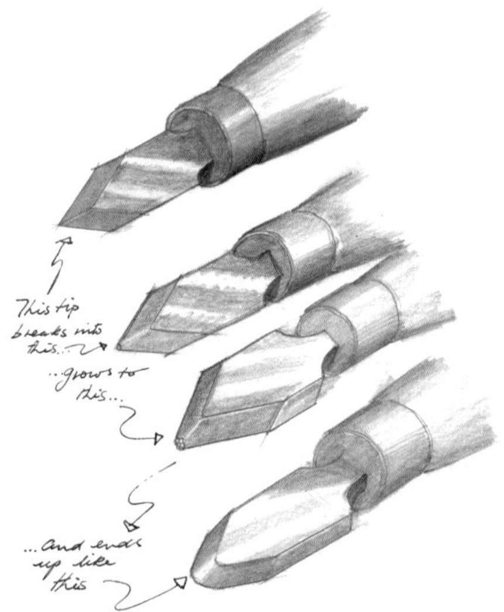

Inevitably the spear-point knife must be sharpened as shown to gain a viable cutting edge and, though this is not much of an issue in itself, I still prefer other knives.

Sharpening Your Layout Knife

To sharpen my knife, I present the blade bevel on the coarse (250-grit) sharpening stone at the same angle that the knife came with, which is generally around 10 degrees to each side of the blade. This combined angle gives us a strong and resistant cutting edge. I rub the blade along the abrasive surface back and forth until a burr comes on the opposite side of the bevel. I then flip the blade over and do the same to the opposite bevel. The blade will be sharp enough at this point but you can repeat on finer grits for an even finer cutting edge, depending on the work you are involved with. If you are using three diamond stones in a holder you can just skip the middle stone and go from the coarse stone to the finest. Generally there is no need to strop when sharpening knives.

An alternate method is to use a small diamond hone as shown below. The one I am using is a medium (400 grit) hone. Use a ⅞" (23mm) thick section of wood as a platform. With the handle of the hone resting on the workbench 5" (125mm) or so from the knife edge you use a circular motion to establish the 10-degree bevel each side of the blade. You can also make your own hones using abrasive paper adhered to a paddle with double-sided tape. This works as well but the abrasive needs replacing from time to time.

The Marking Gauge

Marking gauges provide the guidelines we cut to for exacting fine work. We rely on them for the interlocking of joints and the recessing of hardware, inlaying wood into wood, and thicknessing. In the 1800s the makers and owners of hand tools considered longevity and functionality to be of prime and equal importance. These priorities were what drove the development and evolution of improved versions. I believe that the finest examples of many hand tools existed prior to the two world wars and they reflect how woodworkers considered their importance in their lives. Victorian examples show us that craftsmen considered gauges to be refined instruments for exacting woodworking. Personally I do not think that we should consider them any less than our forebears did.

Artisans in Britain, at this time, enjoyed privileged access to some of the finest woods the earth ever bore, as merchants traversed the globe in search of wood. Exotics, like ebony and incredible rosewood with deeply rich chocolate stripes contrasting with blacks and reds, enriched the lives of the wealthy and the crumbs that fell from the table became the stock and stem (also called the beam) of a marking gauge. The brass mechanisms and wear plates inset gave them added richness and so, when I pick mine from the rack and feel how the ovals fit my hand, I value what was left to me as an inheritance.

Of course there are new and innovative makers using machines to replicate marvellous work. Although I do admire what they produce, I look at the hand work of old gauges and marvel that I am still using those same tools, some of which have been used daily for 200 years.

Marking gauges are used throughout the different woodworking trades from heavy joinery and carpentry to sensitive work of every kind. With finely sharpened pins they give us the exactness we need to guide us in our finer cuts. When the stock is aligned carefully along the edge of the workpiece and the pin (or pins) are not pressed too hard onto the surface of wood, the gauge lines guarantee our depths, widths, and distances to visibly enhance our undertakings to stay true to course. Buy new or old gauges, refine them as needed, and you will grow to rely on these remarkably simple tools throughout your life as I have.

Marking, Mortise and Combination Gauges

In this chapter heading I have lumped three different gauge types under the one generic heading of marking gauges. The specific names, however, identify the tool for our convenience. We use these three different types of marking gauge to mark parallel lines lightly onto the surface of wood. These lines then guide subsequent work with other tools such as saws, chisels, and planes. The lines are made with the single and double pins installed in the gauges on a part called the stem. We use different marking gauge types for a wide range of specific tasks from laying out recesses to marking out the parts of joints before cutting. The three marking gauges are the marking gauge, the mortise gauge, and the combination gauge, which combines the functionality of the two previous gauges in one. A small and inexpensive addition to the common mortise gauge created a major economic development to the tool. Installing an extra single pin to the opposite side of the mortise gauge stem gave us the combination gauge. It is hard to imagine how the early makers missed so simple an improvement. The birth of the combination gauge gave us two tools in one. Here are all three showing the heads of each:

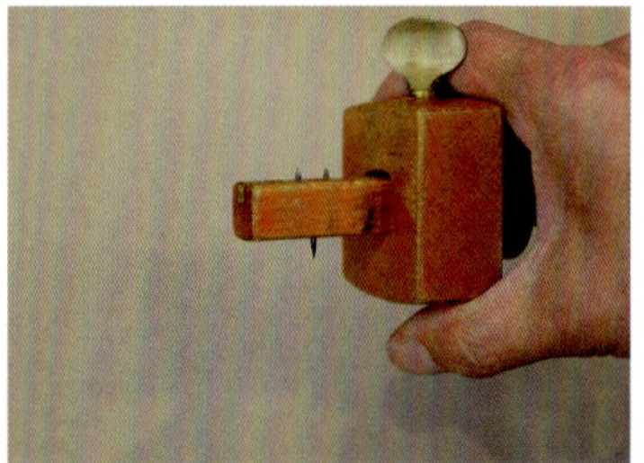

The marking gauge, the mortise gauge, and the combination gauge.

We use marking gauges for establishing guidelines on the surface of wood during layout. The marking gauge comprises a fine pin (or, in the case of mortise or combination gauges, pins) for marking thin lines, parallel to the edges of wood or boards, in preparation for subsequent cutting. Sometimes we use a disc-type gauge with a circular cutter too. Depending on which type of gauge we use, the surface marks are either lightly scored or sliced; the disc-type gauges slice into and cut the wood fibres.

Gauge Locking Systems

The older, more traditional gauge types comprise a wooden stem, wooden stock, and a marking pin. These gauges use a simple locking mechanism that locks the stock of the gauge firmly to the stem. This fixes the distance between the pin and the stock at any predetermined distance. The most commonly used locking method is some type of knurled screw or thumbscrew. Older gauge types used either a slot-headed setscrew tightened by screwdriver, a wooden wedge pressed and tapped to tighten and loosen, or a cam slide using another simple locking mechanism. All of these locking systems work just fine but most marking gauges available today have the benefit of the knurled screw or thumbscrew.

The Modern Engineered Gauges

New gauges have been developed in more recent decades, mostly by newer makers looking to develop new and innovative tools or replicating high-end tools for the more recently developed market. Many of these gauge types have replaced the pinpoint marker with a finely machined thin-edged disc, which is fitted and anchored to the end of an adjustable, round, metal stem. Whereas some woodworkers extol their virtues, in my opinion the traditional marking gauges are still hard to beat. The hardened tool steel disc (or discs) fixed to the end of a single (or sometimes twin) rod is removable using an allen setscrew so that the disc can be sharpened somewhat; but this is limited and difficult to do with any real accuracy. I generally see the two gauge types as different tools and therefore keep one around for alternative functions rather than as a replacement marking gauge. The disc cutters, with sharp circumferences, become actual cutting edges around the perimeter of the discs. These discs then slice-cut marks into the material being worked. The discs do not rotate as is often thought but are fixed at whatever angle or position the user places the gauge to the wood. The stems are usually either centred or offset in a metal stock that guides the gauge along the edge of the wood being worked. The general concept is the same as the traditional pinned marking gauge but, essentially, the difference is that the disc or discs actually cut the fibres with crisp, clean, cut lines. This in no way should lead you to believe that the modern gauge has, in some way, bettered the traditional marking gauge. In my view it simply offers an alternative method. Although both gauges will perform almost identical tasks in delineating cut lines, they can also be applied differently for a more diverse range of tasks. In some cases, one will work better than the other for marking. For instance, the disc-type cutter works quite well to cut surface lines across the grain as well as with the grain if a severed-fibre cut line is what is wanted. Having tried the different disc-type cutters over several years I have decided that they are most useful for two particular areas. Firstly, they are good for developing hinge and lock recesses, and things like that - quite a limited use. Secondly, I also find them very functional for delineating straight inlay work and for developing cockbeading rebates. In most gauge work this is not needed and pin point will work better for 99% of general bench work, say, in furniture making, joinery, and fine woodworking. In my view, the first choice will almost always be the traditional marking gauge. In some situations, the disc type works less effectively and, although the discs can be replaced, in my experience they do not last as long as the pins in pin gauges. All of this has lead me to conclude that the disc type gauges are useful to have around for very specific tasks but they do not replace the essential functions of the pin gauge. Therefore, the traditional pin gauge is my essential marking gauge while the modern disc gauge is a secondary tool that you will only need on occasion, if at all.

Choosing a Marking Gauge

Gauges made in previous centuries sometimes used ornately configured, brass wear plates, inlaid into solid and stable woods such as ebony, rosewood, boxwood, or mahogany. Many gauges, however, are utilitarian with no redeeming qualities other than the fact that they really work well. Others come as highly engineered units but perhaps unnecessarily so. Beyond appearance, the most utilitarian gauge gives exactly the same results as the ornate counterparts. There are many different types of gauges in existence and, at first glance, it could seem confusing to anyone new to woodworking as to what they do, how they differ, what they should be looking to buy, and what to use.

Most marking gauges made through the past three centuries have been made from beech, a remarkably resilient, straight-grained hardwood growing throughout Europe and parts of North America. In functionality and general appearance, the single pin marking gauge remains unchanged after more than two centuries of developed use. The gauge comprises a single piece of wood, known as the stem, a shaped stock designed to fit the hand, and a locking mechanism that secures the stem to the stock. The stock houses the square or shaped stem, which passes into and through the stock at 90 degrees. The stem holds a single, round, steel pin about 1/16" (2-3mm) in diameter fixed near to one end of the stem as shown.

Mortise gauges follow the same pattern as the single pin marking gauge but have two pins, one of which can be adjusted in relation to the first, fixed pin for distance or width. The methods for adjusting the second, moveable pin are explained on page 115. The term 'mortise' relates to the common use for the gauge, which is to set out the width of a mortise for creating mortise holes ready for chopping with chisels. Whether economy of words was the reason that we left it at 'mortise gauge,' I do not know but the gauge is used in equal measure for laying out the corresponding part of the joint, the tenon, too. I suppose if the manuals were rewritten and the jargon redefined, the tool might be aptly and accurately named the mortise and tenon gauge.

Holding the traditional mortise gauge.

Combination gauges give us the two most important gauges in one and, of course, they can be used either way. I think that they are cheaper today than at any other time in history and so owning a few is an option but, if you have the combination gauges, you no longer really need separate, dedicated marking and mortise gauges. On the other hand, I still like using a dedicated marking gauge but this is just a personal preference and something of a luxury. However, I have no preference for dedicated mortise gauges over combination gauges. If I go out of the shop somewhere and can only take one it will always be the combination gauge. This is the gauge I would suggest if you are starting out. It is a perfect first gauge and you can even buy several of them so that you do not need to reset them for different projects or different aspects of a single project. Buy additional ones when you find them at the right price and you will have the benefits of different types to suit your preference. I do especially pick combination gauges when it comes to economy of space for travel, going to shows, or to someone's house or office to work and such.

Access to several gauges becomes especially useful on large projects with many component parts and different joints so you should aim to own several eventually. In the middle of a given project, it is inconvenient to reassign a gauge to another task and then have to reset it, with the same exact sizing, back to the task in hand. Often we need both gauge types set at the same time. These facts are not always easy to anticipate and to plan for.

Compare the single pin of any marking gauge to the twin pins of mortise gauges and you will immediately notice how the single pin has a longer, more slender point. This is also the same with the single pin of the combination gauge. Thinner pins seem more common for single pin marking gauges whereas the mortise gauge pins are usually dumpier. Also notice a slight difference to the slope of the pin bevels, which are at wider angles to the pin point on the mortise gauge.

Here is my marking gauge of choice, with the two types in one gauge.

The double pins on mortise gauges are usually shorter and stouter for increased strength. This is because of the type and nature of the work. The single pin of the marking gauge is mostly used along the grain for tasks such as insetting hinges, lock recessing, and also for marking lines for cutting or ripping along the long grain for sizing wood. Finer pins work better for this and so this is the reason for the differences. Mortise gauges, on the other hand, are used on end grain as well, for marking tenon cheek cuts, which places a higher demand on the points of the pins.

The gauge pictured above, which is made by Sorby, shows the forethought of the makers of the time. The slightly longer and more slender pin shows that the craftsman's design was well considered.

Converting a Mortise Gauge to a Combination Gauge

Converting an existing mortise gauge to make a combination gauge is simple enough to do. The drawing below shows the steps. Use piano wire, often available from hobby stores, to make the pin. Secure the pin into an electric drill (as you would a drill bit) and use the drill's rotation to abrade the pin to a point on abrasive paper and then follow the steps below.

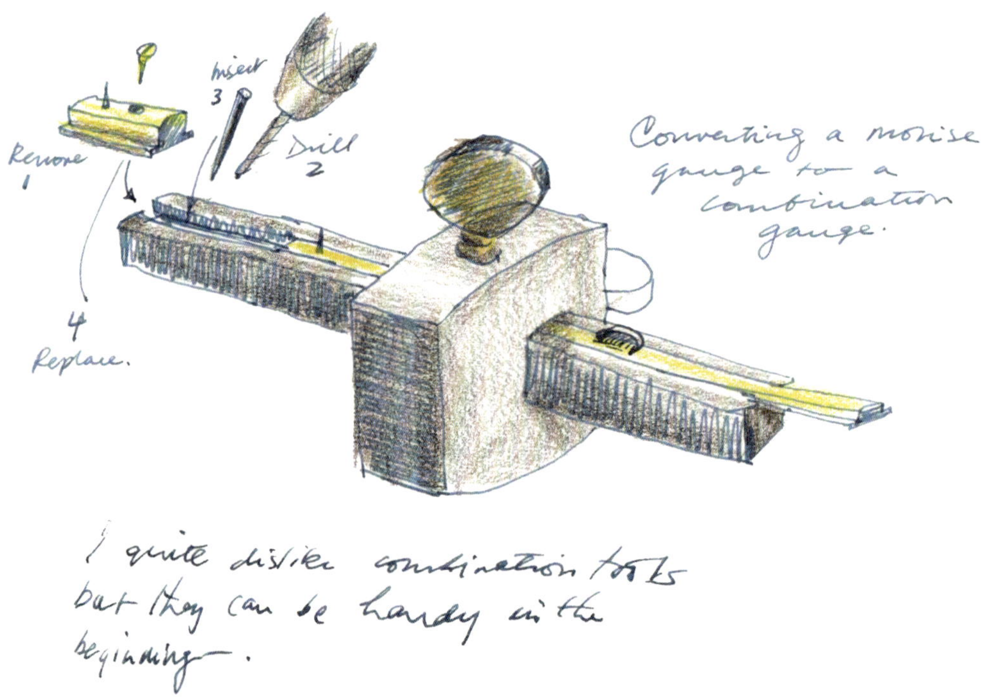

How Many Gauges Do You Really Need Anyway?

I have acquired many different gauges in the form of marking gauges, mortise gauges, combination gauges and cutting or slitting gauges. After five decades of gravitating to the magnetism of secondhand discoveries, it is inevitable that I find tools for a few pennies from time to time. This gathering here (pictured opposite) happened in the last few years and I have many more besides these in the USA. In reality, I would suggest you will use no more than four mortise gauges on most projects and perhaps the same number of marking gauges. You do not need them all at once and so two of each would be practical if you have already got started and decided this craft is for you. I like choices in my tools and so have planes, saws, chisels, knives and so on in excess. I then select specific tools from my vast collection to use in a particular aspect of work. I like to do the same with gauges and find I will pick out one gauge over another for no particular reason but knowing in myself that I did, in fact, prefer that one over all the others. I do tend to prefer long, thin pins over short dumpy ones. Of course, on old gauges, especially mortise gauges, the pins are often filed or worn down to little more than nubs. This is worth checking when you purchase an old gauge.

How to Use the Gauges Correctly

Working with struggling students through the years has helped me to understand the problems and issues surrounding different gauges. In the beginning I find the main problem is the awkwardness students feel in handling the tool itself. As with the square, the gauge often necessitates holding the wood and the tool in direct opposition to one another. Students often do not understand why something that seems so simple presents such difficulty. The fact is that it is one of the more awkward tools in the hand. In light of this, students then often ask themselves "how hard can this be?" The awkward shape makes them feel that they must somehow be more domineering with the tool and so doggedly press it to task. This is usually the exact opposite of what is needed because it increases the pressure to both make it work and to make it stay on course. What is needed is a light but firm presentation, using mostly a lateral (or sideways) pressure to press the stock of the gauge to the face of the wood. Then, keeping that consistent pressure, pressing the gauge lightly down and forward to trace the pin or pins along the surface of the wood. Pressing too heavily into the wood creates deep grooves that often follow the grain of the wood rather than the straight, parallel course it should be following to the edge of the board. This exacerbates the problem rather than resolving it. Heavy-handedness tends to create deepened score lines that become wider, stroke by stroke. The tips of the thin pinpoints are designed to deliver accurate markings rather than deep, ploughed grooves. Therefore, my advice is to relax the hand and keep control by sensing the course, the wood's grain and texture, and the gauge.

These images capture the essence of balanced application between the body, the hand, and the tool to the wood. It seems to me that most people, who are new to woodworking, feel the need to press the tool more rigidly to the material and then lose the sensitivity needed for the better work.

I cannot overemphasise the benefits of using the vise to hold the wood wherever possible. This saves straining against yourself and frees the other hand to help steady the gauge and apply greater pressure if necessary. You can also angle the wood to further improve presentation between the wood and the gauge as shown here.

"*I cannot overemphasise the benefits of using the vise to hold the wood wherever possible*"

Mortise Gauge Adjustment

In general, we rely on two types of adjuster to change the position of the second, moveable pin. Though both are usually locked with a set screw or thumbscrew, the two types of adjuster delineate two levels of engineering complexity. The simpler of the two, shown left in the picture, is the thumb slide, which is pushed or pulled into position and then locked with the thumbscrew. The other, shown on the right, has a screw-thread mechanism operated by a thumbscrew or, in some cases, a screwdriver. Both work just fine.

Sharpening Gauge Points

Traditional marking gauges use sharp pinpoints, as shown earlier. The pins of gauges, when new, will be long and sharply pointed to a conical tip. When the gauge points wear down it is mostly because the very tips break and then the remaining point becomes rounded through additional wear. When that happens they must be resharpened to restore the fine point or be reshaped to a flat chisel tip, filed parallel to the face of the stock. This method improves the tip and is easier to establish and maintain than a rounded point. Chisel tip refinements work equally as well as cone points if the flat of the chisel point is filed parallel to the face of the gauge stock. The lines we mark with the gauge always run parallel to one edge of the workpiece and so, with the chisel tip running parallel to the stock of the gauge itself, the lines we make will be as thin and as fine as a pinpoint. Twin-pinned gauges are often problematic because they are difficult to sharpen to exactly equal heights. It is also important to know that the more modern gauges have extremely hard pins that cannot be sharpened with a file. In this case use a diamond sharpening hone to sharpen them.

Making a Poor Man's Marking Gauge

In a bind, where you do not have access to a marking gauge, you can make a 'poor man's marking gauge.' I have used a flat head countersunk screw with a filed rim in a block of wood for five decades on and off and the gauge works as perfectly as any other. Below I am checking and setting the thickness of a hinge flap. You set the gauge by simply turning the screw. Applying these gauges to the wood is very comfortable and controlled and I can either reset the single screw or add a second screw to cover both width and depth in a single gauge. Marking out for recessing a hinge flap for door hinges, for example, becomes very efficient. The same gauge can then be used for mortise and tenon layout too and it works just as well for other applications including recessing corners for corner inlays and cockbeading.

The Sliding Bevel

The very name 'sliding bevel' suggests movement and adjustability. In this case, the two parts of the tool move, one part to the other, to create any angle between 0 and 360 degrees. These parts, the beam and stock, are locked to the required angle and the angle can then be transferred from one part or piece of work to another or used for some other guidance. This is a simple way of establishing the layout lines we need in readiness for subsequent cuts with saws, planes, and chisels. This helps us to maintain the high levels of accuracy we need in our work. The sliding bevel works similarly to the combination square in providing a thin, straight edge to guide our pencil lines and knife lines but, this time, at any given angle instead of just square and 45 degrees. Just as the square gives us repeatable replication with dead-on squareness, the sliding bevel enables us to work with exact angles for projects that require angled components.

The sliding bevel (also called the sliding 'T' bevel, 'T' bevel, and bevel gauge) comprises two main parts; a thin, steel, parallel blade known as the beam or blade; and the stock, which is the heavier and blockier part. The stock holds the beam within a sawn slit that houses and centralises the beam in the stock. The beam slides within and along this slit to facilitate total adjustability. Subsequent to setting the correct angle, the beam is then locked to the stock by a setscrew or wingnut or some type of levered cam. The stock of the sliding bevel is made of wood, metal, or plastic, or indeed any combination of these.

THE STOCK

The stock allows the thin, plate steel beam to slide half or more of its length along a setscrew at the end of the stock so that the beam can be set at an angle to that stock. The stock of the sliding bevel can be held against a given straight edge or the face of the wood being worked and the beam pivots to any desired angle. Firm pressure by pushing, pulling, or squeezing aligns and supports the stock of the sliding bevel to the edge and the beam then projects at the preset angle onto the adjacent face of the wood. Lines or cuts can now be made along the beam with a pencil, steel scribe, or knife. We can also use the sliding bevel to register an angle in one situation and then create corresponding parts for the work in progress. Completed work can also be checked to make certain that one part corresponds to another.

Here I used a sliding bevel to take an internal, angled corner and transferred the angles to create a frame.

THE BEAM

Depending on the maker, the beam is usually made from tempered spring steel, 1" (25mm) wide and 3⁄32" (2.5mm) thick. The most commonly used sizes measure about 7-10" (175-250mm) from tip to toe along the beam, which is how we size sliding bevels. Smaller ones, say 4-6" (100-150mm) long, can be useful in tighter spaces. The craftsmen I worked with always seemed to have longer ones, handmade and with the beam also made from wood, for larger work such as stair building, timber framing, and joinery work. I am never sure if they each needed their own or whether they just enjoyed making one early on in their apprenticeship.

In most cases today, the ends of the beams are angled so that, when it is folded away, the beam fits neatly into a slit in the stock. In the past, this angle would vary but, on today's sliding bevels, it is usually 45 degrees.

Using the Sliding Bevel

We use the sliding bevel for transferring angles from one predetermined angle or situation to another, mostly to establish angles without using unnecessary math formula or complicated measurements for our work. It is usually the fastest method of transfer and one that delivers the exactness we woodworkers need. This is especially so in more complex aspects of joinery such as chairmaking, stair building and so on. We use a variety of methods to set angles, ranging from direct transfer, setting to protractors, dividing angles using the compasses, and also using preset angle finders too. In most cases we use a protractor of some kind. This is the fastest if we are actually working to specific degrees but it is often unnecessary to actually know the specific angle numerically by degrees. Internal and external corners on old buildings and such are often not square but angled more or less than 90 degrees. We use many different procedures too diverse to show here to determine angles in our work and this includes compound rafter angles, geometric layout and more. Regardless of how we arrive at an angle the sliding bevel offers great versatility in transferring angles to the work.

Sliding Bevel Locking Systems

I like the various locking mechanisms that firmly lock the beam inside the stock to exact angles. Some sliding bevels lock with a thumbscrew located on the end of the stock while others have a thumbscrew located at the pivot point directly adjacent to the beam itself. The main advantage of thumbscrews, of course, is that they are convenient, effective, and fast. This type of sliding bevel needs no third component, such as a screwdriver, to lock the stock to the beam, which can interrupt the setting process when you least want it to. That said, there is something settling about the slot-headed screw lockdown when long-term or permanent settings seem essential. I keep these around, say, for when I am building six chairs consecutively; where the setting may be kept the same for a few days or even weeks. The countersunk screw head is very positive in such cases. It also allows the body of the sliding bevel to lie flush on any surface, on both sides of the bevel, during setting and then in applying the bevel to the work too, which is always very convenient. If the locking mechanism does protrude even slightly past the face, as is the case with many sliding bevels, the tool does not lie flat to a given registration face or surface or it gets in the way, catches awkwardly and so on. When using the countersunk screw head you can cinch the screw semi tight, micro adjust to the exact angle, and then lock down for a permanent setting. I suggest you seriously consider both the quick-locking mechanism, independent of screwdrivers, and also the countersunk screwhead, which relies on the screwdriver. It is very reassuring when you can be sure that the bevel is not going to move throughout a project, which is critical to maintaining accuracy, and they do work so very well.

The tightening mechanisms should always lock firmly and should not allow any movement in the beam of the stock. In and throughout most of our work with sliding bevels, we need to apply knives firmly against the beam to establish and deepen cut lines as knifewalls. We also generally apply firm pressure between the beam and the work itself as we check and affirm an angle, and determine whether we need to true-up any surfaces with planes and chisels. Before you buy a sliding bevel try to make certain that the locking mechanism securing the beam truly locks it tightly and immovably. I have found that not all mechanisms work well. If that is the case, you will never feel any solid level of confidence that you can truly trust the sliding bevel in action at the bench. Also, they do get bumped inadvertently during the work.

Alternative Sliding Bevels

While the sliding bevels I use, and have used for years, are traditional designs, a few current tool makers have changed the way sliding bevels are made and operate. The demise of British entrepreneurialism surrounding traditional tool craft and hand work reflects the lack of investment in formerly thriving industries, such as the tool-making Britain was once famed for. There are some slight innovations from modern manufacturers, however, as well as locking mechanisms that emulate one of several types developed during the early 1900s. Some companies have looked for ways to improve tool design in terms of appearance and materials through the years. The sliding bevel pictured here, for instance, has a resin-impregnated wooden stock that is impervious to water and atmospheric moisture, which is ideal if indeed damp conditions are a problem. Another benefit of this particular design, and one I have enjoyed for over a decade, is that the locking mechanism lies completely flush to the outer face of the stock of the bevel. This allows the bevel to lie flat over the whole surface, whichever side of the tool the stock is placed against. Additionally, this particular mechanism meets my criteria for simple, single-handed locking in tight places using only one finger.

When you are looking for a sliding bevel you should certainly consider modern makers as there is always a chance that they will improve on the traditional models. You should always beware, however, of manufacturers who over-complicate simple tools. Always bear in mind the function of the tool and try to make sure that the manufacturers have taken care, in the case of sliding bevels, to ensure that it is accurately made and has a solid locking mechanism.

Chisels & Gouges

Chisels and gouges are uniquely shaped tools, united by the common functions to chop and pare wood using sharply refined cutting edges. Chisels are simple straight-edged cutting tools, used primarily to slice and chop straight cuts using a variety of techniques. Gouges only create curved cuts but the range of sweeps (curves) is about as massive a range as you could ever imagine. Though the sweeps often follow coves determined by the shape of each different gouge, each gouge is not at all limited to cutting a single shape but can produce an immeasurable range of coved cuts, according to the skilled manipulations of the user.

Unlike many of the other cutting edge tools, controlled by preset depths, adjusters, and soles that determine a thickness of cut, chisels and gouges rely on minute-by-minute judgements coordinated at the hand of the artisan. By skill, dexterity, and careful deliberation, each cut made becomes highly effective in the economy of freehand motion. It is this then that separates chisels and gouges into a category of tools all of their own; to chop and pare, shave and shape, according to the will and skill of the user.

I have used pretty much every kind of chisel made but sometimes I select them instinctively for the different tasks I perform with them. I take a chisel from the tray and apply it to the wood according to what I feel, without deliberation. Sometimes I must elevate the chisel slightly higher before I open the cut and, in a split second,

adjust my angle to optimise a cut and angle in a way that cannot be measured by any machine or the eye of an onlooker. The whole time I am working, I continue to make adjustments. Sometimes I chop and other times I pare; sometimes I go with the grain and other times directly across. When it seems best to me and for what seems, even to me, an unknown reason, I sever the fibres at a seemingly unreasonable angle. This freehand moving from one to the other is constant and no two cuts are ever the same. This then is the stark difference between the measured use of cutting edges held rigidly in planes and spokeshaves and the skilled control of an artisan separating the waste from the wanted, knowing all too well that what is removed cannot be reintegrated.

What I have written about the chisel is the same for gouges but perhaps magnified all the more. The thousand shapes that gouges were made in form coves of every possible type and size but the cuts are not even limited to the shapes of the original profiles alone. Skewing and slicing and glancing effectively changes the profile of any cut in a split second and gives movement to carved leaves and limbs and wings. Just like chisels, gouges are freehand, cutting edge tools that launch every crafting artisan into realms of shapes that can never be defined only by the curve of the cutting edge. Watch a skilled and creative carver working face-to-face with wood and see the thousands of chips beneath the bench as indescribable works of art emerge; then you start to see how much freedom freehand chisels and gouges bring to the work of the woodworker.

Essential Chisels & Gouges

In the following pages I will help you to understand which chisels and gouges you need for woodworking and how to select, sharpen, and use them.

Chisels

Chisels have evolved through centuries of development and are one of the most commonly used tools in the history of woodworking. Along with planes and saws, they are immediately recognised by everyone, regardless of whether he or she has ever worked with them. In their simplest form, they comprise a hardened steel blade held in a wooden or plastic handle. The handle is sized proportionally to fit the hand comfortably and also provides a striking surface for mallet work. The mallet can be used to drive the chisel more effectively than would be possible with mere hand pressure alone. With the chisel, we split, chop, and pare wood to remove the waste from the wanted, to shape it, and to make and refine every different joint type ever made. In industrial woodworking, machines have mostly replaced chisel work but they have not replaced the iconic impression of a handheld chisel driven by a wooden mallet. Even when woodworkers achieve most of their work with machines like routers and such, the chisel refines the final cuts more readily than dialing in final adjustments. In the world of fine woodworking, and especially traditional work with hand tools, the chisel is and always will be an irreplaceable tool.

A whole book could be written about all of the chisels that have emerged from different makers worldwide through the centuries. This is not my aim with this book and I will only discuss a few. I doubt that many cultures developed and produced as many chisel types as the steel-industry capital of Britain's Sheffield alone. This was one of the largest fiery furnaces of the world; the toolmaking epicentre of hand-forged chisels. I believe that this industrious, South Yorkshire town influenced more toolmakers and designers than any other and this is especially so in the world of chisel makers. Amazingly, throughout my life as a woodworker, working in almost every realm of joinery and furniture making, I have generally relied on one chisel type. With this classic, hand-forged chisel, the bevel-edged chisel, I have chopped many thousands of mortise holes and dovetail pins and tails; I have pared down every tenon cheek and recessed all types of hardware ranging from hinges to catches, from lid stays to locks and latches. The bevel-edged chisel still proves itself to be one of the most versatile thoroughbreds of all the chisels ever developed and, all the more amazingly, they still cost very little to buy. With half a dozen well made bevel-edged chisels you have all the chisels you will ever need to work wood with. That said, I would like to discuss two other common chisel types that I find useful for heavier and specialised work too. I pick one of these up when I have many multiples of one thing or another to do, or sometimes just to ease the pressure on my regular bevel-edged chisels in the day-to-day of life.

“

With this classic, hand-forged chisel, the bevel-edged chisel, I have chopped many thousands of mortise holes

”

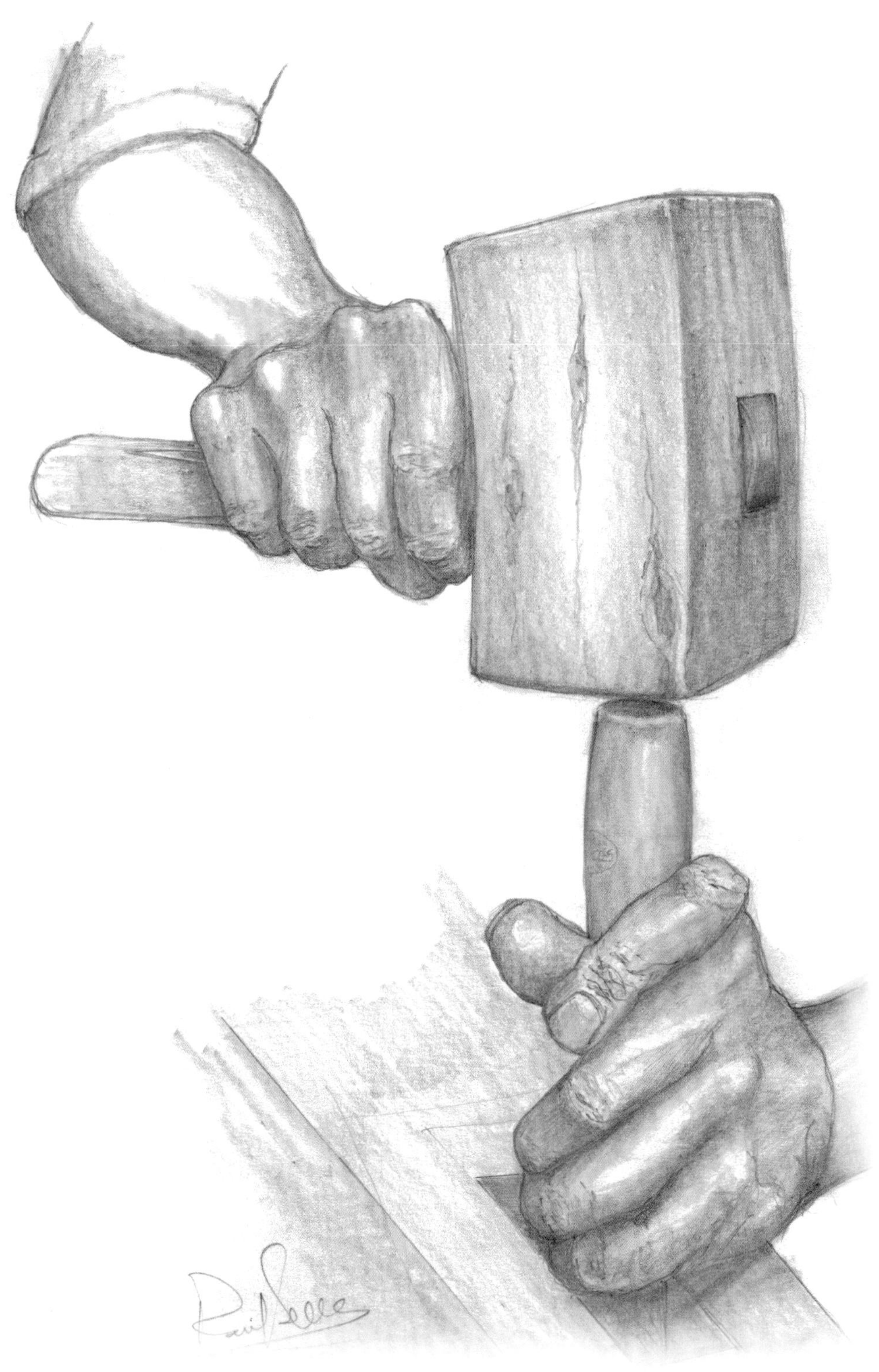

The Bevel-edged Chisel

The bevel-edged chisel has held its own against all competition and I think this is with good reason. They are lightweight yet firm and strong, well-balanced and highly refined. Bevel-edged chisels have survived a culture where hand tools and the traditions surrounding them have generally declined or even, in some cases, disappeared. Alongside other chisels, these chisels might, at first glance, seem somewhat light or fragile. Perhaps they might seem weaker and less likely to last when compared to their heavier counterparts but, in the care of skilled hands, they last crafting woodworkers through many decades of their working life, regardless of the woodworking craft type. I still own chisels I bought as a boy in 1965 and that is after 50 years of daily use or thereabouts. One or two more specialist makers continue the tradition in making quality chisels for anyone looking to buy new; and, in today's economy of global manufacturing and distribution, good chisels can be bought for just a fraction of the price I paid, even 50 years ago, in my youth. By the time I came along to be a woodworker, the bevel-edged chisel had fully evolved as the champion of all chisels. With all the engineering developments of the past centuries, in my opinion, no modern maker has since developed a new chisel to surpass the old design. Makers like Ward, I Sorby, William Marples and many others truly captured the essence of the art of chisel making and pleased working men with the very best.

Most bevel-edged chisels made today retain the grinder marks and the signature of mass-manufacture under economic competition where the expression of quality in what is made has, for the main part, been forsaken. This sad condition developed through two world wars and, so far, tool makers seem to struggle to reestablish the values from when workers were expected to create works of art in common tools. Whereas this may not actually affect the functionality of chisels too much, it does affect their appearance and how we feel about them. That said, the chisels themselves can always be additionally improved and refined by the user. Chisels can be improved by additional remedial work. I took one and removed the brash steel ferrule and hoop; I reshaped the handle and replaced the ferrule with a more solid brass one. I worked on the steel blade to remove the grinder marks and created a tool I would like to own and use for the remainder of my working life. The tapers may not be as thin and refined as my old Marples and Wards but they look and feel good and they do work the wood well.

Other Chisel Types

Few chisels match the qualities that give the bevel-edged chisels their versatility. The bevel-edged chisel is the best chisel for the vast majority of furniture making and many other trades too. There are, however, other chisel types that you may come across and I want to outline them briefly here so that you will be able to identify them and know where they may be useful.

THE MORTISE CHISEL

These heavy mortise chisels were made for general joinery work and especially joinery associated with building work, including all types of framed structures. Mortise chisels are robustly strong, with features designed for easier registration and alignment as the chisel chops ever deeper establishing the walls of the mortise. The thick blade, with its larger, parallel sides, keeps the chisel well aligned as the process of chopping continues to increasing depths. The significance of chisel thickness becomes evident as deeper holes require more leverage. The frames that most woodworkers and furniture makers create today are much smaller and more refined than the large joinery that was common at one time. In times past, door frames, window sashes, window frames, and newel posts used in stair building, gate making, and some timber framing were all built using deep mortise construction that required specialised chisels.

Heavy mortise chisels of this type were once common and generally offered in sizes from ⅛" (3mm) to ⅝" (16mm) in 1/16" (1.5mm) increments.

Chop...

Lever...

Lift.

You should not lose sight of the significant positioning of the thicker bevel heel (or knee) in relation to the long axis of the mortise chisels. This chief fulcrum of the mortise chisel is what we use for leveraging out the waste wood from deep mortises. These chisels have large, oval handles that are ideal for gripping and levering. The bolster of this type of chisel was larger in order to absorb greater pressure and so the large handles stood their ground against heavy mallet blows.

For the majority of woodworkers today the mortise chisel is unnecessary. For most furniture making and light joinery, a bevel-edged chisel is perfectly sufficient. However, the mortise chisel may well become essential if you find yourself cutting many large and deep mortises.

THE FIRMER CHISEL

These square-edged, lighter, carpentry chisels are less common today but in my apprentice days many firmer chisels lay on the bench in the usual sizes. The common use was chopping mortises and fitting tenons. The firmer chisel was also preferred by school woodworking classes of the day. The added corners reduced the risk of bending and breaking by less sensitive 13-year olds proving their strength. However, in the long term, I think it was these square corners, which felt awkward and clunky, that saw the demise of the firmer chisel. I never used one for very long.

It is important to remember that, at one time, joiners mostly made windows and doors and then frames to house them. Sliding sash windows and casements had many a dozen mortise joints in one frame or sash. Often, small and compact mortise and tenons were made from moulded sash stock. The larger mortise chisels were impractical for some of this work and so firmer and registered sash chisels were better suited.

There are actually two basic types of firmer chisel, the square-edged type and the bevel-edged type. So, while I refer to the bevel-edged chisel as a separate chisel type, it is actually a variant of the firmer chisel. The basic difference is that the sides of the bevel-edged chisels are bevelled along the full length of each side on the back of the chisel. Firmer chisels occupy centre ground between mortise chisels and bevel-edged chisels but fail to distinguish themselves as particularly useful for any common aspect of woodworking today.

I have never particularly liked the square-edged firmer chisel and so I have generally eliminated these from any of my personal working chisels and rarely, if ever, use them in any of my actual cutting work. I do, however, keep a ½" (12mm) and ¾" (19mm) near to hand because I find the square edge useful for pressing beeswax filler and regular wood filler into nail heads and other flaws as needed, and for puttying windows. If you happen to have already picked up chisels of this type keep them. They will work just fine for nearly all aspects of woodworking, they are just not my preference.

BUTT CHISELS

These stubby chisels crept in over the years and some might consider them useful but they are not too practical for bench work and fine woodworking. Butt chisels became a favourite with carpenters on jobsites because they are functional and also compact enough for their work pouches. As fully functioning chisels I would not recommend them. Most carpenters working in construction use hand tools only occasionally and cannot generally be regarded as experienced hand tool experts, although there are, of course, exceptions. The butt chisel, for them, is the tool to use when a power saw does not reach into a corner and they need something more to trim it down and out. I have not ever considered these chisels of much value to my work; a full-sized chisel is far more versatile and never lacking.

METAL-CAPPED ALTERNATIVES

Another chisel type started to emerge at the same time as butt chisels and these are the types with metal caps designed for use with steel claw hammers. Again this is a design developed for site carpentry and the mass building of houses, not fine woodworking. It is a strange thing that carpenters, throughout history, used wooden-handled chisels and mallets; all along they could have made steel handles for heavy work with steel hammers and yet they never did. These metal-capped chisels will damage a wooden mallet. I am sure they are fit for some purposes but the new 'refinement' is not really something I would look for. In fact, I would avoid purchasing these chisels for furniture making and general woodworking.

What to Look for in a Bevel-edged Chisel

The full-length bevel of the bevel-edged firmer chisel allows the tool to get into corners more readily. It also increases the sight line along the sides of the chisel and into the corners of the work, where the corner of the chisel slices internal intersections at shoulder lines and such. The square-edged firmer chisels, which I discussed before, are possibly a little stronger but the stoutness makes them less versatile and more awkwardly cumbersome in refining work.

Some makers produce less refined bevel-edged chisels that look similar but, because they are much thicker, they perform no differently than square-edged firmer chisels. They feel clunky to use in finer work. In choosing chisels for fine woodworking, bench joinery, furniture making and so on, I look at the side of the chisels before I buy one. I like the bevel near to the cutting edge to be no more than ⅛" (3mm) but ideally as thin as 1⁄16" (1.5mm). The width of the side can increase towards the handle end to around 3⁄16" (4mm) but no more.

These thinner and refined chisels are not so easy to find new (unless you are prepared to pay a premium) but they can be found secondhand.

These heavier bevel-edged chisels might be better suited to carpentry rather than fine joinery and furniture making.

Sharpening Chisels

Sharpening chisels maximises their effectiveness in severing fibres and eases the passage of the cutting edge into the wood. The sharper the edge, the cleaner the cut and the better the surface created under the cutting edge. Sharpness therefore becomes critical to every chisel and the task of sharpening is undertaken many times throughout the day. Without this, the work and the standard of craftsmanship suffers.

I keep my sharpening plates or whetstones close to hand at the end of my workbench. I use my triple-level set up of coarse, medium, and superfine diamond plates but, as discussed in the sharpening section, there are many types of abrasive that work just fine.

To sharpen, hold the chisel as shown and present it to the plate at an elevation of approximately 30 degrees. On a new chisel this 30-degree angle is usually 5 degrees higher than the manufacturer's 25-degree bevel. Notice that the chisel is not aligned square to the body or the length of the plate but more aligned to the comfort of the hand, wrist, arm and, upper body. Holding the chisel at this comfortable angle allows the greatest energy down to the chisel tip; it allows you to apply the correct pressure, both at the heel and throughout the camber of the bevel. Working across the whole bevel in this way takes you gradually down to the actual edge you want to reach. Push forward and backward keeping the hands and arms as steady as possible and, at the same time, applying firm pressure on both the forward and backward stroke. As you make the motions, allow the hands to slowly lower on the furthest outreach as a natural extension of your arms. When you pull back to the start position on the plate, elevate back to the 30-degree angle. Do this with each and every stroke. Using this method creates a camber to the bevel of the chisel.

Sharpening freehand allows us to start at 30° and tail off to 20°. This thrust forward creates a natural curve and the result is a camber to the bevel of the tool as shown below.

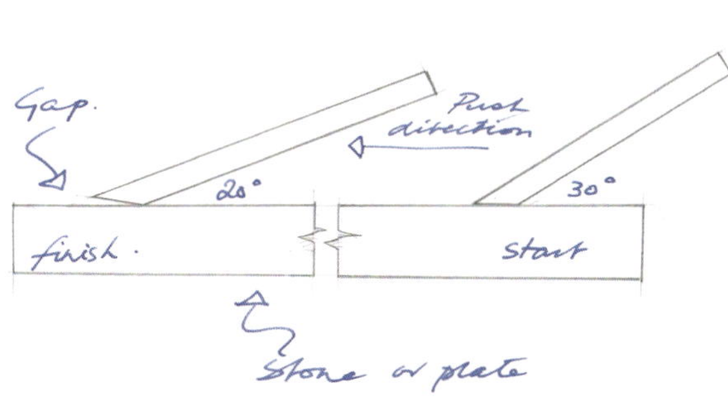

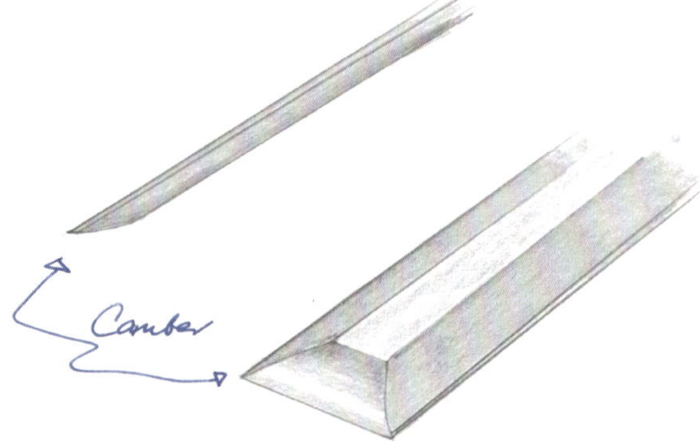

Remember, lifting too high will get you there too, but this creates a 'thick' edge to the beginning of the bevel because you are establishing a steeper angle. This thicker initial edge is not really the desired edge because it takes more energy to effect the cut; the resistance is greater the steeper the bevel. Check periodically to make sure you are, in fact, abrading the whole of the bevel and not just part of it. Also check that you are abrading the whole width of it in a square-like fashion. Otherwise this will effectively develop a bias on the bevel that shows clearly whether you are pressing too hard on one side or the other. Correcting as you go prevents the development of too much of a skew. Any bias should be corrected by pressing harder on the part that needs it. Usually, if you are checking frequently, you can correct a bias in just a few strokes on the coarse abrasive. I think it is also worth mentioning that a slight skew is totally acceptable and does not discernibly affect the performance of the chisel negatively. Just do not allow too much discrepancy.

“ *Check periodically to make sure you are, in fact, abrading the whole of the bevel and not just part of it* ”

Once the bevel is abraded at the coarser level, (and this may take many strokes, perhaps a hundred or so if the edge is very dull) subsequent levels take perhaps 20-30 strokes on both the mid level and then the very fine. The whole process for, say, a 1" (25mm) wide chisel to this stage will generally take a couple of minutes.

As you work on abrading the bevel, a small wire of steel will develop on the back of the blade. This 'burr' is normal and it, in fact, shows that you are properly abrading up to the edge. At no stage before now do you need to remove this burr. Once the three levels of abrading on the bevel are done, flip the chisel over and press the flat face onto the finest abrasive plate or stone. With the face dead flat to the plate, use a single pull-stroke to pull the chisel away from the chisel edge. This is not to abrade the already polished and refined surface of the flat face but simply to force the burr upwards and to weaken the wire edge holding the burr to the chisel. It is not necessary to move it back and forth as the wire edge is all we want to remove and this wire is quite weak. The large, flat face should already be fully polished out (I talk about this on the next pages) and it remains so in this process. All we are doing is forcing the burr up and back onto the bevel side of the edge. This breaks the wire burr along the cutting edge. It is not necessary to ensure the burr is completely removed because that happens with the final level of abrading, which we do on the strop.

With the strop fixed and secured in the vise, hold the handle in your dominant hand and grip the rest of the chisel in your non-dominant hand, wrapping your fingers around the chisel so that the heel of your hand is applied firmly to the back, flat face of the chisel. Then pull the chisel along the strop about 30 times, pressing the bevel to the strop firmly. Strive to keep the bevel parallel to the strop surface rather than trying to follow the contour of the camber itself. It is not really necessary to follow the camber at all as it is nearly impossible not to catch the whole surface anyway. Compressing the bevel into the leather causes the leather to mushroom underneath and this effectively works the whole bevel as we want. By the time you have finished, the surface should have a mirror-finish across the whole bevel and all traces of any burr are usually (but not always) gone. If not, the burr will come away with the first stroke when you start chiseling the wood.

Initialising a Chisel

When we first buy a set of chisels we usually need to flatten the large flat face and polish out any grinding striations left from the manufacturing process. This initialising takes a few minutes per chisel and using diamond plates simplifies the process. The important thing here is that whatever you flatten on must be truly flat. Quality diamond plates will usually be flat to within a thousandth of an inch. Of course, if the chisel has been initialised and polished out at manufacture there is no need to further refine the chisel.

Start on the coarse diamond plate and rub back and forth along the full length and width of the plate surface. Look at the chisel to see the newly abraded sections, which will be highlighted; this will show you how flat the chisel is. The chisel does not have to be abraded over the entire surface. It is actually more than adequate as long the ¼" (5mm) or so behind the cutting edge is flat but often woodworkers take the whole face all the way to dead flat. There is no real advantage to flattening the entire back because it is only the initial cutting edge that really matters.

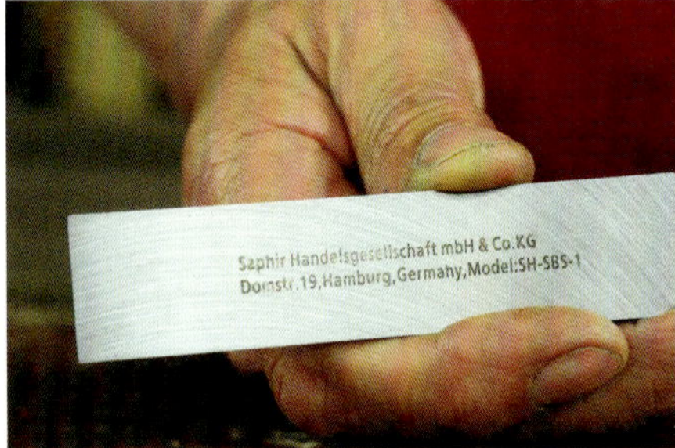

Many chisels are not refined to a sufficient level of polish by the manufacturer.

It is only necessary to fully flatten a small area behind the cutting edge.

On this chisel the bulk of the surface is not flat but this is fine so long as the section behind the cutting edge is.

This image shows a fully flattened and polished-out surface to around 10,000 grit.

After working through the levels of honing I then polish the flat face on the reverse side of my strop using the wood itself, which I charge with honing compound. This initialisation is virtually the same for all the tools that have flat back faces.

Secondary and Micro Bevels

I do not generally advocate secondary or micro bevels, which are usually achieved with rigid mechanical means, because I like freehand sharpening. However, on some occasions, I do change the initial bevel angle to 35 degrees for extra strength if chopping mortises in woods of uneven density. This simple task is a matter of lifting up the chisel on the coarse stone to add 5 degrees to my general 30-degree angle when sharpening. All of my chisels are generally sharpened at 30 degrees and then immediately cut back in a macro camber rather than using micro bevel or secondary-bevel sharpening. Using a secondary bevel increases the bevel angle and strengthens the edge for the higher exertion of pressure when chopping using hammer blows. After the mortises are cut I simply restore the 30-degree bevel in subsequent sharpenings. The fact

This chisel shows a primary and secondary bevel as typical from a manufacturer. I do not advocate continuing this pattern of sharpening but I do occasionally add a secondary bevel for extra strength in certain circumstances.

is that there is almost no discernable difference between 30- and 35-degree bevels but the extra 5 degrees does strengthen the edge to resist fracture when using heavier hammer or mallet blows.

On my mortise chisels I keep the start of my macro-camber at 35 degrees and then drop off to around 25 degrees on the close of my sharpening and honing strokes. I never grind the bevels of my chisels on a mechanical grinder except to remove damage caused by edge fracture, hitting something foreign in the wood, or by dropping it on a hard surface like stone or concrete.

Using Chisels

Most people, even those who do not regularly work with wood, look at chisels with a sense of knowing how they work either because they learned woodworking in school or because they have used them a few times in their lives. Relating to the chisel actually takes a great deal of skill but do not feel discouraged at all. The learning experience is ongoing, always interesting, and often exciting. I am still amazed by aspects of the chisel in the work; I have never stopped learning. I think it is important to feel relaxed and contented in using them and in learning to master them in the work. Watching someone use a chisel, or seeing a picture of it, might give the impression of aggression or heavy handedness rather than sensitivity. I would encourage you to think of them as I do and use them as instruments—instruments transmitting sound and feeling; designed to probe the depths of the grain; to investigate grain structure, direction, and density. That is how we negotiate the cutting action and the wood in the cuts.

FREEHAND PARING

We usually pare with one hand on the handle and the other hand applied to the blade with the fingers wrapped around it. We generally work the chisel in a rocking, side-to-side motion and the chisel penetrates, firstly via the corners and then along the full width of the cutting edge. We can also use the same hold on the blade but, instead of holding the handle, we can use the heel of the other hand to bump the chisel into the cut. This works well on wide chisels, say, ¾" (20mm) and wider. Using these methods, the wrapped fingers correct the presentation, with the inner palm applying downward pressure and the compression between the fingers and palm aiding direction. I initially use my dominant hand on the blade to enter the wood with a firm grip. The dominant hand lifts the chisel and feels for the reaction of the cutting edge in the wood as it cuts. This is critical for feeding the chisel into the wood; you cannot see what the chisel is

doing but you can feel it. Whether you bump the chisel or use continuous firm pressure, the non-dominant hand then takes hold of the blade, after the initial cut, and is responsible for direction from here on.

For narrower chisels, because they are so narrow, I usually pinch the blade of the chisel between the forefinger and thumb of my non-dominant hand; the finger underneath the thumb on the side bevel or corner. My remaining three fingers are tucked into my palm but not clenched. My right hand always dominates the chisel's direction and gives the chisel the main power. Small chisel work, used for paring, usually revolves around recessing hardware, paring the shoulders around joints like dovetail pin recesses, and other finer work. This work is then quite reliant on swivelling the paring cut (as described before) to advance the chisel into the surface fibres and especially on endgrain fibres. I usually choke up on the chisel here. Choking the chisel means that I run the forefinger, which is holding the blade, behind the cutting edge, against the wood to act as a stop so that I do not overshoot and damage the unsupported fibres on the other side (see top image). Remember that, no matter the task, the hands are always behind and never in front of the cutting edge.

I pare both with and across the grain. Pare cuts can remove a lot of material or a just a very fine shaving. One type of paring is a two-handed power cut. Both hands are on the handle with the dominant hand wrapping the handle and the non dominant hand wrapping the back of the other hand and fingers. Both thumbs point along the chisel so that both thumb heels press against one another and against the handle of the chisel. Sometimes the thumbs cross. With this handhold I start to jab the wood at a shallow level until I feel the wood starts to part and I enter the wood. From here I start to swivel the chisel and use the corner of the chisel to separate the fibres, creating a leading edge into the wood. Using the corner is my best strategy for finding levels and removing them one by one until I reach the lines I am working to.

SPLIT CUTTING

Split cutting is best done with thinner bevel-edged chisels. Split cuts are used to remove the bulk of the waste before pare cutting and I love split cutting because it is fast and effective. I use split cutting mostly to get to the cheeks of tenons, splitting from the end by reading the grain direction before applying the chisel. I leave about 1⁄16" (2mm) of wood on so that I can then pare the surface, mostly across the grain but occasionally with the grain also. I also pare the endgrain of the shoulder into the cheek corners.

This, by no means, presents every method of paring and split cutting but it is enough to challenge you to think more deeply about the fibres and the chisel limitations and possibilities.

CHOPPING

It is in chop-cutting that most people find difficulty gauging the work. I tend not to use heavy chisels even though they are designed for much of the heavier work. I feel that I have more sensitive control of the smaller chisels and can feel the work more fully at the cutting edge. Mostly my adjustments are made by listening to the chisel hammer (or mallet) and the density of the sound they transmit to me as I work. The sound of fibres separating is obvious and when I hear a dull thud I know the fibres are resisting and I must change the angle of presentation to take less off. Chopping is systematic. Often people want to cut directly on the knifewall or line without making space for the bevel of the chisel to enter the wood. When they start chopping and place the chisel on the line, the single-sided bevel drives the large flat face of the chisel into the knifewall and this moves the knifewall over because of bevel pressure. It is better to remove the material in stages by chopping away from the knifewall or line on the waste side. Usually about 1⁄16" (2mm) is a good distance but this depends on the density of the wood. Once this margin is established and you have entered the wood, you can move toward the knife wall in a couple of steps. That way, when we chop, we can keep exactly to the line because the knifewall has much less bevel pressure driving against it and so it has the strength to resist.

Sometimes, when I am chopping, I use the handle with my non-dominant hand and, at other times, I use my thumb and fingers right behind the tip of the cutting edge as I feed it into the cut. I find that this gives me greater sensitivity as I feel the chisel against the knifewall just before I chop. Such handholds are always with my non-dominant hand as my dominant hand is always the one using the chisel hammer or mallet.

Gouges

Gouges comprise a complex and diverse range of carving tools that span many centuries of development. Yet I think we use fewer today than at any other time in their history. These unique tools are designed to cut just about any curved shape you care to discover or mention. With them we carve everything from ornate floral designs to massive works of art in the form of sculpted images. Of course, through the centuries, they have satisfied the demands of a wide range of creative and even industrial needs, not the least of which is those of the furniture maker like myself. From their highly refined shapes and cutting edges came mould castings for industrial iron foundries and intricately carved scrolls for violins and cellos. Many millions of carvings, defying description, relied on bent shapes formed by common blacksmithing techniques, unbelievably shaped by the face of a hammer and we often walk past them, completely oblivious to the remarkable carving tool we call the gouge.

As with chisels, there are too many different gouge types to deal with in these few pages. Tool makers have developed specialised gouges to serve the different woodworking trades through the centuries. Carvers and pattern makers, joiners, carpenters and many other trades have relied on these curved-edged chisels we call gouges to create a massive range of items that relied wholly on curved cuts. I keep a dozen or two gouges to deal with my work needs but it is surprising how much work can be accomplished with just a handful of gouges. For the purpose of this book, I can perhaps discuss but one gouge to explain the many. Each woodworking craft might use only a few, in general, and then perhaps another dozen or so for more specialised tasks. Later in this chapter I will recommend what features to look for in your primary gouge, which will handle most carving and shaping used in general woodworking and furniture making.

A single gouge can accomplish a surprising number of tasks.

Hollows carved and shaped using a carving gouge are most commonly formed with a gouge that has the bevel on the outside so that the cutting edge is on the inside surface of the gouge. We call this an out-cannel gouge. When the bevel is on the inner face or curve it is called an in-cannel gouge. This gouge cuts on the outside radius.

This is an out-cannel gouge.

These are in-cannel gouges.

The in-cannel gouge is great for cutting flutes.

Gouges are created in a range of radii we call sweeps. The sweep is the amount of curve on a gouge. They also come in a variety of widths, ranging from as little as 1⁄16" (1.5mm) to 2" (50mm) in increments of approximately 1⁄16" (1.5mm). These sweeps go from straight, No. 1, to No. 11, which is almost semicircular. The sweep numbers correspond to the different radii used to differentiate between gouges. In each of the sweeps there are also width sizes so there might well be dozens of gouges in a full range made by a manufacturer; as many as 200. This number doubles if you consider the two types of in- and out-cannel gouges. In addition, there are bent gouges, front bent and back bent, again in the various radii. A manufacturer may well offer over a 1,000 different gouges in the full range.

Gouges generally have many shapes to their handles; too many to show here. Mostly the shapes come from the makers answering the needs of the majority of users but some are reshaped to suit a particular hand. They can also be designed to suit a specific a task - allowing a certain wrist or hand action that effects a certain cut. Handles can be octagonal, oval, and round as basics but can then be shaped for pushing, pulling, twisting and other ways of manipulating the tool. Chisel and gouge handles are never just round dowel shapes. Octagons prevent the tools from rolling on the bench top but they also allow for alignment

and twisting to counter the effect of opposing the grain, which can pull the hand off course. The wood you work may well determine the type of handle you pick. Some woods, like lime and basswood, work so easily it is often likened to carving a bar of soap or cold butter. Other woods seem always to rebel but must still be carved. Whereas the woods best known for carving and retaining detail can mostly be carved using hand pressures only, other woods need mallet work. Here we usually look at the handle to determine whether the design is suited to this; when the neck is narrow and the end rounded it usually indicates using hand pressure as a rule with some light tapping. Remember that tapping with a mallet is not always used simply to drive the chisel or gouge but can also be used to effect a certain cut type. A glancing blow sends a scallop in a certain direction designed to separate and lift the waste from the cut face and leave a cut that needs no more refining. This brings clarity and definition to the cut. Further abrading to shape often leaves the appearance 'muddy' and undefined.

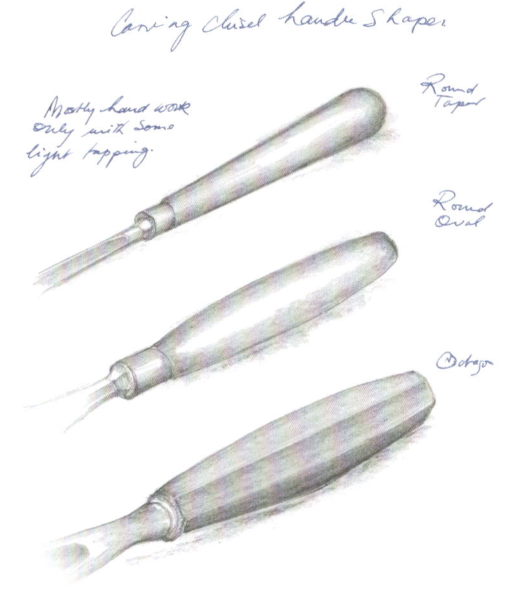

You should understand that the gouges we are looking at here are not the same as the gouges used for woodturning using lathes. The primary difference being that this gouge works static wood, held securely, as the hands work the gouge into the wood. For woodturning the wood is rotated and the gouge held and guided into the wood to form symmetrical shapes in the form of coves and beads. Because of this difference in functionality, turning gouges are made of different steel and are sharpened and shaped differently so that they are not interchangeable with carving gouges.

Gouges Are Lifetime Tools

I usually pick up gouges when I find them secondhand but I would buy new ones as and when I needed them for specific tasks. The thing about gouges is that they truly last and I rarely pick up a gouge that has exhausted its life. Some of the very finest gouges will be those well used and well worn by lifelong artisans. Traditional gouges are still being made today and are made to comparable specifications by European makers, who are linking back to the ancient makers. Aspects of my work include carving spoons, bowls, and chair or stool seats and, for much of this work, I simply rely on a wide 1 ⅜" (35mm) #7 sweep for both roughing out and finessing the last paring cuts. I own maybe 100 or so other gouges of different sizes and sweeps for carving and detailing my work. Some of my work does require carving detail and, though I feel I could carve whatever I wanted to, I am not a carver by calling so much as by necessity on occasion. We often find carving is separated into two categories, carving for need and carving for decoration. It is easy to see carving for need as being purely functional but we often lose sight of the fact that decorative carving can have its uses too. What could mostly be regarded as non-functional, in the sense of use, can be functional in the sense of being a sculpted depiction to show others what might not be seen. Of course there is more to it even than that. I worked on making a cello with my son, Joseph, some years back and during that process I realised that, in many aspects of instrument making, you are, in fact, carving a voice.

Using the Gouge

Like chisels, gouges are mostly used freehand in one of two ways; you either drive them by using chisel hammer (or mallet) blows or you pare them by gripping the handle and pushing the gouge into the wood face using a variety of different techniques. The paring method depends on the gouge type, size and so on, and the type of cut required. Most often the gouge rides either the bevel (if using an out-cannel gouge) or the round of the back (if using an in-cannel gouge). Generally these two surfaces, the bevel or the back-round, move into the wood with the initial cut; the gouge then registers against the hollow surface that is created beneath the cut as we follow through, into and over the surface of the material.

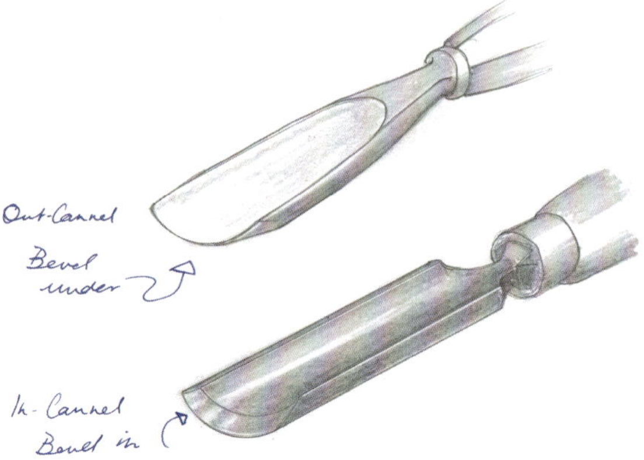

The dominant hand both grips and drives the gouge and the fingers (or grip) of the other hand manipulate the tool into the wood as the cut develops second-by-second. Using this method, we sense the angle of presentation through the tool at the cutting edge to direct the entry cut and follow-through. Wrapping the steel with the non-dominant hand or holding it between the fingers and thumb of the non-dominant hand enables us to apply steady downward pressure over the whole or part of the curved cutting edge. The dominant hand grips the handle firmly and adds further adjustment control as well as further pressure. The dominant hand also directs the cut and, combined with side to side swaying through the upper body to the gouge as a whole, the gouge will scallop and shape to different levels according to how much pressure is applied and the angle of presentation.

Woods Affect the Tools We Use

Wood carving, by its nature, necessitates a working knowledge of the properties of the different species of wood as every wood is different due to its grain structure. Different woods are sometimes worked differently as is the case with the work of the violin maker, who works primarily with perhaps two or three wood types, mainly maple and spruce. Pattern makers, on the other hand, need stable woods that hold sharp and crisp edges for creating moulds. Subsequently the moulds are used to form castings in sand. The sand, rammed around the mould, forms a reverse of the mould and a hollow to receive the molten metal; afterwards, its removal then facilitates reuse for subsequent castings. Other woods are carved in quite diversely different ways for decorative work including the creation of sculpted statues, friezes, door panels and so on. Using gouges in the realms of more general woodworking, such as joinery and furniture making, very much simplifies the range of gouges we actually need.

Sharpening the Gouge

The shape of the gouge can make it look daunting to sharpen. Here you have a curved edge and a flat stone to sharpen the various curves on. I think it is understandable to look at the task with doubt but, when you see it done, all doubt rapidly disappears. There are two simple and practical ways to sharpen the cutting edge of an out-cannel gouge. As I am only recommending a out-cannel gouge as the essential gouge I will not go into detail on sharpening in-cannel gouges but they can be easily sharpened using a shaped block of wood and abrasive paper or a shaped diamond hone or slipstone.

FIGURE OF EIGHT SHARPENING

In my apprenticeship I was shown what we call the 'figure-of-eight' method for sharpening gouges and flat-faced, curve-edged plane irons, such as those used for some non-complex moulding planes; scrub planes and so on. This works best for me, but people often feel awkward using it, especially at first. With a little practice, however, and with increased sensitivity it becomes second nature and you soon develop a rhythm.

Place the corner of the gouge on the stone, as shown, at the end nearest to you and off to one side of the stone. The angle of presentation will vary with different gouges but, in this case, let us say 30 to 35 degrees. The angles to carving gouges vary considerably. For most gouges, I suggest a primary bevel of 20 degrees. I then change the beginning of the bevel to a 30-degree angle. Ultimately the angle will be refined to a camber but this is established over time.

Push the gouge forward and roll the gouge while moving to the opposite corner of the sharpening plate so that, as you move across from corner to corner of the plate, you are also applying the full width of the curved bevel to the sharpening plate.

This rotation of the wrist turns the gouge bevel from one corner of the curved edge around to the other corner of the gouge and, while keeping the same 30-degree bevel, keeps the gouge in constant contact with the sharpening plate.

The hand continues to rotate the gouge so that, although the main thrust is corner to corner, because you are also twisting the gouge to cover the whole bevel, you end up at the far end, towards the middle of the sharpening plate, you have completed the forward thrust. You will have rolled the gouge through a partial rotation following the arc of the particular gouge you are sharpening. The opposite corner of the gouge is now up in the air.

On the return or pull stroke you still have an abrasive quality in the motion, albeit a little less powerful than on the forward stroke. So keep contact with the sharpening plate.

Continue the roll onto the opposite side of the arc and conclude at the end nearest to you, finishing the stroke at the opposite corner.

This completes the cyclical figure-of-eight and now it is simply a question of repeating the strokes over and over, without stopping, until you have established a burr on the inside of the gouge across the whole width of the cutting edge. It is now important to work towards easing the corner, formed by the change in bevel angle, by abrading the hard edge. That is, to round-off the corner of the newly formed bevel and ease it into the main or primary bevel. You will then have created a camber that works well for scalloping cuts, which are ideal for carving spoons, bowls, chair and stool seats, and so on. Working the whole of the bevel means that you do not just work the cutting edge. The aim is to maintain a continuous surface around and onto the whole bevel. We create a camber to the bevel near the edge and then move into the main bevel. This results in the camber being closer to the edge, which is different to a chisel.

The roughed bevel now looks like this. Subsequent abrading on finer stones and the strop polishes out the bevel to the cambered bevel we need.

From this level of abrading we transfer to the fine sharpening plate and repeat what we did on the coarse plate. This level of abrading takes much less work. We abrade only until the coarse marks have been removed.

This is the last level of abrading on the super fine sharpening plate and, again, we follow exactly the same abrading as we did in levels one and two.

Using the Strop

I create a purpose-built strop to polish the inside and outside of the bevels of my gouges. See page 35. With this I can polish-out the final levels of the abrading using buffing compound to charge the leather. The piece of wood is wide enough to use with larger and smaller gouges and it does not have to exactly correspond to each individual gouge.

It makes no difference whether you polish the inside or outside first. Always pull the gouge and trail the cutting edge so as not to gouge the leather. I generally pull about 30 times but sometimes more if necessary. This gouge was initialised by the manufacturer and, as most gouges are, it is sufficiently polished inside the cannel. However, it is simple enough to polish this out with abrasive papers beforehand if necessary.

To polish the bevel pull the gouge along the other side of the strop as before, trailing the cutting edge so as not to gouge the leather. Again, I pull about 30 times, but more if necessary, until the bevel is fully polished.

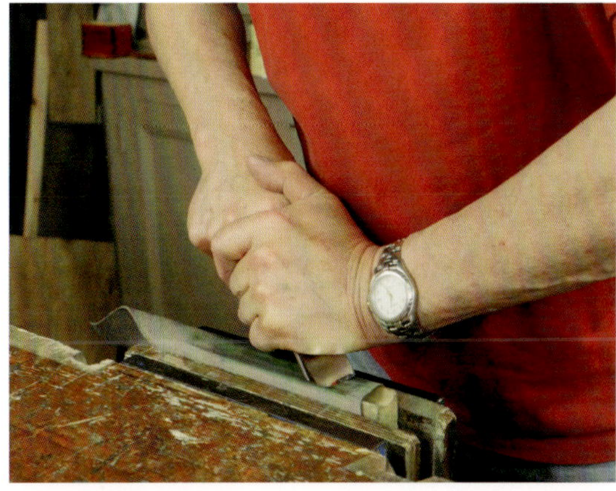

Here is how my gouges look after honing and polishing.

ROTATIONAL SHARPENING

Another method that gives good results is the rotational method. With this method you can also create an equally sharp edge by simply rolling the gouge along its bevel, going from corner edge to corner edge of the gouge, along the long axis of the sharpening plate. Using continuous strokes, rolling the gouge, and elevating the bevel at its angle, as discussed before, we abrade the bevel.

Offer the corner of the gouge to the sharpening plate as shown and feel for the existing bevel or establish a new one. Again, I am shooting for 30 to 35 degrees on the initial edge and trailing off to a shallower overall bevel.

Push the gouge away from you in a forward direction and start to rotate the gouge as you progress the stroke.

Rotating and moving forward prevents flat spots that would occur if you moved forward without rotating.

Continue through until you reach the opposite side of the curve to the cutting edge.

Once we have achieved a continuous burr along the inside of the cannel, we continue with successive strokes to create the curved camber we need, dropping the hand with subsequent strokes until we meet the primary bevel.

Once we have created the bevel on the coarse sharpening plate we follow through in the same way on the fine plate until the coarse abrasion marks have been removed.

“

Gouge shapes and sharpening methods are many and diverse. Every carver has his or her preference. You will experiment and find the shapes, sizes, and techniques you prefer I am sure. This will be just the beginning

Maintaining the lower bevel angle enables me to create a convex profile from the cutting edge to the first quarter of the bevel.

The final polishing now follows the same procedure for stropping, as shown before.

Gouge shapes and sharpening methods are many and diverse. Every carver has his or her preference. You will experiment and find the shapes, sizes, and techniques you prefer I am sure. This will be just the beginning.

Planes

My handful of essential hand planes has brought freedom to the work I do; mostly because they create the clean, sharp, unequalled crispness to the wood I work, which cannot be achieved using other methods. I want to write down how I feel about these tools in the hope that others will be inspired by my experiences as a craftsman working with my hands and earning my living with the same handful of planes. Many experienced woodworkers have returned to these older methods after feeling that something was missing from their work too. Most who master the skills of using them never consider any plane to be an archaic tool. Instead they come to appreciate that planes are uniquely devised and ensure the level of accuracy, which craftsmanship demands. My hope is that these tools and the methods for using them will continue to thrive forever worldwide.

Most types of planes are well proven and tested through centuries of workmanship. Some of these planes may not seem familiar but they are essential to my work as a furniture maker. I have included them because they each perform very unique and individual tasks. The

spokeshave never stops at just curved work and the plough plane will cut grooves and rebates too. The router brings such accuracy beyond mere routing and then, of course, the bench plane offers me a versatility in tasks too many to mention. These are the tools of the crafting artisans around the world; they are well proven to equal the intent of the craftsman's mind and hands and they have found new life by the resurgence and revivalism this present age provides.

It would be hard to number all of the planes that toolmakers have designed and developed over the past millennia in answering the needs of woodworkers. What they all surely have in common and what defines them as planes is the measured control they give in the removal of wood. The plane sole and the cutting iron work together in providing an exact depth of cut that can be changed by control mechanisms, wedges, and cams built into their diverse structures. This uniform control characterises the hand plane in all its different forms and, unlike all of the other cutting edge tools, the hand plane removes almost all the risk to your work once you master them.

Certainly, throughout the world, cast metal and wooden-bodied planes are still used for the smoothing, trimming, and leveling of wood. Even now, the craftsman woodworkers of the past have been replaced by a new generation, unlike any other, with a hunger to become true artisans. Anonymous woodworkers past and present have surrounded us with a legacy of workmanship to emulate, using the same modest assortment of hand tools.

Essential Planes

While planes have a complex history and can seem confusing, I have narrowed down what I feel are the essential planes that are needed to accomplish each woodworking task. I go into detail on each of my essential planes in the following sections:

Bench Planes p. 157
The Spokeshave p. 207
The Plough Plane p. 233
The Router Plane p. 253

Bench Planes

The bench plane category comprises a very specific plane type, designed for surface levelling, truing, and smoothing wood. This group is the most commonly used of all planes and that has been the case throughout the history of plane making. In the past, wooden bench planes (as we refer to them in Britain) were the most common type of bench plane and, in some parts of the world, they still prevail. Metal-cast planes are the product of an industrialised western culture, mostly in the UK and the USA. A large percentage of western woodworkers have ultimately adopted the all-metal design, which we know today as the Bailey-pattern bench plane.

Wooden planes work fantastically well and I highly recommend learning about them and even purchasing and using them when you get the chance. That said, the wide availability and broad consistency in configuration of the metal-bodied planes make them the ones that I will recommend and they will be the focus of my instruction in this chapter.

Plane Sizes

We rely on bench planes for preparing our wood before the laying out for joinery and furniture making can take place. The bench plane series of Bailey-pattern planes were numbered according to length, but increases in width also allowed for slightly wider shavings. This is where the numbering system seems to be the most confusing and some explanation is needed. The numbering for these bench planes goes from 1 to 8 with each number indicating an increase in length starting with the smallest at #1. Plane numbers 1 and 2 are not generally regarded as working models as such though functionally they have the same mechanisms as the full-sized planes. Some people do use them in place of small planes like block planes but, for general woodworking, they have never really featured as viable working bench plane options. Sizes 3 to 8 range in length from between approximately 9" (23cm) - 24" (61cm). Generally I think it is accepted that this length range allows for truing up longer lengths of material but I have found that almost all truing work can be accomplished with planes between 9" (23cm) and 14" (35cm). In the numbering system used for most metal-bodied planes, these sizes will be found in the 3, 4, 4 ½, 5, and 5 ½ models. In this numbering system, the models that have ½, or very occasionally ¼, are wider

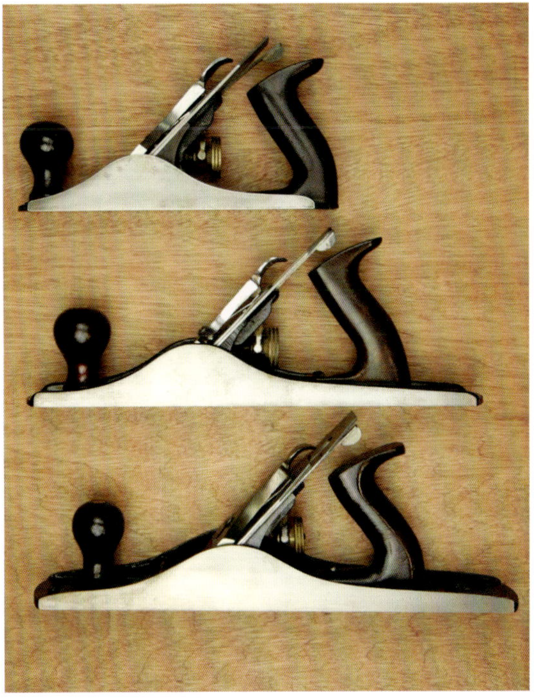

but are the same length as the same number without the ½. The #4 and #4 ½ planes both measure 9 ½" (24cm) long and are commonly referred to as smoothing planes. These are my two most used planes and the ones I have relied on most throughout my decades of working wood. The #4 ½ is simply a wider version of the #4 but performs identical tasks. It does, however, require more power to use it as the extra width means extra weight and also a wider cut. The Bailey-pattern #3 is somewhat narrower, just a little shorter, and performs the same tasks equally to the #4 and the #4 ½ but it takes a narrower cut. Usually this plane is preferred by people with smaller hands and body stature but it should in no way be seen as a lesser plane and it is an excellent starter plane for young people. The main difference between these three plane sizes is that the narrower planes take a narrower cut but are also slightly easier to use. The difference may seem small but, working with students for so long, I have found that it is significant enough to make the work easier for the user and can indeed make the difference between being able to successfully use the plane and not. As with all the bench planes, they smooth and trim the various surfaces of wood and allow us to control the thickness of the shaving by setting what we call the 'depth of cut.' The depth of cut is governed by the amount the cutting iron protrudes past and through the face of the plane's sole - the very bottom face of the plane that registers on the wood as we push the plane forward to effect each cut. The distance between the sole face and the cutting edge will determine the thickness of the shaving; usually hundredths or thousandths of an inch.

Sizes of Smoothing Planes

Lengths and widths of typical metal-bodied smoothing plane soles from #3 to #4 ½ are as follows:

Plane number	Plane width	Plane length	Cutting iron width
#3	2 ⅛" (54mm)	9" (228mm)	1 ¾" (44mm)
#4	2 ½" (64mm)	9 ½" (241mm)	2" (51mm)
#4 ½	3" (76mm)	9 ½" (241mm)	2 ⅜" (60mm)

I suggest you purchase one of these as an essential plane, which will allow you to accomplish most planing tasks.

Jack Planes

The next size up in the series, numbers 5 and 5 ½, are both referred to as jack planes. We use these for leveling and trimming in similar fashion to the smoothing planes. These planes are approximately 14" (35.5cm) long. I think that perhaps these planes would become more essential if you find yourself regularly hand planing long lengths of wood or if you prepare wood from rough. In a world where machined wood is readily available, most people do not prepare wood from rough boards by hand. This is why most people are able to use only the smaller smoothing planes without ever having need for the longer ones.

All of that said, however, the mechanisms and adjustments of the smoothing planes are identically applied to the longer planes and therefore if you do own or choose to purchase a longer plane all of the instructions in this chapter will still apply. Whatever you do to the short planes you do to the longer ones. That is what made these metal-bodied bench planes so simple.

Jointer and Try Planes

Numbers 6, 7, and 8 planes are referred to as jointer planes and try planes. These are much longer, ranging from 18" (46cm) to 24" (61cm).

I do not consider the longer planes to be remotely essential to the vast majority of woodworkers. What I do want to say here though is the same as I said above. The instructions I give for the shorter planes apply equally to the longer ones. In fact most, if not all, of the parts in the # 5 ½ plane interchange with the 6, 7, and 8.

Parts of the Bailey-pattern Plane

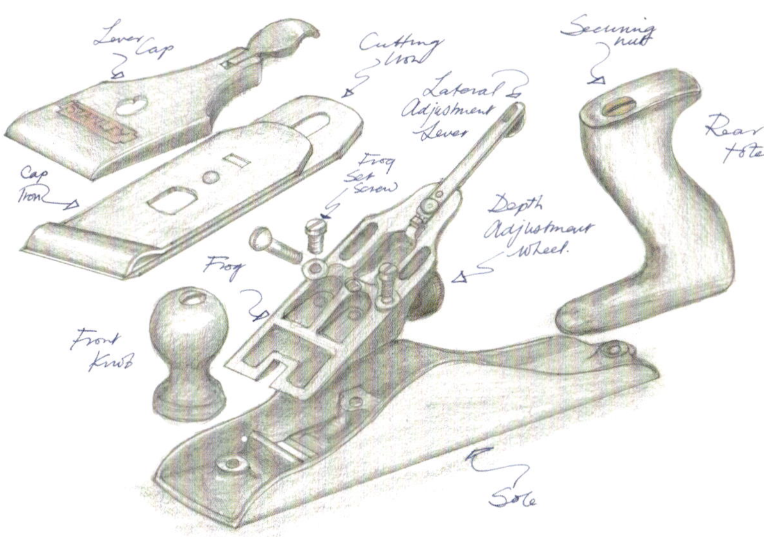

Bailey-pattern Planes – in Praise of Leonard Bailey

Depending on the maker, woodworkers generally differentiate between the two metal-bodied bench plane types by two design features that are not always readily apparent. The working mechanisms and physics of both planes remain identifiably the work of Leonard Bailey and are basically the same in each plane size. The Bed Rock pattern plane retains the majority of the features designed for the Bailey-pattern and so it is essentially a Bailey-pattern plane with a minor replacement, marginally improving the frog. From the outside, these planes look the same and are generally operated the same way. Actually, the two planes have mostly identical mechanisms for adjustment and are nearly identically configured. However, inside there is a difference surrounding the frog of each plane and how these frogs interconnect the soles they relate to.

Even seeing the Bed Rock (left) and the Bailey-pattern (right) frog types side by side, the difference between the two types is not obvious. Removing the frogs reveals the differences between the two.

Some, not all, of the Bed Rock pattern planes have a flat top to the two outer 'wings' that form the plane's sides.

“*The Bed Rock pattern plane retains the majority of the features designed for the Bailey-pattern and so it is essentially a Bailey-pattern plane with a minor replacement, marginally improving the frog*”

The plane on the left is a Bed Rock pattern plane while the one on the right is a Bailey pattern.

The Bailey-pattern frog.

The Bed Rock pattern frog.

It should not be forgotten, in any quest to differentiate between the two plane types, that essentially both planes are attributed to Leonard Bailey. We should not lose sight of or displace his right to being identified with both plane types even though we distinguish one as a 'Bed Rock' and the other as a 'Bailey.' Both designs owe their genesis to Leonard Bailey. Further developments may well be attributed to others who developed improvements but both plane types are actually Leonard Bailey planes. Indeed, you can pick up either plane and you will feel equally comfortable working either one at the bench. It is most likely that many of today's woodworkers around the world will purchase a new or secondhand smoothing plane made to the same patterns and design specifications as the original Bailey-pattern Stanley smoothing plane.

These two planes made on two continents are made internally to the Bed Rock pattern frog.

The Smoothing Plane–a Short-soled Bench Plane

The smoothing plane is basically the shortest of all the commonly used models of the bench plane series. Although its name suggests its purpose is to smooth wood, we also use this plane to true and level the wood, just as much as its longer counterparts. The smoothing plane will not generally be used for jointing long, meeting edges (for tabletops and such) but it will reduce stock rapidly in readiness for truing in many situations. In other words, the smoothing plane is a versatile, small plane that is readily adaptable for many tasks beyond its main remit of smoothing wood.

Once the patent expired on the Bailey-pattern bench planes, many makers copied the design almost to the tee. Though none survived or succeeded as well as the Stanley model, it has led to a little confusion from time to time. The gist of it is this. The list of makers is indeed too long, and unnecessary, to list. Whatever Stanley made, others pretty much copied. Some makers did add their own nuances but mostly they retained the characteristic features we have come to accept as originating with Stanley or designers either working for or transferring the rights to Stanley at some point. In many cases, the parts from the different makers are interchangeable down even to the thread sizes and pitch on screws and bolts. Many of the copy makers produced a substandard plane and the longevity of their availability was short lived in most cases. Others, however, exceeded the standards set by Stanley and Record, the two predominant makers through the last century. You may well find some feature or other that you like in one of the lesser known makers and there are many of these planes that are still available. For instance, I have three planes made by I Sorby that are quite rare. The #4 is of the normal standard but the 5 and 5 ½ are particularly well engineered and enjoyable to use. Whether they perform better than the Stanley and Record planes or indeed others I cannot really say as I get good results with all of them.

While each may have nuances, all of these pictured planes are virtually the same design and I have all of these set up to work perfectly.

My Stanley #4 Bailey-pattern Smoothing Plane

My planes are well settled in my life and I keep them near to me; within an arm's reach. Short-soled smoothing planes answer most of my planing needs and so this is the plane I want to go with me around the workshop in any given day. In many ways, the name on the cap iron and the number on the inside of the sole are of little consequence except to identify the type, the size, and perhaps a level of quality. I will always look for and use the Bailey #4, regardless of whether it is a Bed Rock or not, simply because it is compact and punchy, deliberate and versatile. The reality is that it does not altogether matter where in the world it is made, as long as it is made well. The smoothing planes I reach for are all lighter weight but not so light that they feel low quality. Some planes that are sold as 'premium' planes I consider to be too heavy and less practical. In my view, nothing has replaced the Bailey adjustment mechanisms in terms of centralised proximity to the hands and fingers of my dominant hand. It is a finely balanced weight to strength ratio; one that I have found suits me, and indeed all of my students, without compromise. Stanley and Record produced them throughout a century or so, and more in the case of Stanley. Even now, after a lifetime of using it, this plane still performs over 95% of my planing work and it has proven, through many decades, to be an outstandingly dependable performer. It has indeed been used mainly for the hard work (as well as, periodically, lighter tasks) and this plane performs, by itself, what others might assign to a number of different types and sizes of bench plane.

As I have explained, on today's two most popular models the depth and alignment adjustments perform exactly the same task in exactly the same way. This, to me, is the most remarkable design quality because nothing I have ever seen or tried, in any of the all-metal planes, has proven better. The fact that no engineer has improved on the design concept itself speaks volumes for the designer. The only design features then that remain open to improvement for bettering the regular smoothing plane are perhaps the engineering standards and the steel alloys used to make the component parts. Better engineering standards and materials are indeed available to us today to make this change. For me, improving the quality and functionality of any of the modern planes is simply a question of going back to the drawing board and subtracting some weight from the body of the plane, including the frog. I have weighed many of the 'premium' planes which do have high quality parts but they are 25% greater in weight, which seems quite substantial. This is part of the reason that I prefer the plane that already exists, and has been around for a century and a half, in the form of the Bailey-pattern frog and body. While I simply find it easier to use the lighter plane, I have worked with those who find it difficult to muster the strength they need to apply the heavier weight to the work in a balanced way for the length of time required. I would love to see a modern tool maker create a plane that is the same weight as the original Stanley but with more refined engineering and a higher quality finish. Until then, I have really found my ideal plane in the standard issue Stanley or Record Bailey-pattern non-retrofitted #4 smoothing plane. One day we will see this plane re-engineered to meet these criteria and I will rest my case.

Some New Planes Work out of the Box

I must say that one key difference between the new, high-end manufacturers of planes and those made according to old patterns and standards is that the higher end planes usually come set and ready to use straight from the box. That is, the blades are sharp, the frogs are adjusted correctly for general use, and the cutting iron is installed and set precisely enough to take that first shaving (as long as shipping did not alter the set). This indeed has an appeal because new woodworkers want to know that something works and that it is not their lack of knowledge of the tool that is causing all their problems. Stanley and Record, the two oldest makers of the Bailey-pattern planes, never sent their planes out ready for use. The cutting irons were indeed ground to 25 degrees, ready for further honing, but beyond that they often required further tweaking and even remedial work to get them to perform well. When I bought my first plane I was disappointed. It dug and gouged the wood in my inexperienced hands until the man training me said, "Give it here." He dismantled the whole plane, removed the frog, and took me step by step through every one of the different needs. We filed and fettled and sanded. We saw things I would never have dreamed could cause a problem. Within an hour I understood the plane and all its working parts. I understood certain aspects of its idiosyncrasies, as much as I could, and at least I knew what to check first when the plane malfunctioned.

This is an unrefined plane blade ground to the correct angle of 25 degrees but it is incapable of taking a shaving without further work.

Some Wood Cannot Be Planed

I have come to know that, no matter the plane type and the sharpness, some sections of wood can never be planed and some woods need special strategies and can only be dealt with by tactical engagement. While I will give you some guidance in these pages, some aspects of plane technique can only be learned by experience; by stopping and looking and learning from what is seen, there at the bench, in front of and right beneath the plane's sole. Always remember this, however, some woods, no matter the plane and no matter how good you are at using it, simply will not plane. If a good shaving comes one minute then it might change with the next one. This is a fact of life.

Preparing and Maintaining Planes

Wherever you buy a plane, and this sometimes includes new ones, some additional but simple metalwork radically improves its performance and how it feels to work with it. To fettle a plane is simple enough using a 10-12" (250-305mm), second cut (medium) file and the diamond sharpening plates we use for everyday sharpening.

FLATTENING THE SOLE

The number one area for the plane to be right is the flattening of the sole itself. To do this, use the coarse diamond plate, spray with water or the auto glass cleaner you use for sharpening, and keep the surface wet throughout. This floats off the particles of steel and abrasive, and keeps the cutting action optimized. With the plane fully assembled and the cutting iron withdrawn into the throat without protruding at all, rub the plane sole along the plate several times. Usually 5-6 times is enough. The surface of the sole will now show any high spots with shiny highlights caused by the abrasive. Every plane is different and the highlights can be wide or small, intermittent in spots or localised over an area or two or more. The aim is to get the sole abraded down to a common level; so the wider and greater the surface shine you have, the nearer you are to your goal. From here on it is just a question of moving the plane back and forth until the surface is fairly even on the coarse level abrasive. Try not to apply too much muscle power to the plane handles as this can minutely bend the plane sole and even a very slight bend affects the final flatness. It is not necessary to have absolute dead flatness to every part of the sole but I would aim for a minimum of about 80% total flatness, starting from the fore end and on around the mouth of the plane, full width, and back toward the rear handle.

Note:
Before you apply the sole to the abrasive plate you must make certain the pressure applied to the lever cap is the normal pressure you would apply in the standard use of the plane. You want to replicate how the plane is set up for normal functioning, but with the blade retracted, when you flatten it because this is then reflected in the flatness of the sole once completed.

Some prefer to use abrasive paper and a granite slab that has been tested and certified for flatness but good abrasive plates already have that built in. The plane I flattened here is indeed as flat as possible and matches or exceeds the flatness of all the high-end planes. The diamond plates used here are already flat to approximately a thousandth of an inch and that is all I need. Polishing out the sole with anything more than 250 grit is a waste of effort as the wood itself is quite abrasive too and this will set the final standard of polish eventually anyway.

FEATHERING THE PLANE SOLE

Manufacturers cast the soles and mill and abrade them to a square edge on each side; along the long edges, the fore edge, and the rear edge too. For many years I used mine that way, even though I had flattened the sole some. One day I bought an old and well used plane and, compared to mine, it seemed so willing to glide around the rims of boxes and the faces of doors and frames. It lifted at junctures where two surfaces failed to meet perfectly instead of chewing up the higher points and this was what caused me to look more closely at the sole. The well worn outer edges were so obvious. This feathered edge transformed the plane for me and I knew that replicating this level of wear would take just a few rubs on the coarse plate. Placing an old steel ruler on one side of the plate elevated the plane sole to one side to an exact level. Pushing the plane along the length of the plate with the opposite edge on the abrasive quickly abrades the outer edge to an even bevel. Do this to both sides with about 15 strokes on each side. Once done, elevate the plane with further successive strokes so as to, ever so slightly, round over the corners

For the forepart of the plane, the half moon front edge, simply file the corner at 45 degrees and then use 250-grit abrasive paper to remove the hard edge.

For the rear edges of the sole do the same. For the half moon, centred at the rear of the sole, use the flat file to file it back at 45 degrees and then, again, round over the corners following the edge around. Finish off the hard edges with abrasive paper and then coat all of the surfaces you have abraded with light machine oil or wax to prevent rusting (see section starting page 475).

PLANE SIDES

It is good to abrade the sides of the plane on the coarse stone too, but there is no need to obsess about this as it really makes very little difference to the functionality of the plane's normal performance. You may feel the sides of the plane must be dead square to use it with a shooting board, but that is not the case at all. Although it is best for the sides not to be too far out of square, a little makes no difference; when we use the shooting board, minor discrepancies can be adjusted, through the blade in relation to the sole, using the lateral adjustment lever. This adjustment would need to be checked regardless of how square the sides are because the blade can be out of square in a plane with perfectly square sides. I have never done any more to the plane sides than this and have used all of my planes with shooting boards with nothing less than dead-on accuracy.

“It is good to abrade the sides of the plane on the coarse stone too, but there is no need to obsess about this as it really makes very little difference to the functionality of the plane's normal performance”

THE HANDLES

Often the handles have all the finish removed through wear and deterioration. Sometimes the finish has flaked off in parts and what remains is usually removed quickly with the side corner of a chisel and scraped away. Sand the surface and apply two or three coats of shellac or boiled linseed oil. Stain beforehand if preferred. Once dry, buff out with 0000 steel wool and apply any paste wax. If the plane handle is loose and the screw does not tighten it, remove the screw and handle, and file 1/16" (2mm) from the end of the rod and repeat if necessary.

THE CUTTING IRON

I like to carefully file the side edges of the cutting iron and remove the arrises. This is file work and takes only a minute or two. Avoid the areas right by the cutting edge as this part of the steel is usually too hard to file.

OILING THE PLANE

It is good to regularly oil all of the moving parts to the plane. Before installing the blade, oil the frog bed with two or three drops of oil wiped onto the surface. This allows the swivelling action of the cutting-iron assembly on the frog to work best. You should also oil the lever cam and the setscrews, the adjustment wheel and the lateral adjustment lever.

THE CAP IRON

Do the same to the cap iron edges as you did to the cutting iron using the file. This step is optional but I like to polish the hump of the cap iron out from time to time to reduce friction in the escapement of the plane throat. The image below shows a build-up of resins on the cap iron after having being used for a few days. This resin can drag on the shaving in the throat.

There is another important step with the cap iron. The juncture where the cap iron meets the flat face of the cutting iron is critical because there must be no gap at the leading edge of the cap iron. If there is a gap it receives the leading edge of a shaving, which crinkles up in the throat of the plane. This is a common cause of clogging. By rubbing the underside of the leading edge on the coarse abrasive plate we highlight any discrepancy that might cause a gap. It is fine to slightly 'undercut' this so that the leading edge meets the back of the blade without hinderance. Further abrading levels the edge and, when the cap iron is reunited with the cutting iron, any gaps will be gone. In some cases, you may need to alter the shape of the cap iron to make sure it fully meets the cutting iron. This can dealt with in the same way that we deal with distorted cutting irons on page 172. You will need to think through which way to shape the cap iron before you do this.

THE FROG

The face of the frog should be abraded flat to support the cutting iron assembly and minimise any hindrance to the swivelling of the assembly when aligning the iron to the sole and also the advancing and retracting of the depth of cut.

To fettle the frog face remove the frog from the sole by removing the two setscrews inside.

Now remove the central setscrew, in the middle of the frog on the bed. Turn the frog upside down, onto the coarse abrasive plate, and abrade the surface until flat. You must work around the lateral adjustment lever which is difficult and unnecessary to remove. Once the face of the frog is abraded to completely flat, it can be reinstalled.

Sharpening the Cutting Iron

Sharpening the plane iron follows the same pattern as described for sharpening chisels starting on page 134. Start with the coarse stone, follow through the other levels, and then strop on the leather. Again, the large flat face must be initialised and then polished out as with chisels (discussed in section beginning on page 137). One difference separates the plane iron from the chisels. We must form a small radius to the outer corners of the cutting edge. To achieve this, at each level of abrading, we lift the plane iron so that the corner alone is on the abrasive. The elevation is about ⅛" (3mm). Move back and forth until the corner is bevelled. Once this is established keep abrading but, with each stroke, drop the blade until you return to the full long edge. Do this to both corners. Repeat abrading along the entire bevel and to both corners through the finer grits in preparation for the final stropping. Now flip the cutting iron over and pull the blade across the finest sharpening plate, just once, on the flat face to remove the burr. The last step is to buff out the bevel on the strop to a polished finish, including the outer rounded corners. Any burr should have broken free, if not strop the flat face side a couple of times also. You are now ready to install the cutting iron and set up the plane.

Plane blades should be sharpened at 25 to 30 degrees. You must be careful not to sharpen the blade too steeply; a rounded or very steep bevel angle can prevent the iron from cutting because the heel or centre of the blade bevel makes contact before the cutting edge.

RESOLVING DISTORTED CUTTING IRONS

Sometimes plane irons are dished on one side or the other. If they are dished on the flat face (non-bevelled side), so that the face is hollow, this is of little consequence because as long as the first ½" (12mm) or so of steel behind the cutting edge is flattened then the remainder makes no difference to its functionality. Whichever way the cutting iron is dished, the quickest way to resolve it is with a rubber or nylon hammer. Hold the cutting iron flat on a piece of softwood with the belly up and strike firmly in the middle of the blade. This works every time and it is quick and effective. This will flatten the hump. You can take it further to create a slight hollow on the flat face if you want to. This will give you a good start to abrading the face in initialization.

I am now going to go a little further into detail on the frog of the plane, its functions and configuration. I go through the steps for setting up the plane on page 179.

Tension and Pressures Inside a Plane

I have been learning what happens inside a smoothing plane since I was a boy; the tensions cast into and retained in the sole itself; changes in straightness or flatness due to changing temperatures; how craftsmen, both of my era and those before me, willed the plane in its course to energise their effectiveness in straightening edges and surfaces. The tensions applied through the lever cap to the frog (that holds the whole cutting iron assembly) mean that the frog becomes the central hub through which all mechanical adjustments begin.

For this section I cut away the side of the plane to show how the different parts interact. It is the only way to show just how the design works, building the tensions that counteract the pressures applied with each thrust and thereby absorbing any and all contention into the body of the plane.

One thing I noticed, when I cut the first two inches or so along the side of the plane from the forepart of the actual sole, was that the side closed up on the hacksaw blade with such pressure that the blade could not be extracted without a lot of effort to pull the side away. This shows the level of dormant tension that is present even in a 50 year old plane.

This tension in the sole is something we should really consider when we decide to flatten a sole to true flatness. I say 'consider' and that does not mean making serious changes to the actual physical plane. But when something does not come out dead flat then the tension is something we should bear in mind when trying to work out why. Other things can cause the plane to change slightly such as changes in ambient temperatures from one day to another or even during a single day. These things affect all planes to some degree, regardless of the makers. You can flex the plane sole and alter it to correct or create minor changes in flatness by pulling the handles apart slightly or pushing them together. By 'flex' I do not mean that the plane bends visibly or even changes by more than a fraction of a thousandth of an inch but even this does affect the plane enough to make a difference. Even high-end planes are sometimes not flat, either because they were not made so or because of changes in their conditions.

Mechanics Inside the Bailey-pattern Plane

Most people seem, at first, to see the plane as a complex tool with many mysterious moving parts needing perpetual adjustment. It may initially seem awkward in the hand and unmanageable but you will soon see that, provided the plane is in good condition and assembled correctly, the plane only needs a few simple adjustments to make it totally functional. The steps are straightforward and easy to follow.

The frog is the central hub, lodged squarely within the sole of the plane, and it facilitates adjusting the cutting iron in relation to the sole. There are three adjustments associated with the frog to micro-adjust how the plane cuts. These are blade alignment to the sole of the plane, depth of cut, and the mouth opening (the gap between the fore part of the plane's mouth and the actual cutting edge).

The frog and sole separated.

The frog installed and held by setscrews.

The frog should first be installed so that the front point aligns with the front incline of the rear part of the sole as shown (below). This gives you the widest possible throat opening for the setting of the frog in relation to the fore part of the sole.

Two setscrews inside the frog attach it to the sole of the plane from the top. Once they are set, the frog is locked firmly in place. For general work, the frog needs no more adjusting in relation to the sole's mouth opening but we do occasionally alter the distance of the frog in relation to the fore part of the sole. We talk about this shortly as an adjustment feature.

With the plane side removed, I can now clearly show that there are gaps occurring between the cutting iron and the incline (or bed) of the frog (see the images on the next page). This is the same on both Bed Rock and Bailey-pattern planes. That said, any gap makes little or no difference and you will see why here. The gap is caused by the cap iron (that is the piece of steel with the hump along the bottom edge, also called the chip breaker in the USA), which has some spring in the steel. When the cap iron is locked down onto the cutting iron both the cap iron and cutting iron bend slightly as the setscrew, passing through the cutting iron into the cap iron, is cinched up tight. This is intentional and caused by the start point of the hump, which is lower than the main flat surface of the cap iron. When the two come together, the most evident bend is in the cutting iron. The bend at the centre is about 1⁄16" (1-2mm). When the cutting iron assembly is installed into the plane and onto the frog, a clear gap can be seen in the centre, between the top and bottom of the frog, and a greater gap can be seen between the cap iron and the cutting iron. When the lever cam is locked down, the lever cap raises against the setscrew centred in the frog. This seats the face of the lever cap against the lip of the setscrew. The top cam and leading edge of the lever cap press against the cap iron at these top and bottom points. Further application of pressure via the lever cam transfers the bulk of the final pressure directly along the hump of the cap iron and the pressure closes off the gap between the cutting iron and the frog through the final press of the lever cap and the cam itself. This also drastically reduces the gap between cap iron and the cutting iron just above the hump itself. It is this very unique strategy that firstly allowed the use of thinner irons - half or one third the thickness of irons used at the time of invention - and, secondly, it generally eliminates the reflexing now commonly, but often erroneously, known as plane chatter. While I will concede that thinner irons do not absorb as much vibration as thick irons, I believe that, on balance, the thinner irons are better because they take so much less effort and energy to sharpen.

You can see the small gaps before the lever cap is locked down.

Here, after the lever cap is locked down, these gaps are reduced.

Open and Closed Throats to Bailey-pattern Planes

The following images show how the cutting iron rests firmly against the sole of the plane when the throat is in the normal open position and that an unsupported edge is created when the throat opening is narrowed even by the smallest degree. Discussions comparing the two types of frog system, the Bed Rock and the Bailey pattern, sometimes suggest that the Bed Rock frog gives more support, helping to prevent chatter. In my experience I have not found this seeming lack of support, over so short an extension, to make any discernible difference at all. The plane throat can, therefore, be set to any setting needed on either the Bed Rock or Bailey pattern plane without concern for this particular issue.

Adjusting the Bed Rock Frog Changes Depth of Cut

I think there is an issue, seldom mentioned, with the Bed Rock plane, which is important to highlight now. I often hear that one advantage the Bed Rock has over its Bailey-pattern cousin is that there is no need to remove the cutting iron assembly and lever cap to adjust the frog. The advantages are however, in my opinion, negated by this additional fact that no one really mentions at all: On the Bed Rock plane, adjusting the frog also changes the depth of cut. This is because the surface that the frog rests on inside the plane is sloping. Therefore, moving the frog forward to close the mouth also moves the blade lower. If you alter the frog and do not know this fact then the plane will most certainly gouge much deeper into the surface than you intended. Of course retracting the frog necessitates resetting too. This alone then counters any advantages that others have suggested make the Bed Rock worth rooting for. Having said all of that, remember too that we rarely ever need to adjust mouth openings in the reality of work at the bench. It is just a handy addition, that is all.

Frog Angles

From time to time, you may hear people discuss the bed angle of the frog. I hear it often enough too and it has become something many modern woodworkers get involved in whereas, in times past, almost no woodworker even considered it when it came to the regular bench plane. Does that mean we recently discovered something new? I am afraid not. Altering angles of presentation has been around for centuries and, for some work, it can help. However, in the day-to-day of life, 45 degrees still seems to be the best strategic angle of presentation. This angle tackles about 99% of all the work.

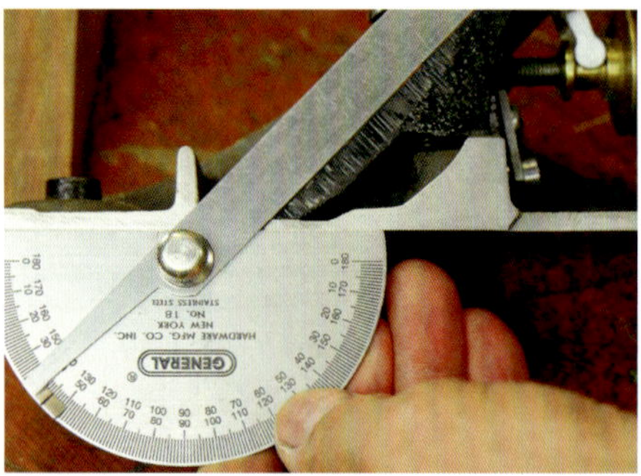

The 'bed angle' is the incline of the frog face that holds and supports the cutting iron assembly. This bed incline is the angle of the front face of the frog in relation to the long axis of the sole. In general, the bed angle of metal-cast bench planes is around 44 to 45 degrees. This is very standard and can vary by half a degree or so. On older, wooden-bodied planes the bed angle was often a few degrees steeper; around 46 to 50 degrees. Once you take into consideration that the cutting iron on wooden-bodied planes is tapered from thick at the cutting edge end to thinner at the top end, the angle of presentation compares to that of the standard Bailey and Bed Rock presentation angle.

The York Pitch

In everyday life we actually rely on a single bed angle to all our bench planes. 44 to 45 degrees will handle just about anything coming our way. That said, on much rarer occasions, when we encounter some very wild and diverse grain that swirls around without any given direction, we might benefit from a steeper pitch to our plane bed. The bed angle will usually be somewhere around 50 degrees. We call this angle a York pitch. It tackles the seemingly impossible by presenting the angle at the steeper pitch. If that is the case, why not make all planes with a steeper bed angle? The fact is that the steeper bed only tackles a small degree of troublesome grain patterns. In general, the standard pitch works best.

The Poor Man's York Pitch

As a young apprentice I was introduced to a slight alteration to my plane iron called the 'poor-man's York pitch.' This strategy took the unusual step of creating the smallest of back bevels on the flat face of the standard cutting iron that came with the plane. By taking two rubs on the finest stone we created a steeper presentation of the blade face to the surface of the wood. This incline was almost always guessed by the craftsman who simply elevated the iron on the stone, pushed it lightly back and forth just once, and then reinstalled the iron. The result was almost always amazing. The grain submitted and the surface became wonderfully smooth. It took only seconds to do and a short time more to restore the original edge, but mostly they carried on with the plane until it needed sharpening again and it worked just fine. York pitch planes were indeed planes specifically made with a steeper pitch. They are rare in metal models but not so rare in wooden smoothing planes and jack planes. Making the alternative from a #4 gives you additional options. You may want to include two or three cutting irons into your arsenal of strategic negotiators of wild grain. By adding back bevels of different pitches you can resolve most grain issues. I keep two, differently pitched, cutting irons ready for my work. I even turn the scrub iron upside down for some issues and this works well too but not for everything.

Setting up the Smoothing Plane

I have learned more from students struggling with planes during my classes at my woodworking schools than from any other area of my woodworking life. I want to unpackage what I have come to understand here, as simply as I can, and to do that I took some drastic action - not the least of which was hacksawing a #4 plane into pieces. This revealed a few things that help us to see and understand what is taking place inside the plane at the throat, where the business end of the plane actually performs its cuts. Regardless of the plane maker, smoothing planes that look the same or similar to the original Stanley #3, #4, and #4 ½ smoothing planes will almost certainly be adjusted the same way. Let me walk you through it.

The cap iron diverts the shaving right behind the cutting edge of the cutting iron, in an upward direction, into and through the mouth to exit the plane. All bench planes of this type are bevel-down planes and generally the cap iron and blade work as a unit together to create what I call the cutting iron assembly.

With the cutting iron sharpened (see page 171 for sharpening instructions), place the hole in the cutting iron over the setscrew and slide it up the slot so that it extends further than the end of the cap iron.

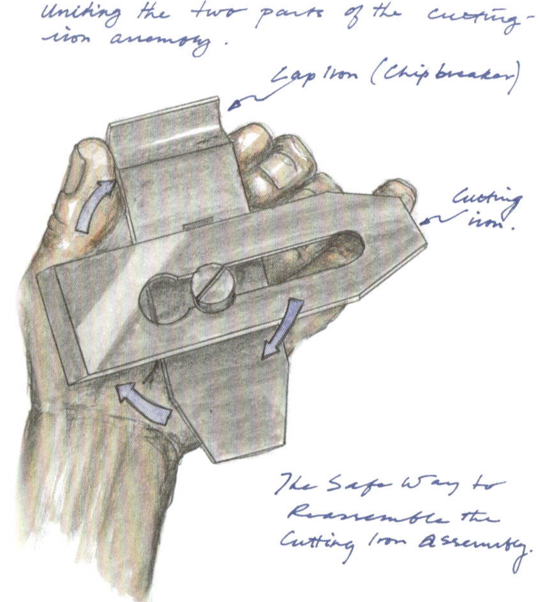

Spin the blade around so that the cap iron and blade are in line and carefully align the sides of the cap iron and blade along their outer edges.

Slide the cap iron along the blade so that it is approximately 1⁄16" (1-2mm) from the cutting edge of the cutting iron.

Once the distance is correct, cinch the setscrew into the cutting iron, taking care not to allow slippage. This locks the cap iron and cutting iron firmly together.

Setting the cutting edge to the cap iron is quite simple. I find it impractical to always measure the small distance from the cutting edge to the fore edge of the cap iron. This is partly because it becomes unnecessary once you can sight what the distance should be. In the beginning, establish the distance visually and then check yourself with a steel ruler until you get used to gauging it by eye. Setting the distance this way becomes fast and effective and soon you will distance-sight with no need for measuring.

Once the frog and cutting iron assembly have been set up, locked together with the lever cap, and located in the plane, the throat opening (the distance between the cutting iron and the fore part of the plane) should be no more than, say, ⅛" (3mm). Very rarely would we ever need a wider opening than this and for most planes the distance will be around 1⁄16" (1.5mm) more or less. It is not generally necessary to measure the opening because this will vary depending on the depth of cut. It will also vary between one plane and another and between one make of plane and another. You can measure your own plane to better assess what you are looking for, but the distance will vary.

The distance measurements for both the throat opening and for setting the cap iron to the cutting iron are much more flexible than you might be led to believe. My experience has taught me to basically set the two the same way as nearly as possible each time, simply to avoid too much variation in the depth setting when the cutting iron assembly is reinstalled. You will still need to reset the depth but the difference will be minimised by using visual assessment to the best of your ability. It is second nature to me now and soon it will be for you too.

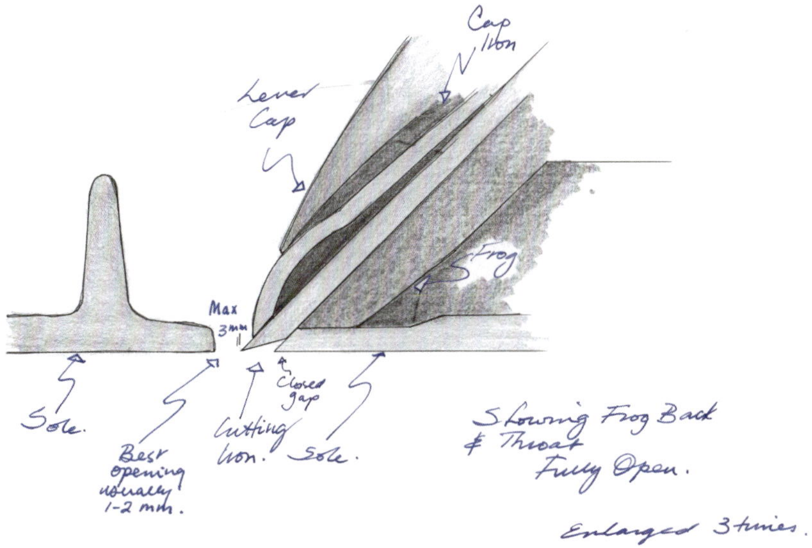

With the cutting edge sharpened, place the cutting iron into the throat of the plane and onto the bed of the frog. Take care to fully locate the rectangular hole in the cap iron onto the protruding yoke just below the lateral adjustment lever. I find it best to align the sides with your fingers on one side and thumb on the other, from the top, and feel for the frog, which is slightly narrower than the cutting iron.

Look to see if the cutting iron lies on the frog with almost no gap. Now load the lever cap onto the cutting iron assembly.

Press the lever cam of the lever cap to feel for the pressure on the lever. The lever cam starts to lift the lever cap away from the cap iron as it presses against the assembly and the assembly against the frog bed. This, in turn, applies leverage via the lever cap against the retaining set screw which is centred in the middle of the lever cap. As you press further, the leading edge of the lever cap presses hard against the hump of the cap iron, which, in turn, applies very direct pressure all along the fore-edge of the cap iron, down in the throat of the plane mouth. This then translates into fully pressing the whole cutting iron assembly against the bed of the frog. In the overall scheme of this applied pressure, the whole of the cutting iron is fully sandwiched in place between the lever cap and the frog and is solidly pressed against the full length of the frog from the bottom to the top of the frog.

The lever cap should tighten firmly when the lever is locked down and, in most cases, you will hear a 'clunk' as the lever sets.

Sometimes people think that the central setscrew, retaining the whole assembly to the frog, is meant to be cinched down as tightly as possible using a screwdriver because the screwdriver slot suggests this but this is not at all the case. The slot does allow for a flat blade screwdriver but it probably would have been better to use a knurled setscrew so as to obviate finger application only. Unfortunately, this design feature and, I think, the lack of information being passed on have led to people using a screwdriver to secure the cutting iron assembly rather than adjusting it by hand to facilitate the use of the quick-release mechanism of the lever cam. Using a screwdriver is far too much pressure and is possibly even the cause of many fractured and broken lever caps. We would never need to use the screwdriver for such setting as, when we loosen the lever cap, the setscrew is freely turnable by finger and thumb only. I do sometimes press the lever quite hard and, at the same time, use the screwdriver or my fingers to set the setscrew according to the pressure I feel on the lever as I press. That way, as I press the lever, I turn the setscrew counterclockwise until the lever clunks down under firm pressure. Generally, the lever pressure is quite high but applying too much pressure means the depth adjustment wheel becomes too difficult or even impossible to adjust for the depth of cut. This is a good way of checking your adjustment of the setscrew. I listen for that 'clunk' of the lever cap when I set this setscrew. If it is too tight it usually does not clunk at all. If it is too loose it lands with more of a rattle sound.

The Two Ready Adjustment Mechanisms

With the plane cutting iron assembly loaded I usually flip the plane over to look for the cutting edge in relation to the sole face. This means that I sight along the face of the sole to see how much the cutting iron protrudes past the face of the sole. The sole face must be as near perfectly aligned with the sightline of the eye as possible so the sole itself is not inclined above or below the sightline. Here you are looking for a black line where the iron just shows through the mouth of the plane. If there is no dark line where the mouth of the plane is, the iron is not protruding at all.

Front and side view of the alignment lever to align the cutting edge parallel to the sole face.

This wheel adjusts the depth of cut by turning clockwise for deeper cuts and counterclockwise for lessening the depth of cut.

You can also use your fingertips or thumb to carefully and lightly hover over the cutting edge and the mouth of the throat to feel for the cutting edge. Usually, if the iron is close, you feel the cutting edge. Do this with care, it is a cutting edge. Do not slide your fingers along the cutting edge as this will most certainly slice your fingers.

Depth of Cut Adjustments

If no iron protrudes you must adjust the depth adjuster, which is the wheel attached to the rear of the frog. Turning the wheel clockwise and counterclockwise advances or retracts the cutting iron. Between forwards and backwards movement there is usually a slack section that must be taken up before the blade adjuster engages to actually move the blade either way. If the iron is not protruding at all, turn the wheel one full revolution clockwise and then sight and feel for the cutting edge along the sole again by turning the plane upside down and using a window, light, or white background to sight against. Carefully use the fingertip test too. I trace my fingertips from the heel of the plane and across the throat toward the toe end so that my fingers are trailing away from the cutting edge as they pass over it.

The depth of cut is governed by the amount the cutting iron protrudes through the sole and we set this according to how much wood we need to remove. For heavy removal we initially set the depth of cut so that the iron protrudes through the sole further. Although it would be nice to have a digital readout for this measurement, it would be difficult to come up with and yet more difficult to make it meaningful. I think the main reason is that we change depth setting constantly, according to something that is quite unquantifiable - the wood itself; the wood type, the type of surface i.e. bandsawn, circular sawn, machined, planed, axed, split, and so on. Rough surfaces usually start with heavy passes and then, as the highs are taken down, we adjust the depth of cut incrementally ever finer until the final refining cuts are less than paper-thin. On other occasions we simply take heavy cuts to reduce stock quickly until we are near to the line and then we micro adjust for finish cuts. Of course, the depth of cut is always infinitely variable, so passes can be anywhere between heavy and light. It does not take long to know when and where to make adjustments and the more you plane, the quicker you learn.

Finalising Alignment and Depth Adjustment

Whether you use sight or touch to see or feel the cutting edge, it is now time to set the plane with its finalised alignment and depth of cut. I set up the following procedure for this and it has helped thousands upon thousands of new woodworkers in getting good alignment straight off.

First set up a narrow piece of wood in the vise. Any wood type will work and I suggest that you use a section about ½" (12mm) thick and 10" (250mm) or so long. Softer wood, without grain defects such as knots, works best for this; pine is fine. Using narrow wood enables you to work at the two extreme outer edges of the cutting iron. You move the plane first over the wood very close to the outside edge of the blade on one side or the other and then do the same again on the opposite side of the blade. Three things will usually be evident when you pass the plane over the wood this way. One, seeing the shavings, you will be able to see whether one shaving is thicker than the other. These two images (below right) show the difference by different levels of transparency as well as the impact of the plane in removing the two shavings from the surface. In this case the shaving taken on the left side of the blade is twice the thickness of the one on the right. Two, you will be able to hear whether one shaving is thicker than the other and, three, you will be able to feel the difference in pressure through the plane itself between one side and the other as the plane passes over the wood. Remarkably, it is the sound you hear as you make the shavings that will give you the highest level of accuracy. Even the most minute difference in thickness will always be detectable, even to the untrained ear, and it will be all the more obvious when you know what you are listening for.

Having determined that the shaving is not even, you must tweak the lateral adjustment lever at the top of the plane above the rear tote and directly behind the cutting iron. Now that you know which side of the plane issues the thicker of the two shavings, and it is rare to get even shavings after first loading the iron and making the initial setup, move the lever from its loose position towards the side that has the thicker shaving. In this case I am moving the lever to the left.

In almost all planes this lever will be loose and will move from side to side, mostly using a medium amount of lateral pressure either way. If it is too hard to move readily then the lever lock down in the lever cap is probably too tight and you will need to adjust the retaining setscrew located in the centre of the lever cap. To adjust the lateral adjustment to create even shavings press toward that side where the shaving is thicker until you feel it register against a resistant point. Once it does, press the lever firmly, but in a controlled way, by a small amount–maybe as little as even 1/16" (1-2mm), but perhaps 1/8" (3-4mm) at the tip of the lever. This pressure swivels the whole cutting iron assembly, from a central point directly between the retaining setscrew and the lever cam of the lever cap. The leverage pivot point however is directly at the point of the setscrew securing the cap iron and the cutting iron to the frog itself. The points of pressure on the hump of the cap iron and beneath the lever cam of the lever cap allows a sliding or slewing movement between the frog and the back of the cutting iron. This then allows minute degrees of alignment in thousandths of an inch.

Sit the plane on the wood again and try once more by taking the same pass to produce two shavings, one from each side of the plane as near to the outer edges of the cutting iron as possible. Listen and look for differences of sight and sound to determine the difference, if any. Go back and forth until you feel the two are the same. If, at any point, you find that the plane is not taking any shaving, this means that the shifting back and forth has pulled the iron up against the yoke of the plane, retracting it into the throat so that it does not cut at all. Simply turn the adjustment wheel a quarter of a turn clockwise and the iron will start to cut or cut more deeply. If not, turn it again in quarter-turn increments until it does. You may need to do this more than once. Also, if the shaving seems overly thick, you must withdraw the iron by turning the wheel counterclockwise. Usually these adjustments, once you have taken an initial shaving, are no more than a half-turn one way or the other and, of course, they can be much less than a quarter turn too.

These two shavings are exactly the same thickness now.

Once you have achieved what you consider to be an even thickness, you can fine tune even this level of accuracy by withdrawing the iron further into the throat. Turn the wheel say a quarter-turn counterclockwise and do the same, checking by taking shavings from each side of the plane. Check to see, feel, and hear if the shavings are the same. If so, withdraw the iron yet again. The shavings will be getting ultra thin. At any given point the shaving may come from one side only. It will be super thin, maybe less than a thousandth of an inch. By minutely tweaking the lever you can still correct even

this minute difference until the iron is perfectly set. Now you can advance the wheel to deepen the cut according to the work in hand. Usually this will be only a quarter-turn or less but it could also be as much as half a turn. From here on, it is unlikely that the plane will be out of alignment unless you place it harshly, bang it sideways, or hit a hard knot or difficult grain that grabs at the plane or the plane iron. Then you simply repeat the steps to correct it. Of course, reading this makes a 20-second process seem dauntingly arduous. It is not. It is fast, effective, and ever so easy.

Using the Smoothing Plane

There is no one way to use a smoothing plane, although many instructors seem all too willing to say that there is. Having the plane in good order is the start but then there is something we now call 'planing technique.' Technique determines how effectively even a well-tuned plane works. Using a plane is very much to do with an interchange of power from one hand to another and, even within each hand, there is a transfer constantly taking place between the heel of the hand to the fingers, thumb, and so on. Knowing where and when to transfer only comes by experience. Sometimes even I do not know how I effect a specific cut to absorb resistance into my whole body through the plane, to make the plane go beyond what it was designed to do. I hope that you will know the plane inside out in a shorter time than I by simply using it and relating to it in the everyday of life. Many of the things I know today are confirmed by science but most of what I know revolves only around feelings and pressures immeasurable even, at this time, by science. I will share a few things in the following pages that I think will help you get started with your plane but you must be patient and observant and learn by doing.

Holding the Bench Plane

It is not difficult in general to explain how to hold a bench plane. Mostly, they have a round knob at the fore end and a handle, often called the tote, at the rear. In general, but not always, the dominant hand latches onto the tote and the non dominant hand clasps around the knob. Sometimes this is reversed but rarely. Sometimes, at least in my case, the hands are reversed because I might occasionally pull the plane toward me rather than push it from behind. Sometimes too, I sideswipe the plane in a double-handed swipe from the side.

Whereas most people will hold the plane with both hands firmly wrapped around the handles, and many people see this as the norm, at the workbench and in the hands of experienced users, these hand positions are actually unusual. Yes, the non-dominant hand may well be used gripping the knob but the wrapped tote is not normally the accepted way simply because it is just a fist rather than a refined hold, allowing for the sensitivity that planing needs. Gripping the plane tote this way drastically reduces the sensitivity we need to orient the plane exactly as we want. There are many different hand positions we use when planing.

Even something that might look less controlled, like this, is a good choice for working the edges of boards.

Many people grab this handle with a fist but the correct hold is actually with the forefinger pointing forward.

Here the rear hand wraps more loosely around the handle and the back of the cutting iron assembly.

Here is another hand position that gives good hold with sensitivity.

Here is another hand position that I find useful on many occasions.

Bailey-pattern planes deviated from the wooden planes quite drastically. The whole profile of the plane is lowered, bringing the drive hand into a more direct thrust, directly behind the cutting iron, instead of a levering overhand action from above it, which tends to lift the rear of the plane upwards. But just because something has a handle does not mean it has to be used and, on wooden planes, many craftsmen gripped the body of the plane rather than the totes to effect their cuts.

Planing Singlehandedly

Sometimes I plane singlehandedly. I do not see people do this much anymore but, as a boy, it was a common practice and I would say that most of the men I worked with planed a great deal using singlehanded planing as shown below. Using the non-dominant hand to pull on a rail, overhand or underhand, adds a power-pull to the work that seems now to be mostly forgotten. Most commonly it is a method we use on larger frames with stiles, cross rails, muntins, and transoms. We may not be able to reach across such an expansive frame on the benchtop if the non-dominant forehand is latched onto the forend of the plane. In such cases, we grab the frame on our side of the bench and pull on the frame, as we push the plane singlehandedly away from the body. The frames I am talking about are mostly doors and door frames, window sashes, window frames, panel frames, and so on. Mostly they are frames that will not fit in the vise or even within bench dogs. When the frame is atop the bench, we pull on the frame as we plane singlehandedly for two reasons; one, it makes the work more stable as we push, countering the pushing pressure, and two, pulling against the opposite hand this way gives us greater strength to effect the cut. We also use singlehanded planing on small sections of wood and smaller frames for such tasks as removing the arris. In such cases we brace the piece against some aspect of the workbench or vise, for example, and use any grip we feel comfortable with to support the wood as we plane down the length to make the cut. It takes practice to gain confidence doing this but the benefits are there when you need them.

Planing Wood Foursquare

You cannot get too far into learning about bench planes before you realise their significance at the most primary level; not just to merely smooth wood but to develop and refine rough-cut, sawn sections in readiness for other

procedures including making joints, panel making and so on. The term we use for this process is 'planing foursquare.' Once the joints are made and assembled, we use the same basic tool type to further refine, trim, true, and level adjoining surfaces into a perfect plane; hence the name 'plane.'

Joint making requires straight edges and undistorted surfaces to establish cut lines from. Before we begin joint making, we usually ensure that all the surfaces of the wood we will be working are planed to a specific standard of exact flatness and that each surface is dead square, one to the other, so that each of the adjacent faces forms a square edge. That means that we true up one primary face first to remove any and all twist from the surface, and to make sure that any cup or bow is removed too. Twist, cup, and bow or crook are common terms describing the three most common flaws in wood after drying has taken place. The drying process both causes this and allows it to take place. It is not generally a flaw with the process but a natural occurrence due to the release of moisture from the wood, which then releases or causes stress within the fibres. Acclimatisation of the wood to the surrounding atmosphere before and after drying also often results in distortion.

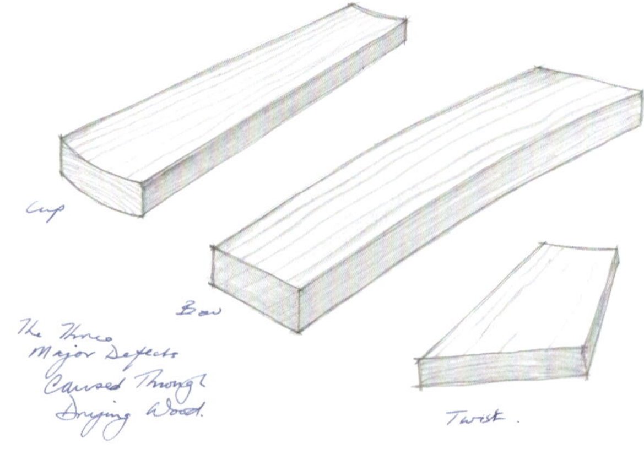

Note:
In times past, when all the work came from rough-sawn stock or even riven or split stock, craftsmen always relied on longer planes, which we refer to as jointer planes and tri (also try) planes. Because today we generally have access to rough stock that is reasonably accurate in its sawn state or even planed stock, we need only use shorter planes like the smoothing plane or its longer cousin the 14" (355mm) long jack plane for final refinement of the wood. The long planes reduce the material to more acceptable levels for further working with shorter planes.

Planing with and Against the Grain

Woodworkers refer constantly to planing with and against the grain. This term is best discovered in the work at the bench rather than with discussion alone. With the right (or wrong) wood you can see how the grain tears when we plane in a direction that causes the fibres of the wood to rise up towards the cutting edge of the plane. Often the plane works fine for the first parts of the stroke but then it hits the rising grain and suddenly we feel, see, and hear the grain tearing beneath the plane. By then it is often too late to correct anything mid stroke and the surface of the wood is badly disfigured by our attempts to make it smooth.

1. This image shows the marks left by the machine planer, going across the grain. These must be planed or sanded out to achieve a good surface finish before adding any protection such as lacquer, polyurethane, shellac, oil finishes and so on.

2. The board, before hand planing, shows the orientation of the grain in relation to rising grain. If you have access to both the end grain and the surface grain you can determine which layer of growth ring is lying on top and thereby determine which direction to plane.

3. In this case, I have planed from right to left, which is against the grain. I should have planed in the other direction for a smooth cut and finish.

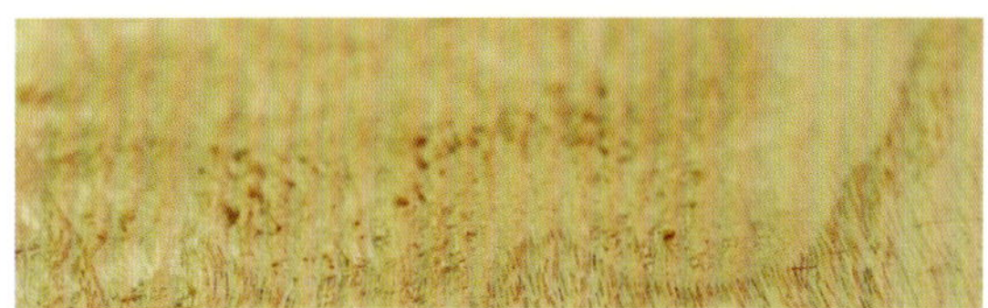

4. This closeup of the same section of wood shows how the grain was ripped from where it was rooted in the main body of wood instead of being cleanly parted. No matter how sharp my plane is, this ripped and torn look will generally be the result if I plane against the grain.

5. Here I have turned the same board end for end to work the surface from the opposite end and in the opposite direction. The surface is now smooth and pleasing.

6. This image shows the grain that once was ripped grain (images 3 and 4) and is now crisp and perfected, ready for finishing with an applied finish or oil.

7. These two images show differences in the results of planing against the grain and then with the grain. It is the edge of the same board we planed the flat faces of above. Ideally you want to be able to plane the board in the right direction straight off. To do that you must learn to read the grain as early as possible in your woodworking.

So, What Caused This Reaction with Planing?

You cannot really talk about planes without talking about grain. What makes planes unpredictable is the grain they work. This causes more frustration to woodworkers than just about any other area. Wood generally grows in layers we refer to as 'growth rings.' As the tree grows the layers forming the stem are encircled by a new ring of growth that with some woods, such as pine, is very distinguishable. These rings develop as the tree grows according to climate conditions, depending on where they grow in the world. In western climates wood grows in more temperate zones and the type of wood that grows here generally has growth rings emanating in concentric circles, increasing in size from the centre of the tree. The rings generally represent the seasons of growth. Any bends in the stem of the tree or variation in width from the base to the top results in different distortions affecting the wood we harvest. Rarely will any one tree grow with perfect uniformity to give perfect grain patterns, parallel to the outer face of the beams and planks we work with. When we offer the plane to the wood the cutting edge responds differently to the grain every time, depending on the direction of the grain and so the terms 'planing against the grain' and 'planing with the grain' describe what is happening when the cutting edge of the plane engages the wood.

This slabbed walnut log shows the bend in the tree stem and its relationship to the wood we end up planing.

I learn more about reading the grain by looking at the endgrain in relation to the adjacent surfaces. Looking at both sides of a board enables us to envisage the layers and also helps us to determine which direction we should offer the plane to the wood.

This image is showing the surface facing to the inside of the tree toward its centre.

This image of the same board flipped over shows the surface facing toward the outside of the tree. Looking at this image, using the oval on the surface part way down, you should be able to work out that this is the lowest layer in the stack of layers forming the growth rings of the tree.

This image shows the layering of growth rings and how they are often actually separate or can be separated.

Here we see one side of a board, which shows the influence of a knot on the wood.

On the other side of the same board we see a point ¾" (18mm) from the other side and how the grain changes radically. These influences complicate how the plane works with the wood.

With the end chamfered back we see the end grain of the board and the face grain on the wide flat face. The chamfer allows us to see the growth rings in the layers in which they grew, with the smaller diameter rings emanating from the centre; the start point of the beginning of the tree.

Characteristic features in grain patterns enable us to read the grain more easily and, after a while, our experience identifies the grain's direction ahead of our planing. You can see now how we flip or turn the board as we are working to best orient the material to minimise any risk of tearing the grain but it is not always possible. The point here is to see that it is usually the grain that dictates to us how we use the plane. Often you are able to get better results just by planing in the opposite direction but that is not always the case. As I said previously in this chapter, not all wood can, or should, be planed.

Softwoods like pine have the most pronounced growth rings because the growth rings usually have more highly distinguishable early and late aspects of growth to them. This means that one part of the ring is light and the adjacent part dark and also that these two areas are harder and softer than each other too. The light and dark, although separated by colour, are really continuations or projections of a single, but extended, period of growth; showing, for example, spring, summer and autumn growth depending greatly on the region, weather influences, temperature, water, sunlight and so on. These rings are helpful in determining grain direction and we use them to guide us when we present the plane to the wood. This initial placement can often be confirmed as we nudge the plane forward slightly into the grain. If the plane grabs too quickly we are likely going against the grain. Flip the plane around and pull the plane lightly and you will feel it working more 'with the grain'. In a single piece the grain can change almost inch by inch and this is the most difficult grain to work with.

Much awkward grain is caused by branches that grew while the tree was still growing. Every branch causes a shift in grain direction in the main stem and all surrounding grain, even inches from the knot, becomes awkward to work with.

Clear growth rings help us to identify what to expect when we plane the wood inside the tree.

First Steps – Dealing with Distortion

Initially we use our eyes to check the wood by sighting along the edges of the board to see what undulations and discrepancies there are in the surfaces. Usually we check all of the surfaces on the adjacent faces to get some feel for how best to approach the work with the plane. In some cases even sawn faces can be near to flat even though saw marks left from the machines remain in the surfaces and the surface feels rough. Surface defects like this are caused by the machine blades when the tree is slabbed into boards and beams or after resawing to other sizes. However, there are other defects caused by the actual drying process itself and these must be dealt with because of the severity of the defects. Drying out wood takes place after the process we call conversion; the systematic sizing of wood into standard sizes for industry. Initially the tree stem is run through massive blades to create flat faces that allow the wood to be planked and beamed according the sawyers decisions. The wood is then dried by either force-drying in kilns or air drying. However, air drying is rarely practised these days. Because wood comprises millions of cells filled with a significant amount of water, wood producers dry the wood down to certain percentages before it can be sold. Through the drying process, the wood almost always distorts in some way, depending on where it was cut from the tree. This is true no matter which method of drying is used. There are three characteristic flaws generally associated with the drying process, even though the sawmill or sawyer did

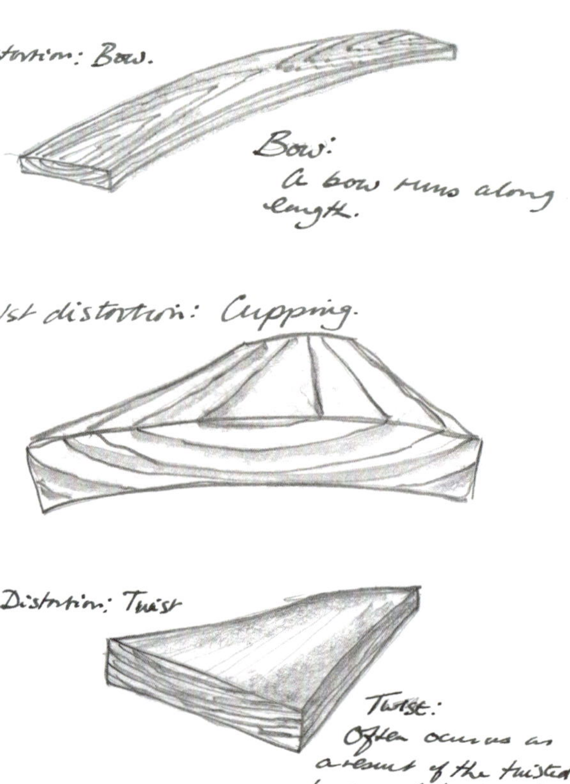

indeed cut the wood dead flat. The three common distortions are cup, bow, and twist. Once the wood is dry it becomes more stable and moves and distorts much less.

Looking at the surface, sighting from one side to the other, often reveals twist. Sighting along the long corner tells us whether the face or edge is curved. What we see on one side is usually the opposite on the other; so a convex surface on one side is nearly certainly concave on the other. This is also true when the board is cupped across its width. The defects in a board must always be removed first but especially any twist. To determine how much twist is in the board we must first endeavour to remove some if not most of the other distortions; the cups and bows. Having cut the material close to the final length and width, we take the bench plane and start planing any high spots. You can use any bench plane for this. Use your judgement and check yourself by sighting as described or by using a straightedge. Though it is not always predictable, often we find that one side of the board has four high points at the extreme corners and a hollow leading from these high spots. The other side then is usually the exact reverse of this and is bellied. Of course, it is not always as simple as this and the number of high spots will vary from piece to piece but, as a general rule, you will find this to be so. Which face you choose to work first, the crowned side or the hollow side, is up to you. The depth of the hollow plus the height of the belly will be the minimum amount of wood you lose in the process of flattening. It is worth noting this if you have a specific thickness of material you need to finish at, which we almost always do. So wood 1" (25mm) thick with a belly of ⅛" (3mm) will be ¾" (19mm) when flattened.

First plane one of the wide faces down until close to flat. Once reduced you can start to sight the edge with your eye or use a straight edge. Sighting is both accurate and fast too. To check across a board we often use the corner of a plane but a straight edge of wood or a square works fine too. When close to flat we use winding sticks to flatten the surface further and remove twist. This is critical to the work as any twist translates into twisted work when we make doors, drawers, boxes and so on. Using winding sticks enables us to sight from one end to the other to see if the edges of the sticks line up with our

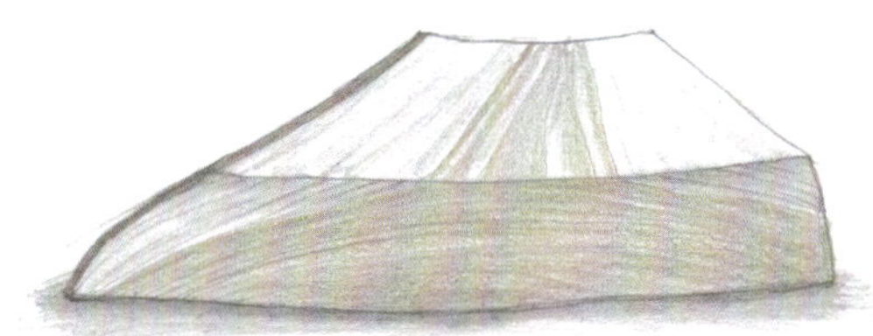

sightline. If they do, then the board is no longer twisted. Sighting along the edges also tells us if that face is flat. If it is, we can focus on squaring one adjacent edge. Usually rough-sawn wood will not have square edges because the wood distorts through drying. We must plane the edge square and straight to the adjacent proven face. Simply sight along the edge to see where the high spots are and plane them down until straight. With one face flattened and trued, we then straighten up the adjacent face. As we do, we make sure it corresponds squarely to the first face, using the square to check our accuracy. This again works well using the smoothing plane or the jack plane. With these two faces square and trued, we then set marking gauges for the final thickness and width we want our wood to be sized to and, if necessary, saw to near width and thickness before planing the wood down to these gauge lines. Once this is done, the wood is ready for joinery or whatever other process we plan for the wood. We call this final stage in the process preparing the wood 'foursquare' or planing 'foursquare.' I have included this brief explanation to help you understand what we regularly use the bench planes for. It is far from exhaustive but I hope you can see the significance. Of course we use the bench planes for dozens of other tasks too, but this one is fundamental to all our work.

Planing Edges Square

An issue people often struggle with is planing narrow edges square to the larger adjacent face. It seems that narrow edges pose the greater problem and I understand why. It seems logical that tilting the plane slightly to counter the discrepancy is the obvious thing to do but few people have this intuitive aspect woven into their woodworking instinct when they start out. Tilting the plane rarely works but what does work, and works well, is to take the plane to the outer edge so that it overhangs on the high side. Taking the strokes now removes more on the high side. Two or three strokes and then checking with the square should show a reduced high and a nearer squareness. Do the same until the edge is near square and then adjust the depth of cut for a shallow pass to finish off squaring.

Note:
Many might tell you that you will need longer planes for wood preparation but, whereas long planes may well have their uses, shorter bench planes do work well for this too. Long planes are useful to own and I might consider using one from time to time but I have them more because I enjoy them and not because I consider them essential to my work. Here, I am talking about the all-metal versions and not wooden ones. I do not consider the longer, all-metal ones to be essential planes. Long wooden ones, on the other hand, while still not essential, perform planing tasks much more effectively in my view. They are much easier to use and almost frictionless on the surfaces being worked. The mistake I often see is people having too high an expectation with regards to long planes, the assumption being that everything you plane automatically comes out straight and flat.

The Scrub Plane

For anyone interested in hand tool woodworking, I would say that a scrub plane would be one of the more useful additions to your plane collection. Some people do have access to machines but many do not and prefer not to. Removing the severe flaws in the wood as described before is much quicker and easier with a scrub plane and retrofitting a #4 smoothing plane to work as a scrub plane is an inexpensive way to own one. You can simply find a second iron and create a curve to the cutting edge instead of the usual straight edge. I keep a dedicated #4 on my bench for heavy removal of material, deep chamfering and so on, before refining with a normal smoothing or jack plane.

The undulations left on the surface by a scrub plane.

The original scrub plane went by a different name and one we might not recognise today. The 'roughing plane' aptly describes its primary task. Originally, the scrub plane was the result of worn down wooden planes where the wear resulted in a wider opening at the fore part of the plane throat, in front of the cutting edge. As the plane sole wore away through use, the throat became wider by the year. This made the plane less suited to fine shaving because it allowed the grain to rise ahead of the cutting edge, under the thrusting of the plane into the wood, and this inevitably allowed grain ripping. Such planes, however, were well suited for rough work, such as scrub work, and so were cycled through for a follow-up life as scrub planes.

A well worn wooden smoothing plane becomes better suited for roughing work because of the wide-open throat that allows for thicker shavings. The finer throat opening is reserved for finer work after the roughing plane.

As use of wooden planes diminished, a specific cast-metal scrub plane was developed by The Stanley Rule and Level Company in the US, with the intention of filling the void. It was a crude and simple plane with none of the complexities associated with the normal metal-cast planes, also produced by Stanley, which were available at that time. It had a single iron with no cap iron and the lever cap, common to Stanley planes, was a simple setscrew knob in a black-japanned lever cap. However, despite its simplicity, as for functionality, it worked.

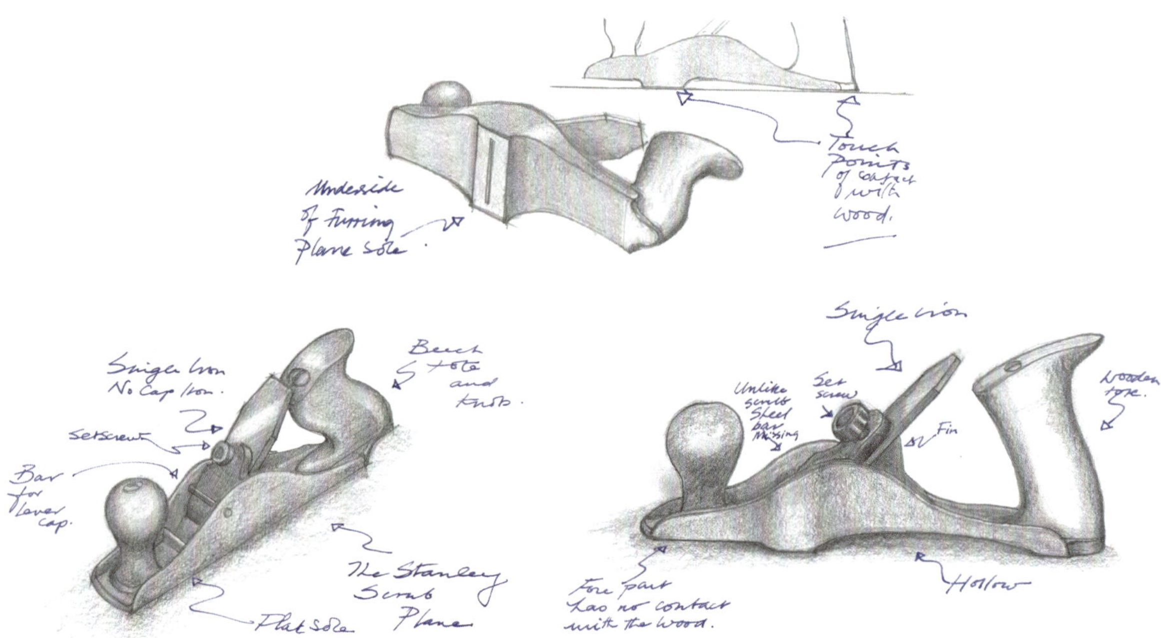

The ordinary Bailey-pattern #4 or #3 planes do make better scrub planes than the wider versions. Personally, my preference is a dedicated upcycled plane fully converted and ready to go with a slightly curved plane iron. I like to use them for a variety of tasks and, with the immediacy my workload demands, this works best for me. My scrub plane nestles neatly next to my regular bench planes, just to the right-hand opposite corner end of my bench, and, on the outside, it looks the same as the rest. Essential? Not really because the basic plane will get the wood down, albeit not as quickly. I am amazed how often I reach for it though. I retrofitted this one with the curved blade for continuous use. Not only do I use it on rough wood, for levelling and such, but also for fast stock removal, prior to surface planing with the regular smoothing plane. I use it for chamfer work, rougher rounding-over before the smoother, artificial ageing to leave planing texture in the wood; the list is endless.

Laying Your Plane on Its Side

It may seem alien to see a plane standing upright on the bench. When people come into my workshop and see my planes standing on the sole face, they feel they have to tell me how wrong I am to do that. It is likely that, when they did woodworking many years ago in school and learned of this supposed 'wrongdoing' at 13 years of age, it stuck with them. However, I see no point in changing what was common to all the men I learned from. I do not think that this fallacy even existed, prior to introduction of woodworking in schools. In my view it is more wrong to place the plane on its side rather than face down. This practice often changes the set on the plane and knocks the alignment out of parallel unless you are very careful. In schools, of course, the children were plonking their planes face down on top of other metal tools and damaging the cutting edges. The way to resolve the issue was to create a law and the law was intended for children, not for craftsmen and women working with planes every day. Placing the plane ready for action and convenient to the lie of the hand makes total sense in the working environment and no damage to the iron or the bench takes place. Here I rest my case and you must do as you will.

Technique and Few Closing Thoughts

There are so many plane practicalities and techniques lost to today's woodworkers. Books mostly convey some of the elementary methods of planing but only rarely do they pass along the full breadth of planing techniques and 'trade tricks' craftsmen of the past used. Apprentices, after a year or two under their belts at the bench, knew to keep the secrets of their trade; except for those they later passed on to trusted followers working under them. Thankfully, those days are long gone. Today I enjoy seeing people share what they know to help one another. In the absence of apprenticeships, passing on what we know and sharing it means preserving it for future generations.

Wherever I begin to explain planing technique for a book or an article, I quickly realise a three dimensional world does not compress too well into the two dimensional without great compromise. The easiest and most practical place to pass on a skill is at the workbench and that is the best place to experiment for yourself too. The plane I have been describing in this chapter is an amazing tool and even more so is its wooden counterpart from the centuries before. With my Stanley #4 smoothing plane I have rounded over many hundreds of feet of bullnosed edges in many wood types and then raised panels for doors and box lids and levelled inlays and fitted hundreds and hundreds of doors of every type. You will soon do the same, I am sure. These things, in general, go beyond the scope of this book. In fact, I could undoubtedly write the same sized volume on the Stanley bench plane alone and not discuss any aspect of it twice.

What I want to close with is this: Do not be restricted by the existing design of your #4. You can alter many things, without damaging the plane, and then you will find yourself building your own outcome. Following here are some of my closing thoughts to address what you might consider as outstanding issues.

SHOOTING BOARDS

Shooting boards give amazing accuracy to the plane work and especially trimming out to thousandths of an inch if the work demands it. I recommend making the one I have drawn here first and then make any others according to task. There really is not much to making them and you can make the standard shooting board for 90-degree end-grain trimming and 45-degree mitres too, following this drawing here.

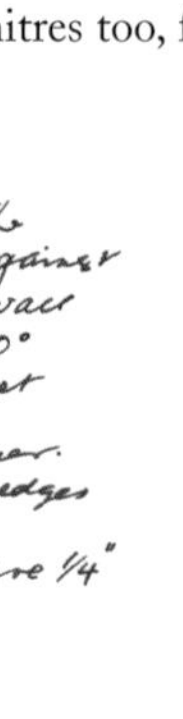

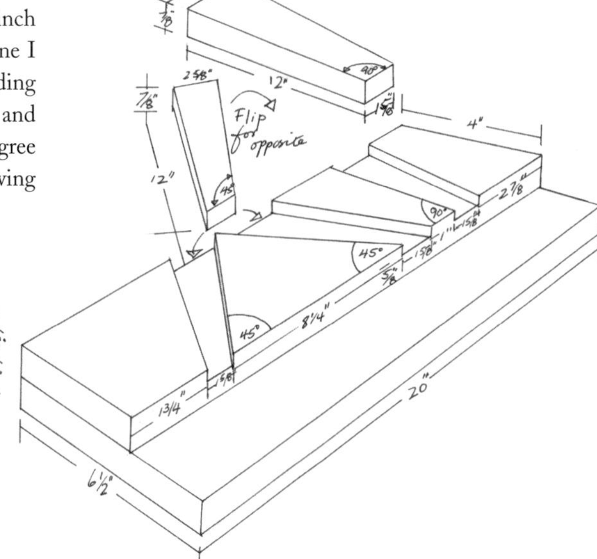

PLANING THE UNUSUAL

It is true that planing the faces of tenons might more generally be given to the rebate plane, shoulder plane, or some other plane of the type. However, the #4 does do a great job of this too. On larger tenons, say 2-4" (50-100mm) and longer, you can surface plane the tenon cheeks to a glass-like finish after first chiseling down to the lines next to the shoulder line and parallel to the shoulder. You can then use the #4 to plane the full width of the remaining tenon; working down to the gauge lines on either side. Planing across the grain this way is very fast and effective.

CIRCULAR PLANING

This is a technique we use mostly on end grain to reduce the risks associated with planing through or stopping over short distances and not achieving the clear results we need. By placing the forepart of the sole on the end grain we use short, oval strokes to return the cutting edge to the start point without ever lifting off. This means we have the plane registered to the surface the whole time and we reduce the need for landing and returning with successive strokes.

OTHER SURFACE PLANING

Surface planing for furniture making is far more than just planing foursquare. A significant part of planing comes after the joints are made and glued up. Whether cut by hand or machine, adjacent surfaces often do not align perfectly and we must trim them down at awkward intersections. This could be the surfaces of doors and the rims of boxes. Inlays too need great care that you cannot get with a belt sander or other means. These are all the different tasks the smoothing plane regularly takes care of but which are rarely mentioned these days.

The Spokeshave

My first success shaving wood came from the edge of a Stanley #151 spokeshave back in 1963. I was involved in restoring older houses as part of my work. Skirting boards and floors, architraves, doors, and window frames were all suspended between fixed, stone anchor points and then trimmed out with moulded wood, and it is here that spokeshaves came into their own. When the floors curved, cupped and twisted after WWII bomb blast resettlement or when a stone wall jumped and settled back on its newly situated foundation, trim and doors, window frames and so on either needed replacing or refitting and that is where I learned to master the spokeshave. Replacing door and window frames with curved headers or circular frames also required the refining work that came from the spokeshave edge. Although we did use the spindle moulder to shape the main frames when they were first made, assembling and then fitting the frames on the jobsite often required extensive use of the #151 spokeshave. This effective tool could refine and scribe any board or frame to an exact fit within a fraction of an inch and could remove much more material than a plane could. This is something few woodworkers would recognise as being necessary today but I cannot imagine how we would have done this work without the humble spokeshave, even though we now have jigsaws, routers, circular saws and more.

I have used spokeshaves almost every day since then. Because spokeshaves operate like planes I have always seen them as planes with short soles, side handles, and knurled adjustment nuts to adjust and control the blade depth and alignment of cut. No matter the type or the age, to me, it is and always has been one of the most remarkable tools. This tool shaves and shapes wood into concaves and convexes; it rounds almost any radius you care to name as well as creating shallow ovals, bull-nosed edges, and walking sticks, and it relies on no other tool to correct its work. Spokeshaves shave wood in the same way that smoothing planes do but they have a dynamic no other tool with a cutting edge has. Though its actual function, in many aspects, may differ from the plane, the spokeshave removes wood in controlled thicknesses, according to the depth of the cutting iron protruding through the sole, in much the same way as a bench plane. A shallow setting gives thin shavings and a heavy set, thicker ones. It is the first tool I gave to my children as soon as they were old enough. I stayed with them the whole time and watched them grow into woodworkers.

As with hand planes, spokeshaves are made with either wooden or cast-metal bodies (or a combination of both) that support and hold the cutting blade at a particular angle, depending on the spokeshave type. The most commonly used spokeshave, favoured through many centuries, was the beech-bodied spokeshave that carried a steel blade held in place by two right-angled tangs. These tangs, tapered to four sides, protruded through the top surface of the spokeshave in a tapered fit. This created compressed friction to hold the blade at a fixed distance to the body of the shave. This simple method allows the blade to be hammer-tapped up or down (in or out) to adjust the cut depth according to task. Further cut refinements came as the craftsman rolled the spokeshave to micro-adjust the angle of presentation in the work.

Spikes and spokes give some limited indication as to why these tools are called 'spoke' shaves but so limited a definition only serves to undervalue the breadth and scope of a tool that multidimensionally defies limitation as a specialised tool. I cannot think of any other shaving tool that so capably spins in the hands of experienced woodworkers and amateurs too. With every shifting, twisting wrist and slight adjustment of hand, the spokeshave creates unlimited possibilities for shaping and shaving wood.

With the invention of Stanley Rule & Level's all metal-cast spokeshave, replete with knurled depth adjusters and low-cost assembly line production, we saw the wooden spokeshaves gradually replaced. This should not go unnoticed as two crafting skills disappeared. Examine any wooden spokeshave blade, made by a blacksmith, or the wooden body holding it, and you witness the passing of an era when the classic workmanship of anonymous craftsmen passed almost unnoticed. The Stanley #151 became the most commonly used spokeshave of the 20th century and relatively few wooden spokeshaves are used today. It is not the case that the Stanley, or indeed any other modern spokeshave, surpassed the wooden model. That is far from true and overly simplistic. At the workbench it is just different and both work well, just in different ways.

The #151 Spokeshave

The #151 spokeshave, made by Stanley, Record, and others, is the workhorse of spokeshaves. It has built-in longevity that guarantees it for a very long lifetime of woodworking. Looking at mine today, I would say that any crafting artisan, who takes it over from me, will pass it on to another in 50 years' time.

Ignore the colours and even the metals. The #151 changed through the years and can be black-japanned or all steel, buffed out to shine, or bronze. I have even seen plastic parts used too.

"Regardless of the maker, this perfectly functional, craftsman-used woodworking tool exists in its own right as a tool everyone should keep close to the bench and close to hand"

Regardless of the maker, this perfectly functional, craftsman-used woodworking tool exists in its own right as a tool everyone should keep close to the bench and close to hand. I say that, not just because of their availability and lower cost, but because of the simplicity they bring to my work and especially their effective adjustability via the knurled adjusters. They rarely clog and, if they do, it is a quick and simple task to remove the blade, reset, and get back to work. Add to that the #151's virtual indestructible longevity, ease of sharpening, and versatility in the work, and you begin to see just why they were indeed so popular throughout the last century; when a good proportion of all curved and contoured work came from a #151 cutting edge. Spokeshaves like these minimise wear on other tools, such as rasps and files, and, at the same time, minimise the need for using different grades of sandpaper too. I like the certainty and punchiness they bring to different aspects of my work, not the least of which is the shaping of curved work. The importance of keeping any spokeshave sharp cannot be overemphasised. This may seem unnecessary to say but, because the spokeshave is such an easy tool to use, it can be overlooked. Candle wax reduces friction on the sole and is a readily available option for frictionless spokeshaving.

Here an arch is spokeshaved to final shape and needs no refinement with sandpaper.

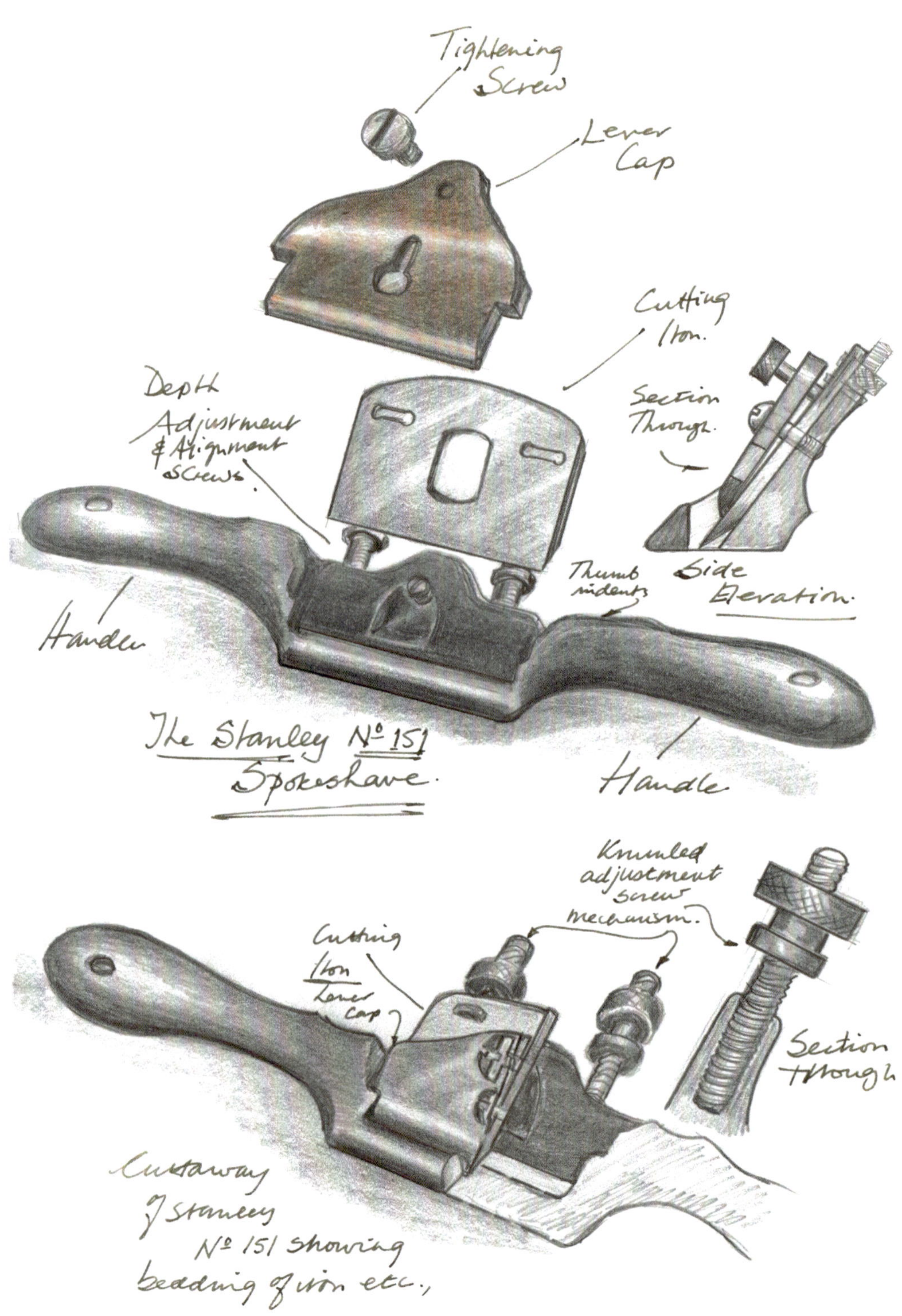
Tightening Screw
Lever Cap
Cutting Iron.
Depth Adjustment & Alignment screws
Section Through
Thumb indents
Side Elevation.
Handle
The Stanley No 151 Spokeshave.
Handle
Knurled adjustment screw mechanism.
Cutting Iron
Lever cap
Section Through
Cutaway of Stanley No 151 showing bedding of iron etc.,

Flat and Round Soled Options

Most woodworkers are surprised when I tell them that the flat soled spokeshaves will take care of all convex work and then most of their concave work too. This depends on the tightness of the concave curves, provided they are not too tight, less than say a 6" (15cm) radius, the flat-bottomed spokeshaves work even better than their convex counterparts. That said, I keep a round-bottomed spokeshave for tighter radii–usually under 6". You can work even tighter radii than 6" with flat-bottomed spokeshaves by extending the blade out further and registering the front and back corner edges of the spokeshave sole on the wood but this is usually less effective.

Longer curves like this are easily refined with a flat-bottomed spokeshave.

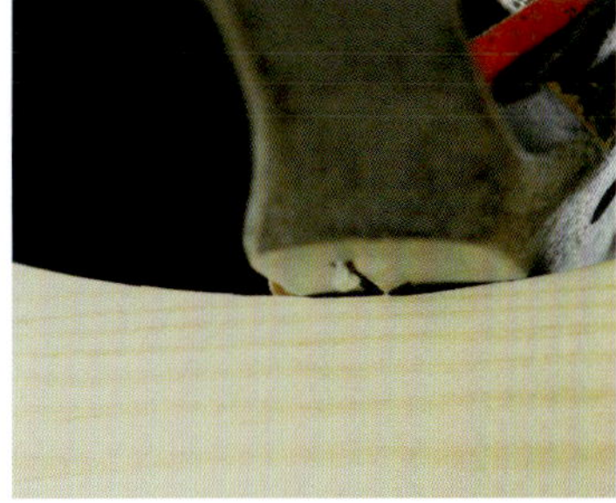

This picture shows the flat-bottomed spokeshave shaving the concave surface of a 6" radius without any issues. This is pine, but it works well in hardwoods too.

Here you see the round-bottomed spokeshave in action on a tighter radius. When the radius is less than 6" (15cm) it becomes necessary to switch to a round-bottomed version.

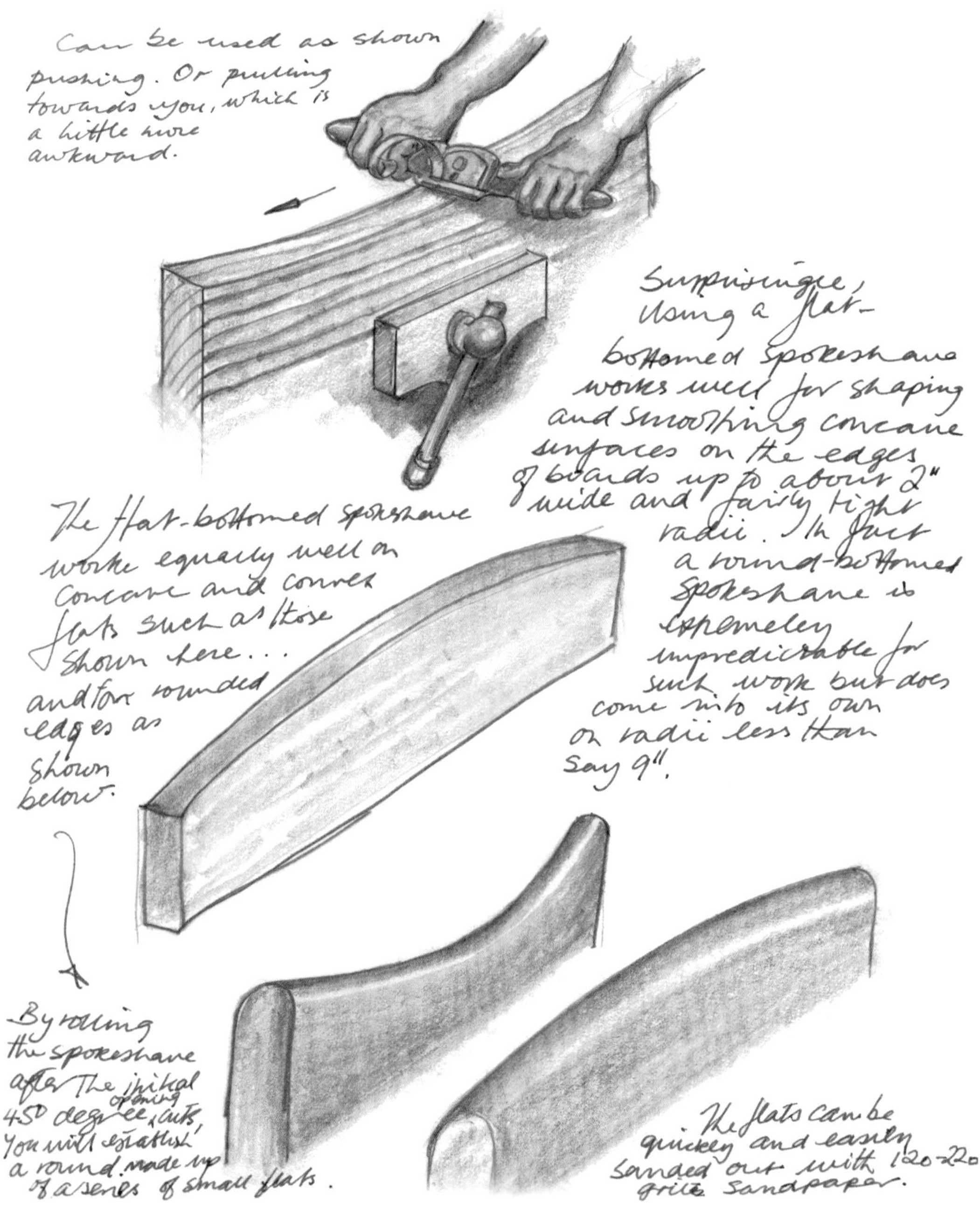

Can be used as shown pushing. Or pulling towards you, which is a little more awkward.
Surprisingly, using a flat-bottomed spokeshave works well for shaping and smoothing concave surfaces on the edges of boards up to about 2" wide and fairly tight radii. In fact a round-bottomed spokeshave is extremely unpredictable for such work but does come into its own on radii less than say 9".
The flat-bottomed spokeshave works equally well on concave and convex flats such as those shown here... and for rounded edges as shown below.
By rolling the spokeshave after the initial 45° degree opening cuts, you will establish a round made up of a series of small flats.
The flats can be quickly and easily sanded out with 120-220 grit sandpaper.

Spokeshaving a convex flat with a flat-bottomed spokeshave.

Spokeshaving a chamfer (bevelled edge) to a convexed surface with a flat-bottomed spokeshave.

Spokeshaving a bull-nosed edge to a convexed edge with a flat-bottomed spokeshave.

Spokeshaving a chamfer to end grain with a flat-bottomed spokeshave.

Spokeshaving a chamfer to a concave edge with a round-bottomed spokeshave.

My Essential Spokeshave

I suggest that you do not disregard any of the older spokeshave models as outdated or outmoded or in any way under par, regardless of what you hear. Yes, there may be more finely engineered models, but the original #151's still have a secure place in my range of spokeshaves. In some ways I like the less tight tolerances because they give me a certain flex that the highly engineered models cannot give me. It is the intuitive aspect of being a craftsman. Were I to have to choose one spokeshave over any other, as a good starter and one to stay the course, it would be the #151 design and I say that guardedly. The reason I do say it though is because it is indeed an important tool and the most general use spokeshave offering many different possibilities in my work. More specialised woodworkers, working in narrower fields, might want something different and I understand that. However, the #151 is far from being an obsolete spokeshaving plane. So if some critics say that they were never any good, just remember that they were used for a century by craftsmen earning their living using them—surely the many thousands of them were not all wrong.

The fact is that even modern makers follow almost exactly the same basic concept, perhaps adding a thicker iron, parts made of wood and perhaps more upgraded metal alloys and such. These are indeed enhancements and I appreciate them but the improvements are marginal rather than major, so it is up to you.

I suggest you start out with the older model #151 by a maker like Stanley or Record or one by a modern maker with the features that follow their pattern. Eventually you may

wish to purchase a second spokeshave. I suggest a traditional wooden beech tanged-type as an additional option. The round-bottomed #151 can be very useful as well if you find yourself working on tight curves.

Some newer tools have surpassed these older models and, in some cases, the engineering standards are better. It is important to know that a #151 spokeshave will negotiate almost all the work any other spokeshave can handle. Usually problems occur only when spokeshaves are not set up sufficiently well. If a spokeshave digs in and gouges the work or does not cut at all, it is almost always because something is misaligned and this can be readily corrected.

The model #151 and similar metal-cast spokeshave types have indeed been in every tradesman's toolbox for a long time. I bought my first Stanley #151 spokeshave in 1965. I have used it almost every other day for over five decades and it is still going strong. It is a lifetime tool and works well. There are several models following the #151 that are excellent spokeshaves. I own several models to use in the woodworking school for students to try out too. But we should never discount the viability of wooden spokeshaves whether old models or new. There are things I can do with a wooden spokeshave much more effectively and efficiently than I can do with other models, including the #151. Despite that, I feel that the #151, or a similar model, should be your first choice because of its versatility and availability.

Sharpening Spokeshaves

We sharpen spokeshaves according to their type. There are two types of spokeshave, bevel up (which are usually the wooden models) and bevel down (these are usually the metal-bodied models). They are therefore sharpened differently too. I will focus this guide on sharpening my recommended bevel-down #151 but I will also point you in the right direction for sharpening the bevel-up model later in this section.

The procedure for sharpening the bevel-down spokeshave is much the same as sharpening many of the other edge tools such as planes and chisels and the angles are the same too. Firstly, see how the blade feels as you offer it to the sharpening plate. The angle of presentation always starts at 30 degrees or less so you should check the angle

“*The procedure for sharpening the bevel-down spokeshave is much the same as sharpening many of the other edge tools such as planes and chisels and the angles are the same too*”

with a protractor if the blade is not new and has been worn. The angle of presentation is important because too steep of an angle can lead to the cutting edge being higher than the heel of the bevel, which prevents the blade from reaching the wood.

Sharpen through the sequence of abrasive levels, as you would all of the cutting edge tools, by pushing the blade at 30 degrees. Start on the coarse plate and establish the bevel. In the progression of the forward stroke, lower the hand just a little so that the blade finishes on the heel of the bevel. This maintains the camber forming the bevel. When you feel the burr across the flat face of the blade you are ready for second-level abrading and then the third level.

Remove the corners by elevating the blade and applying the pressure to create a slightly bevelled outer edge. Do this to both corners. We do this, as standard, to bench plane cutting irons (see page 171) and we treat the spokeshave in the same way.

Having progressed the honing on through the other two levels, flip the cutting iron over and pull the blade on the finest abrasive grit so that the edge trails and this should break off the burr. Finish out on the strop with buffing compound.

When you come to sharpen your first spokeshave blade I am sure you will find the blade length a little awkward because it is quite short. I did it this way for 40 years without using any kind of holder and still do most of the time. However, this mostly relies on the strength you have in your hands, and, in particular, your fingers.

My Spokeshave Blade Extender and the Honing Guide

For #151 spokeshave blades, which are very short, I recommend making an extender to hold the blade. I developed this because, even after my decades of sharpening, I found difficulty holding onto the short blades and applying the even and consistent pressure it takes to effectively abrade the steel economically. The extender enables me to maintain total control in supporting and holding the blade firmly, rigidly, and at a good honing angle. I can also install the extender into a honing guide, which you cannot do with the blade alone; the iron itself is not long enough to be held in the honing guide and still extend out sufficiently to reach the stone. The extender then gives a fixed angle when used in a roller-type honing guide.

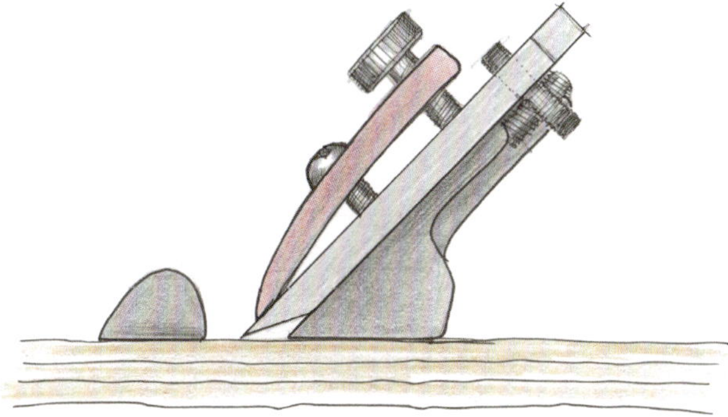

It is important to establish an even 30-degree bevel, from coarse grinding and on up through the finer levels to final honing, with spokeshave blades of this type. Without the extender or some other kind of blade holder, it is very difficult to hold the blade firmly and it is also difficult to maintain any degree of accuracy, in both pressure and angle, throughout the process. Though you can use the extender freehand, freehand sharpening takes a little practice and a period of time to develop hand and finger strength and, of course, muscle memory too. Using the extender in a honing guide does start your training in such a way that will ultimately be reflected in the development of these key areas.

My reasons for suggesting this are not to reverse people from adopting the freehand methods, which I might generally prefer for sharpening, but rather to resolve practical issues. Because new woodworkers do lack the physical strength and applicable precision that I speak of (my students all have this problem), in their early development, they tend to lift the iron and deliver the wrong presentation angle of the blade bevel to the sharpening plates. This then results in a blunt-ended round to the bevel or camber on the leading edge forming the cutting edge of the blade; more so than, say, with plane irons. When the blade is replaced in the body of the spokeshave this blunt leading edge and over-belly cambering on the bevel prevents the very cutting edge from reaching the wood and we end up with burnished wood, not shaved wood and shavings. Eventually, of course, you may want to freehand, using the holder without the honing guide. It is quicker than using the guide and you will develop the correct angle of presentation as well as the right levels of finger and hand strength and accuracy. The guide is really better to start with and well worth using to develop muscle memory and so on.

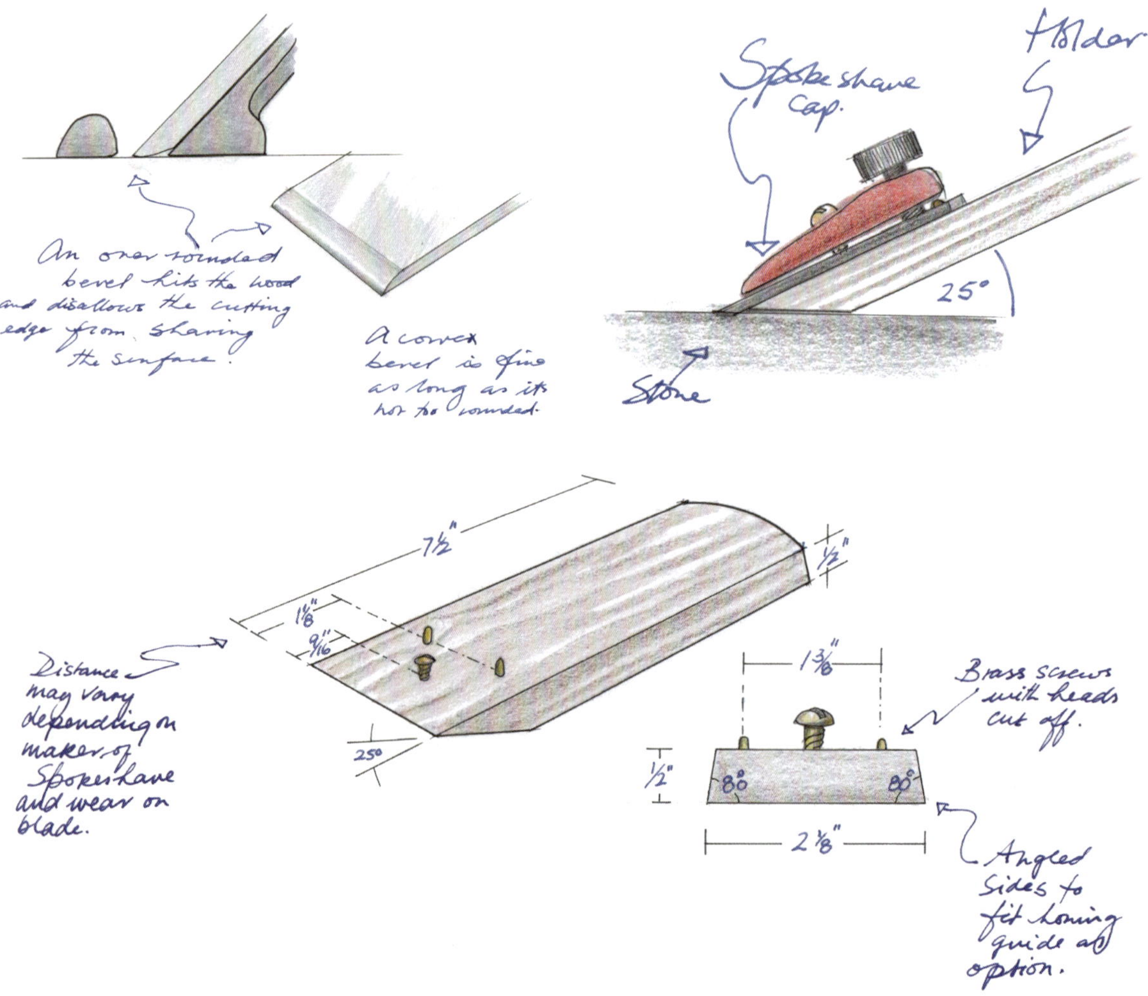

Sharpening Bevel-up Spokeshaves

In sharpening the wooden spokeshaves you must look along the cutting edge to see whether it is straight or slightly curved. If it is straight you can remove a diamond plate or sharpening stone from its holder, hold it at an elevated angle and rub the upturned blade along the edge.

If it is curved along the edge then make some abrasive paddles using abrasive papers in different grits, say 250, 600 and 1200, adhered to lengths of wood. Double-sided tape works well (do two faces of the paddles for economy). If you do the whole length you can turn the paddle end for end too, which adds even further economy of time.

Use a piece of wood in the vise to align the abrasive paddle at the correct angle. Place the paddle on the bench so that one end rests on the bench top and the abrasive connects to the blade somewhere near to the end and sufficient to allow short circular motions to abrade the steel. You may need to adjust the hone length in relation to the bevel, according to what you see after the first few abrading actions. When you are abrading it is ideal for the abrasive to catch both the fore part and rear of the bevel. You can move the hone nearer or further and indeed you can adjust the support wood in the vise too to micro adjust for existing bevels. The important thing here is to shoot for somewhere between 25-30 degrees and no steeper. When the first level abrading causes a burr along the full length of the cutting edge (you will feel it on the large flat face of the blade you are working), you are ready to sharpen with the subsequent grits.

With the bevel established and honed, the last level is to polish out the steel with buffing compound. You can either use leather stretched taut to a narrow paddle and charged with buffing compound or you can charge the actual wooden paddle itself with buffing compound. Both work fine. Push the charged material over the bevel to polish it out for a final finish. This can be done, in like manner to the sharpening, either with the abrasive paddle or freehanded.

The underside of the blade is also polished out and usually this is already polished. Use the wooden stick, charged with the buffing compound, to remove any burr and polish this flat face. Reinstall the blade and tap home. Remember these methods can also be used for all other spokeshave blades too.

Of course, if the blade is straight you can use the very edge of a sharpening stone or plate.

Setting and Adjusting the #151

CAP IRON AND SETSCREW

Regardless of the maker, it makes little difference whether the spokeshave is flat- or round-bottomed when it comes to their adjustment. We adjust all the #151-style spokeshaves in the same way. First of all the centre screw in the middle of the cap iron, the slot-headed one, is not indicative of needing to use a screwdriver to cinch down the cap and blade to the body of the spokeshave, although you can use a screwdriver to help with the adjustment if you want to. This setscrew allows the cap iron to be elevated away from the blade. This cantilevers the pressure from the knurled knob at the top, down to the bottom edge of the cap iron, directly behind the nearest point to the cutting edge. We apply pressure via the knurled knob and adjust the centre setscrew to tip the cap iron nose-forward. Once the setscrew is set at the correct distance we leave it set and, from here on, we apply the pressure via the knurled knob only. Let me say here that it is not unusual to buy these spokeshaves with the setscrew cinched down hard. If that is the case, turn it 4 to 6 turns out. You can use the screwdriver or just your fingers from here on. Install the cap iron and apply the pressure via the knurled knob. Turn the knurled knob and tighten it fully to secure the blade in place.

The setscrew I am adjusting here only needs setting occasionally and, once set, rarely needs changing.

This knurled knob is used to release the blade as well as lock it in place.

CUTTING IRON DEPTH SETTING

Usually the adjusters in the top edge of the blade will turn and adjust with only slight resistance. Clockwise turns advance the cutter into the throat opening for a deeper cut and counterclockwise withdraws the cutting iron.

We check the spokeshave depth of cut and blade alignment in much the same way we set the plane; using a narrow section of wood about ½" (12mm) by 10" (250mm) long, clamped firmly in the vise. With the cutting edge withdrawn from the face of the spokeshave sole, we make adjustments, using the two knurled screws protruding through the top edge area of the cutting iron, until the blade appears to be parallel to the surface around the mouth in the sole. We turn the knurled adjusters, one by one, a full turn at a time, until a shaving appears on each side. If one side appears before the other, focus

on the side with no shaving; again, turning the screw, one full turn at a time, until a shaving comes from that side. You may need to tweak both adjusters at different points as sometimes the blade swivels during these initial alignment adjustments.

We now watch and listen as we take shavings from each side of the blade. The visual check will be comparing the shaving's levels of transparency and so we are looking for thin shavings to be able to check the alignment. Set the spokeshave to one side and take a shaving. Listening also tells us the thickness too. Adjust the adjusters by minute turns until the shavings appear and sound the same on each side of the blade. Once set, we simply turn the adjusters evenly in part-turns according to the depth we want to cut.

Depending on the work type, you may want to set the cutting iron dead parallel, as above, or set it purposely askew. We need it set parallel for shaving surfaces that are flat across, whether they are concave or convex. This might be for curved tops of doors or arches to tables; things like that. However, if we are rounding over corners to create roundovers and quadrants or ellipses, chamfers and such, we usually set the iron askew so that we can take heavier cuts to start with and then refine the cut by moving the spokeshave over to the edge with the shallower depth setting, without actually resetting the blade.

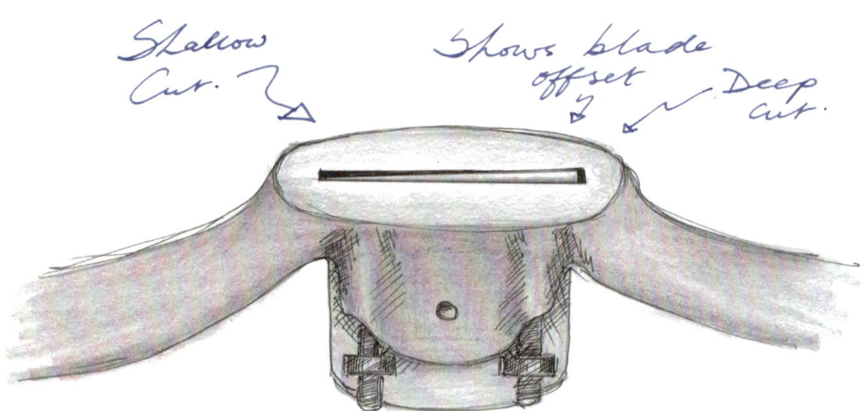

You should be careful not to set the blade to take too thick a shaving. This can develop shavings too thick and heavy for the spokeshave and the throat opening. Another problem is that the iron can be set incorrectly so that it protrudes too much and the back of the bevel rides the wood, preventing the cutting edge from engaging. Because no shaving emerges from the throat, the tendency then is to advance the cutting iron even more and so exacerbate the problem. Tipping the tool forward then takes a deep, ripping and gouging cut and tipping it backwards rides the back edge of the bevel and the heel of the blade in relation to the sole.

Note:
We also set up the wooden spokeshave using the same procedure but, depending on the adjustment type, we either use a hammer or the adjusters, which come in different types.

An Open Throat Offers an Advantage

The #151 has been made by many manufacturers since the Stanley patent expired. Even some of the cheaper ones work really well and I think this is for two reasons. One, the throat is wide open and allows unfettered shavings to rise into and through it, with no grab by the body of the spokeshave; and, two, the lightness of the tool overall heightens sensitivity to micro-adjust for optimizing the lateral angle of presentation to slice-cut the surface. Also, the amount of pressure needed to engage an effective cut is infinitely adjustable, according to user sensitivity. I have never found the open throat to be negative but I have found that tighter throat openings are also good when working with particularly difficult grain. However, it is, in my opinion, definitely more of an advantage to have a wide and open throat rather than a closed and narrow one.

Do You Need the Adjusters?

The #150 was the spokeshave that preceded the #151 and it was made without the adjusters. It is simply adjusted by loosening the knurled knob and finger-pinching the blade to the desired depth. Sometimes I think that the spokeshaves with non-adjustment screws can be more pleasant to use. I think this is because of the lighter weight due to not having the extra baggage of knurled adjusters and threaded rods. Once you take off all the extras you simply have the body, blade and cap iron and a couple of screws. It changes the feel of the spokeshave pleasantly and it works just as effectively as the #151 does with the extra stuff in place. So, the answer is no or not really. I like the adjustment mechanisms - they are handy, of course - but the spokeshave does function just fine without them.

Using the Spokeshave

The only real way to fully understand the spokeshave is to use it, experiment with it and make as much as you can with it; and I suggest that you do this as early as you can in your woodworking. As I have said, the spokeshave is a short soled, side-handled plane. As such, using this power-packed alternative to, say, a bench plane suddenly equips you to engage in work that other planes, by virtue of their shape and size, disallow. I use mine for concaved and convexed working alike; I use it for shaping the rims of chair seats and all types of chair spindles, rails and stretchers. Whereas most chair parts generally rely on woodturning lathes, you may be surprised to discover just how much can be made with a single flat-bottomed spokeshave.

The spokeshave planes wood with greater comfort than many other plane types because it can be flipped, twisted, and turned to work at any angle, on push and pull strokes, so readily and without compromising the work. Grain direction, changing constantly as it does, is effectively managed in very localised areas because of the shortness of the sole. Placing the thumbs in the indents either side of the cutting iron gives the spokeshave very direct support by the blade. The projects often dictate diverse handholds. While working on a project I may need to push and pull the same spokeshave out of necessity because a variety of shapes cause the orientation of the grain to change. Often times you will feel the blade balk in the changeover and it is at these junctures where you skew the

All of the shaping for this Shaker-style Deacon's bench came from the spokeshave and not, as you might expect, the lathe.

spokeshave to the work, which lowers the trajectory and optimises the cutting action. Whether it is a spoon handle or the back of the spoon, a spatula or a walking cane handle, when you master the spokeshave, split second changes create superb sweeps that sweeten the cutting action, in and out and up and down. Suddenly your fingers are tracing new textures following the cuts you made and every one of them with a crisp sharpness no other method or tool can achieve.

The spokeshave works great on both the push stroke... ...and the pull stroke.

It is important to feel for different pressure points in the hands as you work the wood. Combining this with sight and sound enables you to 'read' or, better still, 'interpret' what the grain is saying to you. By doing this you will be able to fully negotiate, with precision, any need for change in a split second and, before long, you can totally predict every action to head-off the calamity of tearing grain.

Employing and Enjoying the Different Types

My experience tells me that it is not an either-or decision when it comes to choosing between spokeshave types. I have accumulated many a dozen and more spokeshaves over the years but I do not really use them all; I just love them when I find them and enjoy owning them. I can share some of them with visiting students and apprentices or give them to friends I meet on my journey. I have found special ones that I sharpen to very specific tasks and having several spokeshaves allows this option in my worklife as an artisan. The very best engineered tools might, in certain cases, be less effective for some work even though, technically, they might be seen as better tools. It is important to keep an open mind when it comes to these aspects of woodworking. I say this because, when you find different tools and take them home, you often find you prefer one over another for different tasks.

This spokeshave, produced by a modern maker, is well designed and a pleasure to use. I have used it for several years now and it is one of my favourites, especially for refining work.

It is too easy to dismiss a particular tool type in order to bolster an opinion, choice or purchase of a tool. Although I do know that a well made, well set and well sharpened wooden spokeshave performs exceptionally, there are many aspects of woodworking that a #151 can do better. The reason for this is the simple fact that the blade of the #151 does not form the sole of the spokeshave but passes through the sole in like manner to a bench plane. In a wooden bodied spokeshave the thickness of the shaving is determined by setting the blade deeper than the wooden body at the fore edge and sides of the cutting iron forming its own sole. This then forms a step-like presentation of the cutting edge to the wood being shaved. In the very narrow fields of chair bodging, green woodworking and such, generally making parts from green wood and even dry wood, the wooden spokeshave is more ideal than the others. That does not mean that the others will not work or even work well, just that it generally works differently. In essence this sets it apart from the #151 and others; the #151 cutting action is very different. In the bedded angle of the #151, the iron is presented at a steep pitch and protrudes through the spokeshave sole so that the sole is continuous and level in both 'fore and aft' aspects of the cutting edge. With the wooden models, the blade forms the sole as the latter part of the cutting action and wood as the fore part as a small band of wood (or inset metal if a wear plate is fitted) that enables the cutting iron to 'lean' into the wood.

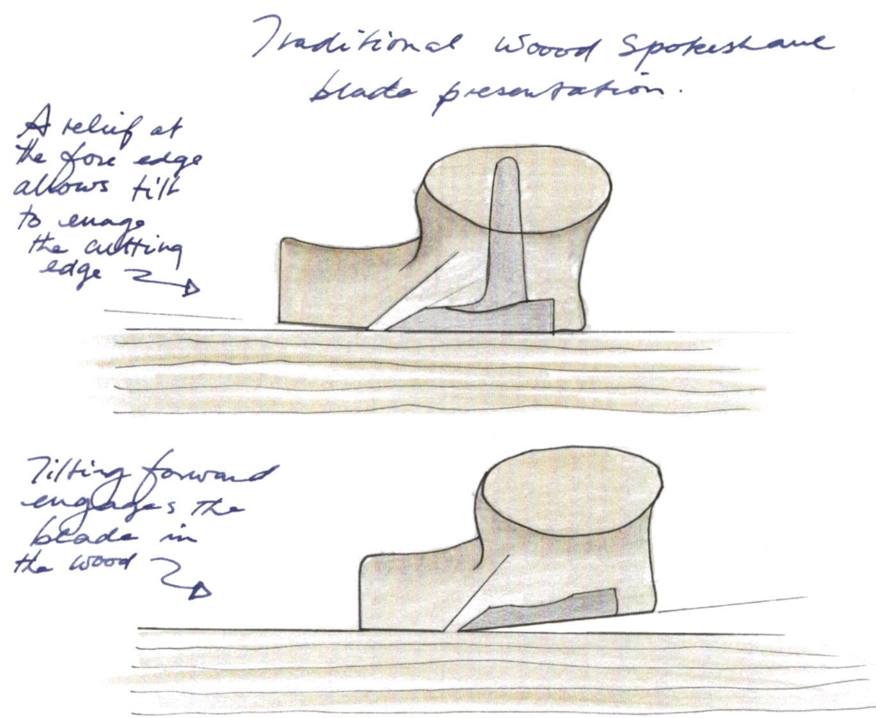

The different woodworking trades or crafts developed specialised spokeshaves according to task. The violin maker had his set and so too the boat builder, the cabinet maker and the instrument makers making precision wooden instruments. From 3" (75mm) to 12" (300mm), these spokeshaves were available with rounded noses or fore-ends for convex work and flat bottoms for larger convex and concave work.

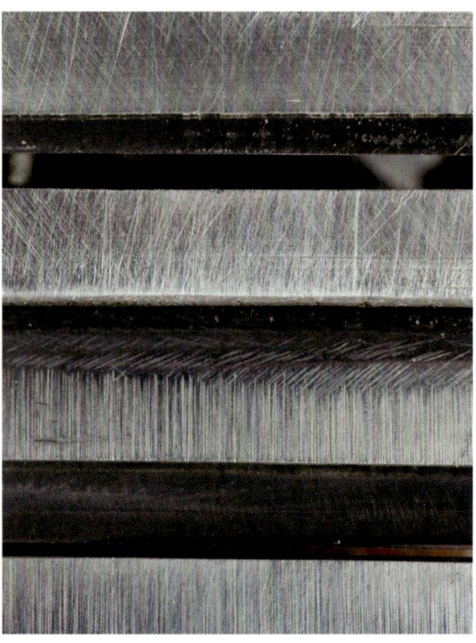

This image shows the contrast between a standard #151 spokeshave mouth opening and that of a modern maker's spokeshave.

As I say, for chairmaking, the bodger might decry the #151 as inferior to the old wooden ones, claiming that the wooden spokeshave works best and is therefore declared superior. On the other hand, others might declare a particular modern maker to be superior to any other because of its tighter mouth opening, superior engineering, and metal alloys and such. The #151, on the other hand, offers us a wide open mouth that enables the removal of heavy stock and the ability to refine our cuts via the adjustment nuts. As I said, I enjoy different spokeshaves for the different strokes they give me.

Wood on wood is light, frictionless woodworking at its best and wooden spokeshaves are a delight to use. This is especially so for long grain cutting. However, when this type of spokeshave meets rising grain the results are often devastating. When this happens the cutting edge of a wooden spokeshave can separate the grain rather than cutting it and as pressure is applied by the user the wood starts to split. Then, as the blade engages the wood at the cutting edge, deep tearout occurs resulting in torn grain. This can then often be remedied by going over the same section of wood with a #151 which cleans up the work substantially, even though still going in the same direction, against the rising grain. I was raised on the Stanley and Record 150's and 151's and have used them all through my working life. These spokeshaves cope with knots, knotty areas, and rising grain far better than their bevel-up counterparts, which is the true for bevel-up and bevel-down planes too.

With spokeshaves there is no "one size fits all," although you could choose any one of these and be happy making adjustments to make it suit the task each time you reach for it. Each of the types discussed will perform differently for different tasks. Bodging chair makers work primarily with long grain cuts and minimal crossgrain work and so they like the wooden spokeshaves best because that is what they do best. The #151 type spokeshave, with its open mouth, is a work horse that tackles a wide range of work types very well; it can even be refined for fine work too. I like owning other, finely engineered, spokeshaves by modern makers for fine-tolerance work but have no hesitation pulling out the #151 for almost anything I do.

Spokeshaves Should Always Be Used With Sensitivity

Sensitivity determines the exactness of the direction, according to pressures at the tool's cutting edge. It is only by sensing the minute-by-minute changes that we can shift and change so as to present the tool's cutting edge at its most effective angle, according to small shifts in grain direction and configuration in the wood. By sensitivity we determine sharpness and the need to sharpen, the need to change the bevel angle slightly or alter the presentation from a head-on force to a slicing cut and much, much more beyond. We may not even be capable of defining, in words alone, what sensitivity means when it comes to the way we respond to a tool's cutting edge or the grain in the wood we work. We may not even be mentally aware of the subtle changes we make by effectively adjusting a hand or finger position as we work the tool but we do it every second if, when we work, we sense what needs to change and make the changes immediately.

The Plough Plane

The popularity of plough (plow USA) planes lessened as woodworkers embraced power equipment in the form of specialist machinery. Industrial machine manufacturers downsized machines and introduced smaller spindle moulders, compact tablesaws with stacked dado cutters and of course the hand-held power router emerged too. Though it is no longer commonly used by today's woodworker, the plough plane may well, even in our age, become a much more sought-after hand tool and reverse some of the trend toward machine-only woodworking. Reversing this past inclination toward using machine methods means the return of such tools as plough planes, rabbet planes, and router planes; and, of course, the restoration of more traditional woodworking skills as well. Most woodworkers, rediscovering these all but lost tools, express pleasant surprise at the efficiency with which they work and a sense of real control at the workbench. To some, using the plough plane might seem more of a backwards step but, when they see how effectively this action-packed workhorse tackles grooves in any and all woods, the option of power routing becomes all the more questionable to them. First of all it is necessary to work through the steps of setting up the plough plane. It is not complicated at all but dismantling and reassembling the parts is the first step to a better understanding of how the plane functions. Understanding a few idiosyncrasies and features becomes intuitive very quickly, and before too long I doubt you will run grooves by machine ever again unless you are working on large scale production.

What the Plough Plane Does

The plough plane, in its basic function, runs grooves parallel to any given edge of a section of wood. Generally, these grooves run with or along the length of the grain rather than across it. The grooves formed then usually house panels of wood, glass, or some type of engineered boarding such as plywood or MDF. They can also be used for inlaying and creating removable stops, such as in sliding sash window frames. You can use the same plane for creating tongue and groove joints to the edges of boards for panelling, floor boarding, matched board-and-bead panelling and such like too.

The plough plane creates the grooves by removing shavings in a very controlled manner and leaving wood either side of the cutting iron, which then forms the groove. The thickness of the shavings is infinitely adjustable by setting the depth of the cutting iron in relation to a narrow sole, which runs the length of the plane both before and after the cutting iron. Some plough planes are provided with special tongueing cutters for cutting the tongue aspect of tongue and groove boarding.

Groove Sizing

Plough planes, old and new, all wood and all metal, come with a series of cutter blades generally called cutting irons. These come in different sizes, which can be metric or imperial depending on where they are to be sold. As the whole of Europe is metric, imperial sizes are made mostly for the USA. Anything pre-1980's and made in the UK will also likely use imperial sizing.

Plough planes using imperial sizing are sold in incremental sizes with ⅛" (3mm), 3⁄16" (4.5mm), ¼" (6mm), 5⁄16" (8mm), ⅜" (9.5mm), and ½" (12.5mm) cutters supplied

as standard. Some models have additional sizes and also tongue cutters. Metric sizing will be close to those sizes too, usually within half a millimeter. Some makers, past and present, make extension supports, which attach to the body of the plane to increase the width allowance in order to accept wider blades from ½" (12.5mm) to ¾" (19mm) as well as special profile cutters. You can usually run extra parallel grooves to increase width possibilities using the standard size blades also. An important consideration in doing this is that the sole of the plane and the depth shoe sit on the wood 'outboard' to the body of the plane which means you must decide which groove to run first so that the plane's sole and depth shoe have something to ride on.

Here you can see how both the sole, the narrower section in the bottom of the groove, and the depth shoe simultaneously ride the wood.

Controlling Groove Depth and Alignment

All plough planes have two features that control the depth of the plane and make the distance from the edge of the wood being ploughed infinitely variable. The depth stop sits almost adjacent to the main blade or cutter of the plane and is often called the 'depth shoe' or 'depth control.' Usually a knurled knob, thumbscrew, or slotted setscrew secures the depth shoe to the body of the plane (see image, next page).

This knurled screw locks the depth shoe in place. The depth shoe allows fine control over the overall depth of cut.

The second control is the fence. The fence attaches to two round arm rods that slide through holes on the fence casting and also the body of the plane. The rods are anchored to the fence and then the body by setscrews. Locking the setscrews in either the plane body or the fence first allows the fence to be set to the distance required from the body. This then controls the distance of the groove from a given edge of the section of wood being worked. Again, on the all-metal bodied plough planes at least, two thumbscrews or knurled knobs anchor the fence to a preset distance from the corner edge of the cutting iron. Whether you use a wooden plough from the 1700-1800s or a new model from a modern maker, these two control features are fairly standard in all types of plough planes.

A wooden plough plane made by the well known US maker, Sandusky Tool Company of Ohio.

Plough Plane Types

Plough planes are no longer made by Stanley or Record but several slightly different models made by both makers are still available second hand and usually they are in good working order with little need for remedial work. A couple of modern makers are also producing great quality plough planes. I will run through the features of the different types of all-metal plough planes that I have worked with as well as the wooden models. All of the plough planes that I discuss here are great options and you are very unlikely to need more than one. I am simply outlining the various types so that you can compare your options.

RECORD PLOUGH PLANES

The Record 043 is punchy, compact, and stoutly built. Never underestimate its value to woodworking. I think every furniture maker should own one if possible. It is very direct, comfortable, and vibration free no matter the grain terrain; and it is quick to set up, easy to adjust, and lends itself to very tight control, even with only one hand if needed. This was the first plough plane I ever bought.

The Record 044 has a screw-drive adjustment mechanism with a slot head for a screwdriver to adjust and set the depth. The depth feed screw prevents the cutting iron from withdrawing from the cut or from inadvertently changing the depth of cut. To the side of the cutting iron is an additional side setscrew that then keeps the blade

firmly aligned in the body. Once set, the blade becomes rock solid and immovable. The metal handle is more comfortable than it looks. However, when using an all-metal plane handle, in a cold shop, it takes a minute for it to warm in the hand. I enjoy using this plane for its lightness and its flexible yet solid dependability.

STANLEY PLOUGH PLANES

Stanley equalled the Record versions throughout the history of the all-metal plough plane era and added many improvements, not the least of which was the knurled adjusters instead of screwdriver driven ones. These work well and lock dead solidly; so do not think that they were not good quality or well engineered. They were. Their plastic handled versions from the 50's are robustly built too and feel really solid in the hand so if you find one of these it will work for you.

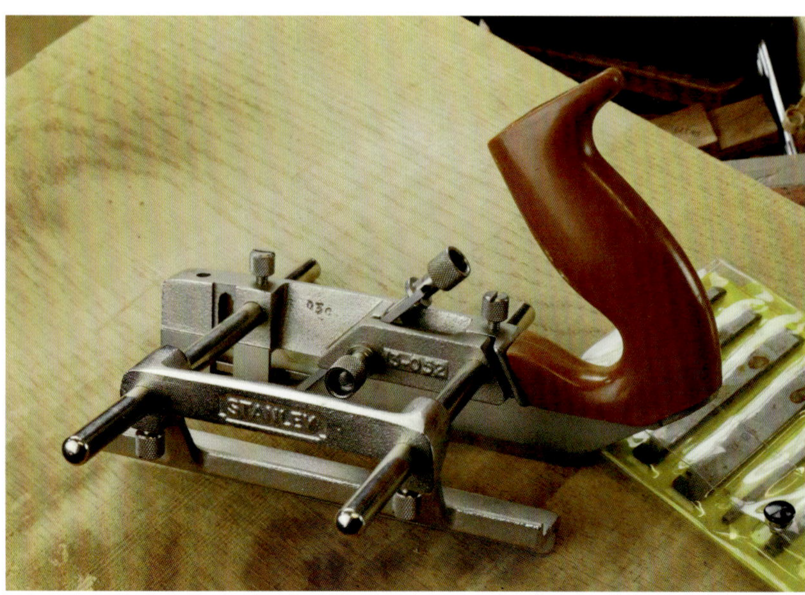

MODERN PLOUGH PLANES

This modern-made plough plane is one of my favourites and, in construction, almost mirrors the Record 044c but with some additional refinements. I think it definitely parallels the 044 and the 044c in the hand and the wooden handle has proven sturdy and comfortable over the years I have used it. Record stopped production of all of their plough and multiplane planes back in the mid 1900's and have not returned to production since so it is important that modern manufacturers work to fill this gap in the market. Even though the originals are solid options there is still room to improve the engineering standards and even the mechanisms. Manufacturers must, however, resist the urge to over complicate these tools, which already work brilliantly.

WOODEN PLOUGH PLANES

Wooden plough planes, even the simplest, are quite lovely when preserved in good condition. I own several of them and keep some just because they are so lovely. More than that though, wooden plough planes work very well. In times past, I am sad to say, some were made from ebony and ivory as expressions of opulence beyond the working man's needs. I hope those days never return.

When you first pick up a wooden plough plane they feel a little cumbersome. They relied on greater bulk in the component parts for the strength needed for the work. Brass strengthening pieces, wedges, and metal holders and retainers combined with the wood to ensure longevity to a tool that necessitated vigorous strain in use.

Not so obvious in the older, wooden plough plane irons is a shallow 'V' groove running down the back of the cutting irons, centered in the iron. This channel sits directly on a ridge on the rear steel skate plate forming the rear aspect of the sole. This sole is often referred to as the skate because, on some makes, the sole resembles the skates used for ice skating. This ridge aligns the iron with the skate and prevents lateral slippage from side to side.

If you like old plough planes made from wood, you can be assured that they do work well and, even though they are generally bulkier to use in terms of mass, in the actual wood itself they are light and easy to use and develop beautiful work. I like the way these old wooden ones feel in the hand when working larger and deeper grooves, as in door making and so on; those frames with long runs rather than short lengths and in heavier material. I still use mine as often as needed but I like to keep them for my best work. They remove material exceptionally fast and can be deep-set for this. Toward the bottom of the cut the set can be adjusted to a shallower setting and the cut cleaned up for a fine finish. The screw-stemmed ones adjust best and the handled ones lower the hand at the heel of the plane and so the centre of thrust is very directly in line with and behind the cutting iron.

The old wooden, handled plough planes are powerful through and through. So strong and resilient, unfaltering in tackling awkward grains, they handle nearly all wood types and, when you get used to them, they always feel equal to the task. I own several and always love pulling them out to use them in my work. I never felt the same about pulling out a router bit and power router, dust mask, ear protectors, or goggles.

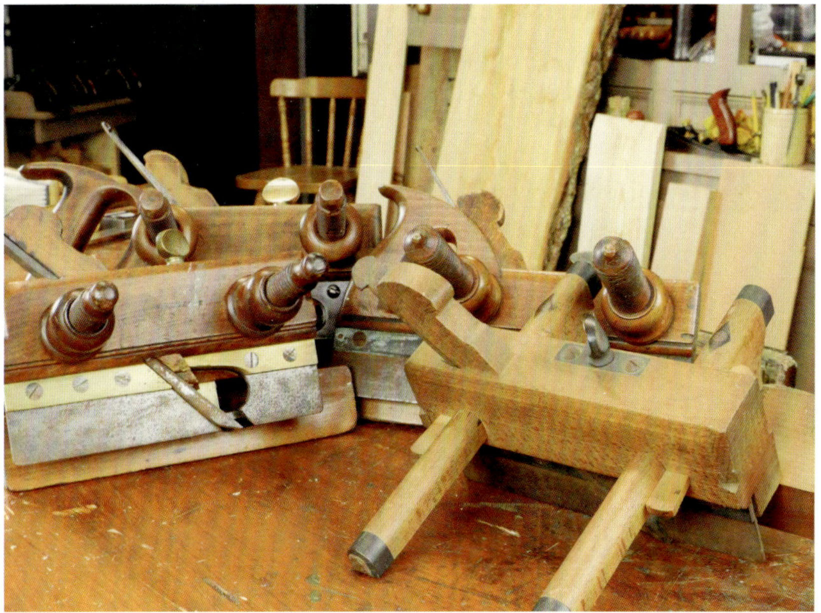

These old models generally came with either wedged stems (for locking off distances between the fence and the plane skate-cutter distance) or the much more refined screw-stem model.

The wedge-stem method locks the fence by the two stems, using compression and friction caused by a wedge to each stem. However, wedges could slip under the sideways pressure being applied to keep the fence to the wood. I do not want you to think this method was ineffective. It was not at all. For the main part, wedges worked really well. The wedge-stemmed ploughs were adjusted by hammer-tapping the wedges and the ends of the stems in or out of the plane body. The screw-stemmed versions offered infinite precision in setting adjustment and immoveable locking. Screw threads to the stems, and also the adjustable depth shoe for depth control of the cut, were refinements to the plane. Such planes are only available second hand but you can occasionally find them at good prices from time to time and they are well worth the investment if you find them.

On the wooden versions, as with other wooden planes, the blade tapers from thick to thin. The reason for this is to create an opposing slope to counter the pressures when the plane thrusts forward into the wood. Without it, the blade would slide up and away from the work in between the wedge and the bed of the plane. This strategy really works because it creates additional wedging action under pressure.

Four Different Developments in Plough Planes

The difference between these four plough planes (pictured right), in terms of practical functionality, is quite minimal but each one does have its own idiosyncrasies you must get used to. The wooden ploughs were the heaviest and bulkiest looking but perhaps the very best and lightest in functionality and use, even though they do generally weigh more than the all-metal ones. That is the effect of wood on wood and it is the same with all wooden planes. Near frictionless motion makes all the difference but, for most, this difference has been forgotten and even lost. I do not know of any modern day planemaker making wooden plough planes but, if they did copy a Sandusky like this one shown, I think they might sell them readily, provided they matched the quality of the Sandusky workmen.

Multiplanes

Plough planes are made specifically for plough work and should not be confused with multiplanes. Multiplanes come with a wider range of cutters for moulding different shapes and they can do all of the work plough planes do but the cutters for moulding do not perform particularly well and so the results are not to be relied on, as they are with ploughing and rebating. These additional blades with shaped cutters are generally less predictable and less controllable than moulding planes. This is what many woodworkers exposed to multiplanes experience but ploughing grooves is very different than the moulding multiplanes are particularly bad at.

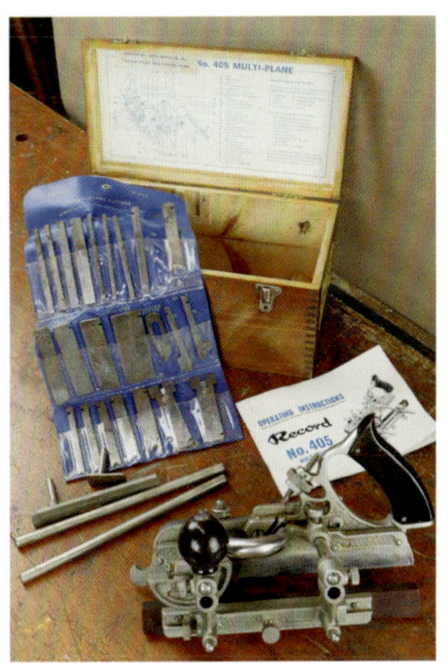

Left: The multiplane was designed to make more than just grooves. It works well within that more limited capacity but, as a plane designed for other mouldings, it works less effectively.

Right: Moulding planes create many different profiles using individual planes made to specific mould shapes.

Features of Metal Plough Planes

On the all-metal models of the plough, the blade sits inside a recess formed in the body casting. The plane iron slides in place and is then locked to the plane with a setscrew.

A setscrew, when tightened, pushes the blade sideways against the wall to prevent lateral movement. A slight back turn on this setscrew allows the cutting iron to be adjusted in relation to the plane's sole.

The cast metal blade retainer, which also serves as a form of lever cap and cap iron to divert shavings up and away from the throat, keeps the cutter pressed down firmly to the bed via a knurled screw.

The adjuster behind the cutting iron advances and withdraws the blade to the desired depth setting, which can be changed to change the thickness of shavings depending on the work and the wood type.

Sharpening the Plough Plane

Sharpening your plough plane irons follows the same pattern as that for narrow chisels. With narrow blades there is less to hold onto than the wider ones and often you are limited to two or three fingers to apply pressure with. Another aspect of narrow blades is the tendency to take off more steel from one side of the blade than the other and bad habits here can translate into a badly skewed edge. Remember though that, because the bed of the plane presents the cutting edge at 45 degrees and the bevel you create finalises at 30, this lowers the discrepancy in squareness too. For this reason a slight skew is actually less problematic because, when it comes to the actual cut, the skew is only a fraction of what you see face on. I say that because it is all too easy to obsess over something that really makes little difference.

Here is how I freehand sharpen the blade:

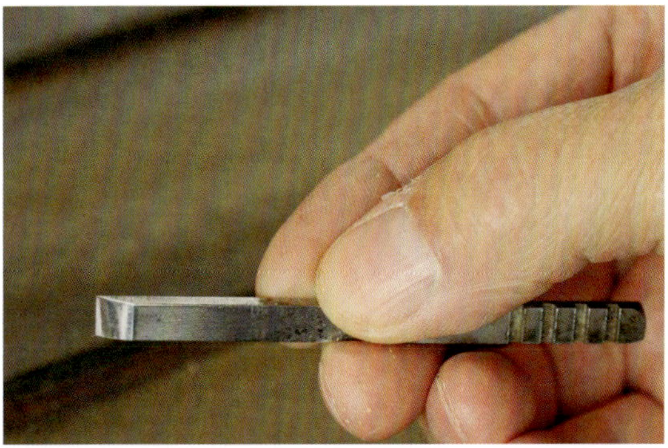

Use your dominant hand and place the forefinger in the centre of the flat face and grip the side edges of the blade between the thumb and second finger.

Present it to the sharpening plate and press firmly, as near as possible to 30 degrees…

…and add the forefinger of the non-dominant hand and, starting at 30 degrees, move forward and, in the extension of the movement, drop the hand slightly, to around 25 degrees, to remove the heel.

You may find room to add another finger too and this will increase the stability and the pressure you can apply.

After working through the grits, as you would with any other cutting edge tool, flip over and pull the blade on the flat face on the finest abrasive plate to break the burr and then polish out on the strop as normal. Take great care never to raise the blade to more than 30 degrees as this often results in the bevel riding the wood and the cutting edge failing to reach the cutting level.

A honing guide, which often has a special narrow blade section, brings an added advantage to narrow blades even though it is only a step towards the freedom of freehand skill development.

The finished blade looks like this and has square edges right to the corners.

I check my work from time to time and you can see how I trail off the heel of the bevel to keep it from affecting the work at the cutting edge.

"*Take great care never to raise the blade to more than 30 degrees as this often results in the bevel riding the wood and the cutting edge failing to reach the cutting level*"

Solving Plough Plane Problems

Sometimes problems exist with both older model metal plough planes and the new maker models. These are not necessarily obvious manufacturing errors but are common things that can go wrong and you should know how to correct them.

CHECK THE BEVEL ANGLE

If you bought a second hand plough plane the cutting iron or irons may not be functional. Assuming the main body of the plane is generally good and so too all of the components, the cutting iron bevels forming the cutting edges are sometimes poorly shaped. Anyone new to the intricacies of these planes might miss this flaw. It is not necessarily glaringly obvious but if the bevel is too steep then the heel of the cutting iron may well hit the wood so as to prevent the cutting edge cutting the surface first.

The bevel in this case is too steep and would prevent the cutting edge reaching the wood as the bevel rides the wood.

The correct bevel should be between 25 and 30 degrees.

MAKE SURE THE BLADE IS SQUARE

Often the irons are out of square at the cutting edges too. This is because narrow blades can be harder to hold square to the stones. This results in the bottom of the grooves sloping one way or the other out of square, showing the iron's flawed squareness in the work itself. You might consider using a honing guide, as discussed before, when re-establishing a square edge.

RELIEVE THE SIDES OF THE BLADE

The sides of the grooves created by the plough plane flank the plane cutter on two sides as the cut deepens, and they always run parallel to the edge of the board being ploughed. Because of this, the iron penetrates the wood and, as you move forward in the cut, the leading edge of the iron is under the wood, forming the two edge corners to the top face of the groove sides. A deep cut, one where the cutting iron protrudes past the skate markedly, say 1/32" to 1/16" (1-1.5mm), tears and lifts the rim corners leaving ragged corners. When the plough engages some more awkward grains such as reverse or short grain then the problem becomes exacerbated a hundredfold. To resolve this I use abrasive paper to remove the hard cutting corner off the top face of the iron on both corners, but I take care to keep this abrading to the barest minimum. I also do the same to the underside of the iron too, as this ensures a smoother operation of the plough in retreat pulls. This seems such a small thing but it makes such a big difference. You can also file the edges of the cutting iron slightly out of square so that the sides are slightly bevelled. Relieving the sides follows the patterns set by the old craftsmen blacksmiths making plough plane irons for wooden plough planes. Retain the full width on the front face of the iron though, this is critical for accuracy of width in the grooves you make. The older plane irons for wooden ploughs always have this relief to the sides of the irons and thereby have a trapezoidal profile. This relief allows much freer passage forward and into each subsequent cut, which lowers friction and, at the same time, prevents binding in the cut. More importantly, it allows the plane the same free passage on the return strokes and maintains the registration of the plane iron to the groove. Some all-metal plough plane irons do also have a slight bevel to the edges of the blade and some, I have found, do not have this. Those that do not will definitely benefit from a few file strokes to create the relief.

Some plough plane cutters have bevelled side edges from 4 to 7 degrees which gives them an advantage.

To add this to a cutter take a flat file and bevel the sides to make them narrow on the underside of the cutter. Stay away from the top face corner as filing this will reduce the width of the cutter.

CHECK THE FENCE ALIGNMENT

Sometimes the fence can be slightly out of parallel. When the fence lock screws are tightened, the fence may be assumed to be parallel when, actually, it is slightly out. If the opening end (between the fence and the plane body or skate sole) is narrower than the rear end, it will work. If it is the opposite, and the opening end at the front is wider than the rear end, then the plane will not work well at all. It is best to check, by measuring, if you encounter too much pressure in ploughing. In using the plough planes, no matter the maker or the type, new or old, you must always check that the fence is, at the very minimum, parallel to the skate sole but ⅟₃₂" (1mm) wider at the back than the front is better. This helps the plane operate freely with near zero friction from the fence and skate. If it is out, so that the fence gap narrows the distance between the rear end of the fence and the rear end of the sole, the plane will bind with each cut. If no adjustment is made, as the cut deepens, the friction increases and the plane ultimately stops or the wood is damaged. Ideally

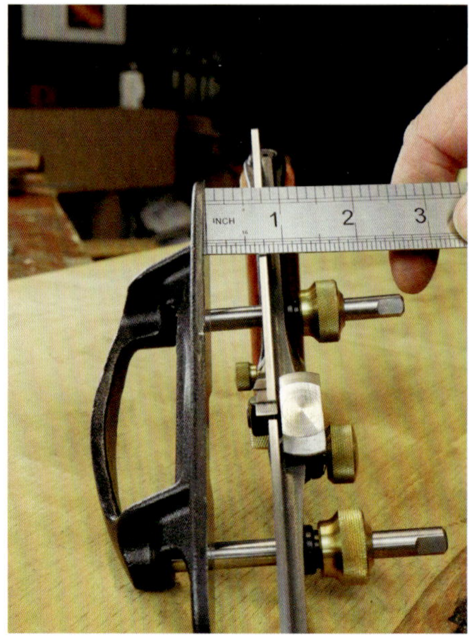

the fence should be set slightly out of parallel with the main body or the skate sole of the plane. Sometimes, especially on the all-metal plough planes, once one fence stem is locked, the other end of the fence is immoveable for locking either parallel or a little more open. In such cases, I found it best to simply lock the front setscrew and leave the other end to 'float'. This then opens up the other end when the plane is in use and the plough will work just fine.

Using the Plough Plane

Because the plough plane irons are narrower than smoothing plane irons they cut the wood more easily and you can usually take shavings two to three times thicker than when just smoothing wood. Plough planing allows for deep setting of the iron but you must take care not to start ploughing the groove with too deep a setting; once the cutting iron enters the wood, the cutting edge is effectively underneath the wood fibres lifting the wood without severing it and establishing the walls to the groove with progressive cuts. As a result, the deep set can rip the corners of the walls if the top corners of the blade within the wood are below the surface too deeply. Start the groove, initially at least, with a fine set to the cutting iron. This creates a shallow groove for subsequent cuts and, as these cuts deepen, you establish well-cut, well-defined, and crisp corners. Once the opening cuts are made, the groove walls become established stroke by stroke and the walls become defined. Once this has taken place, you can further adjust the set for deeper passes and the ploughing then deepens more quickly.

Here is a groove with torn corners, perhaps from taking too deep a shaving.

You should aim to get grooves with clean, crisp corners and walls.

STARTING A PLOUGHED GROOVE

Often people feel a little anxious using the plough plane for the first time and especially so if they start on an actual workpiece they do not want to ruin. Because they do not want the plane to deviate from a true course parallel to the edge of a board edge, they grip the plane in a bulldogging vise-grip and force it into the wood without considering anything except force. They also start by offering the plane to the wood at the nearest end and force the plane down onto the wood, pushing from one end to the other. Both actions are really counterproductive because you lose the sensitivity needed whenever you make a fist to direct any cut. The work should be approached firmly but gently and considerately. The key concerns are lateral pressure, to push the fence against the workpiece, and then alignment, where we align the fence and the main

The first stroke starts near the end.

body along the long axis of the wood to be ploughed. Ensuring the fence is aligned with the workpiece, we start at the far point from us and work backwards in short stages with successive strokes, taking first one cut, say 4-6" (10-15cm) from the far end of the wood and then moving backwards in 2-3" (5-7.5cm) increments. You may be concerned that the far end of the wood gets the successive cuts and deepens the most. However, the plough plane has a depth shoe, which ultimately helps to establish an even depth throughout the length of the groove. This stage-by-stage approach is the typical method and we should look at this as the general pattern we apply to most planing and it is especially important with plough planing.

The short stroke initialises the work and subsequent ploughing cuts start further from the nose and finish at the far end, where we started. The strokes, of course, get longer as we work backwards towards the near end.

Here is the second stroke...

...and the third...

...and the longest.

Once the walls are established we can continue taking ever longer cuts until we reach full depth. It is still advisable to work from the far end and work backwards as we deepen the cuts. This helps to keep the work crisp and neat. When the depth shoe hits the edge and prevents any further ingress into the wood at the far end we continue moving backwards and the cut continues to deepen along the groove. In the final strokes we generally take long passes, even from one end to the other, until we have a fully consistent depth.

Extra Refining – Gauging the Groove Walls

Plough planes will soon impress you with their punch and panache. That said though, and through no fault of the plane's at all, sometimes you come across awkward grain that catches the plane sideways and rips from the body of wood and, no matter which direction you go, it will tear on the top inside corner of the groove leaving an ugly edge. No matter which way you orient the plane to the wood the corners become unacceptably ragged. There is an extra step you can take that really helps with this which is to pre-cut the groove walls before you start ploughing work. For this I use one of the modern marking or mortise gauges, the ones with discs instead of pins for markers. The disc works really well as a cutter to delineate the walls of the groove on either side.

Always begin a groove by making a short start at the beginning edge of the board to just engage the cutter in the wood.

This leaves definite marks to guide you and if there is any tearout you can then use these initial marks to guide cuts with the marking gauge.

Using a marking gauge with a disc cutter can help sever the fibres of difficult grain on the side with tearout or on both sides of the groove and help prevent any further tearout.

If you do not own a disc gauge just use a regular marking gauge to lightly mark the position of the walls, again, on either or both sides of the groove.

You can then follow the gauge lines with a cut with a sharp knife.

Now set the plough plane to work and run the groove. The wall will be clear and neat and should look as good as any machined edge you have ever seen.

The Router Plane

The first time I ever encountered the router plane I somehow sensed it was on its way out. That was in 1965 and I did indeed watch as it all but disappeared. Fifty years have passed since then and today I cannot imagine life without it. I, for one, would be most miserable without this unique and special plane. So I hope to persuade you too, especially those of you new to woodworking, that the hand router, no matter the type or the age, is a wonderful plane you can rely on forever. The router plane was, in recent years, deemed one of the least necessary hand planes because power routers were said to replace them. However, I have worked to expand the vision of their purpose. Today, riding the resurgent wave of revivalism in hand tool woodworking, the hand router plane will always be held in the safe keeping of amatuer woodworkers around the world. If you are a joiner or a furniture maker or any other kind of woodworker, keep one near to hand and get used to owning and using one in the workshop. Like any good hand tool, it will never be far away and it will never let you down.

The first router I ever saw was this type, tucked away in the corner of an old man's tool chest. I liked the look of it, but could see no use for it until I saw him level the bottom housings in a stair string after roughing out with a chisel.

For many decades I saw router planes disregarded, discarded, and left as relics of the past in the wake of power equipment developed for the woodworking industry. Industrialised woodworking gradually invaded every home workshop as some kind of solution, supposedly surpassing skilled hand work but then something slowly started to change. I watched as woodworkers began seeking more of the methods of the past. Today, in a few minutes around the bench with my students, I watch their eyes grow wide when they see just how wonderfully these tools really work. Sensing a level of control without loss in efficiency and the quality of cut has an appeal of its own. People become the power behind the workmanship and the safety aspect is truly invaluable to them. Combine this with the quest for developing correct hand skills and mastery, and most of those I teach need look no further for satisfaction and contentment. Hand powered router planes work really well.

What the Router Plane Does (and What it Does Not Do)

The name of the router basically describes its primary function in 'routing' out (or down) a section of wood from its surrounding plane. Most often, the new surface level is between two adjacent planes to create a housing dado or other housing but, as I have said, the router plane is far from limited to just the one task.

The hand router is not used at all for creating a mass of different mouldings or for making engineered materials like plywood and MDF look like something they are not. It was not designed for that so I hasten to say here and now that any comparison between electric power routers and hand router planes should be set aside. They are not the tools of the past and the present side by side. Neither are they at all one and the same and they should not generally be associated or compared in any such way, even though both will route out housings for hinges and cut housing dadoes too. The

hand router develops housing dadoes in many different forms, to any depth, and that is its primary function in most work; it creates a perfect plane parallel to an original surface as a recessed step-down. We use it to trim out recesses to house other wooden parts as well as fitments such as hinges, locks, and other hardware too. I introduced the tool as a tenon surfacer by adapting it for hand trimming and fitting tenons to mortise holes and to centre the tenon between the outer faces of the stock back in 1980. Today others have adopted this method for perfecting their tenon saw work. So think tenoner, recessor, surfacer, and do not stop there. I am sure there is more that this tool can help to accomplish.

For the main part of our work we use the router plane for surfacing the bottom of grooves and housings or other depressions parallel to the surface of the work. There are many applications in pattern making, cabinet work and, in fact, almost all kinds of woodworking that call for these hand tools. They are particularly practical for routing housing dadoes for shelves and also many other types of housing that require exact depths. I use them for housing all of my drawer backs so the draw can cantilever when pulled all the way for access to the back. Stair stringers route readily to a level and consistent depth, ready for the treads, and then too the recesses for pieces of hardware. It is not possible to show all these possibilities, but the path to discovery will prove their inevitable value.

By now I hope you can see just how essential the hand router is to woodworking in general but especially in fine woodworking and furniture making. Routing recesses and levelling the reception areas for inlays can be difficult without them and they far surpass recessing with power routers when it comes to personal and project safety.

Chiseling out recesses usually leaves the recess bottoms somewhat uneven and generally inaccurate, and the hand router readily adds that final perfecting touch. It is fast, of course, and it is often much faster than setting up power routers for many operations, especially for individual recesses.

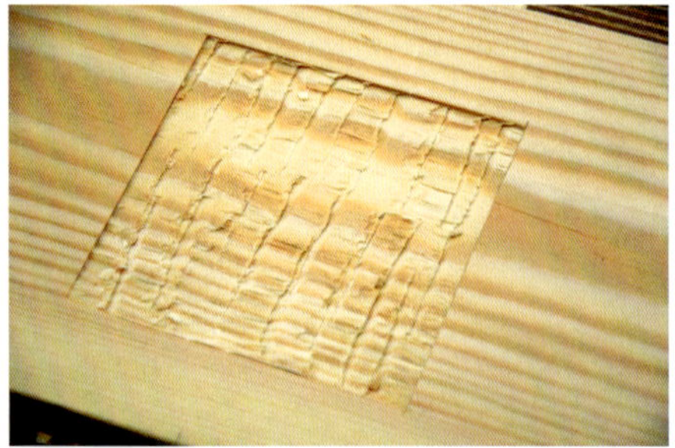

Level one; Surface after chisel cuts.

Level two; Surface after routing with square cutting iron.

Level three; Surface with refining cuts with square cutting iron.

The refined level after using the spear-point cutting iron.

Routers basically offer a planing cut to the surface of wood. They operate, as any plane does, by supporting the plane iron at a fixed height in relation to the sole. As you move the plane forward into the wood, the cutting iron engages and removes thin shavings to an even level and a controlled thickness. The chief difference between this plane and other planes is that the sole allows a protruding blade to cut to increasing depths, by incremental adjustments, and, at the same time, maintaining the surface area surrounding the cut at the same level. The even depth of recesses relies on the registration of the plane's sole to the original upper-level, outer face of the wood. The sole spans the new recess work and allows the cutter to level within the recess.

They do work well and especially so if you follow the methods given here to fine tune them for use. Rarely will you find one perfected in this way but, with an hour or so at the workbench, you will own a stunning router that I'm sure you will reach for, as I do, throughout the day. I think it is important to remember that this tool will often compliment any work you do with a machine router and you may want to own one just to refine the cuts left by the machine.

The Stanley #71-style Router Plane

The most common production-made hand router plane is the Stanley #71, followed by the Record version, which arrived when the patent ran out and they gave us the Record #071. They are almost identical, with the Stanley in typical nickel plating and the Record painted blue. Since then, at least two modern makers have started producing their own versions based on the Stanley original, without really altering the design but improving the engineering standards. As far as performance and functionality goes there does not seem to be much, if any, difference. This proves the efforts of the original designer to circumvent every problem surrounding the use of the tool and its relationship to the wood, the user, and the tasks it was designed for. The Stanley and the Record are basically one and the same tool under different maker names. As far as shape and size goes they are the same. Other modern makers have redesigned and reconfigured certain components but they are either essentially the same tool or only slightly different in size and shape. The instructions given here work for all the metal cast router planes I have come across.

Here are the Stanley and Record models held together, showing that they are virtually identical.

The level of smoothness you can achieve within a recess using any standard #71-style router plane, and indeed most others, is quite remarkable once you have refined the tool and, in particular, the cutting iron.

Hand Router Developments

Most router planes follow the same basic template, designed purely to facilitate the direct needs of the user. These include the ability to micro adjust the depth minute-by-minute to progress the deepening of a recess or lowered surface. Modern makers use exactly the same method, developed by Stanley in their last plane type, the #71, and they keep to a similar sized footprint.

Almost all of the metal cast routers, old and new, use Stanley's screw mechanism, which is a simple threaded stem that stands up from the cutter post (H), which then holds a knurled adjusting nut (B). The adjusting nut fits into a recess in the cutter (N) that lifts and lowers the cutting iron to any depth needed. A collar clamp, surrounding the whole assembly (D), then locks the cutting iron to the cutter post. Simple and very effective. There is a further schematic drawing on page 262, which may be of further help in part identification.

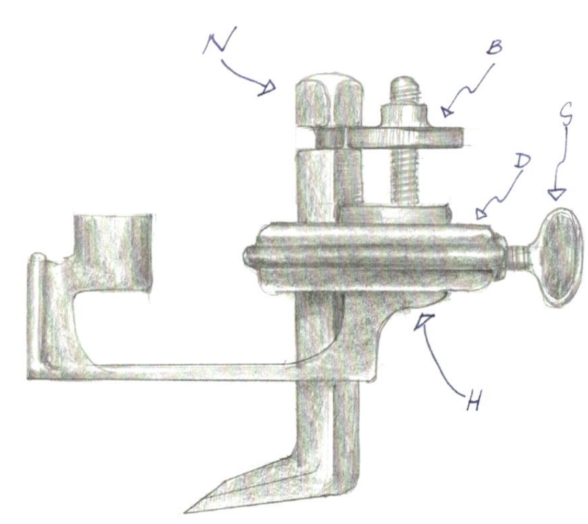

Until you get used to all-metal routers they can seem a little awkward, especially when it comes to loading the cutting iron into the collar and locating it into the screw nut adjuster, but you soon get used to it and load it more readily.

This leads me to a development in the Stanley version, which I think many might not see or understand at first glance. The cutting irons in the Record and Stanley models present the stem of the cutter into a 'V' channel, cast into the cutter post (H), and angled at 45-degree presentation. The advantage of this is the automatic locking of the back vertical corner of the cutter into a channel, which then ensures perfect vertical alignment of the stem of the cutting iron. One modern maker adopted it in their design but improved on it by adding a spring-loaded pressure point inside the clamp collar to assist with loading. Regardless of the model, the 'V' also helps guarantee that the underside of the cutting iron, when sharpened accurately, aligns parallel to the sole of the plane because there is not even the slightest lateral slippage.

The Parts to the Stanley #71 and Record #071 Router Planes

Note:
Letters in parentheses refer to the schematic drawings on either page 258 or page 262.

CUTTING IRONS

Cutting irons are made of high grade carbon steel, hardened, tempered, and ground ready for sharpening. Stanley provided graduated markings in 1⁄16" (1.5mm) increments for the first 1" (25mm) on the side of the cutting iron which help you to keep track of measurements used and then duplicate a depth elsewhere in the work and also to approximate depth adjustments before final setup. Both Stanley and Record provided their routers with three cutters (N), ¼" (6mm) and ½" (13mm) router cutters and a 'V' shaped spear-point cutter called the smoothing cutter because it is used for smoothing. All cutting irons provide a recess to receive the adjusting screw nut (B) and allow adjustment of depth, according to the work. The cutting irons can be held to both the front and back of the cutter post (H) by means of the clamp collar (D) and clamp thumbscrew (G).

VERTICAL ADJUSTMENT

To adjust the cutting iron to depth, loosen the thumbscrew (G), turn the adjusting screw nut (B) up or down to the required depth, and re-tighten the thumbscrew to lock the cutting iron to the cutter post.

SHOE

We use the shoe (F) to close the open throat at the fore end of the plane. This allows the plane to be used on the edge of narrow work if a closed throat suits the work better. The shoe attaches to the depth gauge rod (A) by means of a thumbscrew at the side of the shoe (E).

DEPTH GAUGE ROD

The depth gauge rod can be used in different ways but generally we use it as follows. We use the depth gauge rod when the plane is used as an open-mouth router. Setting the depth distance in this way means we do not need to constantly check for depth of cut. The depth gauge rod (A) is installed into the front pillar arch of the plane by inserting it through the hole. The rod can be used to control the final depth of the cut if the plane is used in its normal function as a router and with no shoe attached beneath the arch of the pillar. To do this, insert the rod and attach the shoe onto the top side of the rod and not inside the arch as normal. By setting the plane onto a flat surface and allowing the depth gauge rod to align with the sole of the plane, the distance between the top of the pillar arch and the shoe can be set by measuring the difference and locking off the setscrew on the side of the shoe. Leave the rod loose in the hole in the arch by not tightening the setscrew, which would usually be used to secure the rod and shoe assembly to a fixed depth. You can now start routing in the normal manner but with the rod remaining loose. Increasing the depth adjuster to the cutting iron incrementally, as you would for general routing, rout down and watch as the depth gauge rod reaches the final depth, which is shown when the shoe hits the top of the arch. Notice too that one end of the rod has a smaller diameter, which allows you to use the rod in a narrower groove.

FENCE

The adjustable fence (L) has a straight edge that allows the cutter to run parallel to an edge for straight work, such as grooves and housing dadoes. The opposite end is used for curved work.

Grooves in the sole of the plane receive the fence and keep it aligned.

The fence can be fastened to either side of the face of the sole (K) depending on the need and is locked in place by a setscrew and washer (M).

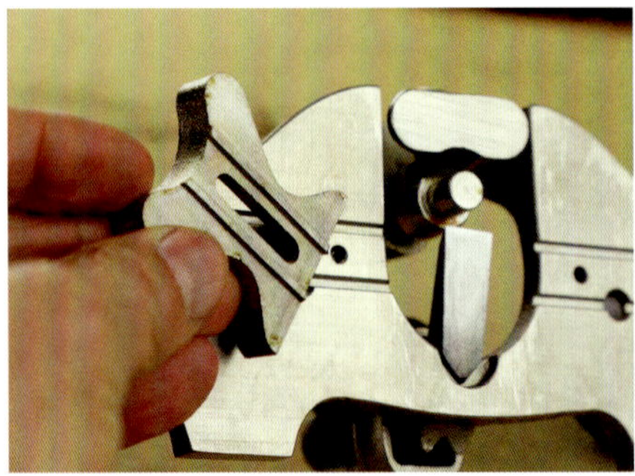

KNOBS

The two hardwood knobs (J) are fastened to the plane body by means of the knob bolt (I), which screws into threaded upstands in the sole.

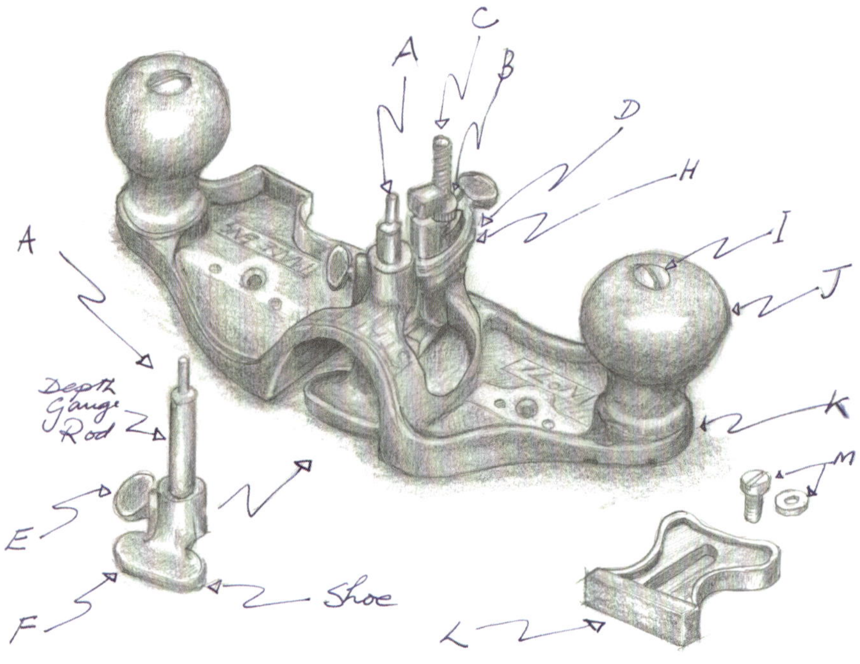

Using the Fence and Guide Post

The tool comes with additional features, as you have seen, enabling different functions for the plane's use. The fence fits to the underside of the plane and its two edges are shaped differently. One end of the fence piece has a parallel, squarely rectangular edge. The opposite end has a two-point contact fence that facilities turns on the edge of curved work.

It is best to use the fence, when running the cutting iron along recesses in the edge of narrower boards, to keep the plane square and parallel to the work. In conjunction with the shoe the fence is especially useful when the walls of the groove are very narrow. Because of the horseshoe-shaped rise in the sole that separates most of the forepart of the sole into two side sections, the plane sole is effectively useless on narrow sections or edges of wood. On such narrow work, with none of the fore part registering the work before the blade, running grooves trips the plane forward because there is nothing to stop it from tilting in the direction of the cut when the cutting edge grabs the wood. Stanley developed the horseshoe shape to the front for a couple of reasons, including holding a depth gauge rod into the body of the plane which, in turn, holds the shoe to align this auxiliary section, level with the sole, filling in the gap between the two halves. This piece then rides the edge of the board, along with the flat of the rear of the plane sole. In addition, the depth gauge rod can be used on its own, without the shoe, inside a groove to align the blade and prevent the cutter from digging into the walls, whilst at the same time restraining the plane from digging any deeper than in fractional increments. This effectively works as an additional sole depth guide for grooved work and the rod itself has two diameters, one for wider grooves and one for narrow ones. We often use both the fence and the depth rod and shoe in conjunction with one another to ensure alignment accuracy in the work.

Preparing the Square Cutters

Just as fettling a regular plane iron or chisel requires you to flatten and polish out the flat face only once, the same is true of the cutter for the router. Any subsequent sharpening is usually done on the bevel alone. Working the bevel evenly and carefully presents the cutting iron parallel to the surface; and it is here that I would stress the value of taking care to initialize the cutting iron so that the bevel is perfected to the underside of the cutting face. To do this, the underside of the cutting iron must first be perfectly ground and honed parallel to the face of the sole of the plane along its long axis. Once this initialization is done it need never be done again. When you start to look at the underside of the foot-shaped cutting iron you will notice that it angles upwards and away from the cutting edge. This might seem a flawed perspective but it actually makes sense; you cannot present the cutter to the work without a relief on the underside of the cutter. If the underside were level it would ride the surface of the wood. Stanley and Record have quite a steep angle to the underside of the blade; others less so. Because of the relief, the front cutting edge of the blade is affected by the top bevel, which must be square to the end. Too much tilt to one side of the bevel or the other lifts or lowers one side of the actual cutting edge. If we could present the underside of the cutter squarely and parallel to the underside of the plane and the surface of the wood, we could skew all we wanted and not affect the presentation.

We must therefore be very careful in preparing the cutting iron for work, otherwise the surface being addressed will never run parallel to the outside face of the wood. The best way to establish a line to work to for the top bevel of the cutter is to start with the underside first. Load the cutter into the plane and set the iron as close to level with the sole of the plane as possible, with only the tiniest protrusion past the sole face. Here I first offered the plane blade to the wood so that I could check for the alignment of the blade to the sole. You can see that the blade takes a deeper cut on the right.

"*The best way to establish a line to work to for the top bevel of the cutter is to start with the underside first*"

I now take the plane and place it carefully on the coarse or medium abrasive plate and move it back and forth lightly on the surface. I have never had any problem but you can put some masking tape on the sole of the plane to protect it if you wish. The goal is to use the shine, created by abrading steel, as a guide to check and, if necessary, slightly change the shape of the underside of the blade to correct the alignment. As soon as the iron traces the abrasive, lift it from the surface and look at the underside of the cutter. A bright area should appear on the cutter right by the cutting edge. If the line is narrow and parallel, the cutter is aligned well and presented correctly and all further sharpening and remedial work can be carried out. Notice, in the picture, how the white lines of abraded metal reflect to show that, in this case, the blade is out of square. To correct this, when I offer it to the abrasive I must press a little more heavily on the side that shows the wider band of light.

The actual cutting edge, created by the new minor bevel on the underside, will be removed by abrading the flat face of the underside of the cutter. This means that somewhere between the top bevel and the underside you must create, working first on the underside and then from the bevel, a leading edge that is parallel to the sole face of the router. Once we have the underside of the cutter corrected it generally never needs doing again and the rest is easier but still exacting.

Placing the underside on the abrasive we now flatten the surface to as near dead flat as possible and this can then be abraded to between 600 and 1200-grit. It is not generally necessary to go beyond this level of abrading and, because the angle of presentation to the work is so shallow, it is best to stop here. My experience has shown that any polishing out of this face tends to round over the very cutting edge and especially the corners. I find it totally unnecessary.

Now the underside of the cutting iron is abraded square.

Once this is done, you must work on the top bevel only and it will not usually be necessary to work on the underside ever again. The top bevel is always awkward but holding the blade sideways and rubbing the bevel along the abrasive plate now refines the bevel and you can sharpen to any level you prefer. Most router work can be finished at 600 to 1200-grit even for the finest work.

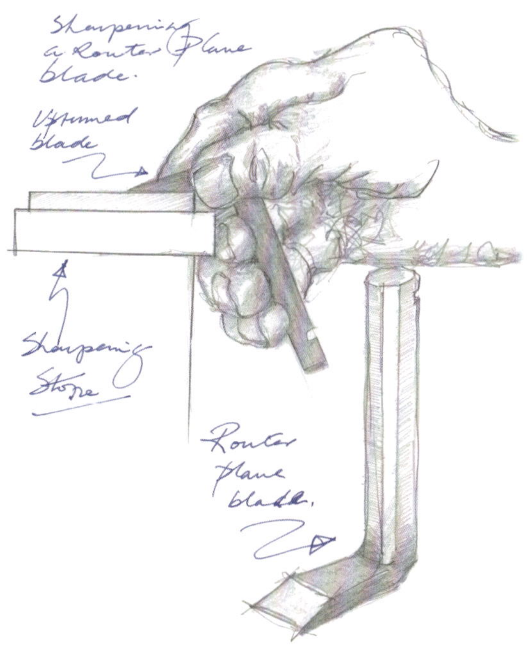

Testing it out after this is simply a question of working it on the surface of the wood again. The square-across surface fibres should be cut evenly. Micro-adjusting is usually as simple as returning the underside to the diamond plate and pressing one side or the other, for just a few strokes, on the finest level.

Visually the iron looks parallel to the plane's sole but the only way to test it is on the wood.

Here you can see the initial cut on the right-hand side and the cut made after correction on the left.

Wooden Router Planes and Tap Adjustment

It is always assumed that better engineering and mechanical adjusters improved our lot; I could argue both ways but, because of my working experience and through examining the work of my forebears, I do not believe this to be the case. Mechanical threads do ease adjustment but pinched adjustment, which can be found in some wooden-bodied router planes, where we loosen the locking set screw holding the cutter and then pinch the cutter to adjust it, works remarkably well. You can pinch to adjust this type of router by a minute amount easily and I find they work equally to some of the more elaborate routers. I think it is also true of wedged routers too. A quick tap to the plane body in the right spot shocks it back a thousandth of an inch and tapping the end of the cutting iron sends it deeper by the same thousandth.

The router referred to disparagingly as the 'old woman's tooth' or 'hag's tooth' is a router that houses a plough plane iron or a chisel instead of a purpose made foot-shaped cutting iron. I only name it here so that you will know what it refers to when you see it. They work fine and, when set and sharpened correctly, give the type of clean surface we might want for veneer, inlay and so on. It is also good to remember that, with these router types, it is much easier to align the cutting edge of the cutting iron parallel to the sole face. Generally the mortise that houses the cutting iron is wider than the iron, which allows lateral adjustments to be made.

We adjust these planes using the same hammer-tap tapping method used generally on all wooden-bodied planes; where we tap on the iron or plane body to set the depth of cut. Once the blade is tapped we tighten the wedge against the iron by tapping the end of the wedge. To loosen the wedge we use the hammer to drive the blade down into the throat. Because the cutting iron is tapered and fatter at the throat than the top end, driving the cutter loosens the iron and the wedge.

We can also use the cross-pein hammer to micro adjust wedge tightness but taking care not to damage the wood.

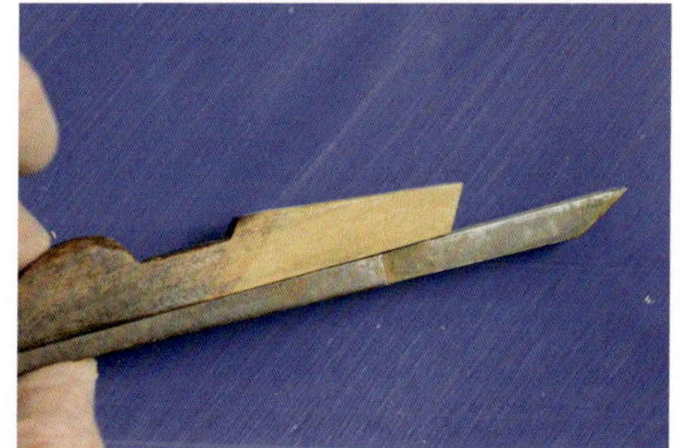

This image shows the wedge countering the wedge shape of the cutting iron as it is arranged within the plane body.

Small Routers

Small hand routers resolve issues in confined spaces both for accessing the work and also working within smaller recesses and joints. They provide an alternative tool to their larger counterparts, that is true, but it is also surprising how well they will work for larger areas too. These routers often measure 3-4" (75-100mm) in length. For many years I relied on Stanley router #271 but then switched to the bronze one, made by a friend as a first prototype in his adventure into plane making. None of these have fine adjustment mechanisms but then they are not really necessary because it is actually simpler to move the cutter by slackening the knurled nut or thumb screw, finger-pinching the cutting iron and then locking it off.

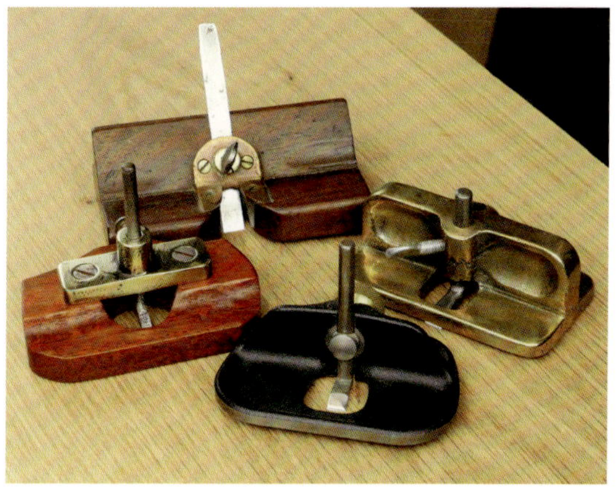

I have found that round stems to the cutting irons often slip under pressure in the cut. Correcting the flaw takes but a few strokes with a flat file to file a flat edge on the back of the stem. The steel is usually mild so they file readily. The setscrew can then set against the side of the flat-filed stem cutter. This remedial work gives surprising rigidity to the cutter.

Do not hesitate to make your own router from a section of wood, a small threaded bolt, and an allen key ground to shape. These work well.

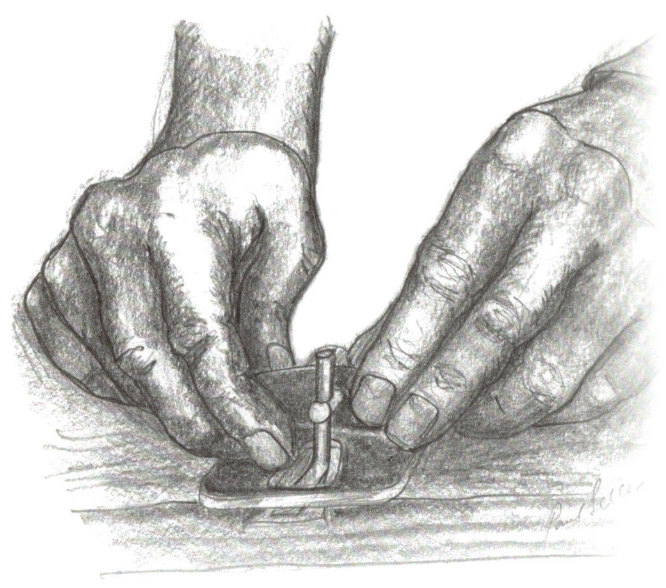

What Are Pointed Blades on Router Planes Used For?

At first glance, this might look much more specialised than it really is and, though it might be handy, it is not necessarily essential. This is what was described as the smoothing cutter in the original Stanley leaflet accompanying the plane I have from the 50s or 60s. This is exactly what this blade works great for; smoothing the bottom of recesses.

The angled presentation, either side of the centre of the spearpoint, provides a sheer cut to the action at the cutting edge and, by manipulating the plane according to the grain encountered, the user can effectively address just about any grain. The end result is a level and smooth cut, which effectively improves on that provided by the square-edged cutters. This is particularly ideal in some situations such as inlays, for instance. Most of the time and for most tasks, the square-edged cutters work satisfactorily and so it is not necessary to install a spear-point. Visually considering the appearance of the cutter, it does look as though the spear-point might dig into the walls or surface being refined but that is not usually a problem at all.

Modern Makers Unite but Disconnect With the Past

Modern-day makers of the router plane sized their planes to the same or similar footprint of the Stanley #71 and Record #071 planes but they have, as yet, omitted the depth rod accessory and adjustable shoe for attaching to the arched front of the plane. It is clear that the original maker felt that there was sufficient need for this to be included, even in the improved model, so you may want to consider this when you are looking for a hand router.

I have used modern-made planes with and without incurring problems but I do like the depth gauge rod for additional versatility from time to time. We use it to ensure alignment to the rim of a recess or along the length of a groove so that the side of the cutter does not undermine the edge of the cut. The adjustable shoe is used to span the edges of boards that are narrower than the opening in the arched edge. One modern maker offers a flat soled router plane as well as the split soled model, emulating the Stanley version of the #71. But, of course, this means buying two plane types instead of one. It is easy enough to add the wooden sole for spanning in narrow-edge work and for general work too. This improves performance and, of course, costs almost nothing no matter which plane type you buy from which maker. Having said that, some of the modern planes do not offer provision for screwing a wooden sole to the plane so that is an obstacle you will have to overcome if you wish to do this.

Underside view of the shoe in line with the sole.

Use a steel straightedge to align the shoe with the sole.

Here you can see the application of the shoe in place.

Adding a Wooden Sole

The addition of a wooden sole, roughly similar in size to the existing sole, does improve performance. I used a ½" (12mm) piece of hardwood and added 1" (25mm) to each end and placed the plane on the wood to determine where the hole should go.

Bore two 1" (25mm) holes side by side but overlapping to give room for the cutting iron and then clearance to clear the hole.

Then use a rasp or a chisel to remove the mid-waste.

Screw the plane to the sole and if the screws protrude through the wood cut them and file them flush.

Making an Extender

Making an extension to lengthen the sole of the router adds new functionality to any basic model. Many years ago I began using the router for surfacing the faces of my tenons because I wanted an exact surface, parallel to the outside faces of my rails. Provided my materials are not twisted, I can achieve a perfect surface on my tenons. The technique creates exceptional surfaces and the exactness means untwisted doors and much more.

This works well on shorter tenons of up to around 1 ½" (38mm) long but, when the tenons are longer, the router tends to tip with the unequal forces being applied over the extended distances because leverage, in these cases, is against us. I have developed an extender to the sole of the router to increase leverage at the hold-down end on the face of a rail. Whatever length you add to the extender increases the ability to overhang to any length you need as you apply the different pressures. This is really determined by the length of the tenon.

As most tenons are rarely longer than, say, 4" (100mm) the extender I am using, at 13" (33cm) long, takes care of all of my needs. My extender is simple enough to make with a piece of plate metal like aluminium or some other rigid material such as heavy perspex (plexiglass US), sign board, MDF or plywood. I devised mine to fit an existing router some years ago, using high-grade aluminium that I salvaged from a scrap dealer. It is ¼" (6mm) thick and the same width, front to back, as the router plane. An elongated section of wood, around ½" (12mm) thick, works for this too, as long as it is flat and true. For mine, I tapped the aluminium to receive the screw thread of one the router knobs so I could remove either knob (depending on left- or right-handed use) and relocate it in the plate. Two set screws through the existing plane body secure the plane to the plate. If tapping is a problem you can pass screws through the plate and use nuts and washers on the topside of the plane.

The tenon shown here is quite large at 6" (152mm).

Using the Router Plane

Most of the time the router plane is used for housings and recesses. I am going to discuss some of the ways the router can be used but first I want to give you a brief safety warning. Because the sharp blade of the router plane is somewhat hidden underneath, you have to make an effort to remember that it is sharp and can still cause damage to you and your work. Personal safety concerns mostly surround the very corners of the cutting edge. These corners are often quite exposed and are always extremely sharp. Get used to handling the plane by the handles and the hands will then be on the opposite side to the cutting edge. The time for concern is mostly during setup when the hands are on the metal sole and you want to measure depths and set distances.

The wood itself is always subject to the greatest pressures of all. The sole of the plane, even if it is a wooden sole, can damage the surface of the workpiece, especially if particles of routed material get in between; this, of course, happens minute-by-minute. Lift out and check regularly and be sensitive to feel and watch for this as you work. If you are working on an enclosed recess, with walls ahead of the cutter, make certain no pieces of material are between the fore edge or corner of the plane and the rim of the hole as this damages the corners by bruising.

HOLDING THE ROUTER

Using different handholds increases sensitivity ranging from a full fisted grip to partial fist and finger to total fingers in some cases.

These three images show increased levels of sensitivity, which we require for different aspects of the work and we change grip accordingly.

TENON SURFACING

I use my router for surfacing tenon faces just about all the time. Using this perfects my ability to fit the tenon exactly to the wall of my mortise holes. Whether I use the tenon saw or rely on chisel work to establish the initial tenon is immaterial. What matters is how I perfect them. I place the router over the tenon and press down on the outer surface of the rail with either preferred hand. Then I use a swivelling action to skim off the face close to the gauge line. As most tenons are centred in rails, we simply work evenly from both sides until the tenon fits the mortise.

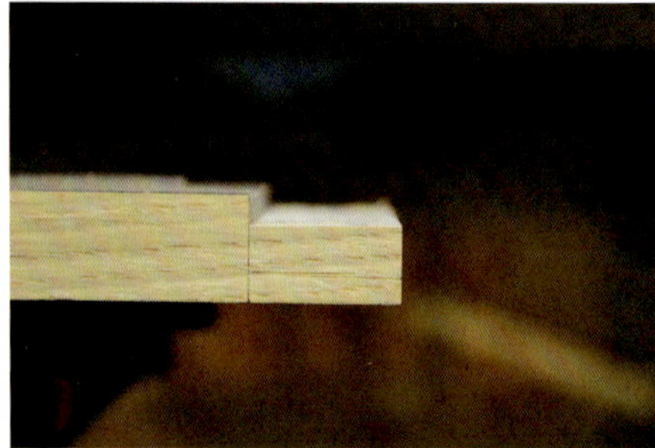

At the end my tenon face looks like this.

RECESS SURFACING

For recesses, I use one of two methods. I either remove the bulk of the waste with the chisel, using cross-grain paring cuts down to near the depth gauge lines, and then use the router to finish it or I go down incrementally using shallow passes with the router. The end result will be the same.

RECESSING HARDWARE

In this situation I have attached the wooden sole to the router sole and I am using it to delineate the depth for a hinge recess.

By using the flap of the hinge as the definitive depth to set the cutting edge of the router, I get pinpoint accuracy right from the outset. I have never seen anyone use this tool as a marking gauge or a cutting gauge but I started doing so decades ago and it works beautifully; it even gives me the knifewall cut I might prefer for some chisel chopping activities. Using it to mark my hinge flap depth in the wood, I can start my chisel work, remove the bulk of the waste, and follow through with leveling cuts with the router, retaining the same depth-setting ready to go.

Refining the recesses generally results in an ultra smooth surface within tight tolerances to an exact overall depth.

This pattern creates a perfect union of teamwork between chisel work, knife walls and using the router as a cutting/marking gauge for recess work.

Translate this then into creating inlay recesses and you start to understand the real value (and comparative safety) in using the hand router with the wooden sole attached. It offers the same advantage all-wooden planes have over all-metal ones but with the

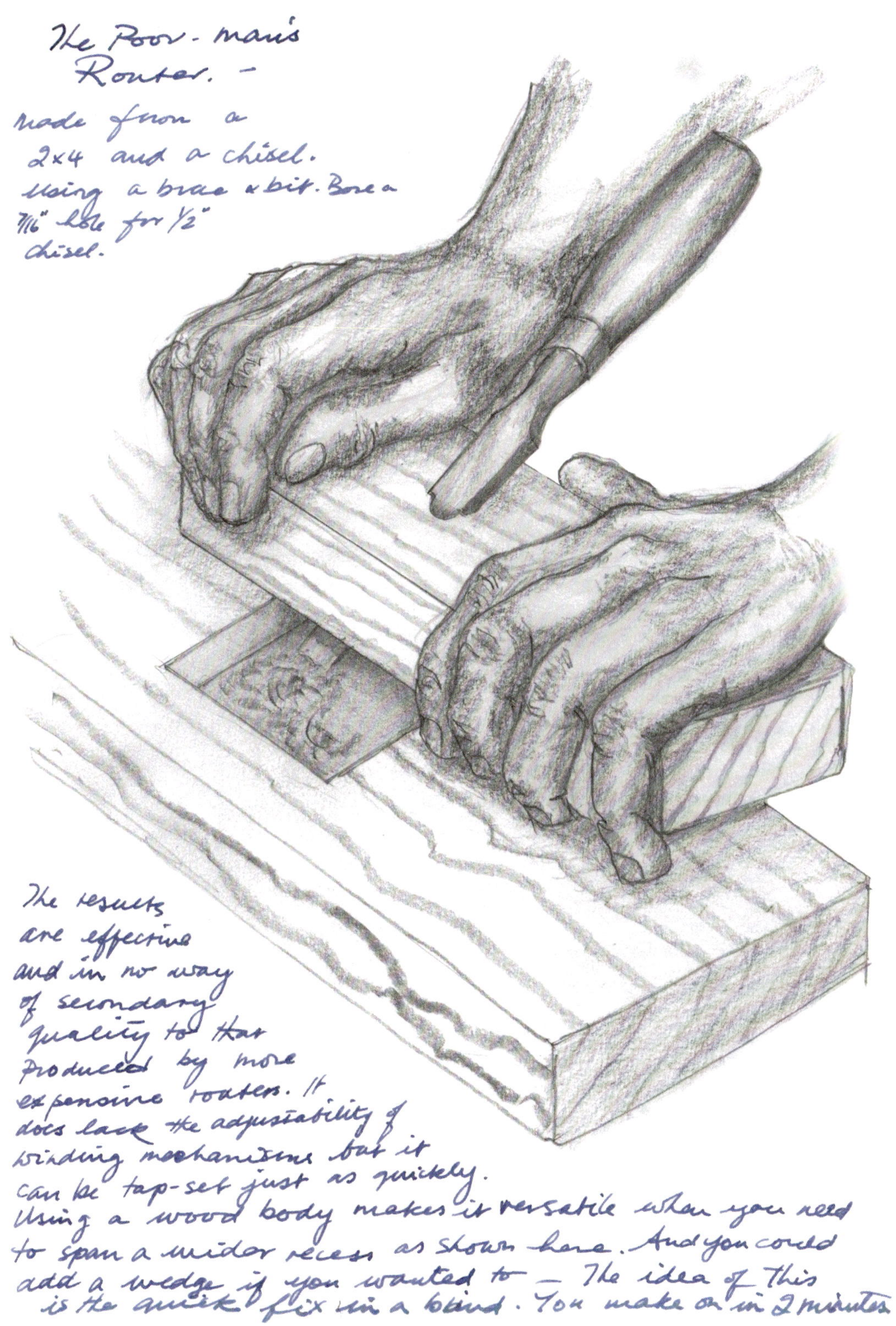
The Poor-man's
Router. -
made from a
2x4 and a chisel.
Using a brace & bit. Bore a
7/16" hole for 1/2"
chisel.
The results
are effective
and in no way
of secondary
quality to that
produced by more
expensive routers. It
does lack the adjustability of
winding mechanisms but it
can be tap-set just as quickly.
Using a wood body makes it versatile when you need
to span a wider recess as shown here. And you could
add a wedge if you wanted to — The idea of this
is the quick fix in a bind. You make on in 2 minutes

added micro-adjustment that makes the work dead-on accurate. You have seen some of the steps for hinge recessing here just as a guide and to encourage you to expand and explore the possibilities.

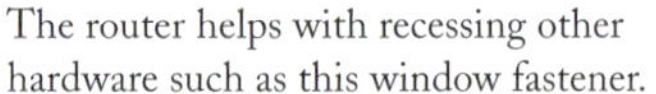

The router helps with recessing other hardware such as this window fastener.

The router helps in recessing locks which often require accurate recessing into two faces adjacent to the corner.

Making My Poor Man's Router

As a lad working the early days of my apprenticeship, a new woodworker like myself did not have a hand router plane and machine routers were barely on their way in. Skilled craftsman at that time could set hinges much faster without a machine or even a hand router and every recess was spot on. For the type of work we did back then, a router as a machine would have offered little value. The men showed me how to make the router I needed from a scrap of pine and a chisel in a matter of minutes. The poor man's router was born and I feel that, in most cases, this tool produces the same results as many sophisticated models.

Use any wood scrap 1 ¼" (32mm) x 2" (50mm) x 9" (228mm) long. Here I am using pine, which works fine, but spruce or any softwood also works well.

Pencil a centreline across the length…

...and then, about ⅓ from an adjacent long edge, mark the position of the start hole.

Bore a hole at an angle somewhere around 50 to 55 degrees. The hole diameter should be about 1⁄16" to 1⁄8" (1.5-3mm) smaller than the width of the chisel you want to use. The 1⁄16" (1.5mm) works well for chisels less than ½" (12mm) and 1⁄8" (3mm) for chisels larger than ½" (12mm). In this case I bored a 5⁄16" (8mm) hole for using a 3⁄8" (9.5mm) chisel.

Scallop a relief on the underside fore part of the block as an escapement for shavings. This is not essential but it helps keep the forepart clear.

Insert the chisel to be used into the hole, bevel down and centred in the hole, and ease it into the passage, trying to centre it as it passes through. Eventually this will need the extra force of a chisel hammer.

This is how it will look when the chisel is installed. Neatness is not really essential for this.

Set the required depth by trying it against either a depth gauge line marked on a scrap or by measuring. If you are taking the level down gradually, without more preliminary chisel work, simply set the depth to say 1⁄32" (1mm) and then take it down in similar increments of 1⁄32" to 1⁄16" (1mm to 2mm) at a time.

Depth setting is simply a question of forcing or tapping the chisel into the block or easing it backwards for a shallower setting. Because leverage against the fore edge and top side of the chisel keeps pressure on the chisel, the cutting depth usually remains to a constant and does not generally withdraw or deepen as you might expect.

Refine the shape for greater comfort if you have a lot of work to do using the router all at once.

Saws

The term 'saw' refers to a tool with specially formed teeth along the edge or perimeter of a plate of steel. The teeth of woodworking saws are designed to separate wood fibres by a little more than the thickness of the plate; this creates a passage for continuing cuts in order to remove wood and thereby separate one part from another. In most cases the saw cuts wood to size, ready for subsequent sizing and smoothing using planes. In hand work the function of the saw can be divided into two main categories—dimensioning the wood to various sizes and then creating joints for joining the parts together. Some saws are used more for dimensioning and others are used mainly for making joints. In both cases, handsaws and backsaws, the saws often cross over to do the same work but this is generally according to proportion. Handsaws cut large joints as well as dimensioning and backsaws dimension wood as well as cutting joints on a smaller scale.

Depending on the manufacturer, the steel used to make any plate for new saws will almost always come from rolled steel stock. Most of the older saws, however, were made from cast steel and often will have the method stamped somewhere in the saw plate or back to identify this as a part of the making process. Both cast and rolled steel produce good saws.

Saw Sizes and Terminology

The term 'handsaw' can, somewhat confusingly, be used to refer to all saws that are used by hand but also, more specifically, the large flexible-bladed saw that is used for dimensioning wood. To better identify the difference it is generally accepted that short saws with backs, known generically as backsaws, encompass joinery saws we call tenon saws, dovetail saws, and beading or gent's saws depending on their size. All of these saws are used by hand and so could be referred to as handsaws. However, for the sake of clarity, in this book, where I use the term 'handsaw' I will only use it to refer to the specific saw type and when I am talking about saws in general I will refer to them just as 'saws,' rather than 'handsaws.' Handsaws take over where the shorter backsaws stop. Backsaws

usually range in size from just a few inches long on up to 14" (36cm); the backless handsaws then take over in ranging from 16" (40cm) on up to 30" (76cm). In the first category of backsaws we have saws used mostly for dovetailing and smaller joint making, these are most commonly 6" (15cm) to 10" (25cm) in length and are generally known as 'dovetail saws.' The next size of backsaw then extends the size up to between 12" (30cm) to 14" (36cm). These saws we call 'tenon saws,' although they can be called by other names too such as sash saws and carcass saws. 'Tenon saw,' as a name, seems sufficient to me.

Western and Eastern Saws

Saws have evolved somewhat differently in different parts of the world. Over the decades, I have seen fine furniture coming from both Asian and Western cultures and I know that both styles of woodworking have long traditions of fine workmanship, fine standards, and high quality tools; and there is a place in our modern world for both styles; this choice need not be a matter of either/or. I have worked, and been taught, using mainly western saws. One of the biggest, and most apparent, differences between western and eastern saws is that western saws nearly always work on the push-stroke and eastern saws typically work on the pull-stroke. Because of this, the western saws are often made using thicker plate stock to give the saw enough rigidity to press into the cut without buckling and yet still remaining thin enough to minimize resistance. Added tensioning in the manufacture of the plate brings the saw up to even greater strength and resilience for the thrusting strokes western saws are famed for. The western saws allow for highly effective overhead overhand power cutting. By this I mean pressing down into the cut from above, using one or two saw horses to suspend and support the wood; or alternatively cutting into the wood from the front face, using the vise to hold the wood either face on or at an angle, as pictured below. Both methods are highly effective.

I favour western saws. This is perhaps just because it is what I am used to. That said, I am in no doubt at all that eastern saws, when they are are set up correctly and used by people who are adept in their use, do work very well. It is better, however, that I share my knowledge of the saws that I am most competent and comfortable using. Therefore, in this book I will focus entirely on the western saws that I am most knowledgeable about. If you have access to good quality eastern saws and instruction I am certain that you will be able to adapt parts of what I discuss here to those saws as well.

Avoid Saws With Super-hard Teeth

Saws, once made for a lifetime of use, are now made with built-in obsolescence by the introduction of impulse hardened teeth, which then limits them to perhaps a year or less of regular use before they must be thrown away or recycled. Many saws, both western and eastern, are made with these super-hard teeth and are made as disposable saws. A whole group of Japanese saws with these hardened teeth are now available. Retailers have become the primary source of sales information surrounding these saws. I suspect that many of these saws are made specifically for western markets and bear little resemblance to those used for millennia by Japanese craftsmen, making some of the finest examples of woodworking.

When students ask me which saws I recommend, my answer is simple. I want them to buy saws of a quality that lasts for decades and centuries, not disposable copies of ancient tools that demand they return to the supplier every few weeks or months. I believe everyone can sharpen their saws to professional standards after initial instruction, followed by some consistent practice. Consistent practice comes naturally through the necessity of sharpening from time to time; a ten-minute job every month or so.

Super-hard saw teeth are difficult, or impossible, to sharpen by hand. They are advertised as being long-lasting but, in fact, while a single initial sharpening may well last a long time, the saw must be thrown away as soon as the edges become dull.

Essential Saws

As with all sharp-edged cutting tools (and that is what saws are), it is not just a matter of choosing the right saws for the different tasks but knowing how to use them, what to use them for, and then, all the more importantly, knowing how to sharpen, set, and maintain them. There can be no doubt that new woodworkers struggle to understand the various dimensions surrounding saws. As you follow on from my introduction here, I hope to disseminate the information surrounding the saws I have relied on throughout my working life. Before discussing each individual saw I am going to outline my sharpening method, which works on most saws. Then, in the subsequent sections, I will discuss each type of saw:

Saw Sharpening

I grew up in an era when DIY saw sharpening was just about coming to a close. In my youth I could walk into most hardware shops with my saws, no matter the type, and a man behind the counter took a manilla parcel tag, attached it to the saw handle, and wrote any instructions on the tag for the 'saw doctor' to work to. The tag allowed for re-cutting new teeth into the plate, pitch changes for more or less aggressive pitch to the teeth, and various other tasks like these. The saw was left on a given day and was returned the following week, ready to go. The joiners I worked with mostly sharpened their own but occasionally they felt they would benefit from additional tweaking by what was then called the 'saw doctor.' I realised later that it was probably more the lack of an eye doctor for the older men, struggling with the small teeth, that sent them to the hardware shop. Once I learned to sharpen the saws, they would buy me a file every few sharpenings and that was my payment for touching-up their saws from time to time.

Those days are gone and the saw doctor has vanished from the streets of the UK and so it is even more important to learn to sharpen your own saws. Of all the tasks affecting woodworking generally, the one that seems to be the most intimidating for new people is that of sharpening saws.

The Need for Saw Sharpening Skills

It is not long after buying any saw, new or old, that you must learn to sharpen it. Sending it away for sharpening is prohibitively expensive but that is not the only problem. All saws dull through use over time and lose the crisp, sharp edge you need, without much forewarning. The work becomes more sluggish as the cut deepens and the cut becomes less crisp too. Also you will rarely find a saw sharpener, who is able to understand exactly what you want from your saw; custom saw sharpening is rare and almost never local. The cost of postage in both directions and then the cost of sharpening on top can soon mount up. On top of this, being without a saw, even for a day, would be totally impractical for me and I risk losing a favoured saw. The option of sharpening them myself then becomes the obvious answer. Once you have learned to sharpen, you are a few short minutes away from sharp teeth every time you need them. After an hour's practice, it is most likely you will be able to sharpen your saw for the remainder of your life. Beyond all of that, when you buy saws secondhand they are almost always dull. I have rarely bought a saw that was suitably sharp. This shows that people use saws until they stop cutting altogether and this is way past the level they should have been used to. I am in the habit of sharpening my saws regularly, even when they do not technically need it. I love that crisp edge to the saw and to my work and also the ease with which a sharp saw cuts. Once you have bought your saw it may well need some remedial work to bring it back to good working condition. This is often the case even if it is brand new.

Saw Files

To sharpen saws we use specially shaped triangular files, generally called saw files, triangular saw files, or three-square saw files. These are discussed on pages 43 and 44, where I give more detail on sizing. Filing the teeth means that we remove a layer of steel, to a uniform depth, to restore the angular corners to the profile of the saw teeth. The teeth will be profiled in one of two ways, as ripcut teeth or as fleam cut teeth, which are the patterns we identify for cutting along the grain and across the grain respectively. The terms 'fleam cut' and 'crosscut' can be used interchangeably to describe the tooth pattern for crosscut teeth.

Crosscut and Ripcut Saw Teeth

When you encounter saw sharpening for the first time you will need to consider the two main types of saws—the crosscut and the ripcut saws. The different types are specifically designed for two distinct areas of sawing; ripcut saws are for sawing with the grain and crosscut saws are for going across the grain.

Images of crosscut and ripcut teeth side by side (crosscut on the left).

When you look at ripsaw teeth and compare them with the fleam pattern (bottom), the difference between the two is quite obvious. The ripcut pattern seems simpler and is, perhaps, easier to understand and to achieve. By comparison the fleam pattern might seem more complex. I should say here that the advantage of sharpening smaller-toothed saws for crosscutting is so minimal that you will most likely follow the same practice I do and save the fleam pattern for sharpening teeth on larger saws. I keep one of my handsaws for cutting across the grain, using the fleam pattern.

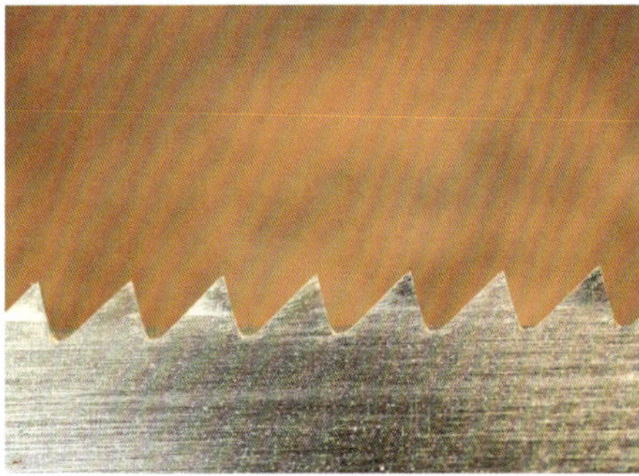

Ripcut teeth are filed straight across to produce square-edged, chisel-like teeth. They can be sharpened from one side only, with the slight bend, called set, in the teeth being added or reinforced by the sawset.

Just to simplify your understanding, rip cut teeth are sharpened square across and perpendicular to the face of the plate. We generally sharpen these from one side of the saw only, but we can sharpen from both sides by skipping every other tooth as we pass down one side and then turn the saw around and file those we skipped on the other side. This means that the burr formed on the outcut of the file strokes is equal on each side and the burr is formed on the non-cutting facet of the teeth—the inside of the teeth. My preference is to work from one side as all of the burrs break off with the first pass of the saw into the wood anyway.

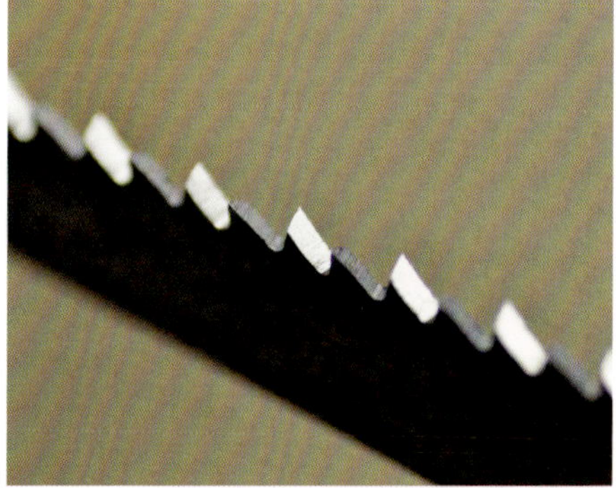

Fleam teeth must be filed from both sides of the plate to produce the pointed tip to each of the teeth. Doing this means that each tooth is bevelled on the inside which allows the saw to sever the grain on the outside of each tooth so that it can cut the grain crossways.

Ripcut teeth are filed 90 degrees to the saw plate.

These newly filed teeth show the rough burr to the outcut.

RIPSAW TEETH

Ripcut saw teeth, when you look directly from the side, show only a flat face with no facets, in contrast to the crosscut saw. We shape and sharpen ripsaw teeth to what has come to be called chisel tips, in contrast to the teeth used with the crosscut saw, but the sawing action for both saw types is generally the same. The crosscut saw uses bevelled cutting edges to shave the side walls of the cut. However, with the ripsaw, the two flat faces that create the cutting edges (the front and back of each tooth) shave out the face of the wood to the width of the cut in a paring action; the set of the teeth determines the width of the cut, which we call the kerf (see page 304). Depending on the thickness of the wood and the presentation angle of the saw to the wood itself, the saw teeth pare-cut long grain shavings that peel and curl wood inside the gullet and carry these shavings away with each forward thrust of the saw. Usually, because rip-cutting with the grain is easier, the teeth of ripcut saws are slightly larger and take a bigger gullet cut than crosscut saws. Saw teeth vary in size and ripsaws are usually available with teeth that are from 3-20 PPI (points per inch). Some ripcut saws are available up to 48 PPI but these are used mostly by modellers.

“

We shape and sharpen ripsaw teeth to what has come to be called chisel tips, in contrast to the teeth used with the crosscut saw, but the sawing action for both saw types is generally the same

”

CROSSCUT TEETH

To best identify the difference between ripcut and crosscut saws look at the teeth from the side. Crosscut teeth show three faces to each alternate tooth and you see a pinnacle point formed by the two sides you can see and the side you cannot see. When the saw teeth are small, smaller than 8 PPI, we can easily use ripcut saws for cutting across the grain but they are still called ripcut pattern teeth, even when they are being used for crosscutting. The reason this works is because we effectively create a shearing cut using the ripsaw tooth pattern. The crosscut tooth pattern is very different in shape to the ripcut pattern. The teeth of crosscut saws are shaped by filing the inside of each tooth with two bevels to create a three-sided point, similar to a diamond- or spear-pointed knife, and these are generally referred to as fleam teeth. Having each of the teeth facing into one another this way creates the unique dynamic of slice-cutting across the grain fibres with parallel knife-like cuts and so creates two parallel walls. The severed fibres between these two 'knifewalls' crumble into small particles as sawdust with each forward thrust and the particles fall from the cut beneath the wood on the outcut, accompanying the thrust of the saw. Saws are available with different sized teeth and the available ranges vary between ripcut and crosscut saws. Generally, crosscut saws are available in 6-12 PPI.

Do You Need Rip and Crosscut Saws?

First of all it is good to remember that all saw makers want you to buy two saws in every saw type and size they make. It makes good business sense to persuade you this way. I suggest that you buy only their ripcut saw pattern at first. Use the saw sufficiently long enough to get used to it and break it in - I would say a month of daily use or the equivalent over a longer period. That way you get to know its idiosyncrasies. Ripcut the tenon cheeks with the larger tenon saw (14 PPI) and use the ripcut dovetail saw (16 PPI) for crosscutting the tenon shoulders. You have lost nothing by practising exactly what craftsmen did for centuries this way. I almost never use any crosscut backsaw for any of my work, even though I own several for the research work I do. Remember that, by using a knifewall, you can guarantee crisp crossgrain shoulder lines (see page 343).

However, you will need a specific crosscut saw if you are making cuts across the grain that necessitate a saw with teeth bigger than around 8 PPI. This will often mean that the only dedicated crosscut saw you need is in the larger handsaw or perhaps a larger-toothed tenon saw too. You will also need a dedicated crosscut saw if you are cutting plywood and other such materials because the alternating layers are cut better with fleam teeth.

The Pitch on Ripcut Teeth

There are three angles to consider when presenting the file to sharpen ripcut teeth in any ripsaw; regardless of the size of the saw, the saw maker, the size of the saw teeth, or the name of the saw. Two of the angles are 90 degrees and the third angle can be varied according to task or according to preference. This angle is the one we call the pitch (also called the 'rake') and it is the angle to which we file the front of the saw teeth. The pitch determines how aggressively the saw cuts into the wood. If the front pitch of the tooth is steep, that is, near to vertical, then the teeth will cut aggressively – often too aggressively. By altering this to a lesser pitch, we create a less aggressive saw cut. The usual pitch from manufacturers is around 8 to 12 degrees out of perpendicular to the line of the saw teeth so that the front pitch of the teeth is 98 to 102 degrees or thereabouts. There is no hard and fast rule for this. We can lessen the pitch much more than this and the saw still cuts well. I want you to understand that the saw will cut at almost any pitch to the front of the teeth as long as it is within reason. The other two angles mentioned are both 90 degrees. So, the saw file files across the saw teeth at 90 degrees to the length of the saw plate, and also at 90 degrees to the width of the saw plate too; by that I mean the file is level and square to the plate in both directions. These angles are not rigidly critical and may vary a little with each hand stroke but this will not generally affect the saw noticeably in the cut or the quality of the cut.

This is a very high (aggressive) pitch.

This is the lowest (most passive) pitch of all.

90°

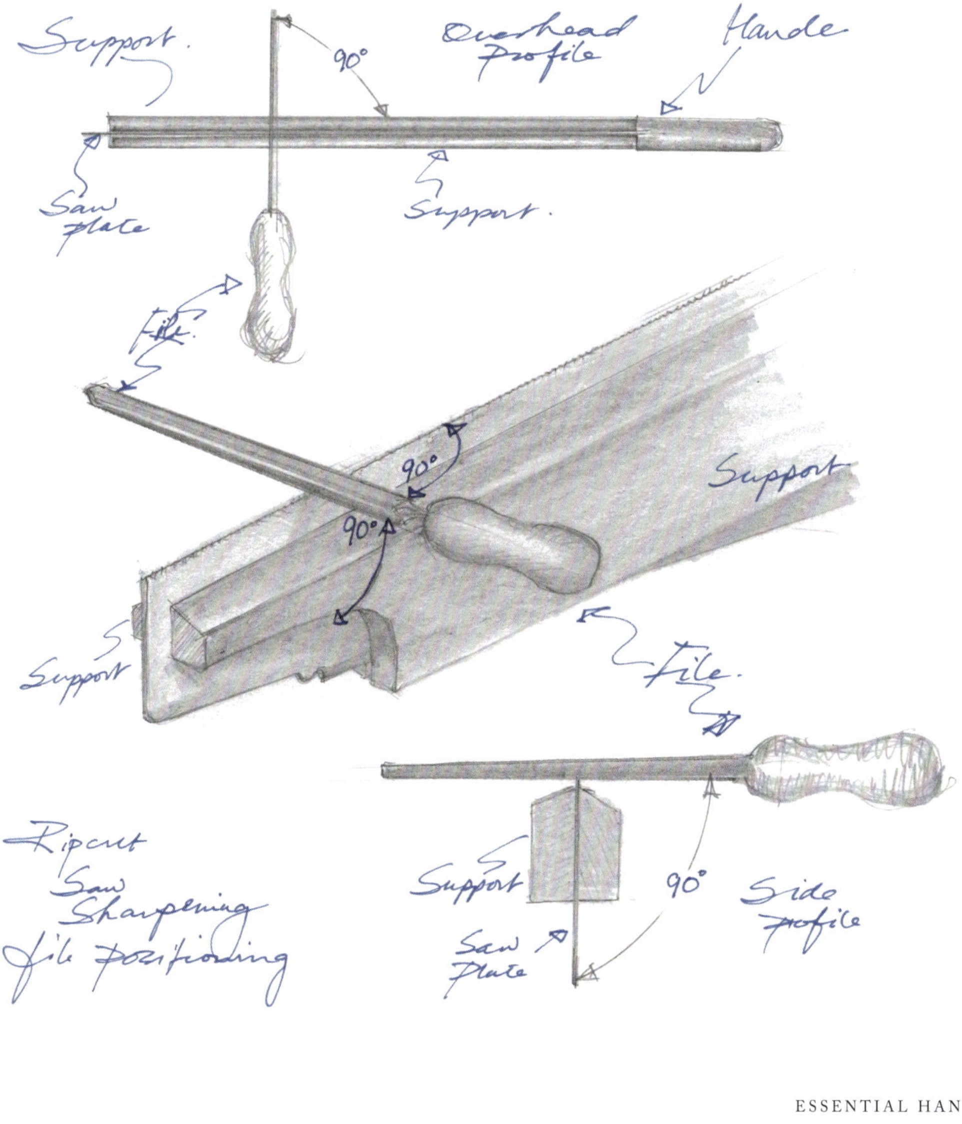

Support.
90°
Overhead Profile
Handle
Saw plate
Support.
File.
90°
Support
90°
Support
File.
Ripcut Saw Sharpening file positioning
Support
90°
Side profile
Saw Plate

Passive pitch. In this and the following images the saw handle is to the right and the toe end to the left.

More aggression. Here the file is tipped forward from the level-on-the-top position to steepen the pitch to the front of the teeth.

Most aggression. This time we ignore the top face of the file and look to the face against the front of the tooth. This is the most aggressive presentation.

The pitch can be anywhere between 0 and 30 degrees. Rotating the file forwards from being level across the top creates a steeper pitch to the tooth pattern. By this we can govern the amount of aggression we get to the teeth in the cut. The least aggression comes when the top of the file is level with the tooth line of the saw. By rolling the file and tipping the top face of the file slightly forward toward the toe end of the saw, the cut becomes more aggressive. A full roll forward means that the file face on the front of the teeth now becomes perpendicular to the tooth line of the saw. This is the most aggressive tooth pitch. The front pitch to the teeth also governs the back of the adjacent tooth because the file uses two adjacent faces in the gullet. The gullet in this case is the 'V' formed by the tooth cutter in manufacture, which is then maintained by the file we use to sharpen the tooth. The back bevel on the tooth is generally inconsequential to the front pitch as far as sharpness goes. The file faces are formed to an equilateral triangle and therefore the file creates a 60-degree 'V'.

Different Pitches Are Suited to Different Types of Sawing

As I have already explained, the front pitch of the tooth determines the level of aggression the tooth cuts at. In some saws I will use a perpendicular front face or something near to that vertical pitch. This would be for overhand ripping of a board or plank that allows me full power to bear down into the cut, applying the greatest shoulder and upper body pressure and thereby the highest speed in the cut. I would use this pitch on large-toothed saws of, say, less than 6 PPI. On smaller-toothed saws I will usually assume a less aggressive pitch and this is usually because I am cutting at the bench and in the vise. For this type of cutting the saw is often perpendicular to the face of the board so a perpendicular front to the tooth will usually be too aggressive because the teeth are more engaged.

Jig Guide for Beginning

After you have sharpened a few saws a few times you will be able to assess how the saw works in the type of work you do and then shape the teeth accordingly. It is not complicated to do this but, to get you started, make this simple jig I devised for beginners. The jig is used to help you hold the file at a fixed angle while you sharpen the saw teeth. You could make three or four with the different pitches we use the most. The different pitches generally are: 90, 98, and 120 degrees. The 98-degree pitch is standard, the 60-degree pitch is very passive. The aggressive 90-degree pitch is for an aggressive rip tooth. As the jig always aligns to the level of the tooth line, it makes clear the angle of file presentation.

To make the jigs we initially mark the wood to show the pitch we want. Here I am making the most common of all the jigs which gives me a 98-degree pitch.

To make the jig you will need a piece of wood around ⅝” (16mm) by ⅝” (16mm) by 2 ¼” (57mm) long (the measurements are actually fairly arbitrary).

1. Mark a line onto the wood at 98 degrees, square the line across the adjacent edge and then do the same to the other side remembering to reset the protractor to 82 degrees.

2. Bore a ⅛” (3mm) hole all the way through. The edge of the hole should line up with the angled line you have marked and it should be only just large enough to receive the tip of the file.

3. Use the saw to cut a wall along the 98-degree line you have already marked, about ⅛” (3mm) deep. This should line up with the hole you have bored. Flip over and follow the same pitch to the opposite side (if it was 98 degrees on the first side it will be 82 degrees on the other). This allows you to work with the same jig from both sides of the saw if needed.

4. Chisel into the sawn walls to create step-downs of about ⅛” (3mm).

5. Push the toe end of the saw file into the hole, aligning one flat face of the file to the saw cut and give a light tap to compress the fibres in the hole.

6. The walls of the hole will now be triangular like this.

Be careful; files are very brittle and fracture easily if pulled on too much. When you pull the file out it can snap. Also watch out for your face and eyes when you are pulling upwards. You may want to use an old file to shape the hole instead of a new one.

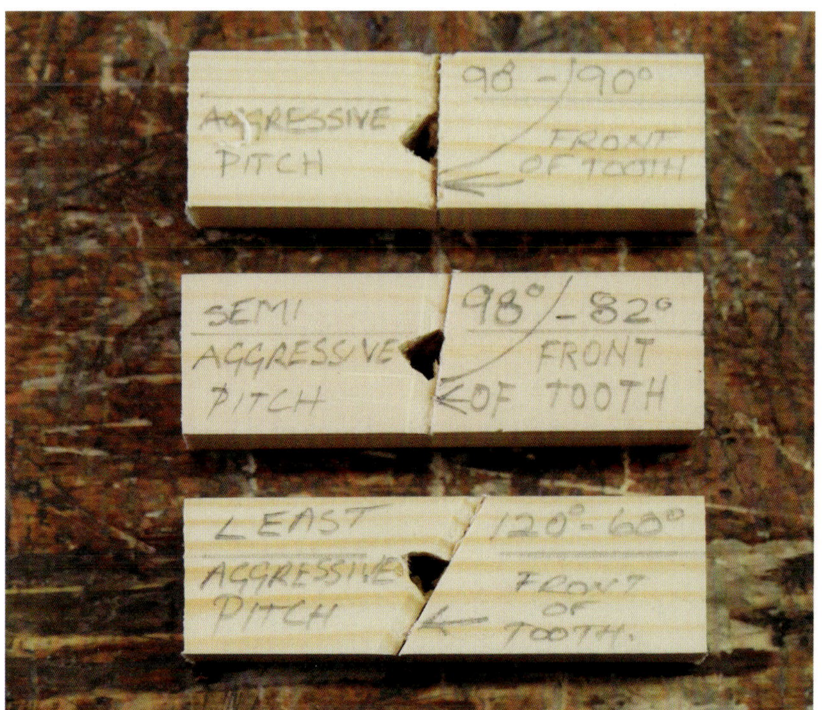

Here are the jigs I recommend for students, which help to get consistent results.

When you offer the file to the saw teeth simply align the top edge of the guide, by sight, to the tooth-line and all the teeth will be filed at the same pitch, from one end to the other. You can make additional guides as you develop your preferences for different saws.

Holding Saws for Sharpening

Regardless of the saw type, the saw plate must be clamped firmly before filing can take place, otherwise the plate flexes under the filing pressure. Make certain that the saw is fully supported as near as possible along the tooth line. As a general rule the extension above the clamp, holder, or chocks should be ⅜" (10mm) and no more, otherwise the saw flexes away from the file and the negative vibration causes uneven, ineffective filing.

Here the teeth are ⅜" (10mm) above the supporting saw clamp.

My simple split stick clamps readily in the vise and aligns both sides of the saw simultaneously as you clamp the vise jaws tight.

Sharpening Ripcut Saw Teeth

New saws are easier to sharpen because you still have the original pitch set by the maker to guide the file as it engages the gullet. In this case, it is just a question of choosing the right file size and pressing it in between the saw teeth so that two faces of the file engage the two opposing faces of the adjacent teeth. Sensitivity is the key to good sharpening and certainly not aggression or force. You must feel for both faces so that the lowest corner of the file reaches to the bottom of the gullet. If you are happy with this established pitch then you are ready to start filing.

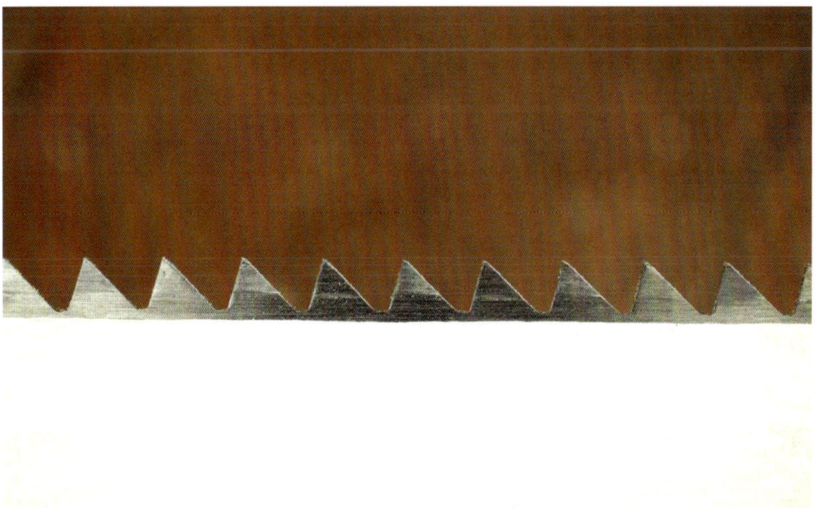

It is important to know that files do wear out and reach a point when they must be replaced. Some new files have higher fracture rates and fracture along the critical row of teeth on the narrow corners of the file. This prevents the large faces of the file from cutting and it can then only be used for narrow flat file work and not saw filing.

The small corner of the file should have teeth that look like this, with no broken sections.

We begin filing at one end and work consistently through each adjacent tooth, from that end to the other. Starting at the end helps us to keep track of where we have filed. No matter how dull the teeth, take a single stroke only. Until you have gained mastery in saw sharpening this gives the best approach. It will also help you to develop sensitivity and the saw may not need more than the one stroke anyway. You should only use the file on the push stroke and should disengage before drawing the file back. If the strokes you make create a fresh cutting edge at the tip of the tooth then the tooth is sharp and needs no more. All the strokes you take should be the same length and the same weight or pressure. This ensures a well managed and even depth of cut to each gullet and helps to maintain the evenness we need. If the faces to the saw teeth are shiny but not to the tip you will need to make a second or even a third pass but finish the row first and then go back and start over. This is the safest way. After you have learned to sharpen you will be able to better gauge how many strokes to take but, in the beginning, one stroke is the best way. With the file placed into the gullet, apply medium pressure to the file. The stroke should feel firm and productive but it may take a little time to interpret what you hear and feel from the vibrations. Maintaining the same pitch, apply medium pressure to the file at the tip and in the handle evenly, and make a single continuous pass into and through the gullet. It is important to establish a rhythm whereby we mentally gauge a measured length of the file stroke and also the amount of pressure we apply, according to tooth size and the thickness of the plate. In my view, no beginner should start out filing with teeth smaller than 16 PPI. It is all too easy to file out the whole tooth. This is especially the case on small-toothed thin-plate saws but do not be fearful, just careful.

For an easier start to your cut with a saw you can, for the first two inches or so at the toe end, have equal pitch to each side of the gullet and then adjust to a steeper and more aggressive angle. This gives you an easy start and can be done using the 120-degree guide.

Sharpening Crosscut Saw Teeth

The work we do in sharpening ripcut saws is good preparation for learning to sharpen crosscut saws too. Most of what I have written for ripcut sharpening can be applied to crosscuts, with the only differences being that you must sharpen crosscut saw teeth at an angle and you must sharpen every alternate tooth from each side of the saw plate. The filing strokes are very similar but at the two opposing angles, from each side of the saw plate. We create these teeth by filing into every alternate tooth gullet to form the two bevels to the teeth, using two of the file faces with the strokes we take. We cannot form these two bevels just working from one side of the saw plate, as we can with ripcut saw teeth. It must be done from both sides. Passing the saw file through the teeth sharpens the front of one tooth and the back of the adjacent tooth. That being the case, first we focus on sharpening each alternate tooth from one side of the plate and then we turn the saw around, end for end, and change the angle of filing to file from the other side. By filing alternate teeth, so that the bevels are inside the teeth, we place the actual cutting edges to the outside face-point of each tooth. This creates two parallel rows of counterpoised teeth and the saw passing into the cut forms a channel for the plate of the saw to pass into and through the cut in the wood.

The pitch of the teeth can be the same as we use on ripcut saws; we use a passive pitch for the first two inches of the saw and then follow the normal 98-degree front angle to the teeth.

You can sharpen any tooth size to a crosscut configuration but my recommendation is to sharpen only the saws dedicated for crosscutting as a dominant cut. Remember, I suggest that only saws with teeth larger than, say, 8 PPI need to be dedicated to crosscutting. Smaller saws can be sharpened to a ripcut and will work for cutting both with and across the grain. You may eventually want to change this and sharpen smaller-toothed saws to a crosscut once you have practised on larger-toothed saws and so adjust to your personal preference. To develop the fleam tooth pattern means that we file through the tooth gullet at an angle of 65 degrees. This action creates an angled 'V' between the front of one tooth and the back of the adjacent tooth. It is angling the file across the line of the plate that creates one half of the pinnacle tooth. With the full length of one side of the saw plate done, skipping every other tooth, we turn the saw around, end for end, and change the file presentation to 65 degrees the opposite way to sharpen the gullets we skipped.

Start out by facing the saw plate with the plate mounted in the saw chocks or vise, with the toe end of the saw on the left and the handle on the right. You can start at either end but my preference is to start with the passive rake at the toe end, the same as we do with the ripcut pattern, and work toward the handle end. First of all, you must look at the teeth to follow the existing pattern in the saw plate. The set to the teeth, if there is any, is important as a guide in this. You will be sharpening the back of the tooth leaning away from you. If this is the first time sharpening a saw with an existing crosscut tooth pattern then you can choose to follow the existing pattern or alter the rake to a more passive one by keeping the top face of the file level. We generally only do this to the first two inches on saws and then, for the rest of the teeth, change the pitch to match the existing pattern where the front rake is around 98 degrees. If you change the rake to the first two inches for a more passive start then the first file stroke in each gullet will seem abrasively harsh but the second stroke, and it will take two strokes per gullet to make a change, will be smoother. Place the file in the gullet with the tip pointed toward the handle end of the saw. As I said, you will be sharpening the back of the tooth leaning away from you and thereby the front of the tooth leaning toward you. The rest is easy. Skip the alternate gullets that counterpoise your current angle. Take a single stroke into each of the gullets, with a steady and level forward thrust following the angle existing in the gullet. Starting at the toe end you then continue on to the handle end of the saw, taking care not to miss a tooth gullet. When completed turn the saw around and change direction with the file to an opposite 65 degrees and do exactly the same to the other teeth; you will again be working from the toe end and work along toward the handle.

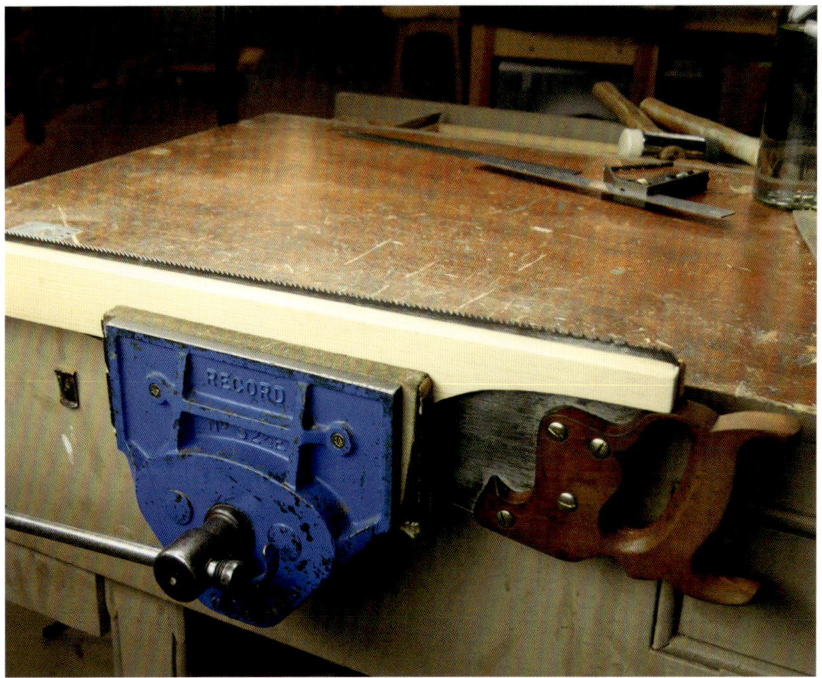

Depending on how worn and dull the saw teeth are, a single stroke to each side may not be enough to reach the pinnacle point of the teeth; still, you should take but one stroke and then move on to the next tooth. As you gain experience, you will be better able to gauge the number of strokes for uniform sharpening. Taking one stroke on every tooth and then repeating the whole process, if you do not achieve a pinnacle point on the teeth, is a safer way to start out. The single stroke from both sides may well be enough but you will only be able to tell when both sides of each tooth have been filed. If the tips are still rounded then start again from the side you are on and repeat the same filing action, turn the saw around and do the same to the other side. Using this method will give consistent depth to each gullet, which is very important. Depending on how dull or rounded the saw teeth are, the saw should now be sharp. If not then you have not yet reached the very tips of the teeth points. Repeat equally from both sides until you do and the saw will be sharp.

Consistent Filing

Consistency in file stroke direction, angle, pressure and length of stroke is ever important. Regardless of whether you are filing a crosscut or ripcut pattern, keep the length of the file stroke the same to each tooth gullet and generally this means using most of the length of the file. Apply even and equal pressure throughout each stroke, pressing the file fully down into the gullet and maintaining the same consistent angle. I suggest marking the saw holder with the 65-degree (for crosscut) or 90-degree (for ripcut) angle marks at 1" (25mm) intervals as a periodic guide to check yourself for angle as you progress down the length. Alternatively you can mark a board or piece of cardboard and lie it next to the saw as you file (see images, next page).

Saw Set and Kerf

After the teeth are cut into the saw plate to create the saw, the teeth are bent alternately, opposite to one another, along the full length of the saw, from tip to handle. This saw set needs to be maintained, or in some cases re-established, by using the sawset to slightly bend every other tooth from one end to the other and then bend the skipped teeth from the opposite side. This increases the passage width (or thickness of cut) of the saw as it cuts into the wood fibres. The term we use for bending the teeth this way is 'saw setting'. The sawset, along with its settings, are discussed in detail in the section starting page 53.

Saw kerf is the narrow gap created by the passage of the saw into and through a section or segment of wood. The distance between these two walls is known as the kerf, regardless of whether ripping or crosscutting and regardless of the size of the sections of wood being cut. The kerf is determined by the thickness of the saw plate plus the set of the teeth on either side, which can vary.

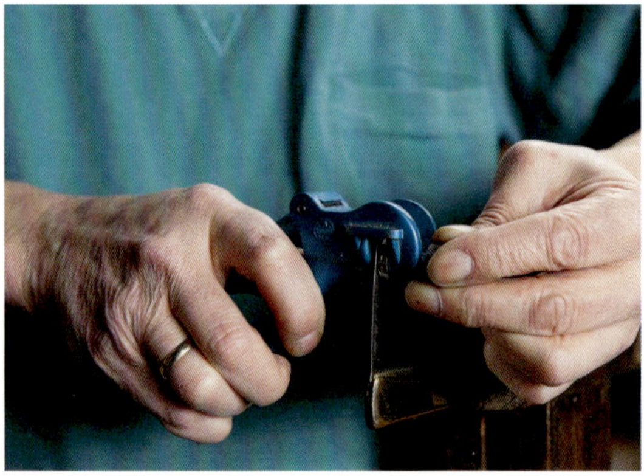

The set is generally adjusted according to the saw being used but, for most saws, the bend is relatively slight unless the wood fibres are wet or have a higher moisture content than usual. Saw kerf allows the free passage of the saw into and through the wood.

Generally the saw set varies according to the size of the saw teeth; large teeth requiring more set and small teeth, less. I usually set all my saws with a fairly small amount, especially for bench work. Were I to use the saws for soft-fibred woods, green, or wet wood, I would set the teeth to create a wider kerf and use a larger-toothed saw. Cutting such woods with smaller-toothed saws, which have small gullets, tends to clog the gullet with the soft and saturated fibres.

Saw set has little to do with the saw's sharpness but it does affect the effectiveness of the saw in use dramatically. A sharp saw without set binds in the cut and the saw does not progress very far. This is because of friction between the sides of the blade and the walls of the cut, as the saw deepens and the fibres then become compressed on the sides of the saw blade. This worsens if the wood is even slightly damp and is all the worse if it is still green. Saw set provides a relief area behind the very tip of each of the cutting teeth. Friction on the plate sides eventually stops the saw completely if it has too little set.

Most saws of old were made thinner than mass-made saws today and older, second-hand saws have usually been worn thinner still by constant use. These saws are usually improved by use and, while thicker saws do still work, they usually require much more effort to push through the wood due to this extra thickness. To check the amount of saw set, pass the saw into the wood to see how much of a gap there is on either side of the plate, as the cut deepens. You can also check by carefully holding the saw teeth between the fingertips and the thumb. If it feels quite pronounced it probably has too much set. If there is too much set you can remove some by tapping the teeth, all the way along the length of the saw plate, between two hammers or by using a steel base and hammer-tapping the teeth onto the plate. This will reduce the set if you tap first from one side and then the other. There is enough memory (spring) in the steel for it to bounce back somewhat but still reduce the set and it is surprising how even the set is afterwards too.

Saw Teeth Cut on the Tip and on the Side

It might seem that saws just cut the wood from the chisel tips of the teeth but the cut actually relies on two cut types, with each pass of the saw into the wood, at the same time. The cutting tip to each of the teeth, which, on ripcut teeth, results from filing square across, creates a chisel tip to the teeth; that is one cut type. The second aspect to the cut is the vertical, when sawing straight down. The outer face of the slightly staggered tooth line is dictated by the tooth set. On this outer face, the sharpening stroke creates a squared edge that then gives the side walls of the kerf a shearing cut, as the saw passes into the wood. Combining the shear cut from the sides of the teeth with the chisel-type cut of the edge of the teeth results in a clean wall in the ripcut, and then, with smaller toothed saws, across the grain also. What I am talking about here is especially significant when using the ripcut saw for crosscutting. This feature makes the ripcut saw a winner when it is used for making strong cuts either with or across the grain because the shearing action cuts the side walls quite smoothly in both cut types. This is why most of the artisans I worked under in my formative years of training never sharpened their saws for crosscut but simply used their ripcut saws.

Side Honing the Teeth

To improve the shear cut I use an approach I developed after seeing a particular Asian saw; the outside face of the teeth were abraded, to further refine the cutting edge of every alternate tooth on each side of the saw. On my saws I periodically, every six sharpenings or so, hone the outside facets of the teeth too. To do this I place the saw on its side and add a double layer of masking tape to each side of the saw plate, just below the tooth line. I then place the saw on the finest diamond plate (or whetstone) and hone the sides of the teeth. This is generally done after saw setting and saw setting is done when the saw starts to bind a little in the cut; usually after between 6-10 sharpenings, I find. The abrasive only catches the protruding teeth caused by the set, which is on the outer edges of the teeth. Three or four passes is usually enough. This is a step that I often take for ripcut saws but it can be used on crosscut saws as well to even up the set and create a truly flat and even face to the outside facets, whilst the inside faces have the two filed bevels that form the pinnacle-tipped cutting points.

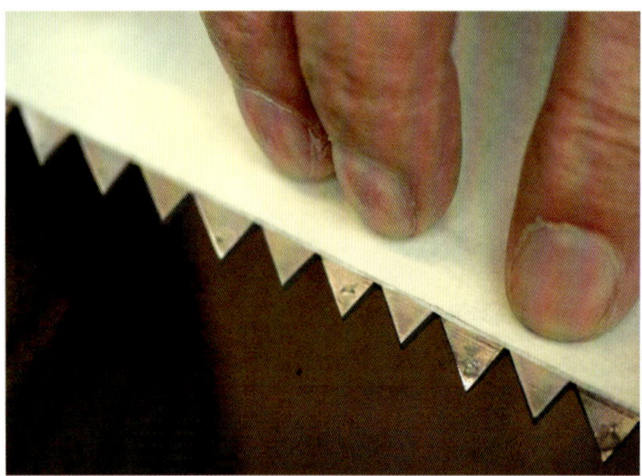

The outsides of the teeth then look like this. The saw cuts very nicely after this added step.

Progressive Tooth Patterns

Some saws do have what we call a progressive tooth pattern which means that the teeth decrease in PPI along the length of the saw; with smaller teeth at the beginning or toe end and progressing toward a standard tooth height and size after a short distance. Some have progressive teeth all the way through from toe to heel but this is a rarity and not common at all. In fact, progressive tooth patterns are more rare altogether. Instead of changing tooth sizing it is equally effective to simply change the pitch of the teeth, as I have discussed, to a more passive pitch for the starter teeth at the toe end.

Topping the Saw Teeth (Jointing USA)

To top the saw teeth is to use a flat, single-cut file to trim the heights of the teeth so that no single tooth protrudes higher than the other and to guide us as we then file the individual teeth. This is something we do to a saw when the teeth are uneven. A saw with too many uneven teeth jars in the cut and makes sawing difficult, which results in uneven cutting. Topping also straightens any undulation along the teeth, which can also affect the smooth action of the saw. By supporting the saw, on either side of the plate, with a split stick in the vise, the thin saw plate remains firm so that the file can pass over the teeth from the handle end of the saw to the toe end. In most cases the aim is to file the teeth straight, but sometimes, in the case of very large ripcut handsaws, we form what we call a breasted saw. This is a long, even curve from the toe to the heel of the saw. Breasted saws work well for deep and long ripping cuts.

Passing the file along the tops of the teeth, from the handle to the toe end, creates a small flat on the teeth tips. You can see variance in the width of the bright spots in the image below. The wider the bright spot the higher the tooth. Usually the difference can be very small, depending on how bad the teeth are. The bright areas show us that we need to file the teeth to even out discrepancies in size to match the adjacent teeth. Sometimes we file one side of that tooth only, whereas other teeth must be filed on both sides to even out the size and centre it between the adjacent teeth. An individual tooth makes little difference to the functionality of the saw but several uneven teeth can result in jarring in the cut. Some areas take extra work, relying on sighting to correct irregular tooth sizing. Only when there are very severe issues with saw teeth should you consider sending the saw away for recutting or file all of the teeth off yourself and reprofile new teeth into the edge of the plate. Most often, even topping will not be needed, unless the saw has been poorly sharpened over a number of sharpenings.

This saw shows the refined teeth on the left and the topped teeth awaiting refining on the right. This saw was particularly bad.

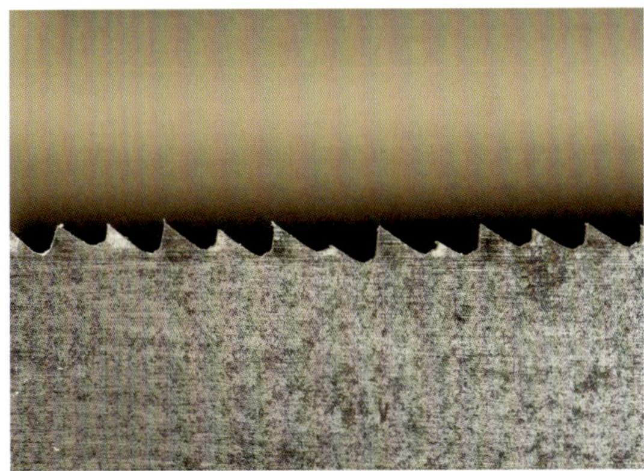

Here two teeth are below the level of the others, these will emerge with subsequent sharpenings.

Identifying Tooth Problems

Problems with saws are made most obvious by the course the saw takes in the cut. This image shows two curved cuts caused by damaged teeth to one side of the saw where the saw hit something in the wood. The straight cut to the right is from the same saw, after correcting the teeth. Common problems are ragged sides to the kerf, curving in the cut, and binding in the cut. Knowing how these can be corrected comes by experience but the following should help. Most sawing issues are identified by a curve in the cut, as the saw progresses down or along the cut line. Sometimes we can cause curved cuts by bending the saw and misaligning the hand and eye as the cut progresses. This is a technique issue and the more sawing you do the more you will feel for self-correcting.

DULLED OR DAMAGED TEETH

I am often asked about saws that seem constantly to curve in the cut to one side or the other. If the saw plate itself is undamaged then this usually relates to issues with the teeth themselves. Sometimes the saw plate is curved from the back edge of the saw to the opposite tooth edge, usually because someone trod on it or some other force caused it. Such damage to the plate will not be worth the effort of repair and requires skill and knowledge to achieve, but the teeth issues can almost always be resolved. More often, curving cuts are the results of either uneven sawsetting or dull teeth; common flaws occurring when one side of the teeth or the other, or even both sides, caught something hard like an embedded stone or a nail. It is not unusual for woodworkers to catch the metal vise jaw either. The dulled teeth, to whichever side, cut less effectively than the other (or not at all) allowing the saw to cut with the sharp side only. With the other side no longer cutting effectively, the biased passage curves the cut and, after a few strokes, the curving cut binds the saw and stops it from deepening the cut. Where the teeth are damaged to one side you must sharpen the saw, working on all the teeth, to take them down equally to a consistent level. Filing only the damaged teeth can mean that one side of the saw will engage the wood and the problem is not really resolved.

Catching the saw on the vise can both dull the saw and cause it to curve in the cut.

In this case it is damaged teeth that jeopardize the saw's passage.

UNEQUAL SET

Another issue causing curving in the cut is if the saw teeth are unequally set. This means that the set to the two sides of the saw is unequal, so the efficient and inefficient sides create an unequal cutting strategy and curve the cut. Sometimes the knurled setting screw on the sawset that locks the anvil loosens and allows the anvil disc to turn as it passes along the saw for each tooth set. This can go unnoticed and the imbalance is undetected.

OVERSET TEETH

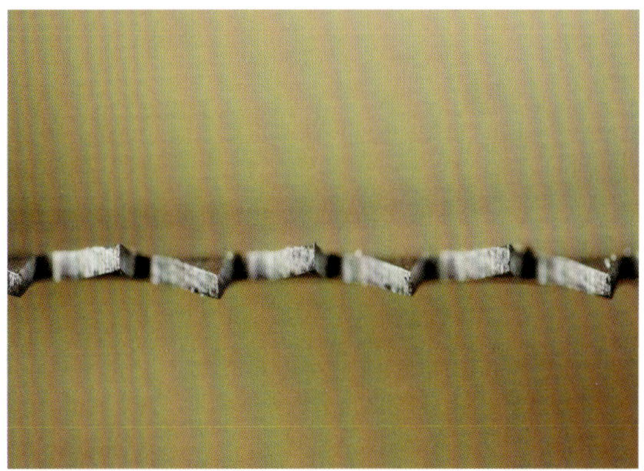

Some saw makers send their saws out with too much set on the teeth. This causes the saw to wander in the cut and leaves a jagged edge to the wall of the cut. Overset teeth also increase the effort needed to push the saw through the wood and this can be very significant. To check this on a saw simply rip along a board to see how wide the gap is and also to see if, indeed, the walls of the kerf are ragged and jagged. You will also feel the saw waggle in the cut. This can be true of second-hand saws too but with second-hand saws the problem is usually that the saw is underset. If they are underset you simply reestablish the tooth set with the sawset.

If the teeth are wrongly set it is usually easier to reduce the discrepancy using one upturned hammer, held in the vise, as an anvil and a second hammer to carefully tap the teeth between the two hammerheads; this is the same method we use for reducing set generally. I recommend that you do both sides of the teeth quite gently and try the saw. Sometimes this still leaves enough set in the teeth for the saw to be used and may well take care of the inequality. If, after doing this, you do not have enough set, then you simply reset the teeth using the sawset.

MISSING TEETH

When you encounter a missing tooth through breakage or misfiling, treat the saw as if it were there; go on to filing the next tooth by skipping the broken one but making sure that the alternating sequence is maintained, just as if the missing tooth were still there. Subsequent filings will gradually see the new tooth emerge and you will set it again when it reaches its full height. This usually happens in four to six filings, depending on the tooth size.

Restoring Saws

Second-hand saws can be an inexpensive alternative to buying new, even if they need restoration work. That said, be discerning; heavily rusted saw plates will be pitted and saws with uneven, irregularly spaced, and wrongly sized, misshapen teeth can take a great deal of skill to restore. That can lead to a lot of unnecessary work and disappointment. One or two teeth missing is not usually a problem but avoid more than that, for a starter saw, unless it is just to practise on.

While it is great to pick up second-hand saws to work on, I think it best to avoid saws if the teeth look like this. That is not to say that rough saws are no good, far from it; just that, in the early days, it is best to pick your battles and match them to your skill levels.

Restorative Saw Sharpening

It takes time to establish accuracy and confidence in your sharpening skills. At first, the strokes seem imprecise and faltering and this causes irregularities. A saw in poor condition is not really the best place to get started. On the other hand, a second-hand saw can give you a good saw to practise on and is often a lot less expensive than a new one so it is less costly if things do not go well at first. I usually recommend students and apprentices find any old saw that needs sharpening. The experience can be exactly what they need. If they succeed they have a saw and if not they can start over. I have found that, with care, you can find a good saw with reasonably shaped teeth in a condition good enough to start on; more in fairly good condition than bad. If the teeth are sized correctly and are even, it may well be a simple question of filing the gullets with a saw file and establishing a clean and sharp profile again.

Practice makes perfect and the resultant skills gradually become permanent. You must take these initial steps at some stage, even on your own in your own workshop, so you may as well start early on. Handsaws are better to learn on than, say, small saws with smaller teeth. A handsaw with 8-10 teeth per inch is ideal in size because you can see the teeth and the result of the file strokes clearly. It is also good to start on a saw with teeth that are well shaped and equally sized to begin with. The last ingredients are to use a sharp saw file (it is best to use an altogether new one), matched to the tooth size (see page 44), and to use a saw vise or to make a 'split stick' holder to secure the saw throughout the sharpening process.

Derusting Saws

Derusting is simple enough using fine abrasive, provided the rust is not too deep or pitted. Pitting is caused by rust eroding the surface and creating a cratering in the plate surface. This does not usually affect the saw functionally but it can.

We look at the rust from the point of view of restoring the plate to a fully functioning and usable condition and not as a preservation procedure only. Superfine surface discolouring, with a powdery coating of rust comes away with fine steel wool or some worn 250-grit abrasive paper. Surface coating the steel with some light machine oil reduces friction on the plate and protects the steel from rusting over again. I use my oiler rag-in-a-can (see page 476) for this and use it almost daily. This way my saws never rust. Any abrading should always be with or along the 'grain' of the steel, that is along the length of the saw from toe to heel, as much as possible. It is best to remove the handle, if possible, so that you can continue uninterrupted sanding with the grain. Take care not to damage the brass screws or the handle if you do feel the need to take this course on older saws, especially those with nuts and bolts that are flush to the surface.

Handle Nuts

The handles on all saws should be tight and firm, with no movement between the saw plate and the handle, no matter the saw type. Any movement at this important juncture makes the saw less punchy and leads to wobble and inaccuracy in the cut. The nuts that hold the handle firm to the plate sometimes come loose through use and sometimes the wood itself shrinks too. The nuts allow the handle to be re-tightened or removed for whatever reason. When you want to buy a saw for restoration, look for saws that allow this; i.e. saws with slots in the nut heads to receive a screwdriver.

These nuts are relatively easy to tighten and loosen. It is easier to restore a saw with nuts of this type because you can use a simple screwdriver to remove the handle.

Modern manufacturers have, in some cases, replaced the traditional nuts with a type of stud rivet fastening, even on saws considered to be of better quality. These fastenings rely on a type of stud compression where the two-part fastenings are hammered together and rely on friction or compression to hold them, which means that they cannot generally be removed. Usually you can identify this type by the fact that they have no slot for a screwdriver. However, when woodworkers stopped buying saws with these rivets because of this, some makers cut slots in the heads even though these pretend slots do nothing. These stud fittings can usually be tightened if the handles have shrunk or feel loose. Simply place the saw handle on a hard surface, like the tail of a metal working vise or an upturned hammer secured in the vise, so that the protruding stud is supported. Tap the opposite side of the stud with a steel hammer and the fittings will almost always tighten just fine.

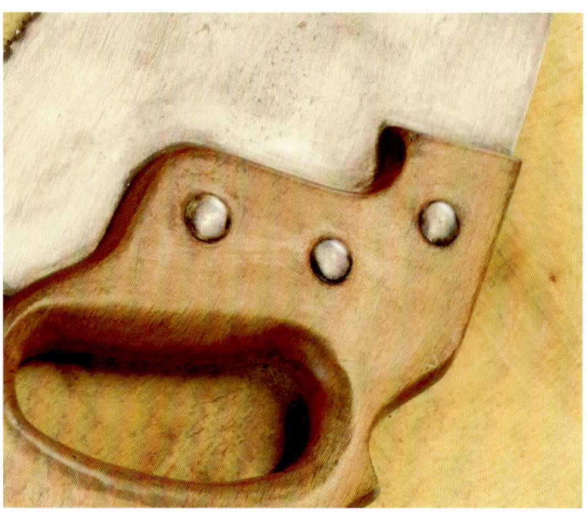

Split-nut Screwdrivers

On some saws, especially the 18th century saws, the nuts are split nuts of brass and the studs are brass too. For these we use a special twin-pronged screwdriver to turn the nut tighter or looser, as needed. Some makers sell such screwdrivers but they are simple enough to make yourself. You can grind out the midsection of a regular flat screwdriver for this.

Restoring Handles

Sometimes the horn to the top of the handle may be cracked or split off, which is often caused by dropping the saw on its end. It makes the saw uncomfortable and difficult to use as the hand relies on the saddle part there to push against. If this has happened, saw a flat surface on the existing part, plane flat and glue on a square section of hardwood. Reshape when the glue has set and fit to your hand. It may not look as nice, but it will work and feel fine.

The Handsaw

The handsaw comprises an expansive group of saws with wide blades made from thin plate steel. Though all the saws we use in hand work are indeed hand saws - that is any saw held by hand, using its handle - the term also refers to this specific type of saw. The handsaw range comprises the larger saws, which vary in length anywhere from 10" (25cm) and on up to 30" (76cm). The limit in length is generally governed by the length of the arm stroke. Where 10" (25cm) is particularly short and not normal at all, 30" (76cm) is a long arm stroke and not many people can use the full length of so long a saw.

Most woodworkers rely on handsaws sized between 16" (40cm) to 26" (66cm) long, and they are usually available in 2" (5cm) increments but not always. The short saws were originally made for more specialised work as well as for amateur woodworkers forming, at that time, a class of UK society known as the gentry. These men were less disposed or inclined to heavier work, living as more affluent land- and/or property-owning upper-class society. Woodworking, in terms of working manually for a living, was an issue of social class but, for those who simply enjoyed woodworking as a hobby, it seemed quite classless. Hence the term 'gent's' or 'gentleman's' saw, which refers to the shorter saws in this range.

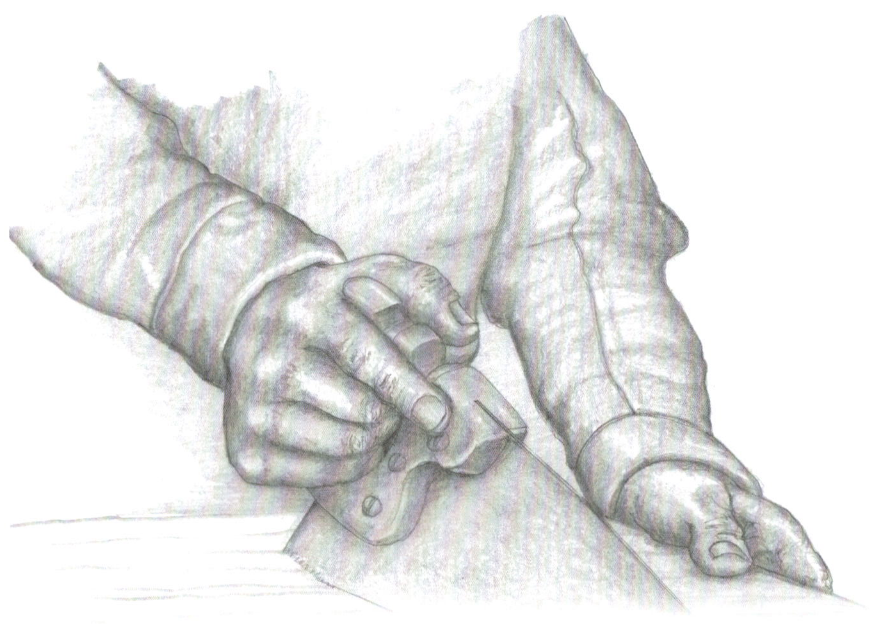

The longer handsaws require more strength and arm length to use them effectively. Most working craftsmen, by consistent use and upper-body exercise, become trained to manage the longer lengths and the thicker kerfs that such large saws produce. Of course you do not have to use the whole saw length and often we do not. The mid range lengths of 20-24" (50-61cm) cover the saws more commonly made and used today as new saws. With woodworkers today combining the use of machines like bandsaws and tablesaws with handsaws, the need for very large saws in general is markedly less than in times past. It is fairly easy in the UK and the USA to find old handsaws of every size, well used by working artisans but still in fully functioning and even excellent condition. Throughout the past century, with machine methods replacing much of the heavier sawing work, we have inherited a legacy of quality handsaws abandoned in toolboxes.

Handsaws, as a category, comprises saws with teeth often ranging from 12 PPI (points per inch) down to 4 PPI. This means that saws are generally sized in two ways; by their saw plate length (from toe to heel) and by the number of teeth points there are to the inch of saw length. All saws, no matter the type or size, are sized using these two measurements. Most saws made up until the 1960s are marked with a number at the heel of the saw, representing the number of points the saw has per inch of run. The size of the teeth does not determine the saw length at all. Here are three saws stamped stating 7 points per inch run of saw length but ranging in size from 18" (46cm), 24" (61cm) and 26" (66cm).

Hande.

Skew back.

.62

.70 max

Heel.

Taper Ground back

.43 .58 .62

.70 max

My Disston Panel Saw shows these taper grades measurements.

Tooth line.

Toe

The taper grind is phased to remove more to the back edge of the Saw.

What Handsaws Do

Handsaws are the means by which we convert wood into specifically sized sections. The process begins in the raw when trees are severed from their roots. The subsequent process is called conversion. Conversion generally begins in the sawmills of the world, when the tree is reduced down, using massive sawing machines. The subsequent squared-off sections are further converted into smaller sections and subsections ready for drying, usually in kilns. At certain points after drying and sometimes seasoning, these sections of wood reach the workbenches of woodworkers and it is at this point that the size of the saws we use becomes relevant to us as woodworkers.

In furniture making, bench joinery, and other areas of more general woodworking, I make most initial cuts, with and across the grain of wood, using different handsaws. This means that the saws cut across the tree grain and also along the main, long axis of the tree – that is from the root upwards toward the top of the stem. This is after the bark, roots, and limbs have all been removed. To do this I rely on saws of different sizes. Whether the saws are machine driven or driven by hand, wood is always cut and converted to rough size by sawing except when it is split for sub-sizing, which is a rarity for most woodworking and woodworkers and is definitely not common today.

Ripcut and Crosscut Handsaws

Searching for a new saw, it soon becomes apparent that most outlets and manufacturers offer both crosscut and ripcut tooth patterns, regardless of what type the saw is. Comparing ripcut and crosscut handsaws or ripcut and crosscut backsaws, side by side, they have the same general appearance, with no apparent difference until you get to the smallest parts, which are the teeth. When you look at the actual saw teeth themselves the difference shows, but, even then, if the teeth are small you may not be able to tell. In that case, it is when the teeth need sharpening that the shape of the teeth becomes apparent because of the way they must be approached by the saw file. This is the best place to bring clarity to the differences between ripcut and crosscut saws. So it is best to follow the section on saw sharpening, starting on page 288, to fully understand the differences.

Hand sawing with the grain, or along the wood the long way, is called ripcutting. When we cut at 90 degrees to the grain we call it crosscutting. Some saws will cut both with the grain and across the grain equally, whereas others will only cut one way or the other. This depends on how the saw's teeth are shaped and sharpened. In general it is true that custom sharpening for ripcut or crosscut produces the most efficient and effective saws. However, almost all of the saws I use in bench work have teeth smaller than 8 points to the inch. These are the handsaw, tenon saw, and dovetail or gent's saw and I sharpen all of these saws to a ripcut pattern, even though I also use them for crosscutting. The reason I can do both ripcut and crosscut cutting with the same saw in each type or size is that the teeth are relatively small and commensurate to the size and type of grain I am sawing. Further refining the shape of the teeth, even by a small amount, enables me to customise my saws to task. Smaller teeth work best for crosscutting, as they take a smaller bite in the cut. Were I to use say a 6 or 4 points per inch saw I would need to sharpen them to the different cuts as either ripcut or crosscut according to purpose. This, again, is due to the size of bite the saw takes, which is governed by the depth of each gullet and thereby the spacing of the teeth. This is discussed in the saw sharpening section on page 291. This does not mean that saws with smaller teeth cannot be sharpened specifically to crosscut or ripcut but, for the main part, it is unnecessary and inconvenient. Also, it does make a significant difference if you duplicate all your saws in ripcut and crosscut teeth patterns because you effectively double the number of saws you use and must then keep track of. I would only sharpen a saw with more than 8 points per inch specifically with a crosscut pattern if I needed it for a significant amount of dedicated crosscutting.

Here I am crosscutting using an 8 PPI handsaw sharpened to a ripcut.

Here I am using the same handsaw with ripcut teeth to rapidly cut along the grain.

Another reason that I can use my saws to ripcut and crosscut using the same saw is that I sharpen the initial first inch or two of saw teeth, at the toe end, to a more passive rake or pitch. The saw starts more easily in the opening strokes, starting with the toe end, and then, moving the stroke into the cut, the more aggressive pitch along the main part of the body of the saw teeth engages. This means that, after that introduction with the passive rake, the teeth change to a steeper angle and they then cut more effectively.

Choosing a Handsaw

The handsaw I choose for bench work, and that I recommend as a good all-round saw, is the one we refer to generally as a 'panel saw.' Panel saws are the general-purpose handsaw, relied on for most handsaw tasks and the title suggests one of the main aspects of its use. We cut panels from boards with this saw; ripping and crosscutting sections of wood to different widths and lengths to suit the size we need for making rails, drawer parts, and much more. The best size is a 20-22" (51-56cm) long saw plate with 10 PPI but an 8 PPI works well as a panel saw too. What is the difference? Well, only a little; a 10 PPI will generally crosscut better than an 8 PPI and the 8 PPI will perform ripcuts more quickly because the teeth are slightly larger and further spaced, point to point. This detail also gives the saw deeper gullets, which means they are better disposed to ripcutting. The choice most often depends on the thickness of the wood and then the type of wood. Hardwoods are sometimes, but not always, harder, more dense-grained woods. Larger-toothed saws work better for this type of wood. Some woods, especially exotic species such as rosewood, clog the gullet of the saws and larger-toothed saws cope better than finer toothed saws. As you grow in your woodworking, you will acquire an additional saw or two and then perhaps eventually a larger saw for heavy ripping in thicker and harder, more dense-grained woods.

Good Handsaws Should Be Flexible

In times past, a craftsman took his saw and whipped it into a quick bend and bent the tip, in a large arc, into the handle. Some tucked the tip of the saw into the handle hole itself and if the saw returned to its former state of flatness, with no bend or breakage, it was deemed a good saw. I have bent my own saws this way and found them to do just that, with no deterioration. The trouble is that if it fails the test you have a useless saw. I do not recommend that you do this, even though it is a good test. Also, the length of the saw plate makes a difference and short saws are definitely disadvantaged so be careful not to lose a good saw.

This is an old Henry Disston saw about 100 years old.

If a saw is too thick you will not be able to bend it very far without damaging it and, because the saw is thick, the work is much harder. Many makers' standards, in this regard, have diminished over a half century and the new generations of saws are not generally the same or as good. This 1950s version is stiff and difficult to bend beyond what you see here.

The spring in the steel is an important feature to good saw making. Tensile recovery matched to resistance of pressure is not something we can particularly measure so we often go off the reputation of the makers. This is not so easy today. Pushing and pulling saws into and through the hundreds of thousands of cuts a handsaw makes means it must have resilience and resistance to all manner of strains. The spring in the steel gives the saw these characteristics and at least some of the modern makers seem to have sidestepped this issue. So I like old saws for the main part. They give me what I want in a saw. Almost any pre-1940 handsaw will be a good saw. After the Second World War saws became more questionable. There is always a possibility that a modern maker will step up and fill this space. They must, however, work hard to achieve the correct level of flexibility in saw blades.

Features for Traditional Handsaws

I own handsaws made in the 1700-1800's. There can be no doubt that the workmanship in the saws is exceedingly good and, when you hold a well used and cared for saw, you sense the importance the craftsman placed on refining every aspect of the saw. The artisan was indeed speaking from a different era in workmanship and life, a different world and something no one spoke of back then; lifestyle. My take on this is that everyone can enjoy what I have enjoyed in using and owning old saws. The old saws are still plentiful and can be restored and sharpened to parallel the very best of the best and they can, and should, last for 50-100 years of daily use, provided they are cared for, sharpened properly, and used correctly. Unlike the degenerate non-sharpenable modern-day counterparts, the teeth respond well to saw files and can be sharpened many hundreds if not thousands of times. How amazing that is to me. I hope never to take such things for granted. Of course, there are modern makers but most of them produce saws that are too thick and they often arrive from the factory without being sharpened well or correctly. Even those striving for the former qualities in the old handsaws we once knew rarely achieve what they had.

Handsaw Handles and Hardware

I do like wooden handles for saws. I think that they have served us well for centuries and most saws using plastic composites are made that way to cut costs and cancel out the need for skilled labour. Of course, today manufacturers have access to sophisticated machinery to shape their handles and flap sanders to refine and remove marks left by the routing machines. The telltale signs are there and generally they do not match what past craftsmen sawmakers worked into their handles by hand, with auger bits and rasps, gouges and scrapers, but this is a different age. Little sandpaper was used and there was no excess and waste of energy; it was economic, direct, and purposeful. Their efforts produced some of the most beautiful and thought-through shaping of handles for over a century. Fruitwoods, such as apple, pear, and cherry, held fine detail in the carved designs.

Compare the two saw handles here, made by the same company, Disston. The bottom saw is the older, more refined model.

Carbon steel is the standard material manufactured for saw makers by steel suppliers. Today's makers use rolled steel stock, where the plate is created between a series of massive hydraulic rollers. The remaining metal work revolves around threaded bolts and nuts, securing the handle to the steel saw plate. The earliest models used nuts that lie flush with the surface of the wood forming the saw handle. These are often what we call split nuts. On most of them you can see that they were hand cut with files and then fitted to the recess that was, again, hand bored with an auger bit corresponding to the diameter of the bolt and nut heads. This flush-to-surface appearance looked aesthetically pleasing but this era came to an end. Over the following decades, saw

makers replaced the flush bolts and nuts with raised and slightly domed heads. The replacements did improve the nuts and bolts because they left more wood in place for strength. They were formed into a barrelled stem, inserted into the hole in the wood, and they had triple the length of thread engaging the bolt inside the nut. The split nuts of old had been much weaker as there was but ⅛" (3mm) of thread in the split-nut versions. They also required much less skilled work to install them; the split nuts were hand threaded and chased and then fitted into recesses before being filed flush and scraped to the surface of the wood.

These two images show both sides of the same saw to show how the fastenings were flush with the faces of the saw handle. I must say that they do look lovely.

The Taper-ground Saw Plate

Handsaws, developed through many decades, had very gradually improved in performance and functionality when two seemingly simple changes transformed them all the more. These improvements might be obscured by their simplicity at first and often one of these improvements might go completely unnoticed, primarily because it cannot be seen in the constructs of the saw itself. Looking through old manuals and manufacturers' catalogs we see that these improvements - the taper-ground plate and the skew back - markedly changed how the saws performed on sawhorses and at the workbench. They changed carpentry work on remote worksites away from the workshop too.

Taper-grinding was a method of refining the saw plate by thinning certain parts of the steel from the wide and thicker level, near to the heel (the handle end), to the narrower toe or tip of the saw and from the teeth toward the back edge. This feathering of the saw plate reduced the amount of set needed to the saw teeth and so improved the free passage of the saw into and through the wood with subsequent strokes. Remember that any reduction in set at all means removing less wood in the cut and this translates into energy saving for the user. Some more recent saw makers have copied and maintained some of this tradition through the decades but not all. The development of the taper-grind allowed for a two- or three-degree tilt in the cut one way or the other over and above that allowed by just the set of the saw teeth alone. This simple tilt enables a gradual change of direction after the saw enters the wood; a point when the course is generally being set. If we then stray a little from the line, we can generally use the narrower forend of the saw to effectively redirect the cut and, by keeping the stokes short until the direction seems corrected, we can realign the saw plate. Subsequent strokes are then elongated until the full width of the plate enters the cut to a full saw-plate width again. That is the advantage given to us by the advent of the taper-ground handsaw plate.

Skew-backed Saws

Just when they seemed to reach their pinnacle, another change transformed the handsaw. We began to see two saw types side by side; one with a straight back and another with a skew back. That is, a long curve along the back edge of the saw. Many modern-day hardpoint-toothed saws have reverted back to a straight back saw. These are mostly the mass production models favoured for crosscutting dimensional construction lumber such as 2x4s, 2x6s and so on as well as sheet goods. The straight back works fine when few people rip boards along the length by hand and it provides both a straight edge for drawing lines and a square, formed by the handle, to use as a convenient on-site squaring tool. These disposable saws with hard-point teeth have straight backs because few of them are used for much more than crosscutting dimensioned wood.

I think it is important here to know that the skew back to handsaws was a design concept intended to make sawing an easier and lighter task but, more importantly, to provide the extra flexibility to help 'steer' the saw in the opening cuts. The first few strokes of a saw are more critically important than people know when they first start to work with wood. These opening strokes set the saw's course and, of course, there is almost nothing steering the saw except the user's hand and eye coordination. Very soon the course is set to the point that it can be almost unalterable without some major effort if it drifts more than a millimeter or so. Here the user, pushing full length strokes, finds that the course will not change. Often, if the saw strays, they keep pushing in the hope that somehow, by sheer force of will, the saw will come to change its course. Mostly that is unlikely. Using the full plate nearer to the handle prevents any change of course but withdrawing to the narrower end at the toe, and also the lower sweep of the skew, enables the flex you need and, again, using the same short stabbing strokes used with the taper-ground saw, the side of the teeth shave fibres and the course changes stroke by stroke by stroke. Soon the strokes elongate all the more; a new course is set and longer strokes begin to follow along the correct line. The skew-back and the taper-ground plate unified two simple strategies to create a unique and dynamic marriage. It happened where you would least expect it, on the opposite side from the teeth, to the top aspect of the saw. This enabled directional shifts along the cutting teeth; minor changes that brought major improvements to performance.

Disposable Handsaws

In woodworking today, many of the saw manufacturers that once produced the traditional handsaws we know from history now make mostly disposable saws for mass international markets. They cater to a demand for high efficiency and the utilitarian workmanship of modern design. If the teeth cannot be sharpened then they must be discarded and, even if they are recycled, it still makes little economic sense in terms of the real costs to the woodworker. Over half a century, the changes in manufacturing processes have downgraded the need for hand skills and that includes how to sharpen and set saws for basic or specific tasks. On the other hand, I now see many people, once reluctant to sharpen saws whether old or new, are now becoming experienced as they learn that it takes only a short time to learn the basics. In an hour or two anyone should be able to learn how to sharpen a ripcut saw for hybrid ripcut and crosscutting wood. Over the space of a few weeks the skills can be expanded and will become intuitive for a lifetime of saw sharpening. The lifestyle woodworker, searching out the old ways and uniting them with the best of the present, will find a greater level of skill, self-sufficiency, and sustainability.

“ *The lifestyle woodworker, searching out the old ways and uniting them with the best of the present, will find a greater level of skill, self-sufficiency, and sustainability* ”

Distance Sawing

The lack of back spline means the handsaw can pass into and through the wood unhindered, which facilitates unlimited distance sawing over long lengths and spans. That is the main advantage handsaws have over backsaws and frame saws too. It also means that the saw can be used for large tenon cutting, where the spline of a tenon saw would otherwise hinder the saw on things such as tenon cheeks that are deeper than 3" (76mm). Sheet goods, such as plywood, are impossible to cut down with tenon saws and frame saws over large distances. Here the handsaw comes into its own. Ripcuts are the more common cuts for the handsaw but we do work across the grain too. Again, handsaws are ideal for wide crosscuts, which are also quite common to handwork. Generally, and most commonly, handsaws are used in reducing wood in its width and length.

Backsaws

Some saws rely on thicker plate steel for rigidity, while other blades are stretched between two fixed points to tension what may be a thick or thinner blade. In this section I will discuss a third saw type, which relies on the addition of a second component that stiffens the plate along the back. We call this stiffening bar a 'spline' or 'back,' hence the name back saw or backsaw. Another way of describing saws is by their action. Saws that cut along or with the grain are called ripsaws and those used to cut across the grain we call crosscut saws. Just as the term 'handsaw' can describe every saw used by hand, 'backsaw' describes every saw with a stiff back or spline. Within that group of backsaws we then have additional names that relate to the saw's intended purpose. The 'tenon saw' describes a group of saws we use to make tenons and other joints like half lap joints, bridle joints, and dovetails. Tenon saws come in a range of sizes but generally they are the larger of the saws in the backsaw category. The term 'tenon saw' can actually be used to refer to any of the backsaws other than the gent's saw, which has an inline handle. For the sake of clarity and differentiation, however, I am going to use the term 'tenon saw,' in this book, to refer to only the large backsaws. I will use use the terms 'dovetail saw' and 'gent's saw' for shorter saws with somewhat narrower blades than full size tenon saws. Backsaws provide us with the most rigid form of hand saw. Their common purpose is to cut the parts of joints, which always rely on dead straight cuts. Beyond that we use them to cut mouldings and beads, dowels and small sections of wood. Larger tenon saws may also be called 'carcass saws' but even then can still be known simply as tenon saws. Smaller backsaws such as the dovetail or the gent's saw, identified by the handles, are best known by these two names and so need no further explanation once

you understand the fundamental differences. Calling them all backsaws is perhaps quite common but can become somewhat confusing so it is useful to use the other terms when discussing a specific backsaw. The specific backsaws I consider essential and will be discussing in this section are the gent's saw, dovetail saw, and tenon saw.

Backsaw Sizing and Tooth Sizing

Backsaws are identified by their handle type and their length. Generally the ones we refer to as 'tenon saws' are the larger backsaws, 10-14" (25-36cm) long, and anything shorter, be it dovetail or gent's saw, is known as a dovetail saw. Both groups can be used for any aspect of sawing that they are suited to and not simply for cutting the specific joint referred to in the saw's name.

Here are the three main types of backsaw:

TENON SAWS

Tenon saws are available in three general sizes for joint making and general woodworking 14" (36cm), 12" (30cm), 10" (25cm). The most practical tooth size for both 12" (30cm) and 14" (36cm) tenon saws is 14 PPI. I also keep two additional 14" (36cm) tenon saws close to hand; one with 16 PPI for finer cuts and the other with 12 PPI for more progressive and heavy work, especially in larger workpieces. In my 12" (30cm) tenon saw I keep only one extra saw with 16 PPI as I would be less likely to use the shorter saw for any work requiring teeth larger than 14 PPI.

Here you can see a range of tooth sizes against a 1" (25mm) length, for comparison.

These teeth are 14 PPI, which is quite typical for tenon saws.

DOVETAIL SAWS

Dovetail saws are available in three general sizes for cutting smaller joints, including all dovetails; 10" (25cm), 8" (20cm), and 6" (15cm). Dovetail saws should generally have a maximum tooth size of 16 PPI on all sizes, 6-10" (15-25cm), though you can go finer, perhaps 18-22 PPI. The difficulty with these finer sizes is that it becomes more challenging to maintain the shape and size of the teeth when sharpening. Usually, on the smaller sizes, the saw plate is thinner than that of the larger saws and it is all too easy to file out a whole tooth in a single stroke if the file is moved too far left or right. It takes much higher levels of sensitivity to sharpen so fine a tooth. However, a 16 PPI tooth size should be small enough to cut good joinery, even in fine joints.

Dovetail saws are smaller and have smaller teeth, such as these 16 PPI teeth.

GENT'S SAWS

Gent's saws are available in several sizes less than 10" (25cm) and are used for fine work including small joint making, inlay cutting, model making, and instrument making of different kinds. They are generally available in the following sizes, 10" (25cm), 8" (20cm), 6" (15cm), 5" (13cm) and 4" (10cm). In some ways, these saws seem less popular and I am not sure why. My thought is that, though the saw is not necessarily essential for, say, joinery, it is indeed an extremely useful saw and one everyone should own. The very fine teeth are precisely cut, which makes them very direct and purposeful saws. I also like the fact that I can align it very precisely to my work, both vertically and inline, in a way that I feel to be much more accurate than the other types of handled backsaws. I use two basic types, the 10" (25cm) 16-18 PPI and the ultra-fine modeller's 6-8" (15-20cm) saw with 24 PPI.

Gent's saws are often the smallest saws in a workshop and suitably have very small teeth, such as these 20 PPI.

I find little use for any gent's saw less than 8" (20cm) long, though even a 6" (15cm) works fine and I can see that modellers, as well as those involved with inlay and veneer work, might prefer the short versions. I think my preference for longer versions is mostly because I am more used to saws that are at least 8" (20cm) long and I find myself running out of length in the stroke when using something shorter. The difference in cost for longer and shorter saws is often negligible.

These are very fine teeth at 24 PPI and are very difficult to sharpen. That said, because they are only used very occasionally, they do stay sharp for a long time in my work.

Choosing Backsaws

Saws, both new and secondhand, can often be collected from different sources inexpensively if we shop around and look for them. My best saws did come from secondhand markets but this usually means having the ability and necessary experience to be able to sharpen and set the saws. With three or four saw types (i.e. handsaws, such as a panel saw or a slightly longer handsaw, tenon saw, and dovetail saw in one or two of the various sizes offered) you will have enough saws to tackle any woodworking.

For closer work, and especially joint making, we rely on backsaws. Most people want to cut smaller joints, such as dovetails, half laps, bridle joints, and tenons; and, as long as the tenons are not overly large, the 10" (25cm) dovetail saw with 16 PPI is a good first purchase. However, within a short time, you will need to purchase a full-sized tenon saw. By 'full size' I mean a larger backsaw that suits you and your stature, weight, strength, and such. For me that size is 14" (36cm) but for some it will mean 12" (30cm). For a smaller person that extra 2" (51mm) makes the saw unwieldy and less accurate. The tenon saw should have around 14 PPI but you may want to downsize the teeth to 16 PPI on a 12" (30cm) saw to best match your body size and strength. So my essential backsaws are:

1. A 10" (25cm) dovetail saw with 16 PPI
2. A 12" (30cm) or 14" (36cm) (depending on your stature) tenon saw with 14 PPI

While this should give you a starting point when you are looking into buying backsaws, you certainly should not be constrained by it. The dovetail saw could easily be exchanged for a gent's saw with the inline handle. Also, if you are looking for a 14" (36cm) tenon saw but come across a wonderful 12" (30cm) saw, you should probably just go for that. I have ended up with many more saws than I really need but I find that I enjoy setting each one up in a slightly different way to suit specific tasks.

For my joinery, I generally reach for one of three tenon saw types. The 14" (36cm) with 14 PPI cuts almost all of my tenon cheeks and the long grain cuts on other joints too. I do keep a tenon saw of this size with 12 PPI too but this is not so essential. If the long grain cut is smaller, for example, small tenons around 1" (25mm) wide and 1" (25mm) long, I would then reach for my 12" (30cm) tenon saw, which also has 14 PPI, and I will also consider my dovetail saw for this too. I would most likely cut the shoulders with the smaller dovetail saw. For almost all of my dovetailing and small joint making I do use the dovetail saw with 16 PPI. If the wood is thicker or the joints, including dovetails, are marginally larger or sometimes if the wood is harder, I will find myself reaching for the in-between saw, the 12" (30cm). So, after you have acquired the 10" (25cm) dovetail

saw and 14" (36cm) tenon saw I do suggest adding a 12" (30cm) tenon saw. With these I can complete all of my woodworking joinery. If, on a rare occasion, I need a much larger tenon I simply reach for the handsaw.

Now we see that the range of backsaws cut all types of joinery ranging from tenons to housing dadoes, notches, and recesses too. We sometimes adapt them for other tasks, such as channels, and I even use them for creating rebates, especially across the grain, where a rebate plane might not work. All of the backsaws work well for mitre cuts, cutting beading and so on, where cross-cutting small sections of wood and the like is necessary.

Folded Backs Maintain Rigid Control

Most backsaws follow the same principle methods with regards to the metal aspect of manufacture. The gent's saw is made the same way as the rest of the backsaws except for the handle attachment, which relies on the spline of the saw entering into the handle for an inch or more to keep the necessary inline rigidity. The rigidity of the saw relies on a tight, friction-fit spline extension, passing into a drilled hole, which is centred in the handle to hold it securely in place. Tenon and dovetail saws, on the other hand, rely on the handle enclosing the saw plate and the spline, which enters a recess in the top of the handle. Bolts pass through both the wooden (or sometimes plastic) handle and the saw plate to lock the metal parts and the wood together.

Traditionally the backs, used to stiffen tenon saw plates, were made of folded brass or steel and the meeting line, where the two edges of the folded strip came together, created tensioning to the saw plate itself. When the plate is inserted, the spline pinches the steel plate firmly and permanently along the entire length. This clever strategy maintains the straightness of the saw. It also means that, if the saw plate ever bows along its length, the spline can be tapped with a hammer or slammed, carefully, edge-on onto the bench top and the saw will generally return to straightness. Unfortunately, many modern saws are made with a machine-milled groove to fit onto the plate, which does not allow you to straighten the plate if needed. This works to stiffen the saw but, if the plate is ever bowed by misuse or accidental uneven pressures, it cannot be so readily restored to straightness without removing the plate. The plates are almost always permanently installed and cannot easily be removed.

The saw plates in tenon saws do bend due to the wide range of pressures applied to the saw. Pushing or pulling the saw, standing on it accidentally, and catching and jarring the plate all have the ability to distort the plate. Sometimes saws are kinked, with a tight crease in the steel, through misuse and accidental damage. A kinked saw is not usually fixable.

Brass or Steel Backs?

All backsaws are made with either steel or brass backs in roughly equal measure. Brass-backed saws are heavier than the steel-backed versions and were considered better for this reason alone. The extra weight adds even pressure in the cut and so the heavier saws do generally cut more effectively than the steel ones. There are no rust issues with brass and so I was told, in my apprenticeship days, that there would be less rust occurring on the inside, between the saw plate and the brass spline, than there would be with steel on steel. The only difference I have seen, with regards to functionality, is in the weight. I prefer the extra weight I get from the brass and also the look of the brass too. I suppose brass always has a look of quality. The pictured brass-backed Groves saw still weighs more than its all-steel counterpart by the same maker, even though the brass one is now a little narrower at the toe end in the plate, through use. The saws weigh in at 1:11.8oz (787g) for the steel one and 1:12.6oz (811g) for the brass; if the plates were exactly the same I think the difference would be around 2oz extra. A seemingly small difference but noticeably weightier in the extended hand.

Here the two saws by the same maker, side by side, are basically identical, except that one has a brass back, the other steel.

Holding the Saw

Holding a saw is simple enough. The main thing to remember is that the forefinger of the dominant hand is always pointing forward and never part of the grip. This forefinger aligns along the side of the saw handle and points toward the tip of the saw to give direction to the saw and bring vertical alignment and squareness to the plate in the cut.

The main thing to remember is that the forefinger of the dominant hand is always pointing forward and never part of the grip

Here I show the correct way to hold the tenon saw, from both sides of the saw handle, in the conventional, closed handle tenon saw.

Holding the pistol grip saw is the same but sometimes we slide the little finger underneath the handle.

Here I show how to hold the gent's saw.

Using Backsaws

All saws work on both a pull and push stroke, one negative and the other positive. The direction of the teeth, in relation to the handle and the user, determines whether the saw actually cuts predominantly on the push stroke or the pull stroke. Whichever saw type is used, push or pull stroke, one direction cuts and the other, the returning stroke, prepares the saw for the subsequent cut and only cuts minimally, if at all, on this return stroke. When I was a boy, the men I worked with said 'let the saw do the work under its own weight.' Saws should be started with an extremely light pass, as if suspending the saw in the work, rather than forcing it downwards into the wood. A light and confident stroke should start the saw and, once the saw has entered into the wood, stronger and more progressive strokes can, if appropriate, be used. Many people, who are new to using backsaws, use too much pressure at the start of the cut by pressing down and it is this that makes a well sharpened saw difficult to start. In most cases people are not used to using sharp saws but applying the wrong pressures severely impairs the functioning of the saw.

All of the backsaws are used in much the same way but for different aspects of our work. The fuller sized 12-14" (30-36cm) tenon saw is used mostly for cutting larger joints or aspects thereof. The gent's saw parallels the shorter 8-10" (20-25cm) dovetail saw and performs many of the same tasks at the bench.

Although the tenon saw describes perhaps one of the larger backsaws' primary uses in the cutting of tenon cheeks and shoulders, we also use it for cutting all the other joints too. Tenon saw sizing depends mostly on its use. When you are choosing which backsaw to use in joinery it is actually very simple. Use large saws for large joints, mid-sized for medium-sized joints, and then smaller saws for smaller joints. That said, there are crossovers between the sizes; only you can gauge, as you work the different wood types and assess the grain in the working of it. The fine-toothed saws work well for all crosscutting work, such as shoulder lines, mitres to picture frames and things like that. The larger saws will

work well for larger crosscutting and mitre cutting intended for further refinement with planes and shooting boards. Most often, with a finer-toothed saw with newly sharpened teeth and the correct set, the cut needs no more refining, so cuts across the grain or at angles can be used straight from the saw cut itself with no planing or truing.

Cutting Joinery

For different joints we use different approaches and tactics to develop optimal performance from the saw. When I cut tenons, for instance, I always begin by cutting the crossgrain shoulder lines to the knifeline, which has first been established with a surgically-sharp knife together with the square.

It is always best to secure the workpiece in the vise from the start, whenever possible. This reduces the risk of slippage and makes the work solid and safe. By establishing the knifewall first and then making an angled cut, on the waste side of the cutline, into the knifewall with an inclined chisel cut, we create a slight step-down for the saw teeth to rest in as we cut.

Drawing of knife walls - showing two knife walls & saw between
Handsawn ends should be planed to the knife wall. Shallow setting.
Surface plane all surfaces - and edges - clamp two together in vise to increase support for plane

Wanted wood

Wanted wood.

Two side-by-side knife cuts allow passage into and through the wood without splintering to the outcut side. These knife walls pass around to all four faces.

I do the same on dovetail shoulder lines to the outside edges of dovetails too but usually I do this after I have cut down the angles forming the dovetails first. Slicing across the fibres to cut the shoulders means the saw readily snugs up to the knifewall and then follows the knifewall across its width, down to the interconnecting point at the cheek or dovetail with subsequent strokes. The shoulder, elbow, wrist, and hand are aligned in synchrony to follow the sightline as I cut. This alignment ensures squareness of the shoulder both crossways and vertically. As long as the cut moves away from the knifewall, further trimming can be exacted, using a 1" (25mm) chisel, if needed. Working to the depth lines or adjacent cuts along the grain shows me where to stop.

The interaction between crosscut and ripcut cuts, be that cheeks or shoulders, can often be done using the same saw but this usually depends on the size of the saw's teeth. In practice I find myself reaching for a smaller-toothed saw for the shoulders even though all of my backsaws are sharpened for ripcut identically. The smaller-toothed saw works the crossgrain fibres more cleanly and the saw moves more freely into the cut. The traditional techniques we use generally follow the same patterns and techniques, even though we may well be working with different saw types and sizes.

In almost every case we place the saw on the waste side of the line, the part we are removing in the formation of the joints. Cuts should always start on the forward stroke rather than a back stroke, as many are taught. With a push-stroke western saw these opening strokes push the grain fibres in the direction of a proactive cut stroke rather than pulling fibres toward the user. Pushing the saw on the thrust cut thus aligns the fibres away from us and subsequent cuts become much more fluid and easily worked into the wood. Also, these opening saw strokes should be light, not heavy or hard, allowing the saw teeth to lightly 'kiss' the wood fibres, rather than forcing the saw into the wood without allowing a positive saw kerf to develop.

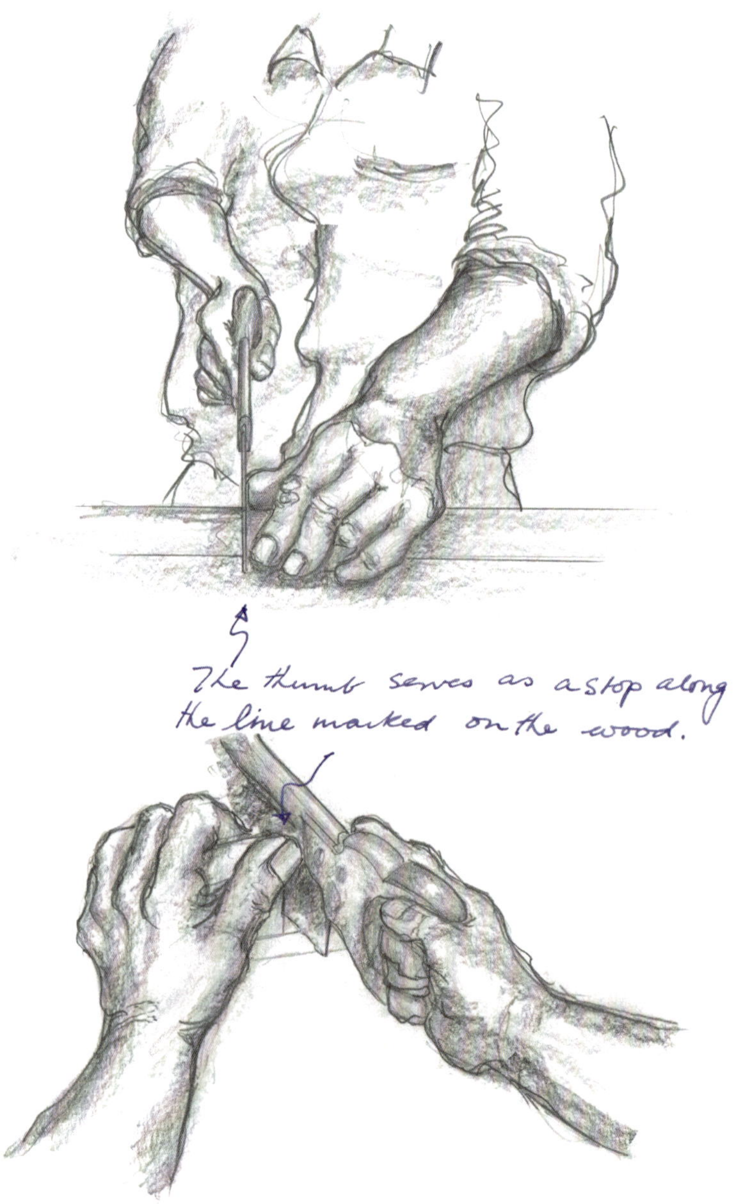

Once entry is begun, the subsequent strokes can become stronger as the saw aligns to the line and we drop the angled presentation to work into the grain and on into the cut. Remember that it is the first half dozen strokes that set the course for the saw to progress deeper into and through the cut. Once deepened, it is difficult to reorient the saw. After several strokes have taken the saw down into the wood by around ¼" (6mm), we then adjust the hand with each stroke, according to how we feel the saw is in relation to the wood we are cutting. Using that initial long saw kerf to align the strokes, parallel to the outer face or onto the cut line, we progress the cut down into the work of, say, a tenon cheek until the saw reaches the intersecting line or pre-cut corner. Ultimately, as the saw closes in on adjacent cuts, we level the saw and cut down to the shoulder. Any trimming to final depth, using the knifewall as a guide, can then be done with an appropriately sized chisel.

The tenon saw works on most other joints too and so should never be seen as being purely for tenon cutting alone. When I was young we used the tenon saws to cut the housings for stair treads and risers and then to cut and fit treads, risers, wedges, and returns for dogleg staircases into return posts. It cuts wedges for wedging tenons and also trimming them off. The list goes on.

Crosscut Tenon Saws

I advocate a no-nonsense ripcut sharpening for everyday work, which works well for most woodworking. There are rare occasions when a crosscut profile refines the cuts I need in my work and I refine my saws ever so slightly to give fleam to the teeth to give me the edge I want. It is important to know though that the smaller the ripcut saw teeth get, the better the cut. In my view there is a point where the tooth size makes little difference between ripcut and crosscut pattern. I discuss this in detail in the saw sharpening section on page 291.

The reason saws will crosscut, even with a ripcut tooth pattern, is that the rip cut tooth cuts with a shearing action. As long as the tooth has set (see page 304 on saw setting), with the actual teeth having been pushed outwards, the side edges of the chisel point to each tooth give a shear-cut alongside the face edges of the teeth. It is this developed cutting strategy that then allows the saw to cut well both with and across the grain, using the same saw. Whereas the ripcut pattern allows for versatility in use, the crosscut generally does not work as effectively for rip cutting and, though a crosscut saw will still rip, its effectiveness is markedly reduced. It is important to see that a shearing cut works well and that the only problem area might occur on the outcut face of the wood, depending on the sharpness of the saw teeth, the front pitch of the rake, and then the size of the teeth and the effort used. Using a knifewall method to delineate cut lines prevents any risk of breakout on the outcut fibres and so such problems can easily be eliminated.

The fleam teeth that create a crosscut tooth pattern are mostly used for special work requiring a more highly refined cut.

I find it somewhat debateable whether the best tool for crosscutting is alway the pinnacle-shaped tooth of the fleam pattern saw. Experience tells me that my cuts with smaller ripcut teeth parallel the crosscut quality when the teeth are hand filed rather than sharpened with the sophisticated machines used by manufacturers to initialise saw teeth. There can be no doubt that, with good saw makers, the teeth are indeed highly refined and accurately cut. Whether we achieve the same results with hand-eye coordination is doubtful unless we have a great deal of experience and consistent file quality. However, I want to reiterate that hand filing, even by an amatuer, produces good results. Most of the saws I buy, as refined handsaws and tenon saws, need extra refining by my hands. Whether or not sharpening to a crosscut profile is worth doing is up to the individual and the work he or she is involved in. Some work can demand the extra step and it is easily done, but generally it is not necessary and this is especially so with smaller-toothed saws such as those we use in small and mid-sized backsaws.

The Coping Saw

It is all too easy to dismiss so common a saw as the simple-looking coping saw; after all it is a commonplace saw, included in almost all toolboxes. I first bought and used mine when I was about fifteen and I still remember my children's faces when they cut with one for the first time. For me, it remains a most essential woodworking tool. Apart from the sentimental reasons for which I have enjoyed this saw, it really works for a wide range of uses ranging from metal cutting to shaping wood and, of course, no other saw 'cope cuts' better than the coping saw. Serious developments to improve its engineering design and quality have given us a lifetime tool for very little money. The intricate profiles and fine scrolls cut by the coping saw can be very simple or as complex as any you might encounter; including scribes and circles of just about any size, when most of the other saws merely cut straight lines.

As far as saws go, the coping saw is a relative newcomer to the world of woodworking, in that I have found no catalogue references by makers before about 1920. Also known as a 'scribing saw' because it is commonly used for scribed cuts, the coping saw was preceded by the wooden bow saw, which held narrow saw blades in stiff frames of wood for cutting larger profiled shapes of all kinds and also for piercing work in wood and softer metals for inlay work. The coping saw is closely related to two lightweight cousins used for cutting thin metals and veneers. Still made from spring steel and similar in construction and function to the coping saw, are two other metal-framed saws; the jeweller's saw and the fret saw. Though closely allied as trade saws, and very similar in appearance and functionality, the coping saw is much more robust as it is designed to work through thicker stock, which requires much greater rigidity to push or pull the blade through the wood.

The user of the coping saw is most likely the joiner, carpenter, and furniture maker, rather than those involved in more refined work such as jewellery making, intarsia, and, inlay marquetry, to name just a few. It was the development of steel alloys and metal working processes that permitted the inception of the coping saw. Its lightweight, narrow, spring-steel frame and thin blade offered a high-tensile steel saw that could be rotated along the blade's long axis, full circle, and then further turned in its entirety, as a frame, using hand manipulation, according to the exact shape needed. Effectively, this saw replicated the wooden versions of the turning saw but with much higher levels of tensioning and tighter tolerances because of the strength in the frame and the fineness of the blade itself.

The lightweight frame gives the tool the essential rigidity, spring, and strength to cut through wood by providing enough built-in power to withstand almost any and all alternating forces. It must have sufficient strength and rigidity to maintain consistent levels of tautness on the blade throughout cuts, whether used on the push or pull strokes. This makes it one of the most versatile and compact shaping saws we use today in woodworking. Once the blade is tightened, tensioned, and aligned in its frame it becomes very stable. This gives very direct and positive control for precise cutting of intricate and irregular shapes. Because the blade rotates a full 360-degrees between the two anchor points along its axis, the blade can be presented to the wood at any angle and then changed at intervals, if necessary, throughout the course of the cut. Imagine cutting jigsaw pieces in ¾" (19mm) oak and then you will understand how the blade spins and turns according to the artisans hand direction and control.

Most western coping saws take a 6 ½" (165mm) blade length and the blades are usually sold in packs of six or ten. Most coping saws have a 5" (125mm) cutting depth we call the 'throat,' which is the distance between the blade and the back of the frame. This limits the depth of cut or reach. However, often we can reorient the blade and use it turned to 90-degrees to cut parallel to an edge as if cutting sideways.

It is not just curved work that we use the coping saw for. You can also use it for removing waste before paring the surface to a finished level with a chisel.

Here I am removing the waste to create a twin tenon for a project. It is quick and effective to use the tenon saw for the two long cuts and then slide the coping saw blade into the cut and turn the corner.

What to Look for in a Coping Saw

I have used the same Eclipse coping saw since 1966 and today a similar saw costs a small fraction of what I paid, which was half a day's pay when I bought mine. The importance of this saw type depends on how much you will need such a saw in your work but, for most woodworkers, they become quite the indispensable tool simply because there is really no substitute for the kind of work we use them for.

A SOLID FRAME

Substandard coping saws with insufficient tensile frame strength allow the blade to buckle in the stroke, even when there is little pressure, and this frustrates the work as the blade springs from the frame mid-stroke. It is important to find a reputable maker that offers the ideal combination of light weight, rigidity, and, of course, strength.

A WOODEN HANDLE

One of the ideal components used in the manufacture of a coping saw will always be a comfortable, well-shaped handle. Despite the introduction of elastoplasticized composite handles to replace most wooden handles, the wooden handle still remains my favourite. Of course, it is important that both the wooden handle and the steel frame holding and directing the blade are equal to the task. The union between the handle and the frame must be rock-solid once tensioned and immoveable in the work to give directness in the cut. Any give between the working parts of the handle, frame, and blade reduces accuracy in the cut. Confident cutting results in the kind of precision we depend on as we work.

A FINE CUTTING BLADE

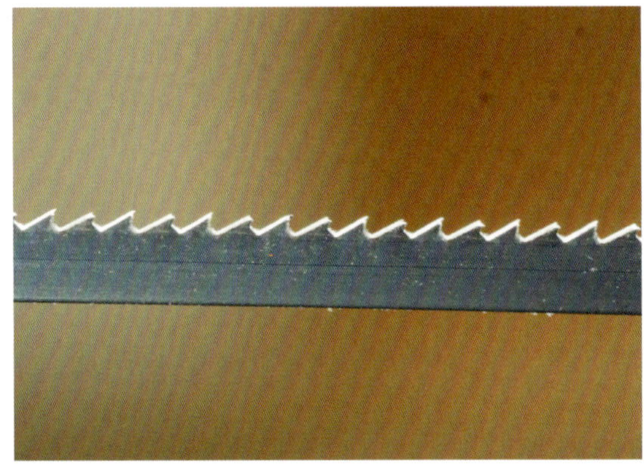

Coping saw blades are hardened and cannot be resharpened at all. However, the blades last well for several months, depending on usage. The blades are inexpensive and they can be used on softer metals, even up to mild steel. That is why they last a long time when used for wood alone. They come with a ripcut tooth profile only and there are no crosscut blades. The reason is simple enough, the finer teeth cut both ripcut and crosscut effectively; just as the smaller, finer teeth in other saws, such as dovetail saws, cut with and across the grain using a ripcut tooth pattern. Fine teeth cut smoothly both ways.

The tooth sizes vary from coarse cut to fine cut. Usually the 14 PPI blade would be the coarser end for me but I like to use these for long rip cuts and also for rip cutting thicker material, which is when they really come into their own. The 24 PPI blades cut a fine and smooth cut for much of the work I might do, whereas a good median blade of 18 PPI is a useful and practical size of tooth. Buying coping saws more cheaply secondhand is a good idea if you identify the maker. Each continent or country has its own makers and older ones do not generally degrade through age alone so secondhand is often a good way to go. I buy them inexpensively so that I can load the three different grades of blade in the different saws and be ready to go, no matter the task.

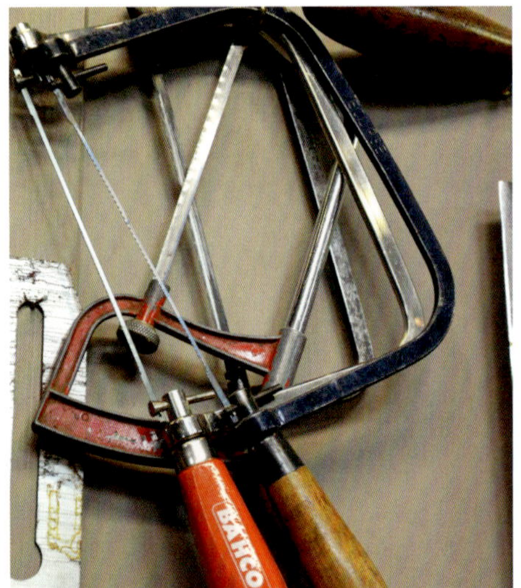

Coping Saws for Children

As my children grew up with me in the workshop, I gave them the coping saw over all other saws. Of course they were supervised, as all children in a workshop must be, but those early experiences laid the foundation for them to become skilled in their own right. With this simple coping saw they had exactly the right amount of friction-free cutting they needed to make productive cuts in their wood. They made many a dozen spatulas and wooden spoons with their saws and even their first dovetails. Soon they were working alongside their dad giving him the best memories.

Coping saws are especially good for children to work with for, say, sawing out shapes for spoons, spatulas, and cutting boards or even puzzle pieces.

Using the Coping Saw

The coping saw can be held with both hands on the handle or with just the dominant hand on the handle and the other on either the frame or on the wood to give support. This depends on how much power you want in the cut. Most commonly we start cuts with one hand on the handle and the thumb by the side of the blade to ensure the blade stays to the initial cut line. Otherwise the blade tends to dance around. Once started, two hands can go to clasp the handle or one to the wood to reduce vibrational flexing.

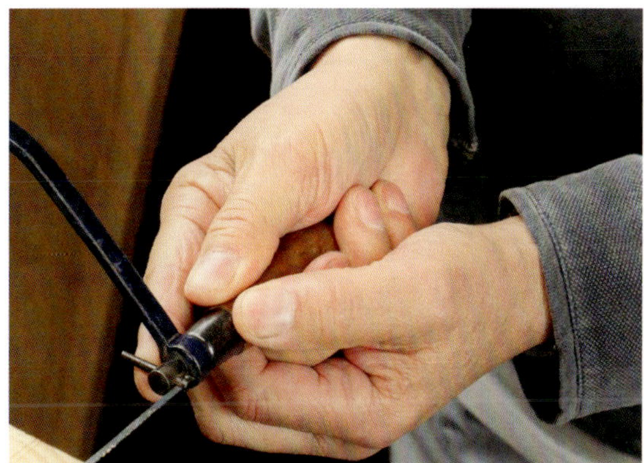

Here I push the saw into the cut and use my non-dominant hand to counter the pressure of the stroke. This reduces vibration and also stabilizes my body too.

Using my dominant hand for force and guidance, I also use my non-dominant hand to direct the saw and stabilize the extension at the top extreme of the saw.

Regardless of whether you orient the saw teeth to cut on the pull stroke (teeth facing toward the handle and you) or the push stroke (teeth away from you), turning a corner to change direction relies on making the turn on the actual cut stroke. Whichever way you use the saw blade, push or pull, determines which you become accustomed to and which habit you develop. I use the push stroke only. Careful cutting with the right blade allows me to turn a virtual 90 degrees in two strokes, as I turn on the forward cut strokes. The blades are also well resistant to breakage even though they can and do break from time to time.

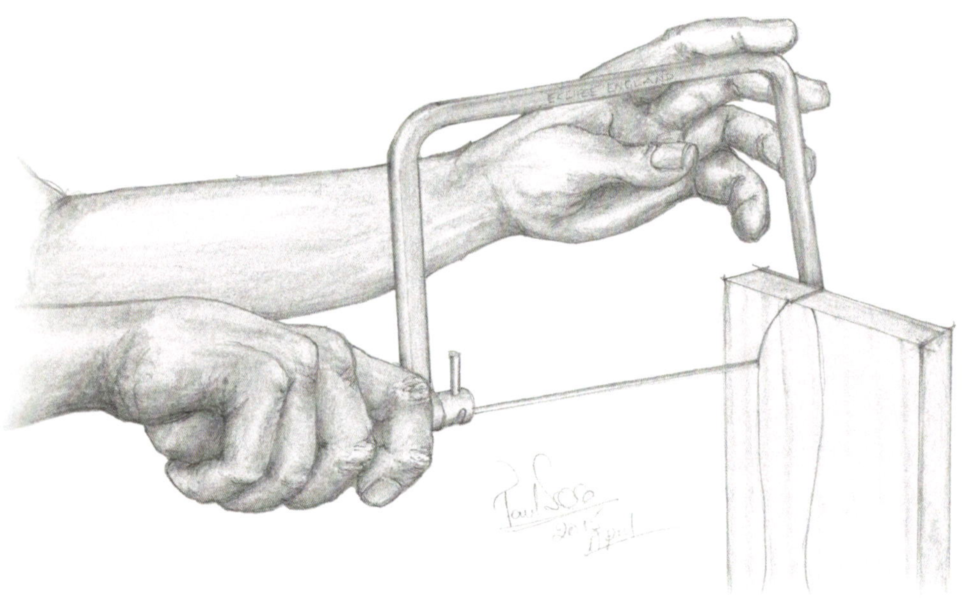

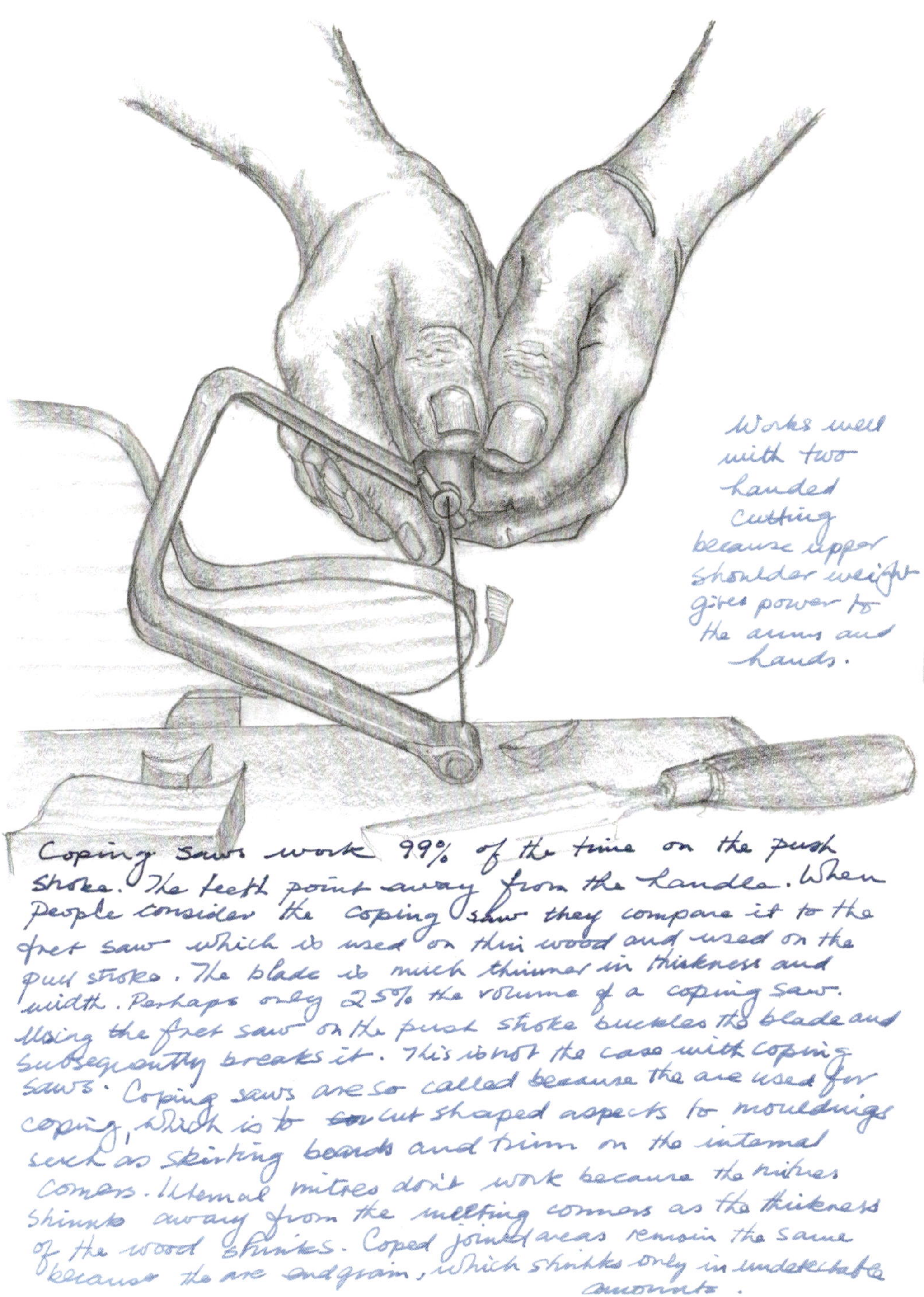
Works well with two handed cutting because upper shoulder weight gives power to the arms and hands.
Coping saws work 99% of the time on the push stroke. The teeth point away from the handle. When people consider the coping saw they compare it to the fret saw which is used on thin wood and used on the pull stroke. The blade is much thinner in thickness and width. Perhaps only 25% the volume of a coping saw. Using the fret saw on the push stroke buckles the blade and subsequently breaks it. This is not the case with coping saws. Coping saws are so called because the are used for coping, which is to cut shaped aspects to mouldings such as skirting boards and trim on the internal corners. Internal mitres don't work because the mitres shrink away from the meeting corners as the thickness of the wood shrinks. Coped joint areas remain the same because the are endgrain, which shrinks only in undetectable amounts.

Cutting on the Push or Pull Stroke

The coping saw offers us both push and pull strokes in a single saw, according to how we orient the blade in the frame of the saw. This, of course, is the advantage any frame brings to thin- and wide-bladed saws. There are advantages to both options, according to the task in hand. By simply loosening the handle and flipping the blade end for end we can change the way the saw works. People often tell me it is wrong to position the teeth pointed away from me but that is not the case. Throughout my training, the men always used the coping saw on the push stroke and never the pull. You get much more power in the cut this way and, of course, cutting through the face and leaving the visible face crisp and clean with no breakout is always an advantage.

Using the coping saw on the pull stroke works well too and when you use an underhand pull stroke with the wood supported on a platform, such as in fret saw work, the marking then is on the top side and you can follow your line. In other situations, say, for thicker material, I find it is much harder to pull than push. In many cases the work cannot be flipped and you must work into the visible face. This then becomes problematic and here you can see me pulling the saw where the line is fractured and so too the outer face, which matters. Cutting the same material on the push stroke leaves the line visible and the surface unfractured. We should, however, never say that only one way is the right way when there can be good reasons for reversing for a specific advantage.

Replacing the Coping Saw Blade

To load the blade and unload or replace it you must loosen the handle by rotating it counterclockwise, whilst holding the small lever that changes the direction of the blade firmly to the frame. This reduces tension on the blade and stops the lever and blade from turning too. The screw-threaded handle tightens and loosens the blade from the frame to allow blade changing and directional changes also. Turning the handle clockwise tensions the blade and counterclockwise turns loosen the tension and allows the blade to come free. Usually you need to pull the two ends of the frame in toward one another to actually withdraw the blade ends from the slots. The blades have a pin through the blade ends which slips into the slit and an angled notch that holds the blade into the frame. With the blade in place and, again, holding the lever to the frame to prevent it from turning, tighten the handle by turning it clockwise all the way. This then holds the blade solidly in place. From here on, we can use this locking mechanism to adjust the angle of the blade to the frame of the saw to allow for any turning in the cuts we make. To change direction simply loosen the handle one turn counterclockwise, adjust both levers either end of the saw frame and tighten to lock the angle and the handle. The blade can be adjusted to perform at any angle we need. Notice that both levers, at opposite ends of the blade, must be rotated close to the same angle to work effectively.

Confusing the Saws

I think it can be confusing looking at some of the frame saws. The confusion really arises when people think that the coping saw is the same as the fret and jeweller's saws, which, though sized differently can look as though they are just an alternative option. These saws definitely favour the pull stroke but as an underhand pull down rather than a pull towards the user; a very different approach and task altogether. These two saws were used on a platform with the work supported on top and the blade pulling on a downward cut-stroke through a hole. Generally the workpiece was moved around on the platform support to optimise the angle of presentation for the cut. The blades, being much, much finer and thinner would buckle if used on the push stroke.

It Is Called a Coping Saw for a Reason

A coping saw is so called because it cuts copes but what is a cope? A cope is the cut we make to shape the end of one piece of wood to fit over a second, moulded piece, often using the same shaped stock to intersect perfectly to the face of an adjacent corresponding mould. The common reason to use a coped cut rather than a 45-degree cut is to do with wood shrinkage. For example, when cutting skirting boards, because the wood is fixed to the wall, all shrinkage must shrink in from the outer face toward the wall. This then means that any internal mitre automatically shrinks inwards toward the wall and away from the front face resulting in a visible gap at the meeting internal corner. Though the adjoined piece of a coped cut still shrinks, coping the other piece reduces the total shrinkage and so minimises the probability of gaps.

A coped cut is created like this:

Mark, cut and plane the mitre to 45-degrees.

Now cut the straight cuts with a fine toothed saw.

The curved cuts are then cut using the coping saw.

The internal corner is very neat and exact using this traditional method.

Coping Saws for Dovetails and Pin Recess Cutting

As a boy, we often used the coping saw to remove the waste between the tails or pins of dovetails close to, or even right on, the depth lines. It was fast and effective if a little crude. You can use finer coping saw blades for this and they work well. I generally do this if the work is coarser and less refined; a beehive, a garden seed tray, or tool carrier for instance.

Scraping & Abrading Tools

Working with something as raw as wood fibre, where the strands often grow in ungoverned ways and a combination of natural influences affect the trees as they grow, our efforts can be frustrated as we work to tame the grain. No matter the sharpness of the tool's cutting edge, grain lifts and tears in ways that defy description. Although we can and do sharpen an edge tool to tackle a very particular challenge in a piece of wood we might be working, such localised refining of a tool edge is often too time consuming to keep setting up to task. As skills in using hand tools diminish, most woodworkers have turned all the more to abrasives, such as sandpaper and sanding machines, to resolve difficult situations. Commercial equipment, such as large drum sanders, are often beyond our more domestic needs and resorting to power sanders introduces a range of dangers to the environment and the workpiece. Most of us cannot or do not want to go down that road and yet we still have to resolve the issues surrounding difficult grain patterns and that is when we reach for one of the tools in this category of scraping or abrading tools.

Scrapers slice the surface of wood in a very unique way and most of the files we use present a series of broad teeth that actually cut the surface too. Even the rasps we use cut the surface with fairly regularly shaped upstanding teeth 'stitched' into the surface of steel. None of these tools compare to the abrasives we use for making sandpaper, which generally comprise irregular shaped particles of abrasive adhered to paper or some other material to abrade the surface. In woodworking we look mostly for tools that sever and separate fibre by a cutting strategy. Though we do indeed call these tools 'scrapers' and 'abrading' tools, they actually refine our efforts by using sharp teeth in the form of files and rasps, and the cutting edges of scrapers. We should not misconstrue the actions beneath the tool by the names we give them. Scrapers slice and cut the fibres and indeed rasps and files cut the surface too. So, in this chapter, we investigate a series of tools that offer us the control we need to tame what otherwise might be impossible with the other tools we have.

There can be no doubt that scrapers are indispensable tools for woodworkers, redeeming projects that might

otherwise have to be abandoned. To date no other tool has been invented to replace them or better them. A well-sharpened and honed scraper will indeed refine almost any and all grain configurations and the harder the wood is, the better it works. Therein lies a clue as to its limitations. Generally the softer the wood, and I mean very soft woods indeed, the less effectively the scraper works; the tool can actually tear the surface fibres rather than slice them where the surface is more spongy and fails to give sufficient resistance for cuts to be made. You will learn how best to address these issues as you develop your understanding of the different scraper types and by using them for yourself. The amazing thing, still for me today, is that we have inherited a tool like no other used in woodworking.

Files look common enough but woodworkers generally allocate them more to the filing of metal and rarely consider them important to woodworking, beyond sharpening edges and refining the metal parts of tools. When you look more closely at the cutting edges, you discover a series of neatly cut teeth, arranged meticulously, to refine the surfaces of different materials ranging from plastics and metal to wood and other resistant materials too.

My Essential Scraping and Abrading Tools

I will now discuss the file, rasp, and scraper types in more detail. They can seem challenging at first but I think, over the years and beyond my initial guidance here, you will discover your own favourites and tie them to the type of work you do:

Scrapers

The term 'scraper' is the accepted name for two tools we use for removing fine shavings of wood in order to develop a pristine surface to our work. The cutting edges we develop for scrapers are perhaps the most uniquely refined and developed of all the edge tools we use. The concept for developing so fine a cutting edge is simple once you know how to create it. It was indeed a brilliant development. It is most unfortunate that we failed to match the tool with an appropriate name. 'Scraper' hardly describes any of its functions or at least its key attribute of shaving wood like no other tool.

In many ways I find difficulty describing the two tools for fear of failing to express their intrinsic value and significance in our work. We reach for one or the other of them hour by hour when we work the final surfaces of our wood, at that critical point where other tools have already failed us. When I reach to the well in my bench, where I keep these tools, I do not think at all of scraping my work but shaving away the most refined shavings in ribbons that leave everything smooth, level, and in order.

Scraper and Burr, Two Misnomers to Working Wood

The term 'scraper' is indeed quite strange because it does not scrape at all but slice-cuts with a pristinely sharp and continuous edge. Another consideration as to the terminology is the use of the term 'burr.' This is the term used to describe the tiny edge that is created in sharpening the scraper, which gives it its unique cutting action. It is a strange anomaly here that we use two terms, which have been used in conjunction with one another for centuries, and yet neither of the terms, in their commonly accepted definitions, accurately describes the true condition developed to make the tool function the way it does. The scraper does not scrape but slices in a unique slicing motion and the term burr, a name that might suggest a fractured corner resulting from through-filing, is a highly refined continuous cutting edge that knows no equal in sophistication and functionality. Indeed it is as though both names were accepted by default in the absence of someone troubling themselves to find an appropriate name. Perhaps we will never rename these elements now but I think both names do a disservice to one of the most valuable tools used in refined woodworking.

I hope that, by writing this, I can bring greater clarity to the general understanding of this tool. Both the created edge and the action of the tool are the highest level of simplicity and yet they stem from such considerate thought, showing a certain sophistication; probably the most sophisticated cutting edge ever used in woodworking. All other edge tools comprise two polished-out faces forming a cutting edge. The scraper is sharpened by the consolidation of steel that is effectively compelled into itself until the edge thickens, stroke by stroke, and then is turned in more or less than six further strokes with the burnisher (for more information on the burnisher see page 61). The result is the thinnest cutting edge possible for cutting wood.

An Alternative to Sandpaper for Surface Finishing

Sandpaper has become the standard means for smoothing and creating an acceptable surface in preparation for applying finishes. This is especially so for machine finishing methods. In the last half century, as machines became the standard method for manufacturing production in woodworking, using sandpaper to correct surface flaws left by machines has become the norm. Hand tools, such as scrapers and planes, can be used in such a way that they leave no such marks. Machines work on rotary cuts, which generally leave undulations in the work, whereas planes and scrapers take wide shavings with long strokes and leave the surface smooth. I believe we use more sandpaper today than ever in the history of woodworking as a direct result of using machines in industry. Unfortunately many industrial methods have now replaced the simpler methods and left a deficit in the skills of sharpening and using cabinet scrapers and planes. Good planing and scraping techniques almost eliminate the need for sanding simply because we hone and turn the edge to such fine levels of abrasion - 12,000-15,000 grit in some cases - or we burnish the steel into itself to smooth the edge as we turn with 'iron-on-iron' pressure, which, of course, has no grit as such. Sandpaper might still be used even when you have mastered the scrapers. However, instead of using sandpaper to smooth out flaws in the wood, you will use it more to give 'tooth' to the wood's surface to give the applied finish, such as varnish, a surface to hold and adhere to. Without this tooth the wood can be too smooth for the finish to stick to. Any applied finish then pulls away from the surface as it cures.

Wood Types Affect the Scraper

It is important to identify that the type of wood you are working plays a major part in what kind of finish you can achieve with scrapers and this is important to remember.

Both scraper types rely on surface firmness in the wood grain; a certain level of density, structural strength or resistance, and closeness of grain structure is necessary for scrapers to work effectively. Softer grained woods cannot generally support the pressure of the type of cut you get from a turned cutting edge. The soft surface fibres tend to compress under and away from the cutting edge as pressure is applied. So, to achieve any decent results, you must scrape softer wood surfaces with a newly sharpened edge, lighter pressure, and angled slicing cuts, which allow the edge to better cut the fibres.

A pine board can only be scraped with a super-sharp, newly turned edge but even then the surface is not generally going to be as good as can be achieved on dense-grained hardwoods.

Oak works well with both card and cabinet scrapers.

Steel Consolidation

Something that I notice is mentioned less and less these days is what we once referred to as 'steel consolidation.' It is a critical step in sharpening scrapers and it is an important concept to retain. I cannot see what exactly is happening on a molecular level but, in theory, consolidation compels the steel into itself to enable us to develop the super-thin edge we need. We press the hardened steel burnisher (or 'ticketer') hard down on the large face, either side of the edge to be burnished, and move the burnisher back and forth heavily. Usually 30 of these consolidation strokes, back and forth, is enough for each side or flat face of the plate. Keep the burnisher flat throughout as you present the strokes. This process gives out a ticking sound as the burnisher drops off either end of the scraper blade in the action of consolidation.

Sharpening the Scrapers

THE CARD SCRAPER

To sharpen the card scraper we file, abrade and then use the burnisher to create a turned edge on both sides of the two long edges of the plate to create four individual cutting edges. We generally turn all four long edges at the same time for convenience and efficiency. Do not put off developing the intuitive side of filing as it is a readily developed skill. We generally file the card scraper in one of two ways. We can use the file perpendicular to the edge of the scraper and draw the file to develop a clear edge. This results in the file drawing off a continuous spiral of steel that spins out from the gulleys of the file to the side of the scraper. Alternatively you can slightly angle the file as a through-filing technique, from one end of the scraper to the other, with the file working along the plate of steel. Keep the file as square to the edge of the scraper as possible and,

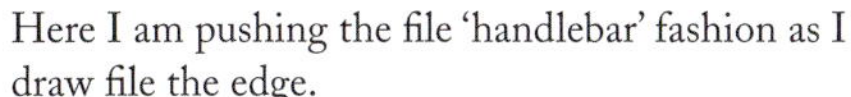

Here I am pushing the file 'handlebar' fashion as I draw file the edge.

This magnified image is of continuous spirals about ½" (12mm) long.

if in doubt, add a square edged piece of wood to ride the file on. Leave the wood $1/64$" (0.5mm) below the scraper edge and file until you hit the wood (see page 375). Once you have a clean, continuous, filed edge, polish out the edge by holding it to the 1200 grit (superfine) diamond plate and push back and forth about ten times keeping it as perpendicular to the plate as possible. Place the scraper flat on its side and polish the face of the plate by rubbing a few times on the 1200 grit plate. Do this to both sides of the scraper and repeat the entire process on the opposite edge. This usually removes the unwanted burr too. If it does not, do not worry as the next step of burnishing does. With the edges polished out we are ready to turn the long edges with the burnisher.

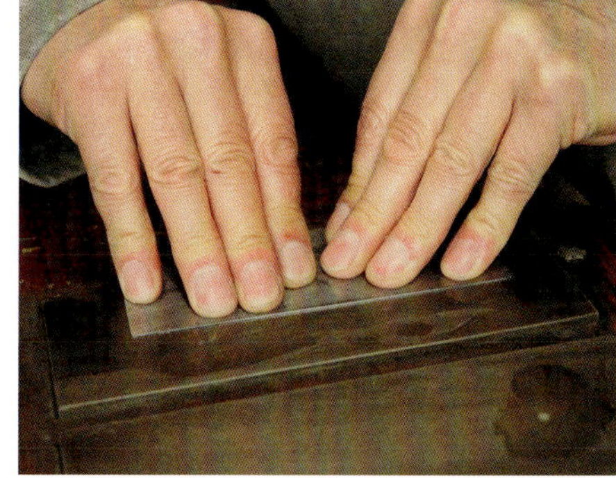

THE CABINET SCRAPER

To sharpen the cabinet scraper we file, abrade and use the burnisher to create a turned edge on both the long edges which have 45-degree bevels. As with the card scraper, we usually do both edges at the same time for convenience and efficiency, though there are only two edges that can be sharpened on the cabinet scraper blade whereas there are four with the card scraper. 45 degrees is the goal but if you end up under or over by a few degrees it makes little difference. Unlike the card scraper, we generally file the cabinet scraper with the file slightly angled for comfort and to maximise the probability of developing continuous spirals in the gullets of the file teeth. Work in a continuous stroke from one end of the scraper blade to the other. Keep the file as close to 45 degrees as possible and, if in doubt, add an angled piece of wood to help guide the file at 45 degrees (see page 375). Leave the wood 1⁄64" (0.5mm) down from the edge and file until you hit the wood. After filing, polish out the edge on the 1200 grit (superfine) diamond plate and push back and forth about ten times, keeping it as close as possible to the same 45-degree angle. You definitely do not want a second bevel to form at the edge. Then, place the scraper flat on its non-bevelled side and polish the flat face of the plate by rubbing a few times on the 1200 grit plate. Do all of this to both bevelled edges of the scraper. Polishing on the 1200 grit plate usually removes the unwanted burr that is created but do not worry if it does not as the next step of burnishing will take care of this. With the bevelled edges polished out, we are now ready to turn them with the burnisher.

“*To sharpen the cabinet scraper we file, abrade and use the burnisher to create a turned edge on both the long edges which have 45-degree bevels*”

Turning the Edge With the Burnisher

'Turning the edge' is the term we give to developing the final cutting edge to scrapers. This comprises three basic stages of development:

1. Flat face consolidation

With the card scraper you should consolidate the large faces on either side of the long edges of the scraper by pressing hard and moving the burnisher along each face back and forth repeatedly (usually 30 strokes). Repeat this for both sides of the two long edges.

With the cabinet scraper blade we consolidate the large flat face opposite the bevel by pressing hard and moving the burnisher back and forth repeatedly along the face (usually 30 strokes). We then repeat this on the other large flat face.

2. Square-edge or angle-edge consolidation

We now consolidate the long thin edge of the card scraper by, again, pressing hard and moving the burnisher firmly along the edge repeatedly (usually 10-20 strokes). Take care when holding the scraper blade and, on the card scraper, keep the burnisher as close to a right angle as possible.

Now as for the angled bevel of the cabinet scraper blade we push hard against the angled bevel with the burnisher and pull up repeatedly (usually 10-20 strokes). Hold the blade carefully and keep the angle at 45 degrees.

3. Turning the edge

While continuing to pull with the burnisher, with successive strokes, begin to, very slightly, change the angle from square to force the edge over, first on one side of the edge and then the other.

For the cabinet scraper continue to pull the burnisher and, with successive strokes, change the angle very slightly from 45 degrees and only on one edge (on each side).

These drawings show the developing stages of turning a scraper edge for both the card scraper and the cabinet scraper. The developed edges are exaggerated for clarity.

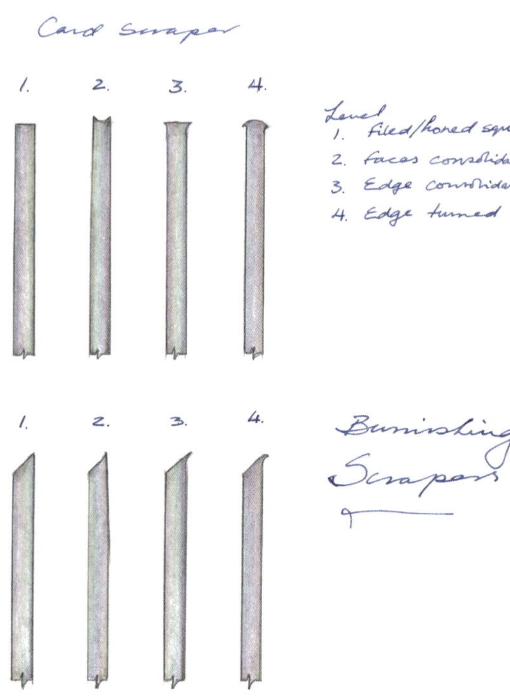

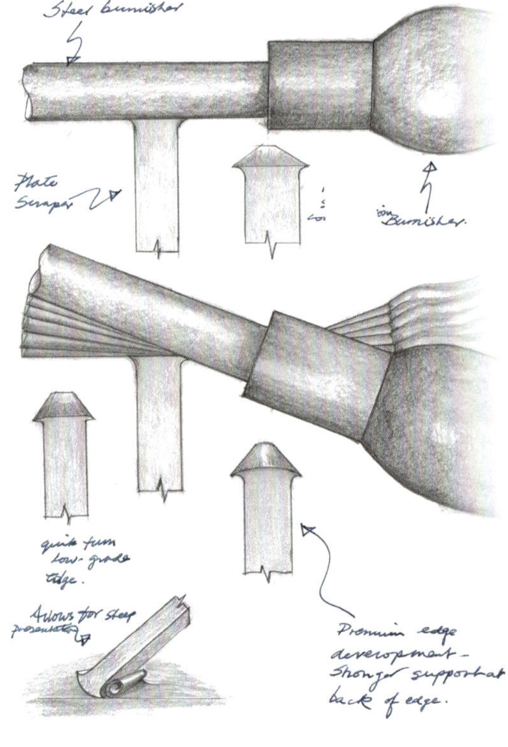

There are two ways I hold the burnisher and scraper blade simultaneously and both ways work on both types of scraper for consolidating and turning the edge. Singlehandedly - that is pulling the burnisher along the edge of the scraper and applying firm pressure evenly, end to end, with the scraper blade pressed to the benchtop with the non dominant hand - or two-handedly - with the scraper blade anchored, edge-up, in the vise and using both hands to pull and/or push the burnisher against the edge of the scraper. Both methods work equally well and at different times I might choose one over the other but for no obvious reason.

I like to lightly lubricate the burnisher, before applying it, with a wipe of light machining oil from my rag oiler, which I keep on my benchtop (see page 476). This reduces friction-grab and allows the burnisher to glide freely without the dragging effect steel on steel often has. This makes the whole operation of burnishing much smoother. Holding the burnisher requires strong hand pressure, confident strokes, and a good firm grip. If the scraper is supported on the benchtop the action is a series of swift upward pulls, directly from the benchtop, up the full length of the scraper edge, and off the top end, while keeping continuous contact to the edge with each pull. Burnishing and consolidation are really one and the same but, when we consolidate the steel plate on the flat faces, we refer to this as 'consolidation' because we are effectively preparing the nearest corners to the proposed cutting edges. Skipping this side-face consolidation leads to earlier edge fracture.

Setting up the Cabinet Scraper

Once sharpened, the card scraper is ready to use but you must set up the blade of the cabinet scraper in the main body before you can use it. The cabinet scraper blade is loaded flush to the sole of the scraper and, once installed and fastened tight, we adjust the blade via the thumbscrew centred in the body casting. The strategy for installing the blade after sharpening is specific.

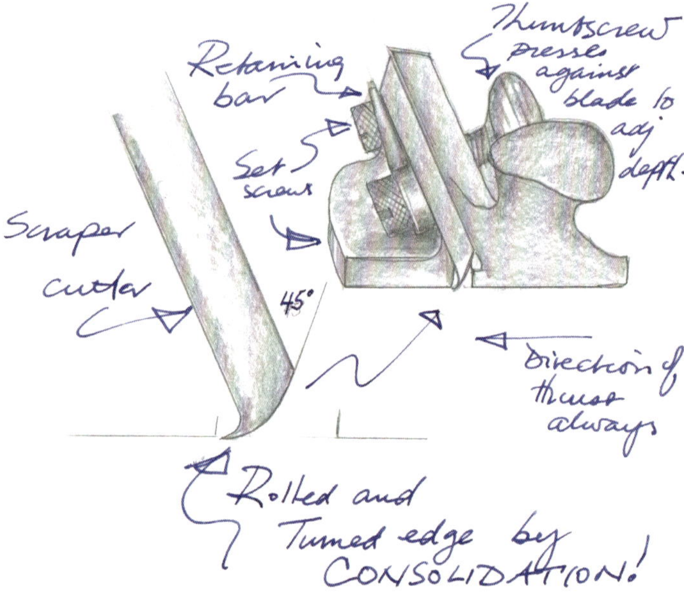

Note:
Cabinet scrapers often arrive with the blade facing the wrong way. This is because many people do not understand that the 'turned edge' works completely differently to regular cutting edges formed between a bevel and flat face. This drawing, which exaggerates the sharpened edge detail, shows the only way to load the blade into the tool body. You can see how the turned edge engages the wood to remove shavings.

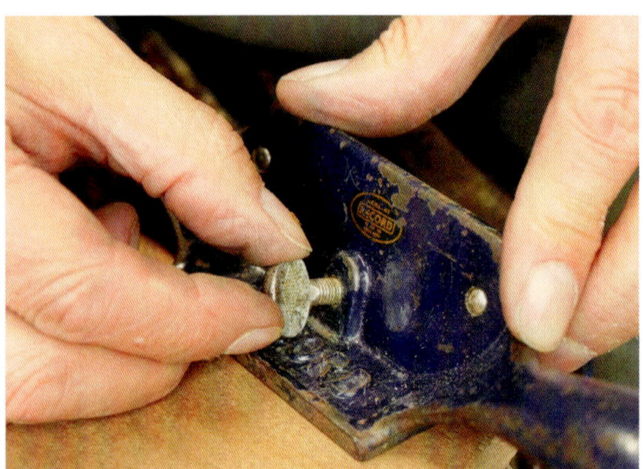

Step 1: With the blade removed, turn the thumbscrew counter-clockwise to make certain the end is not protruding past the inner face of the casting.

Step 2: Loosen the retaining bar, if necessary, and insert the blade between it and the casting. Make certain to keep the sole flat against the surface you are resting it on which could be a machine top, granite block, or a smooth, flat board. This will keep the blade flush to the sole. Then squeeze the retaining bar and the blade against the bed of the scraper.

Step 3: Tighten the bar-retaining screws to the back of the blade, making sure to keep the pressure even between both setscrews. Note: Different makers use different fastenings. Some use knurled nuts and some use thumbscrews.

Step 4: Use a hard object (like a tool handle or nylon mallet face) to push the blade down, flush to the surface you are supporting the cabinet scraper on. Press both sides of the blade. Cinch the bar-retaining screws as tight as possible.

Step 5: Offer the scraper to the wood to see if any blade is protruding. Push forward and test for thickness both sides of the blade. Usually it will take nothing or very little off at this stage. Turn the thumbscrew clockwise half a turn to touch the back of the blade and try again on the wood. Continue to adjust incrementally as necessary.

The scraper should produce a shaving immediately.

Making a Filing Guide

A simple wooden filing guide, can be made for both card scrapers and cabinet scraper blades. It is simple to make and highly effective, especially for those starting out. It pretty much gives guaranteed square edges to card scrapers and bevels to cabinet scrapers. Of course it may wear out or become inaccurate after many sharpenings because you may catch it with the file causing it to lose its shape but it is made from scrap in a minute or two and so this should be seen as a worthwhile sacrifice. When I made mine I planed one edge square and the other to 45 degrees. I then used a handsaw to cut a kerf to receive the blades.

I clamp the filing guide with the blade in the vise, leaving the scraper blade protruding just barely above the guide surface. Half a millimeter is plenty for either scraper type Once secure I file until flush or close to flush.

These images show the two scraper types being used in the same guide.

Why Scrapers Work and the Differences Between the Types

Looking at the card and cabinet scrapers side by side, the superficial difference is obvious. The two types of scraper, though their blades are shaped and held differently, achieve the same results. The chief difference between the two cutting edges is how

they are presented to the wood in use. The cabinet scraper always presents the blade to the wood at the same fixed angle every time because it is held in the handled metal-cast body. The card scraper, on the other hand, is constantly altered according to feel and cutting capability. By altering the presentation angle it is easier to optimise the cutting potential by minute degrees, which can be infinitely varied minute by minute as the work progresses and according to grain change. The handled cabinet scraper only offers variance in direction of cut as the rake presentation remains fixed in the holder. That said, changing the angle of presentation along the long axis of the scraper allows us to change the type of cut from square-on to a more shearing cut. This effectively narrows the bandwidth of the cut for slicing, which again optimizes the performance at the edge. Occasionally, because of the angle of the grain, particularly with what is known as 'standing grain,' 'reverse grain,' and 'spiral grain,' we benefit from altering the rake of presentation slightly to tackle a particular area. The card scraper offers this additional flexibility, especially on localised areas where differences in grain structure fluctuate markedly. We cannot really see what is happening at the cutting edge but it is right at the cutting edge that you discover the main advantage the scraper has for tackling different grain. Often, when we look at wood, we see grain patterns and configurations that defy planes and planing for different reasons, not the least of which is the angle the plane iron is presented to the wood. In general planing, this angle is usually around 45 degrees. On low angle planes this can be between say 10 to 20 degrees but is almost always over 12 degrees. With some grains, especially crotch grain, curly grain, bird's-eye figuring and so on, even bevel-up planes, that generally fare well, often cannot work. Also, such planes rarely work over wide areas anyway. The scraper, on the other hand, and particularly the card scraper, can present the cutting edge at the lowest working angle of any tool we know of for shaving wide, elongated areas with. Perhaps even as low as two or three degrees to the surface of the wood and it is this that makes the strategy so dynamic in tackling wild and awkward grain. Add to this the fact that the shape of the cutting edge on a scraper means that all shavings taken are immediately forced back on themselves and you can understand how the scraper can accomplish this without causing unsightly torn grain.

Another key difference between the card scraper and the cabinet scraper is the support that the sole of the cabinet scraper gives to the tool. The expanse of the sole area spans the wood surface which then serves to maintain much greater levels of flatness to the

work beneath as it lowers the high points. This control is especially valued for close-tolerance work and reduces the risk of creating localised dips in the surface, something which sometimes happens inadvertently with card scrapers. At the workbench and in use we see the different strategies in using the two scraper types. Both have their own intrinsic qualities and both are highly valued for fine woodworking. To get down to the bottom level of a particular flawed area using the cabinet scraper we must work all the surrounding surface around the discrepancy, to reduce the overall height, until we can reach the central flaw. This effectively means that we must see the area surrounding the low spot as the offending wood and not necessarily just the lowest extreme. Larger areas need greater levels of energy and the cabinet scraper is especially good in giving the ability to bear down on the work because of the upper shoulder weight and arm muscle. This means we can remove material more quickly and, at the same time, keep the surface reasonably true to plane. On the other hand, with the card scraper, though we can use the same principle of razing the surrounding surface area too, if needed, it enables us to directly tackle the lowest of low spots in the surface area. This is especially useful when the flaw is very shallow and it is unnecessary to tackle the wider area.

Whereas the cabinet scraper is highly effective at removing material and maintaining even levels with good results, the card scraper enables us to take much lighter and more refined cuts than when using the cabinet scraper and it usually, but not always, follows the cabinet scraper. The handles to the cabinet scraper do give a more secure feeling as you work the surface and it is also easier to adjust the blade in the scraper to take deeper cuts.

An unseen, but often felt, aspect of the two types of scraper is the heat build up taking place at and behind the cutting edges. After ten or so swipes with the card scraper the steel often becomes very hot to hold. Heat in cabinet scrapers is high too but your hands

do not touch the cutting iron itself. When working large areas needing card scraper work I use two scrapers alongside one another, which means I can switch them out for an intermittent cooling off period and keep working. On small surface areas this may not become noticeable, but on large surfaces, such as tables, you must take special care.

Hands and Handling the Scrapers

There are different hand positions for using the card and cabinet scrapers. The cabinet scraper and the card scraper are not handled the same way at all because they are indeed two quite different tools as you will have seen in the earlier text and images. What unites them in the scraper category is that they both create a unique dynamic for slice-cutting surface fibres with a very specific turned edge. The main difference between the two is that one, the card scraper, is held in the hands and fingers and the other, the cabinet scraper, is a blade held in a cast metal carrier that supports the scraper blade. Both rely on a flexed bow to the plate or blade to present the cutting edge to the wood. One is mechanically applied using a setscrew or thumbscrew and the other is applied through hand and finger pressure.

USING THE CABINET SCRAPER

The cabinet scraper can be bulldogged to task and perhaps there are times when we do this. The practical elements determining the shape of the cabinet scraper do not allow the thumb to wrap around the whole handle. Often people tuck the thumb along the side of the forefinger and rely on finger power to grip with but the cabinet scraper is designed to benefit from the thumbs pressing to the back, inclined face of the scraper. This close proximity levers the thumbs to their highly effective use, giving very direct thrust right behind the cutting edge and, at the same time, reducing skudding. The fingers are often quite close together but slightly open, spider-like, rather than clenched. This too is an act that gives good transfer leverage from the fingers of each hand to the thumbs in the back of the scraper.

Though the cabinet scraper is generally applied to the wood from a pushing stance, away from the upper body, in thrusts, there are occasions where it must be pulled. Pulling is less productive and lacks the power you get from forward thrusts. We might use the pull stroke for a couple of reasons such as working surfaces on the inside of a cabinet or when we cannot reach from the side or end of a panel such as a tabletop.

When using the pull stroke, it is always best to work with a new and freshly sharpened edge. It slice-cuts more readily and pulls itself to the surface all the way through instead of tending to glide over the surface.

USING THE CARD SCRAPER

The most common hand position used with the card scraper is three fingers either side, on the short edges, and both thumbs then flexing the plate to create an arc to the length of the plate. At this point the scraper is presented to the wood leaning forward and pushed, away from the body, along the surface of the wood being refined. The thumb pressure flexes the bow into the scraper and the more you apply pressure, the greater the bow and the more localised and narrow the contact area becomes. Yes, this does create a hollow in the surface being worked, but it is not usually discernible. The card scraper has four cutting edges, one to each side of the long edges of the plate. This means that when one edge dulls or fractures you can flip or turn the scraper to another edge. It also means that you can sharpen each corner slightly differently too; one corner with a larger and more aggressively burred or turned edge that cuts more deeply and another with a finer wire edge. When all the edges are dulled you must turn them afresh to restore them. Most turned edges to card scrapers can be re-turned 3-4 times using the burnisher on the edge before full restoration is needed. By this I mean that you can simply burnish and turn the edges without filing them. After this you must restore the edge by filing, honing, consolidating, and turning. You will always get the best edge, however, by starting with a freshly filed scraper. This is worth bearing in mind when you are working on a special or difficult piece.

> *The card scraper has four cutting edges, one to each side of the long edges of the plate*

This exagerated drawing shows the card scraper with four turned corners forming what we call the 'hook', the four cutting edges we use to cut with.

A second hand position I saw most commonly used when I was a young woodworker, and one I adopt regularly, is where we use the heel of the hand to flex the plate into an arc. In this case, it is the last two or three fingers of the hand that hold the plate against the heel of that hand along with the forefinger and thumb of the other. This means that the heel is centred in the back of the scraper plate and the fingers counter the pressure of the heel until the arc is formed. The other hand serves more to support the scraper when using this hand position. Experiment to see which hand position suits the work best.

In its simplicity and its complexity the card scraper is prized by craftsmen for its highly refined and developed cutting edge as much as for its simplicity of use. Thousands upon thousands of diverse grain permutations exist to stump the artisan in surface finishing wood; this tool tames them all, providing the wood is densely grained enough.

Assuming the card scraper is sharp, this scraper shaves the surface of most wood, as long as it is presented to the wood correctly. In time, you, as the user, will come to truly understand the flexes and techniques in the different moves and you will find yourself taking decisions on these minute by minute. Narrow edges to curves can be readily refined after the spokeshave or even the bandsaw.

In instrument making, card scrapers can be curved and coved to create the shape best suited for working the front and back plates; and they work well for levelling the purfling to the outer edges around the ever-changing grain direction.

Very thin card scrapers can be bent to various shapes but I also like to cut card scrapers for specific uses. One of my favourites is one that I have shaped especially for use in the bowls of carved spoons. I made it by taking a normal card scraper, cutting it using a hacksaw and then refining it with a file and diamond stones. This just shows another of the many great ways that scrapers can be used and enjoyed.

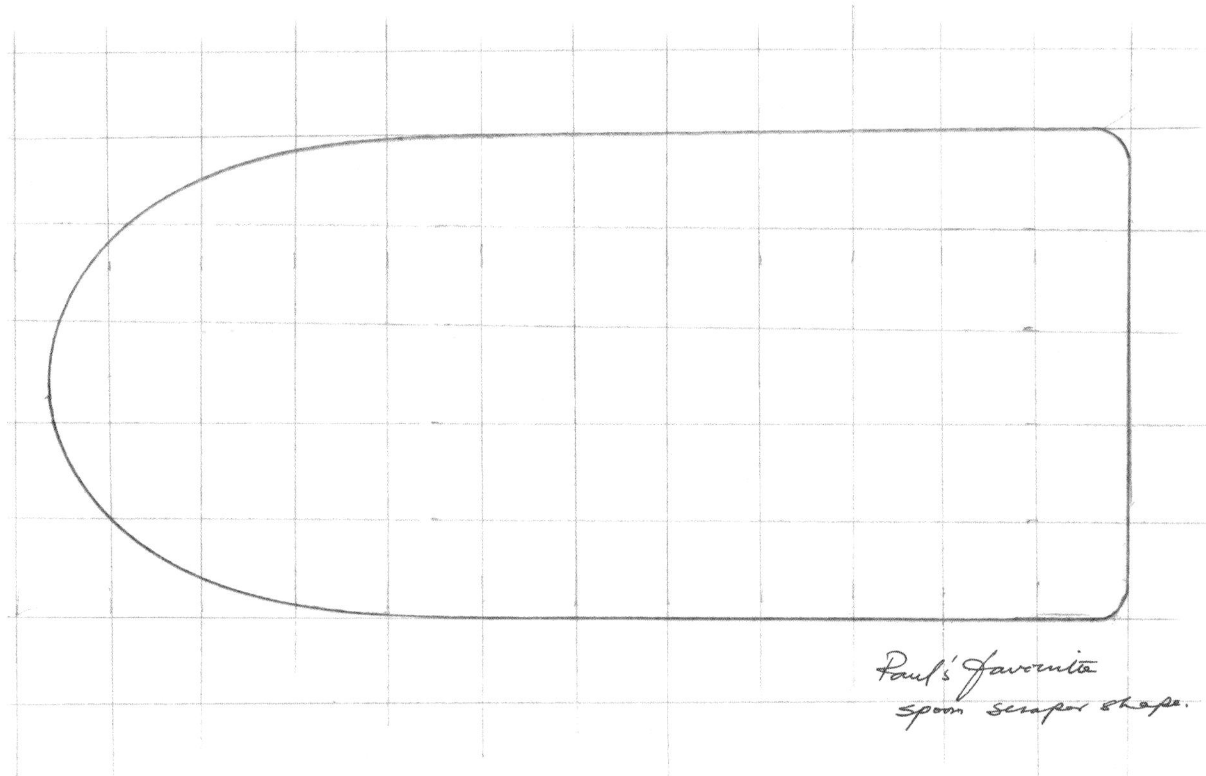
Paul's favorite
spoon scraper shape.

Rasps & Files

It may be surprising but writing this section on rasps and files inspired me. These tools are hard, the very hardest of all the tools we woodworkers might use. When I look at them on my rasp and file shelf they seem inflexibly rigid, even harsh, and somehow counterintuitive to what I do in crafting my wood. My work is more gentle to me, more soft and absorbing and less mechanically austere. But then, when I pick out the exact rasp and file to suit the work, when I choose the right one for an area of wood I see, all that changes. The tool becomes something more adaptable and my work emerges into something I cannot create using any other tool.

Rasps and Files Are Two Different Tools

Rasps and files are not so much general-use tools for the main part of woodworking but we pick them up, from time to time, to shape and refine our work. Carvers use them more extensively, as might more specialized artisans building gunstocks, guitars, violins and so on. In general woodworking, we may only occasionally see them used whereas if you are a chair maker, creating individual chairs by hand, your perspective may well be radically different. Rasps and files are often seen to be one and the same tool but that is because they have the same general shape, are made in similar sizing, and because we use them in the same fashion too. However, they are uniquely different tools and are only marginally alike. On the one hand, files have broad teeth that span the full width of the file face to designated widths, according to size. Though similarly sized, rasps are different in that the faces have raised individual bumps, uniformly placed across the working face of the rasp. Rasp teeth can be cut into the face by hand or by machine. The machine takes only a few minutes whereas a hand-stitched rasp can take up to an hour or more, depending on the grain number; the finer the grain (size and spacing of teeth in relation to rasp width), the higher the number of teeth per pass. Both the rasp and the file are made to different lengths also. Most of the ones we use for working wood are between 8" (20cm) and 12" (30cm) long but we do use shorter ones for finer, closer work.

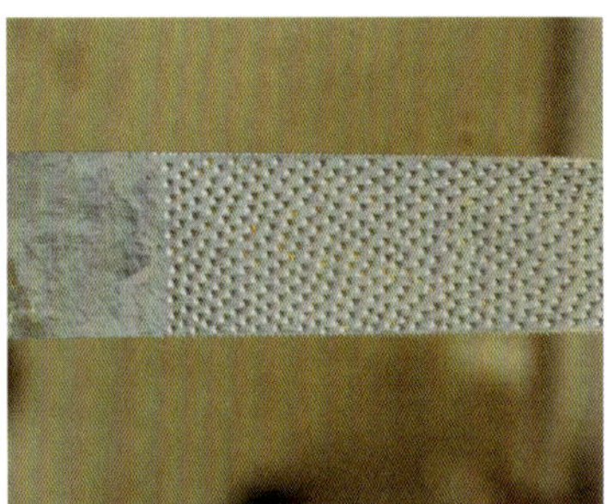

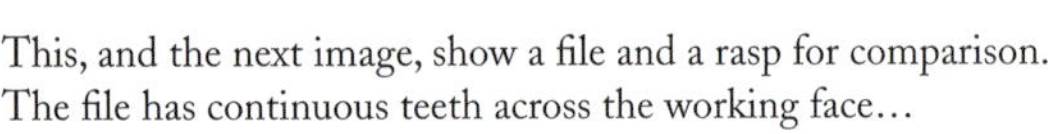
This, and the next image, show a file and a rasp for comparison. The file has continuous teeth across the working face…

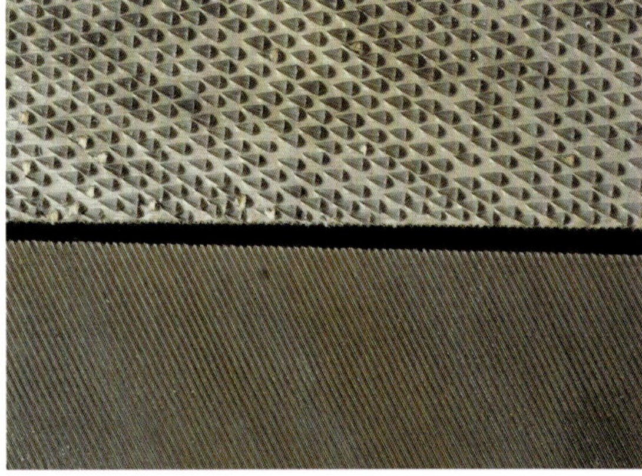

...the rasp has what might be described as more barb-like teeth, although they are not actually barbed as such.

Rasps

Rasps are in a class of their own when it comes to shaping wood. They have evolved through many centuries and there may well be only a handful of people in the world that can hand-stitch a rasp, using their own two hands, a pick, and a rasp-maker's hammer. Most of the rasps used today are mass made by machine methods whereby the teeth are punched into the surfaces by a mechanical process. This, of course, works but I have yet to use a mechanically made rasp that matches the work of those stitched by hand. Some do come close but they are not the same and this is because hand stitching creates a slightly more irregular pattern that tackles the wood more effectively and gives a smoother, more even finish.

This is a closeup of the hand-stitched teeth on the rasp. They are randomly placed which, perhaps surprisingly, aids in smooth and efficient cutting.

What makes the file and rasp different to all of my other woodworking tools is the unalterable condition in which they come from the maker. These are the only tools I can never adjust by redefining their shape or their cutting edges. The depths of cuts are internally built in and constrained by the depth of the gullet in front of the teeth. I never alter or refine the cutting edges because I cannot. This seems counterintuitive to me and to who I am simply because I can better the working edges of all my other cutting tools by making minute changes. Accepting this means I must work within the limits set by the makers. Finding the best rasps and files available and supporting the makers is therefore ever-important. Paying a larger amount for a good quality rasp, stitched by hand, is a worthwhile investment if it supports the individuals making them and then supports you in your work too. Whether there will be a rasp maker stitching in the ways of the crafting artisan in a decade or two I do not know but I sincerely hope that to be the case.

Hand stitched rasps show a certain unevenness in configuration that, when well executed, guarantees the efficient removal of material you do not usually get with mechanically produced ones.

For the reasons given here I prefer, and recommend, hand stitched rasps. They are truly remarkable tools.

CABINET RASPS

We use a category of rasps generally called 'cabinet rasps' for as wide a range of shaping work as you could ever imagine. For general woodworking, instrument making, and furniture making, most work can be accomplished with two or three as long as you are planning to use them in synchrony with other tools such as spokeshaves, saws, and scrapers. Proportionally, these rasps are relatively wide compared to their length and may seem disproportionately sized when compared to general engineer's files but that is because the action in using them is more sweeping and omnidirectional rather than a forward thrusting as with files. This enables us to sweep across surfaces, varying the stroke weight and direction to give us a level of control where we are able to adjust pressures for removing material, according to what we see and feel. This way we can achieve a surprisingly smooth finish to the work and, by using different pressures, we can control the quality of finish to the surface too.

Cabinet rasps are often slightly tapered at the end so that they can reach into hard to access areas.

FOUR-IN-HAND FARRIER'S RASPS

If you are starting out and are unsure about the expense then definitely go for a cheaper rasp like the 'farrier's four-in-hand rasp,' which comprises a round face and a flat face in a single abrading tool. This tool has no handle as such and is simply flipped from face to face and end to end according to task. The two opposing faces have a rasp and file at opposite ends so that you have a flat file and flat rasp on the flat face and the same options on the round face making the tool very versatile and effective. Usually these tools are low-cost and competitively priced, which often means the quality is compromised but they are functional and inexpensive tools to get you started.

My Rasps

My most frequently used rasps are the 12" (300mm) by 1 ½" (38mm) cabinet rasp with a grain #10 stitch, followed quickly by a 7" (175mm) by ½" (12mm) grain #13 stitch. I have other rasps but these would be my recommended starter sizes. The smaller the number on the rasp the larger the teeth but not all rasps are numbered. Some makers distinguish the fineness by using terms such as fine, medium, and coarse or by an in-house numbering system of the company making them. This can make it a struggle to find the size best suited to your particular work. Personally, I would avoid the coarse rasps to start out unless you know you want something that removes a mass of material. In choosing, visually look at several rasp faces. The tighter the grain, that is the number of teeth you see over the surface, the smaller the teeth will be and the finer the cut. This will usually then be denoted by a higher number marked on the rasp if numbering is used. The larger the teeth, the wider the surface face of the individual teeth and the deeper they cut because they protrude much further out from the surface.

This image shows one of the coarsest cut rasps available.

Choosing Your Rasp

You must pick your rasps by considering their relationship to the other tools you use. For heavy stock removal I use spokeshaves and saws of different types. This use of tools that can be sharpened minimises the stressful wear on tools like rasps and files, which cannot readily be re-sharpened. Good rasps are expensive to produce because of the skilled handwork involved in making them. By using edge tools and saws, like the coping saw first, I reduce the number of rasps I need in my work. Rasps are sized by length and width and then by the number of teeth stitched into the surface. The more economical versions are those with a round and flat face in one rasp. Flat rasps also often offer two rasps in one by changing the stitch grain on the two faces. Cabinet rasps taper to a narrower point to offer easier access in tighter areas.

"Good rasps are expensive to produce because of the skilled handwork involved in making them. By using edge tools and saws, like the coping saw first, I reduce the number of rasps I need in my work"

A coarse-grained cabinet rasp is the 12" (300mm) grain #3 stitch, which removes a lot of material very efficiently for those who prefer to simply work with rasps and do less with saws, chisels, spokeshaves, and planes. Rasps give a wide range of choices to best match the work you do and they are graded accordingly; so #1 is the coarsest grain and #15 is the finest grain. Loosely, you could grade them this way for simplicity: 1-3 Coarse, 4-7 Medium, 8-11 Fine, and 12-15 Extra fine but they are not always graded or labelled in a simple or consistent manner.

This chamfer in sapele shows a range of cuts with different rasp grains from coarse to extra fine.

If you are buying your first rasp for general work then I would suggest a 10-12" (25-30cm) grain #9 or #10 stitch cabinet rasp—around this sizing you have the most practical of all of the rasps for general work. This is my essential rasp.

RIGHT-HANDED AND LEFT-HANDED RASPS

In general, rasps are made specifically for right-handed or left-handed people and with good reason. Unlike other tools, such as saws and planes, which can be used by both, rasps are developed according to body and arm movement and thereby hand dominancy. Because of the tooth orientation on the rasp face, left-handed people cannot readily adapt the right-handed rasp to their work, using left-handed actions, reversing the stroke for the opposite presentation. This is primarily because the teeth are not oriented to directly face into the wood when used this way. The teeth on hand-stitched rasps are designed according to our natural body alignment to the work. The positioning of the hands naturally pushes the rasp in an arcing motion across the workpiece. As such, the teeth are designed to face that arcing motion. Reversing the stroke simply presents the teeth to the work wrongly and the teeth cut at about 50% efficiency. The same can be true of files in certain work but files are more adaptable.

“*The teeth on hand-stitched rasps are designed according to our natural body alignment to the work. The positioning of the hands naturally pushes the rasp in an arcing motion across the workpiece*”

Practise Using Your Rasp

When using a rasp for the first time, it is best to practise on different woods and at different angles until you have familiarised yourself with the different pressures; to see and understand the impact the tool makes on the wood. You will be surprised by just how much stock you can remove with these tools. Even the fine ones require a sensitive action so as to not remove what is irreplaceable. With practice, you will soon discover the exact angle to maximise efficiency and economy of cut, and achieve a certain refinement in your work.

In using the rasp, we develop confidence as we gain a working knowledge of the properties and characteristics of the tool. Sweeping strokes into the work shift the wood in a way no other woodworking tool can and, compared to any machine method, they are often safer and more accurate because there is no machine vibration to filter out sensitivity. In some applications they are actually faster and more efficient than a machine. Even the coarse cutting rasp must be used with sensitivity and phased through levels as we work the wood. Opening cuts start with more aggressive strokes and are refined with firm but ever lighter strokes to end with as smooth a pass as possible. Moving to a finer rasp is the same. Start with confident strokes and pass over the surface with ever finer passes. Generally it is best to remove material this way until we close in on the final level. From here we take a card scraper to remove any trace of the rasp teeth or, depending on the shape, we can deploy the use of the file.

Use a stiff bristle or nylon brush like a toothbrush or nailbrush to clean rasps. Do not use a file card or metal brush as these will damage the cutting corners of the rasp teeth.

Applying the Rasps to Task

Rasps are primarily shaping tools and they are especially useful for refining end grain work. The rasps form roundover work and refine rounds such as those found on saw and plane handles as well as some table and chair legs and many other aspects of woodworking. First we shape everything using care and judgement as we fit the shape to our hand or create the shape we want visually, depending on the project. There is an advantage to having round and flat faces in the same rasp. After using the rasp, we generally remove all the marks left by the rasp using a thin card scraper that flexes to the round to also remove any flat spots.

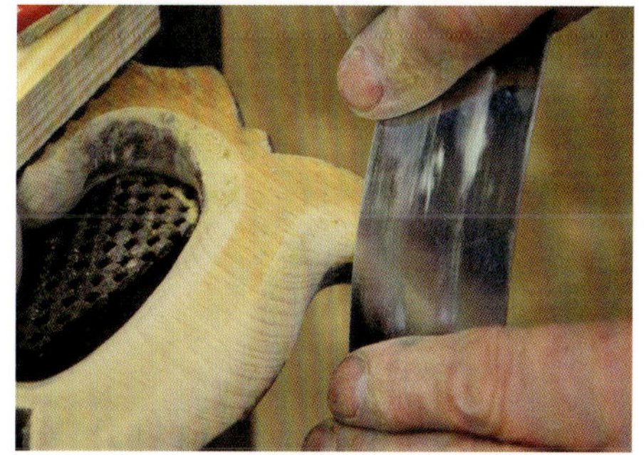

Additional Rasps

There are other rasps available too, in smaller sizes and in different shapes for sculpting, carving, and shaping work in stone, plastics, fibreglass, wood, and soft metals. Disguised under unusual names such as habilis and riffler, they offer the same essential tools of file and rasp but in much smaller sizes for accessing tight places and also in unusual shapes and profiles. In my work I have little need of them generally but, every few months, I am glad to have them in my shop. If you intend to get involved in making carved furniture with cabriole features or ball and claw table and chair legs, such tools become

indispensable, as they do for utility items such as wooden spoons and spatulas, cutting boards and walking canes too. It is not necessarily just new work they are actively used for but conservation and restoration too.

Files (for Working Wood)

Files are radically different than rasps by virtue of the teeth cut into the work faces. Though both tools may be made and sold by the same makers they should not be confused with one another. In this section we take a closer look at the teeth and then the work we use them for in working the wood. By their nature and the nature of wood they are limited. The limitation is the depth of the cut you can make with them. Fine files with close teeth are of less use when working with wood but medium and bastard files are without doubt invaluable because the depths of the gullets are a little deeper.

Choosing a File

The files we use for shaping and smoothing wood are the same as those used so extensively in engineering. Because of this, we have the advantage of an inexpensive refinement tool. The file I recommend for use on wood is the same as the 12" (300mm) second cut (medium) single-cut flat file that I recommend for sharpening on page 44. It is best, however, to keep the ones you use for wood separate from those used for sharpening metal as this keeps the cutting edges all the more suited to the task at hand. Because wood is so much softer and easier to work than metals, we need to keep the edges of the teeth in the best condition we can. Less resistant materials need sharpness and damaged teeth tend to burnish the surface we are working rather than cut it. Our filing techniques do vary and are somewhat different for working wood, compared to when we file metal; so this is another good reason to keep the files dedicated for wood and for metal.

This single-cut 12" (300mm) file is my file of choice. I have added an old chisel handle for safety and comfort.

The surface shows the white, reflective lines to the teeth edges where they have worn too much to work wood effectively.

Files come in every size up to 12" (300mm) but they can be longer. For practical reasons 12" (300mm) is usually the longest file used in woodworking. I talk about the different grades of file when I discuss sharpening files on page 40 but, in the day to day of woodworking, the files I rely on are 10" (250mm) to 12" (300mm) flat file with 2nd cut teeth. That means the teeth are large enough and the gullets deep enough to work without constant clogging with wood fibre. That said, they do clog and you do need to clean them regularly; ideally with a special wire brush, with widely spaced, short wires, called a file card but a wire brush works in the absence of one of these.

This closeup gives a glimpse of how the file works.

A wire brush works great for keeping the teeth of the file clean and operational.

There are many file types you will come across, dozens even, that are different from the ones we have shown here. Many of them are developed specifically for other, more modern, materials such as a plastics and fibreglass. These too may well be adaptable to our work and especially so if we build structures using multiple medium types such as fibreglass with wood and plastics, compressed fibreboards and plywoods. This might be more typical in, say, boat building and canoe and kayak making.

There are many different types of file which may, or may not, be useful in woodworking such as this circle cut file.

Using the File

The teeth on files are generally cut at an angle across the working face at 60 degrees to help the material being removed spiral from the teeth, which, for the main part, prevents clogging. Pushing the file forward in a thrust cut also peels the wood grain away, and the angle of the teeth develops a paring cut, shaving the surface; it is this that creates such a pristine finish to the work. You can experiment and use sweeping cuts in an arc so that you feel the teeth in the wood. This then reveals the quality of the cut in progress and gives you a visual as you look for the telltale signs to your work; any change in direction shows in the texture. You can then make changes according to what you see in the face of the wood.

Because the teeth to files are regimented in strictly sized rows, one behind the other, from toe to handle, we can rely on them for creating pristine surfaces after concluding preparatory work with rasps and even sandpaper. Filing certain components, like through-tenons and such, we actually get a pristine mirror finish on wood that is very different to a sanded finish; and for curved edges, such as bullnosing, the result is excellent. This is especially so on endgrain and dense-grained woods even before any finish has been applied.

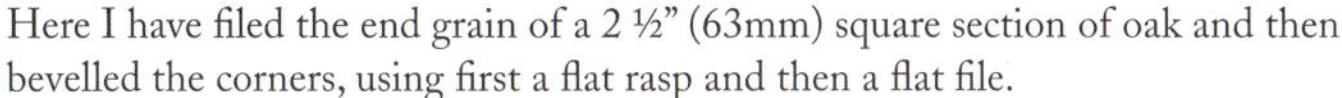

Here I have filed the end grain of a 2 ½" (63mm) square section of oak and then bevelled the corners, using first a flat rasp and then a flat file.

Through-tenons (tenons passing all the way through an adjacent piece) and square tenons, protruding with cambers and roundovers, can be stunning straight from the file teeth and with no further sanding. That is as a good a reason to use files as any.

Boring & Drilling Tools

With the advent of the ubiquitous, battery powered drill-driver and, of course, its predecessor the electric drill, anyone might think that the traditional swing brace (bit brace USA or joiner's brace UK) and auger bit, and the hand drill with twist drills have, for the main part, been displaced. While I do have both of the usurpers running alongside my brace and bit power, I never, at any time, gave up my early models; they still take preeminent place for boring the holes I need in almost every piece I make. They seem, to me, to have a rightful sense of belonging the others just do not have. Both types are the safest to use of any and they are highly efficient, inexpensive, and totally functional. They know no equal, as far as sustaining self-sufficiency goes, and they are lifelong tools that will never run out of power until I do. The power source, of course, is on demand and instant to the cause. In my view, every workshop should contain both types.

Like all of my tools, both brace types provide a practical way to work wood and they bore perfectly clean and clear holes; I find them much more controllable than any other drill type offered. These braces require two-handed use, together with arm and upper body effort and strength. Because you provide the energy and direction this way and because both hands are on the tools, it stands to reason that the feed rate is more governable and that there are fewer hidden surprises than there are with their electric and battery driven cousins.

Very different from boring tools with cutting edges, spurs and such, is the square awl. This tool relies only on the twist of the wrist and no cutting spurs or blades as we might consider them. The more common awls, with round points as the main stem, separate the fibres of the grain when used in woodworking. The square awl can be used to separate the fibres in the same way, leaving all of the wood in place for some work, but can also remove wood by a unique reaming action. Every woodworker should have one of these, as an essential woodworking tool, over any other awl. Mostly we use the square awl for starting holes to receive screw threads and such, and the points of auger bits too.

Essential Boring and Drilling Tools

It is important to understand how different these hand powered tools are, in applying them to the work, compared to the powered versions. When working on a project that is well progressed, I would prefer to use a tool that I feel I have total control of so there is less risk of damaging the work I have done. Imagine taking a powered drill, even one with a soft start and clutch control mechanism, and applying it to cut holes into a near finished drawer or a tabletop, inlaid with decorative work. This, for me, is unnecessary risk and these are good reasons to reach for hand power and control. I discuss my choices for essential boring and drilling tools on the following pages:

The Brace & Bits

Braces date back through many centuries and, at one time, they were mostly made from woods like beech, elm, ash, and oak. Woodcrafters working in woodlands and forests used them to fashion every kind of wooden chair; so too the bench-working cabinetmakers and joiners for making a wide range of woodworking parts, ranging from ladders and carts to wagons. They used them to make perfectly round holes to receive spokes and spindles of every type and size too. Woodworking braces ultimately came to be made from both wood and steel. The mechanism holding the auger bit must withstand the intense pressures of turning the bit and drilling in to remove the wood. Though other non-boring bits, used to perform other functions, do fit into the brace to countersink holes and turn screws, the brace has a mostly singular use of combining with a range of twisted auger bits, designed and used to bore out waste wood and create holes of different sizes.

At one time, most braces were made from wood or wood reinforced with metal. Most braces you will come across today, however, are made from metal, with wood or plastic handles.

A Disappearing Tool?

In today's world of woodworking the swing brace has generally been displaced and replaced by battery-driven drills/drivers and, of course, the electric drill. Developed initially for heavier industry production, powered drivers provide fast and efficient ways of assembling components and other such work. Over the decades, they have become more available for the independent contractor in various trades as well as for the consumer market. They now come with their variable speed controls, forward and reverse mechanism and so on, offering increasing levels of manageability. Of course these tools rely wholly on electricity in one form or another, whereas the brace and bit relies totally on you and your energy. Unfortunately, especially with the invention of the battery-driven drill, most woodworkers have abandoned the commonly used brace almost without considering their actual functionality, durability, and safety values both to the user, others in close proximity to the work, and the safety of the work itself. Although there is no doubt that high speed drill-drivers have their place, I think it is important to remember that every revolution of the brace actually cuts a circumference and removes a level of waste with no excess. The battery drill driver makes up to 2,000 revolutions per minute and drills a 1" (25mm) diameter hole through a 1 ½" (38mm) section of pine in 7 seconds. A brace and bit takes 33 revolutions and takes 17 seconds to do the same. In the home shop the time difference is insignificant. The brace and bit is much safer to use. In my youth every workshop craftsman relied on the instant dependability and constancy they offered for boring larger holes. For me, it still offers a perfect symbiosis for almost all large hole boring needs. The bits never overheat and rarely tear the wood unexpectedly. You do, however, have to know how to sharpen the bits but that is simple enough and a low cost task, taking only a very short time per bit. Are the swing braces here to stay or tools of the past? I have recently asked myself this question, more than ever before, so that I can help others make a decision about their validity in our present world. It mostly depends on the way you live, how you like to work, and what you do in your personal woodworking. For boring clean-cut holes, without excess energy and without much of the risk of high speed equipment, I think they are an excellent choice. I believe that they are here to stay. In my view, no modern methods offer the simplicity, the quiet, and the total independence the combination of the brace and bits bring to my work. The sense of control equals comfort and wellbeing for me.

Parts to the Brace

Metal Frame.

Sweep Handle.

Pad or Head.

Chuck or Shell.

Jaws.

Sequence of Cuts

The spiral snail forming the point of the bit starts and pulls the bit into the wood with each revolution.

The perimeter-cutting spurs trace-cut the perimeter wall of the hole.

The raker cutting edges, on either side of the snail, pare-cut and lift the waste from the hole.

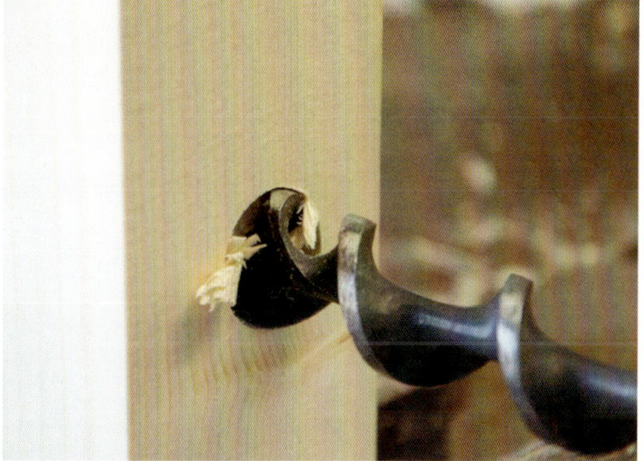

The continued revolutions deepen the hole, removing the waste wood at the same time.

What to Look for in a Brace

Throughout history, many braces have been developed and manufactured for sale to craftsmen. Early models made from wood were mostly craftsman-made, with most of them being made from wood with metal inserts to receive and hold the bit. With the Victorian era of fine cabinetry and furniture making came the zenith of tool making and some of the most beautiful braces ever made, using ebony, rosewood, boxwood, brass, and steel. That said, these older, wooden braces had holding mechanisms that will not receive more modern-day bits and that means most bits less than 100 years old. I suggest you avoid these, as working braces, in favour of their modern counterpart, the ratchet brace. Many of the older, metal framed braces could be made to work but are not too practical and, again, it is more than likely that they will not accept the bits we would most commonly want to use with them. Most of this concern does surround the auger bits themselves, which have undoubtedly evolved to cut better holes than most, if not all, of their predecessors. That being the case, you should choose a brace that works with the bits and most, if not all, Stanley brace types work the best, regardless of the different makers. Models that follow the Stanley model (most available braces) all receive the square tang-type bits and many have the forward and reverse ratchet. This swing or ratchet brace (American brace in old catalogues) is common enough and can be readily found secondhand. Rarely are they worn down or worn out to any discernable level and almost any old ratchet brace will work well. I use two or three braces made by different makers, including a Stanley 73-10" and a Stanley 144-10" Mk2 that I have acquired through the years. My favourite is the one with the wooden handle and pad. I bought my Stanley 144-10" Mk 4 with plastic handle and pad, all the parts of which have held good for decades now too. Of course you need only one brace really. While I like these particular braces there are other good braces available with different model numbers and made by different makers.

Many of the beautiful wooden braces have custom-made bits that are not as easily exchanged as their more modern counterparts.

Ratchet Braces Are Ideal

I prefer a brace with a ratchet mechanism as this allows the bit to be turned in short, partial sweeps of the handle when needed. This helpful mechanism becomes essential where a full turn of the handle is not possible because of space confinement, say, in cupboards or between joists. However, it is also useful when extra torque is needed to maximise arm, hand, and body position, where short strokes from one position increase leverage. The ratchet allows the handle to be worked forward into the wood and then pulled back to take a fresh stroke. It is also useful for reversing the bit to back it out of the bored hole. Turning the ratchet selection ring allows the ratchet to be locked in one of three positions; forwards, backwards, and fixed. Where the brace is locked, without the ratchet mechanism engaged, the brace can be used forwards or backwards at will. This only works when a full sweep of the handle is possible. Sometimes, when using larger bits of, say, ¾" (19mm) and up, it is best to have the brace on the forward ratchet position and take short strokes so that the body/hand positions are synchronised to maximise leverage. This is also true when using the brace to bore more densely-grained hardwoods.

This ratchet mechanism is a great innovation and braces that have this are preferable to those that do not.

The Sweep of the Brace

The brace is generally sized by its sweep and that is twice the distance from the centre of the jaws in the chuck to the centre of the handle we turn the sweep or swing by. So the diameter of the full sweep from side to side determines the overall size of the sweep. Many braces will carry the sweep size stamped into the frame of the brace. The sweep of the brace affects the amount of leverage you get when you turn the handle. A 10" (25cm) sweep is usually the most practical size and gives good leverage. Leverage becomes all the more necessary when using the larger bits or an expanding bit, which generally expands from 1" (25mm) to 3" (75mm) in diameter and needs much more torque. The two most common sizes of swing brace are 8" (20cm) and 10" (25cm) but there are smaller braces, which were made for tight spaces between joists, inside cupboards, and under stairways too. I like the miniatures for my children and grandchildren to use, even though they were very much made for adult usage.

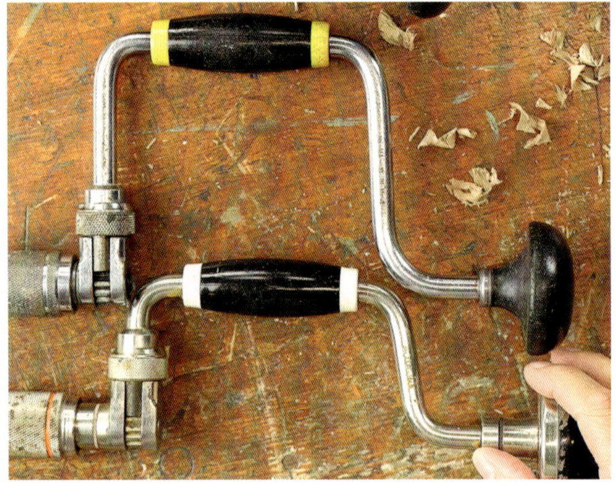

The image here shows two braces I own. The top one is very standard as a 10" (25cm) sweep brace but the bottom one has a shorter sweep, which is especially well suited for tight spaces.

Check That the Parts Move Freely

The handle that turns the brace and drives the chuck-held bit should be loose enough to turn freely throughout the operation of boring, otherwise friction on the hand builds up and causes discomfort. Usually this part is bearing-free but generally the handle revolves quite freely. Occasional oiling keeps the parts moving. The pad of the brace should also freely turn for the same reason of comfort. A bearing is usually fitted where the neck connects to the pad and there is usually an oil port to deliver oil to the bearings inside. If this is immovable then the brace becomes very uncomfortable to use because, in normal use, we either grip it tightly or press it into the hollow of the chest and push with the chest.

The ratchet mechanism, chuck, threads, and internal jaw parts all need occasional oiling with light machine oil to keep the parts fully operational and moving freely. One or two drops is usually all that is needed. There are different points for oiling and then there are accessible components with free access. Here they are:

The chuck and ratchet mechanism.

Beneath the pad there is a hole for oiling.

On the side of the ratchet area is an oil hole.

The threads holding the chuck need regular oiling.

Auger Bits

The auger bit radically differs from all other early bit types in its use of a spiral stem that lifts and ejects waste wood from the hole as it cuts. Prior to this development most bits bored holes but left the waste behind and so drilling generally necessitated the irksome removal of waste throughout the boring process. Twist drills and auger bits both lift and convey the waste from the bottom of the hole to exit at the top, within the spiral of the drill bit or auger stem itself. Whereas the twist drill relies solely on hand, arm, and sometimes upper body pressure to push the bit into the material, the auger bit pulls itself into the wood. However, at the same time, it does require some upper body effort to continue boring. This is chiefly because the auger bits bore the larger sized holes, which require much greater effort.

This vintage blacksmithed centre-bit type scores the wall of the hole to create a rim but the shavings remain in the hole.

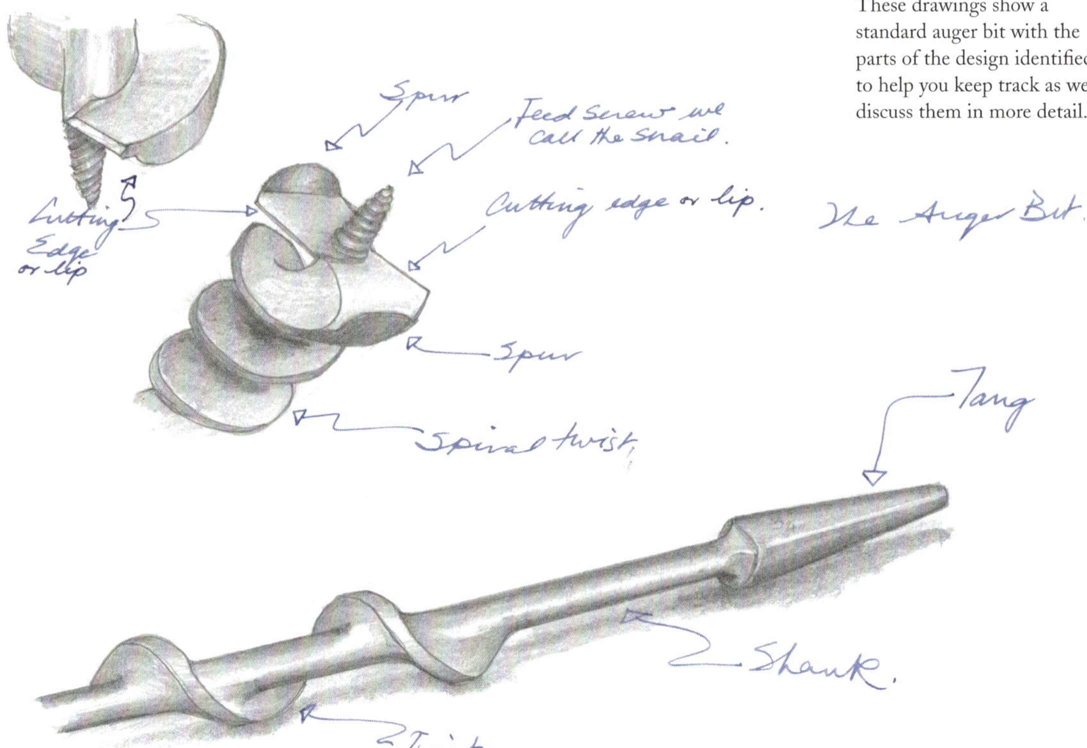

These drawings show a standard auger bit with the parts of the design identified to help you keep track as we discuss them in more detail.

The auger bit generally comprises two spirals that have two different functions within the bit. The first is a spiral tip called the 'snail' or 'feed screw,' which is a tight screw thread, designed to function in the same way as a wood screw; and this engages the wood fibres in like fashion to the screw. This thread advances into the wood with each revolution of the brace, prior to the two side spurs and cutting lips, which actually cut the circumference of the hole and pare away the waste wood. The snail pulls the bit into the wood to start the cut and continues this pulling action when the bit starts to cut the wall of the hole. It is at this point that the second spiral comes into play by paring the surface inside the perimeter cut. The spiral lifts the waste wood into the bit's stem and the waste spirals up or along the stem as the bit deepens and is thereby ejected from the hole. Once the bit reaches the opposite side of the wood being bored, it stops pulling itself into the wood and extra effort is needed to push the bit through. In some situations it is fine to bore all the way through from one side, inside a stud wall for instance. However, if a neat, flawless exit rim is required, as soon as the snail pokes through it is best to then withdraw the bit and, if possible, bore from the opposite face, using the point left by the snail as a guide to centre the bit. Alternatively a second waste piece of wood can be held in place for the snail to pull into and the wood fibres on the exit side of the hole will be supported by the scrap piece to prevent any splintering.

For the brace and bits to function fully, the bits must be in pristine condition and that means the cutting edges must be sharp and well shaped, the stem must be straight, and the metal free from rust. Beyond that, these bits need only care and occasional sharpening to keep them working. I think the fact that they were always stored in strong and protective canvass bit rolls and compartmented trays in boxes speaks of the obvious care that owners took with them. Boring wood does take its toll on the edges but sharpening takes only a few minutes if you sharpen them before they become very dull.

Sharpening Auger Bits

1. Secure the snail point onto a scrap of wood, orienting the incline of the bevel so that the file can be used to sharpen the edge. In this position, you will file from the start of the cutting edge, up into the spiral, toward the heel of the bevel. You can also rest the side of the bit on a support and file the incline in the opposite direction, from the heel of the bevel to the cutting edge. Try both ways to see which you prefer.

2. To file the spurs press the side of the bit against a support and file the half moon shape.

Do not file the outside of the spurs as this reduces the diameter of the bit and causes it to bind in the cut.

Damaged Bits

Boring any hole means cutting with and across the grain with every rotation of the bit. The outer spur cutters are critical to the function of the bit in that they crosscut grain that would otherwise split and splinter. Because the spurs are filed as part of the sharpening process, they are sometimes worn down level with or even below the inclined cutting edges. This results in uncut fibres around the circumference so that the bit no longer cuts cleanly and becomes unfit for purpose. It is possible but difficult to repair them. Sometimes heavy filing will reintroduce spurs to the rim of the bit. This is definitely worth checking for when you are choosing auger bits to purchase.

Bit Sizes

I think it is important to recognise that there is generally a dividing line between the bit types used with hand powered drills. This difference is between auger bits designed for boring larger holes and twist drill bits designed for drilling smaller holes. Both types have spiralled stems but, beyond that, they are very different. The crossover here is usually around the ¼" (6mm) diameter size, but this is an arbitrary limitation. The difference between both bit types is most apparent in the bit sizes but, taking a closer look at the cutting edges of the bits, the area around the points, and you see the unique difference that separates the larger auger bits from the twist drill counterparts. The twist drill bit has two bevelled facets on the end that form two cutting edges. This is simpler than the tips of the auger bits, which have been shown and described. Auger bits mostly range in size between 3⁄16" (4.5mm) and 1 ½" (38mm) in 1⁄16" (1.5mm) increments. Larger sizes are available as additional options but the standard bit set contains 13 bits.

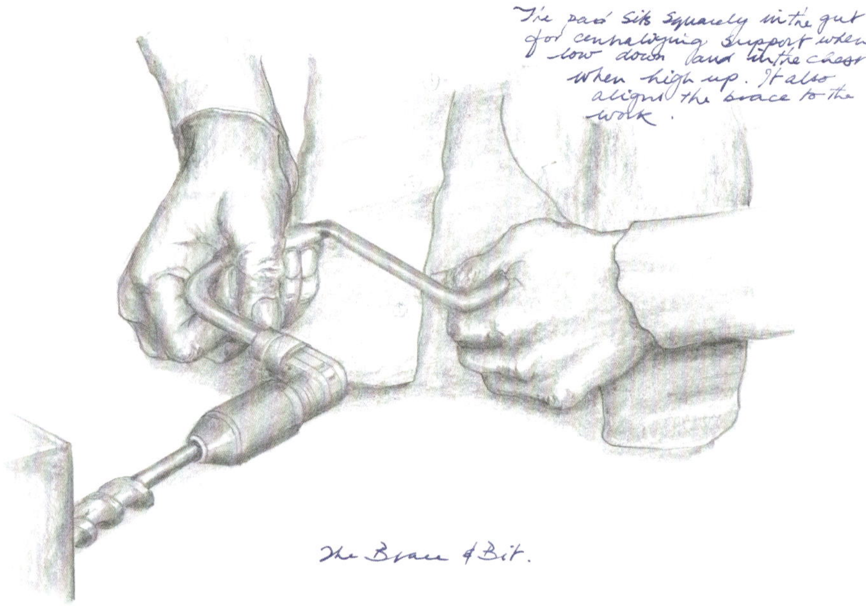

Using the Brace

The chuck mechanisms that hold the different sized bits in place vary a little between makers but generally they all work in a similar fashion. The chuck opens and closes two jaws inside that receive and release the square tang of the auger bits. These two jaws are connected to make them spring-loaded in opposition to one another so that they open and close within a tubular metal sleeve called the shell. A more modern and recognisable term is the chuck and that is the term used in this book. Holding the chuck firmly and turning the sweep handle counterclockwise loosens the jaws and disengages the bit; turning clockwise tightens the jaws on the bit. These jaws enclose the tang of the bits when pressure is applied and, when the chuck is loosened, these enclosing jaws release the bit. The bit tangs themselves have been developed as a four-sided taper that fits inside the two jaws of the chuck; when the chuck tightens along its screw thread enclosing the jaws, the jaws close over the tang like crocodile jaws and latch onto the bit tang. When the jaws are fully tightened they lock the bit solidly.

Sometimes closed and locked jaws stick inside the chuck at the exit hole or inside the mechanism itself. Press the ends of the jaws sticking through the exit hole with your thumb or finger or against the bench to free them and they will usually spring into the chuck a little and then spring open inside the chuck. As it loosens on the thread, the chuck, acting as a sleeve, travels along the threads and the jaws continue opening ever wider inside. Pressing the point of the tang into the jaws assists opening them, which allows the tang of the bit to be fully installed inside the chuck and within the jaws.

I removed the jaws from the chuck to show how the bit tang fits inside the two opposing jaws.

Insert the tang inside the chuck and then turn the chuck to tighten the jaws onto the tang; jiggle the tang inside to help locate it within the angular jaws. Once the tang of the bit feels located, the brace handle is then turned slowly, using the dominant hand, in a clockwise direction, with the non-dominant hand still holding the chuck. It is important here to feel for the tang inside the jaws so that it aligns and seats properly along its long axis. The tang is square and corresponds with angled facets to each half of the jaws. This action causes the jaws to close and tighten fully over the tang with the bit centred in the chuck. Gripping the chuck firmly, with everything fully aligned and closed, and firmly applying pressure via the handle anchors the chuck to the brace and the brace is ready for work. Reversing this procedure loosens the bit and the bit can be removed or changed as necessary. To do this, hold both the chuck and the bit with the non-dominant hand, so as to catch the bit when it loosens, and use the dominant

“

Gripping the chuck firmly, with everything fully aligned and closed, and firmly applying pressure via the handle anchors the chuck to the brace and the brace is ready for work

”

hand to turn the brace handle. When the chuck is fully tightened it takes more effort to release it. In both cases of tightening and loosening the chuck, the pad of the brace is generally lodged somewhere between the stomach and the chest to secure the brace more fully for the lateral pressure to be applied to the handle.

To start drilling, place the point of the bit against the wood and start turning. The threaded snail pulls the bit into the wood. Additional hand and upper body pressure ensures the auger bit cuts productively when the two outer spurs and the cutting edges begin making contact with the wood. Once the snail has pulled the cutter part way into the cut, the spurs on the outside rim of the bit then cut the outer circumference of the hole delineating the rim. Each turn clockwise deepens the hole by about 1⁄16" (1.5mm), depending on the snail thread, the amount of pressure we apply to the pad of the brace, and then the wood type and grain itself. Generally we rely on the threaded snail to govern the depth of cut by rotation as it draws the bit into the wood. All cutting of the fibres takes place around the snail and not with the snail itself. On each side of the snail are two inclined cutting bevels that slice the wood fibres by the rotation of the brace handle. Continuously, the cutting bevels both slice-cut and lift the wood fibres from the cut into the auger spiral itself and eventually out from the deepening hole. The threaded snail works effectively to pull the bit ever deeper into the bored hole but often it can become clogged and the threads it created in the wood strip out. If and when this happens you need to withdraw the bit, clear out the threads of the snail, and then return to the task. Turning the handle counterclockwise unscrews the snail from the wood and allows us to withdraw the bit from the wood and the resultant hole. This helps us to pull shavings from the hole at the same time. On returning to boring you generally need to apply more pressure, at a consistent level, to re-engage the feed threads. This reduces the possibility of re-clogging the threads. Thread clogging usually depends on the wood type. Oak clogs the thread easily and strips out the thread in the wood too because of its coarse and brittle grain. Sometimes the auger itself traps waste fibres between the wall of the hole and the bit itself and the bit must be removed to free the shavings.

Auger bits cut less readily into end grain but they do bore. The threads of the snail clog more readily on end grain and are much less effective in pulling the bit into the wood. Extra upper body pressure usually works to engage the cutting edges. Knots too clog the feed thread in the snail and serve more as a barrier than a help. To get through the knot may require repeated clean-out of the threads.

Holding the Brace

There are different ways to apply the brace to the work and this usually relates to the position and weight of the work. If the workpiece is loose from the main project then loading it in the vise works best. The vise offers the most secure place and greater versatility to adjust the work to your body height and position. If the piece is too big for the vise then anchoring it to the bench becomes another option. Use clamps for this or clamp or screw a temporary piece of wood to push the work up against. In some cases, your workpiece or project can stand on the floor and you can apply the brace vertically to the work. There are many options. Just make sure that whatever you are boring into is as secure as possible.

Boring Into Thin Wood

If the wood is thin, say ½" (12mm) or less, then it is not unusual for the snail of the auger bit to cause the wood to split. This often happens when the hole is near to an outer edge of the wood. You can help prevent this by first making a small pilot hole with a twist drill bit or square awl. Often a ⅛" (3mm) hole will still allow the snail to bite and pull into the wood but there is no 'wedging action' to risk splitting the wood. Smaller auger bits may need a smaller diameter pilot hole. Another alternative is to ensure that the wood is supported on both sides in the vise so that the wood cannot split but this may not always work because of the thinness of the material.

Preventing 'Blow Out'

We use a couple of techniques to prevent 'blow out,' which is when the bit bursts out the other side of the wood, causing splinters on the far side. Because the snail of the bit pulls into the wood with successive turns of the handle, when the bit snail reaches the other side it runs out of wood to pull into. This means that more pressure must be applied and this is where things go wrong. Pushing harder causes the wood to split without being cut by the spurs; there is insufficient support and so the wood breaks away instead of being neatly cut. For guaranteed clean exit holes we must stop when the snail point first appears. We then withdraw the brace and approach from the opposite face, using the hole point to guide us. This way, the rim of the bit scores a fresh wall to the perimeter of the hole to meet the opposite wall. If we can only approach from the one face we should tightly clamp a piece of scrap wood to the back of the work, with no gaps, for the bit point to pull into and thus prevent blow out as the rim of the bit scores the remaining wall, supported by the scrap piece.

To prevent 'blow out' you should stop drilling once the tip of the snail appears on the far side and then use the small hole created to locate the bit and drill from the opposite side.

Other Bits Can Be Used With the Brace

There are screwdriver bits specially developed for use with the brace, which are cleverly devised as tang and driver bit all in one. The bits are flat bits for use with slotted screws and so usually have a large and small end. The old sizing systems for screws were numbered according to diameter in imperial sizing whereas, throughout most of the world today, screws are sized using the metric system. Using the old sizing system, the smaller end of the old screwdriver bits drive screws from number 4 to number 10 and then anything larger was driven with the larger end.

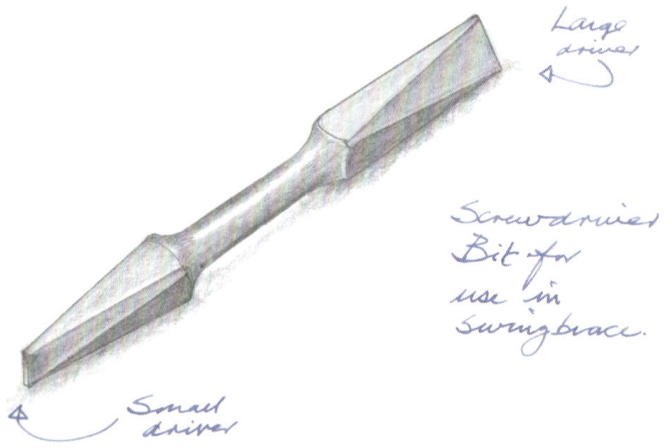

There are various types of countersink bits too. Usually they are rose or rosette shaped but some look like snail shells and blacksmiths were very inventive with their designs too. Deburring bits were also used to deburr the rims of holes in metal.

Square reamer-type bits cut normal through-round and tapered holes in the same way as square awls work but with more power.

Spoon bits, shell bits, centre or spur bits, and several others cut circles in wood to sever the fibres and form the wall of the hole. Each of these bits appears radically different but they all create one and the same thing - round holes. The bits used with the brace all slice-cut the opening circumference ring, using the rim of the bit in some way or other. This ring delineates the size of the hole and all further action is primarily to deepen the

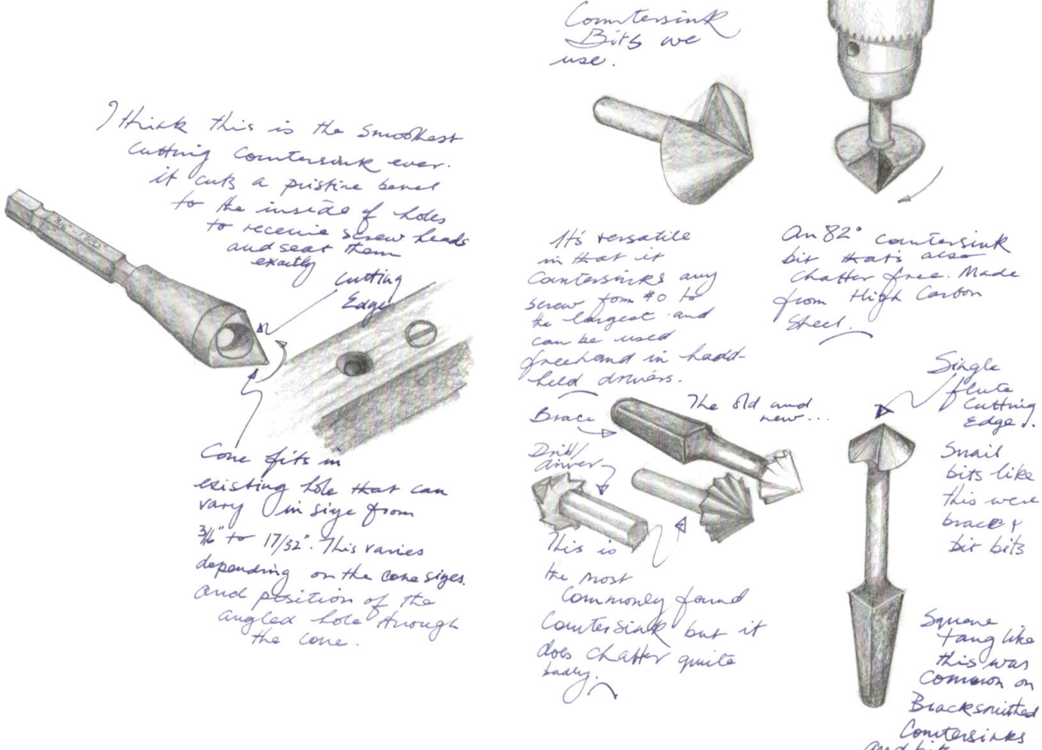

wall either to a specific depth or to go all the way through. The centre bits mentioned previously have a single prong centred on the long axis of the bit. This centrepoint is the initial contact point that centres and guides the bit, keeping it central until the rim of the hole is scored and the required depth is accomplished. These bits rely on applied pressure only and cannot pull themselves into the work as the snail-pointed auger bits do. Subsequent turns with the brace allow the bit to be aligned by the rim, as much as the centrepoint, and centering is generally more assured as the bit bores deeper.

Spoon bits, gimlet bits and shell bits are somewhat odd looking to today's woodworker and yet these bits were highly effective. They start the hole on the nose of the bit and each turn of the brace enlarges the hole, increasing from the centre toward the outside, curved aspect of the long axis. The long, leading edge of the bit then trims the hole wall, as the bit deepens in the cutting action of the nose, and enlarges the wall to the radius of the main stem. I should also point out that the spoon bit can be redirected once the bit has been started. This makes the bit popular with chairmakers because many of their holes are angled and sighted by eye to splay legs and spindles as needed. These initial holes then accept conically shaped chairmakers' tapered bits that create tapered holes to receive correspondingly shaped tapered legs and spindles.

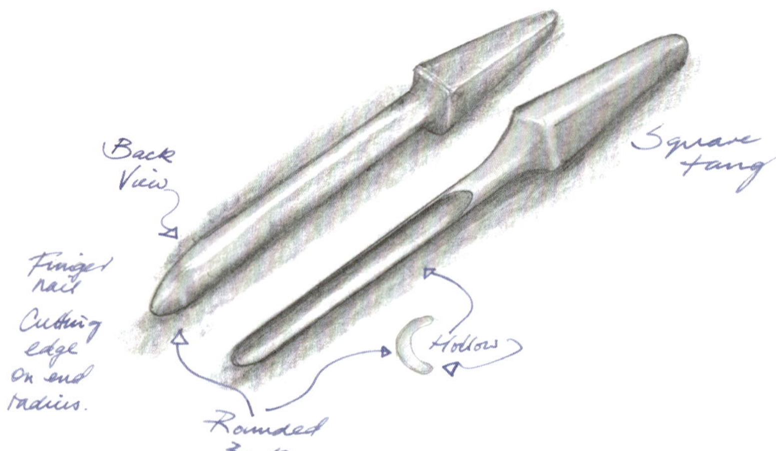

The spoon bit, which is popular with chairmakers, can change direction in the cut.

Can You Put Round Bits in This Chuck Type?

You can indeed. They may not always fit as well or grip as tightly but often they do and, if you are careful, you will get the hole bored even though it is much slower than using a hand drill. I use older bits with squared and tapered ends in the ratchet brace. You can also use bits with hexagonal shafts and round stems, provided they are tightened as tightly as possible. They do slip though so be aware of the possibility. Also, remember that many bits have been designed for high speed cutting; spade or paddle bits, for instance, rely on much higher revolutions per minute than can be achieved with the brace to cut cleanly and are designed to that end; these bits will not work in a brace of this type. Many other bits are also designed for modern methods using power equipment and rely on high speeds that cannot be generated using hand methods. Forstner bits and spur brad bits are just two more of them.

Round-stemmed bits can be used in the brace but the chuck must be well tightened to avoid slippage.

Flat bits look like this and rely on higher speed drivers to bore into wood.

Although, over the centuries, bit types have seen several radical changes and today's auger bits are mainly designed with power drivers in mind, they still mirror what has long been in existence in the form of earlier auger bits. Most of today's mass-made auger bits can therefore be used in traditional braces almost as well as the square tanged version of old; but because they do not have the square tang the jaws must be well tightened to hold the bit securely.

Expanding Bits

For larger holes we use expanding bits that can be set to any size, usually to take over from the 1" (25mm) size and on up to 3" (76mm) in diameter. This bit is adjusted by loosening the setscrew and sliding the spur cutter to the desired size. Notches marked at 1/32" (0.8mm) increments increase the diameter size by 1/16" (1.5mm) distances. Obviously the larger the circumference the more leverage needed and, at 3" (76mm), it takes much greater strength to drive the bit. This is especially so in the more dense-grained hardwoods. The hole is not always as accurately aligned as the holes made with smaller, fixed diameter bits and this shows in imperfections on the wall of the hole; but this detail can be evened out with a fine rasp. As usual, when boring all the way through the wood, we firstly bore half the way through (or until the snail of the bit shows on the reverse side) and then use the centre hole as a guide to continue from the other side and complete the hole with no risk of blow out.

The Hand Drill

The hand drill, also called a wheel brace or egg-beater drill, offers convenience for my benchwork. It is always primed and ready for action and it needs nothing more than some light energy from me. It is also a relatively safe tool in that it stops immediately the hand stops with no fraction of a turn more. I personally feel that powerful drills/drivers and electric drills require a lot of strength to counter their torque in use. The two cannot be compared in terms of safety levels. A set of twist drill bits ranging from ⅜" (9.5mm) down in small increments to less than 1⁄16" (1.5mm) offer compact convenience in both drill and bits. Most jobs needing small holes in metal and wood can readily be achieved using this basic hand drill and, in wood, it works easily and offers total self-reliance. It is no wonder every toolbox I ever peered into as a boy had a Stanley hand drill in it somewhere. I own and use the electric and battery drill alongside the hand drill but I still find many instances where I prefer to use the hand drill over any other tool, which is why this is still an essential tool for me.

Choosing a Hand Drill

Ideally it is best to feel the hand drill in your hand before buying but if you cannot that should not stop you as there is so little to go wrong with them anyway. If you can, hold one and turn the wheel to see that it turns freely without jamming or jarring. Most commonly any jamming is caused by friction in the cog mechanism because the moving parts need a light oiling. Rarely, but sometimes, the cogs misalign and stick when turned and this lack of synchrony can cause issues. I suspect that this is more common with the double pinion models, which seem to jam more than the single pinion models and I think this is caused by vibration, looseness, and the fact that there are more parts to synchronise and align in rotation.

The chuck mechanism itself should be checked before purchase if possible. Inside the chuck are three triangular sections of metal that are held to form a cone. In one type, the sections of metal are loosely connected by compression springs, in between the parts, and are registered in holes in each facet, either side of each jaw. In the other type, the springs are replaced by thin wires connected to each jaw piece, which retain the jaws in place. Generally we never need to enter the cone of the chuck as light oiling takes care of most needs. If one of the wires breaks or a spring escapes the enclosure and needs

Here are the internal workings of the chuck.

This is how the jaws should look from the outside.

replacing it will show by the jaws not aligning fully with one another when the chuck is tightened and the triple parts misalign. Again, this is not the norm. These are usually well designed tools and generally the parts are safe and secure inside. Sometimes a previous owner may not align a drill bit before cinching the chuck jaws up and the parts get forced, which is what causes this type of damage.

I have used the Stanley range of hand drills throughout my work life; I enjoy their simplicity and the functionality they offer every hand tool enthusiast. Hand drills are very reliable and, because of this, are a part of my daily life. There are two basic types suited to woodworking and both of them are the same size and use the same chuck mechanism for locking twist drills inside. The only difference between the two Stanley hand drill types is that one has a single pinion driving the chuck and the other has a second, top pinion that balances out pressures applied via the wheel. As an apprentice, the men I worked with declared the double pinion to be the superior model but often owned only the single pinion one. Over my five decades of working with them I have found little or even no difference in functionality at the bench. I have owned and used both types throughout my working life and both seem equal to one another so whichever you buy will most likely last you a lifetime of woodworking.

Above left, the single pinion type. Lower right, the double pinion type.

The Moving Parts

With its cleverly contrived three-jaw chuck, the hand drill accepts any size of round drill stock. By turning the crank handle and holding the chuck firmly, the jaw opening receives twist drill bits up to around ⅜" (9.5mm). This depends on the hand drill size and the maker but, for most woodworkers, this is sufficient; many hand tool users use the ratchet brace and auger bits for larger diameter holes. The hand drill is a useful tool but, like the brace and bit, it has been steadily replaced by the battery-driven drill/driver and the electric drill because these work so effectively and can be used single handedly whereas the hand drill always requires two hands to work it.

The hand drill comprises a cast metal frame, a drive wheel with a series of cogs or teeth, and one or two pinions with corresponding cogs that then drive the chuck, causing the rotary motion of the drill. The drive shaft, centred in the long axis of the drill, holds the chuck, which in turn holds the twist drills used for boring the holes. The cranking

action of the wheel handle gives continuous motion at controllable speeds. The moving parts revolve around the central, long axis of the drive shaft, where the pinions turn and the chuck opens and closes. The centre of the drive gear or wheel also rotates to crank all mechanisms and at these points we need to apply modest amounts of oil to keep everything moving freely and quietly. The hand drill has built-in oiling points to make oiling easy.

Apply oil to the drive shaft at the top of the cog if there is no oil hole.

Oil the centre point between the drive wheel and the centre of the frame.

Drip one or two drops of oil into the oiling hole, where there is one.

Frequent oiling reduces the possibility of rusting. Apply the oil and wipe away any excess. Leave the hand drill on a cloth or paper towel to drain out.

Sometimes the three jaws inside the chuck stick within the round exit hole of the chuck sleeve and jam together. Loosen the chuck and press the points of the jaws to free them. By 'freeing them' I mean that friction and spring pressure on the inside of the conically shaped chuck allows the jaws to retreat back into the chuck. If the parts are rusted or gummed up, they will not move back and will need extra pressure. Sometimes you must remove the parts from the chuck and degrease and derust them. Once this is done and the parts are lightly oiled, the jaws readily spring back to an open position with a little thumb pressure.

Using the Hand Drill

To open the drill chuck, ready to receive the drill bit, grip the main wheel crank and frame together with the thumb next to the handle so as to stop any movement. With the free hand grip and turn the chuck to open the three jaws inside. This moves the chuck along a threaded drive shaft and allows the three jaws to slide down the inside of the cone shaped end of the chuck. As the jaws slide into the chuck they open ever wider, the more you rotate the chuck. When everything is oiled and maintained properly, the chuck can be rolled along an open palm and this opens and closes the chuck quickly. To close the chuck jaws against the twist drill bit, hold the bit in your non-dominant hand, between the forefinger and thumb, and place it as near centered in the jaws as possible. The nearer you size the jaw opening to the bit size, the easier this is. At the same time as holding the drill bit in the jaw, wrap the remaining fingers around the chuck to hold it still while you turn. With the main, long handle resting on the bench or against your stomach, turn the crank handle clockwise and the chuck jaws will close onto the drill bit. Once snugged up to the bit, tighten the jaws fully by gripping the crank wheel firmly against the frame and tightening the chuck.

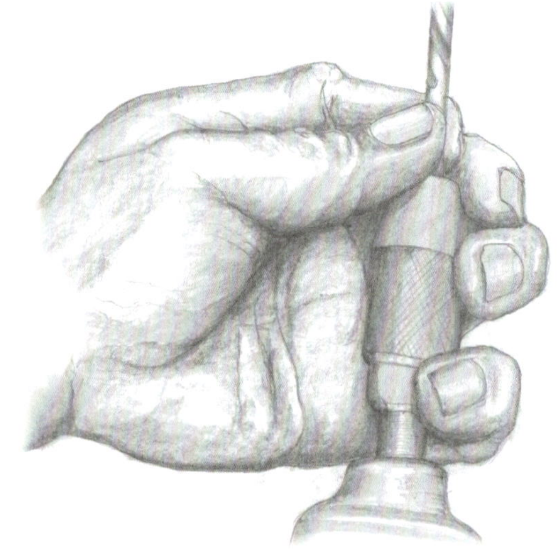

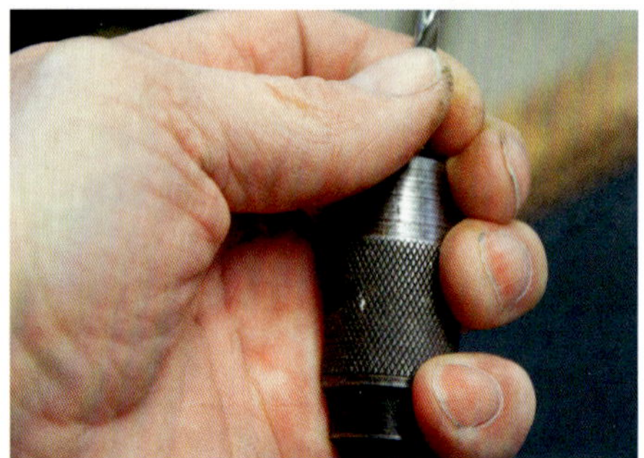

To free the bit for change or removal, grip the crank handle against the frame body at the upper end of the hand drill, that is by the long handle again. Now turn the chuck with a firm grip and as the chuck loosens remove the bit.

As with the brace and bit, the hand drill can be used vertically or horizontally or indeed at any angle, depending on the work in hand. Most holes will be perpendicular to the material but sometimes angled holes are necessary. If that is the case it is often best to start the hole square and then, after a few turns, and in the started hole, change the direction of the drill to the desired angle. That way the bit is unlikely to slip from its starting point. Often such work takes place on a project already large enough to push against. Sometimes the work is held upright or horizontally in the vise. Pushing the drill and bit into the work horizontally gives more upper-body power to the action, whereas pressing downwards relies mostly on the arm muscles and the weight and force of the arm. The amount of pressure you apply directly affects the amount of wood in the flutes of the drill bit and so care must be taken not to clog the flutes, which can prevent the drill from cutting. The amount of pressure needed is usually governed by the speed of the drill. Finding the balance is important and knowing how much speed you need in relation to pressure only comes by experience.

Clearing the Hole

Generally, and especially on small diameter twist drills, the flutes get choked up with wood fibres. Clogging stops the cutting action of the bit and, depending on the wood type, can occur quite frequently. Unlike with the brace and bit, the more speed you give to the drilling process the more cuts you take per depth of cut and the more cuts you take the cleaner the hole. Clogging usually happens through using too much turning speed and too much pressure at the same time. Withdrawing the bit frequently allows you to clean out the flutes regularly and this makes for easier drilling too. It is a good habit to practise and, as you do so, varying the speed according the size of the drill bit becomes automatic and controlled. If you back the bit out with reverse strokes the wood waste will usually remain in the hole. It is best to withdraw the bit from the hole whilst turning the crank clockwise. That way the waste remains in the flutes and the waste is thoroughly pulled from the hole. Remove the waste from the flutes by twisting the bit carefully but firmly between the fingers and thumb. Take care, remember that the wood and the drill bit can be hot through friction in the hole and can burn the fingers.

Twist Drill Bits

Modern twist drills seem to have changed very little since they first came into production. These bits have two bevelled facets at the end and between two spiralled flutes machined into the stem of the bit. Mostly they are a development of engineering for metalworking and so mill-engineering created an inexpensive process for making these bits affordable in the every day of life. Though originally designed for drilling metals, these bits are equally at home in the workshops of woodworkers worldwide. They range in size from ⅓₂" (0.8mm) on up to and beyond 3" (76mm), going up in minute incremental sizes. For the woodworker, the torque needed to turn much beyond, say, ⅜" (9.5mm) in wood using this type of hand-powered drill makes the larger sizes prohibitive and we resort to the auger bit for larger diameter work.

Twist drill bits should not be confused with brad point bits (pictured) which, at first glance, look similar. Brad point bits rely on higher speeds than can be achieved with the hand drill.

Twist drills dull after several hours of continuous work depending on use, speed, and wood type. Because they are made from hardened steels they must be reground to restore the sharp edges to the cutting bevels. This then necessitates a machine process, using a bench grinder; the steel is too hard for filing and usually it is cost prohibitive to use diamond abrasives. It is a quick and simple process to sharpen them on a bench grinder grinding wheel. Small diameter twist-drill bits, because they are small and made from hardened steel, and because the flutes forming the twist create a weakness in the main shaft, snap readily under any duress such as heavy torque or lateral pressure causing bending, buckling, or misdirection. They do work best in drill drivers and drill presses as the speed is higher and cuts per depth of cut distances are higher than with, say, a hand drill. That said, they still work just fine in a hand drill and that is cordless too so you need no electricity for driving or battery charging. Snapped bits can be reshaped and sharpened, if there is still enough length in the bit, by grinding on the grinding wheel.

The Square Awl

In its most basic form, the awl seems a simple enough tool and takes almost no understanding but hidden in its simplicity are issues that can easily be taken for granted or misunderstood. In general, an awl comprises some kind of pointed blade or point fixed in a handle; at first glance, that is. Awls come in a variety of shapes and sizes, mostly catering to a range of different crafts for marking, creating holes, piercing materials, and creating starting points. Although, in woodworking, we may use different types defined by their points, the square awl is the one designed for working wood and the one I find to be the most practical and the most versatile. I doubt that, once you use a well-made square awl, (preferably but not essentially blacksmith-made) you will ever return to any other. I still keep different types in my workbench drawer but, for the main part, I only ever use the square one. To the uninitiated, the square awl might look, perhaps, a little primitive and especially if it has been hammered square and to a sharp point, under the hammer, on the face of an anvil. This would be a rare find. In reality, the square awl was cleverly devised and simply developed as a tool used mostly by peasant agrarians, woodsmen, and craftsmen alike for centuries. The history is indeed interesting when you understand how the tool takes different turns to work the wood.

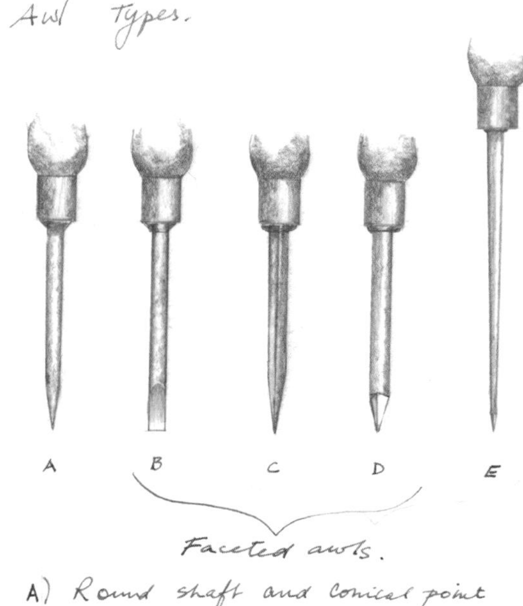

Most awls comprise a round, thin rod of steel, usually sharpened to a conical point. Mostly you push it into wood to start holes for screws or other similar tasks. In general, awls have one of three points; a conical point, a chisel point, or a four-sided squared point. Regardless of the point type, the metal blade is held in a round, triangular, or oval shaped wooden or plastic handle. The handle material depends mainly on the era it was made, with pre 1960's models being made of wood and post 1960's models having either plastic or wooden handles. Both work fine but I think that generally the better quality awls have wooden handles and square, bolstered tangs, hammer-drawn to a point by traditional forge work. For added strength and quality, the handle is often fitted with a brass ferrule to enclose and constrain the wooden handle and awl blade to prevent splitting under the pressures and torque of use.

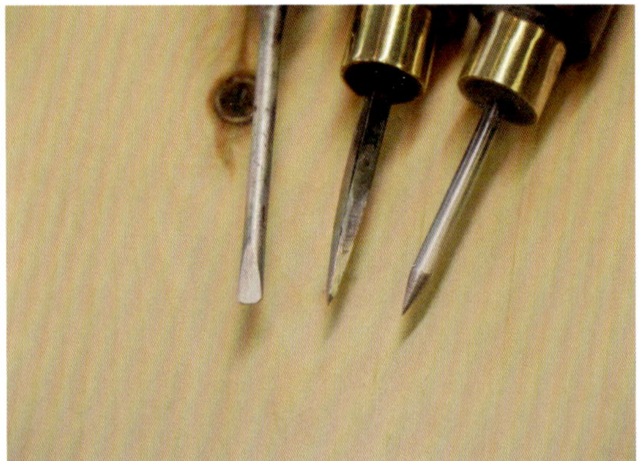

With the awl, as with many simple tools, a lot of the subtleties of the way it works might escape the attention of most people. It is not just a question of forcing a steel point into wood fibres but rather sensing for a course into and through fibres at the point where we cannot see. Some awls, the rounded ones with conical points, are piercing tools with no edges as such, unlike the woodworking awl I use in all my work, which is the very traditional square awl, and for very good reason. This tool differs from other craft awls, which might be used more as general piercing tools that part fibrous strands and puncture skins, such as plastic and leather, leaving all of the material in place. Such awls are used for leather work, paper crafts, fibre crafts and many others. The square awl, used in woodworking, is designed and fit for purpose and that should be well remembered. In woodworking we use them mainly to create holes by either parting fibres but leaving all of the fibre there or reaming out conical holes to take the shank of say, a screw, hook or handle.

The woodworker's awl usually penetrates deeply into thick materials rather than through them, as is the case with skins and fibres, paper and cardboard. The start hole we want and need from the awl allows the point, ahead of the screw threads, to first start in the wood and then allows the threads forming the screw to spiral progressively into the wall fibres. This easing ensures the wood does not split as the intended fixing is inserted.

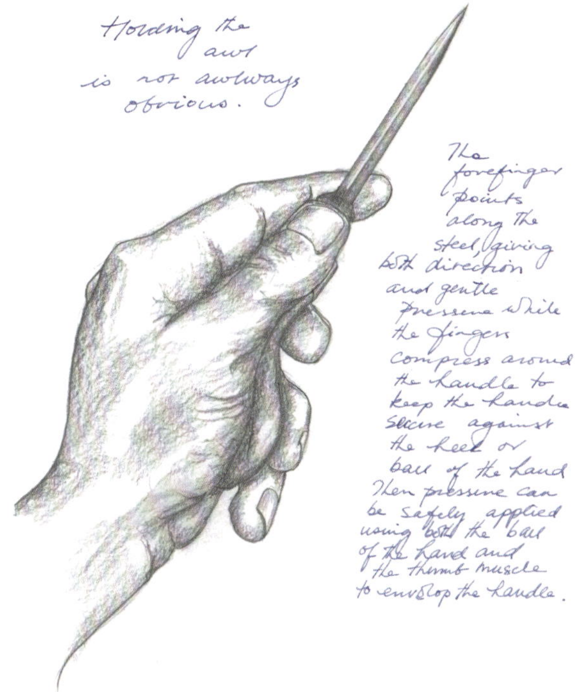

Using the Square Awl

Many of the woodworking crafts may have now forgotten the square awl or indeed do not know of its existence, yet this awl can separate fibres without removing material or, on the contrary and unlike the other awls, remove material in a very controlled way. As the point is pressed down into the wood and then partially rotated, less than, say, a quarter turn back and forth, the wood grain parts to allow deeper penetration with each part rotation but without actually removing any wood. Each partial turn also allows a slightly deeper entry to the desired depth. This method actually compresses the fibres into the main body of wood and so relies more on force than reaming. On the other hand, a full back and forth rotation along the long axis of the awl reams out wood which attaches itself to each corner of the awl. A full rotation of a square awl creates an exact hole size, the same diameter as the corner to opposite corner width of the awl blade. Successive wrist twists deepen the hole to the desired depth and can even pass entirely through a section of wood if a through-hole is needed. The tool relies on the square corners of the blade to act as actual cutting corners in like manner to any cutting blade but, in this case, the blade cuts on both forward and reverse rotation equally. It is usually necessary to sharpen the sides of the tapering part of the awl blade

by filing each facet flat occasionally. The advantage this tool has over all others is that it creates a conical hole that matches the shape of different sizes of screws. The goal is to leave enough wood for the screw thread to bite securely into the walls of the shaped hole.

The Bradawl

Bradawls usually comprise a round-stemmed, chisel-tipped cutting point, sloping to form a shaped tip that looks like a miniature screwdriver. Newly made ones are fully squared and angular but after longer periods of use the tip becomes rounded at the corners through wear. We often use these awls as small screwdrivers for tinier slot-headed screws.

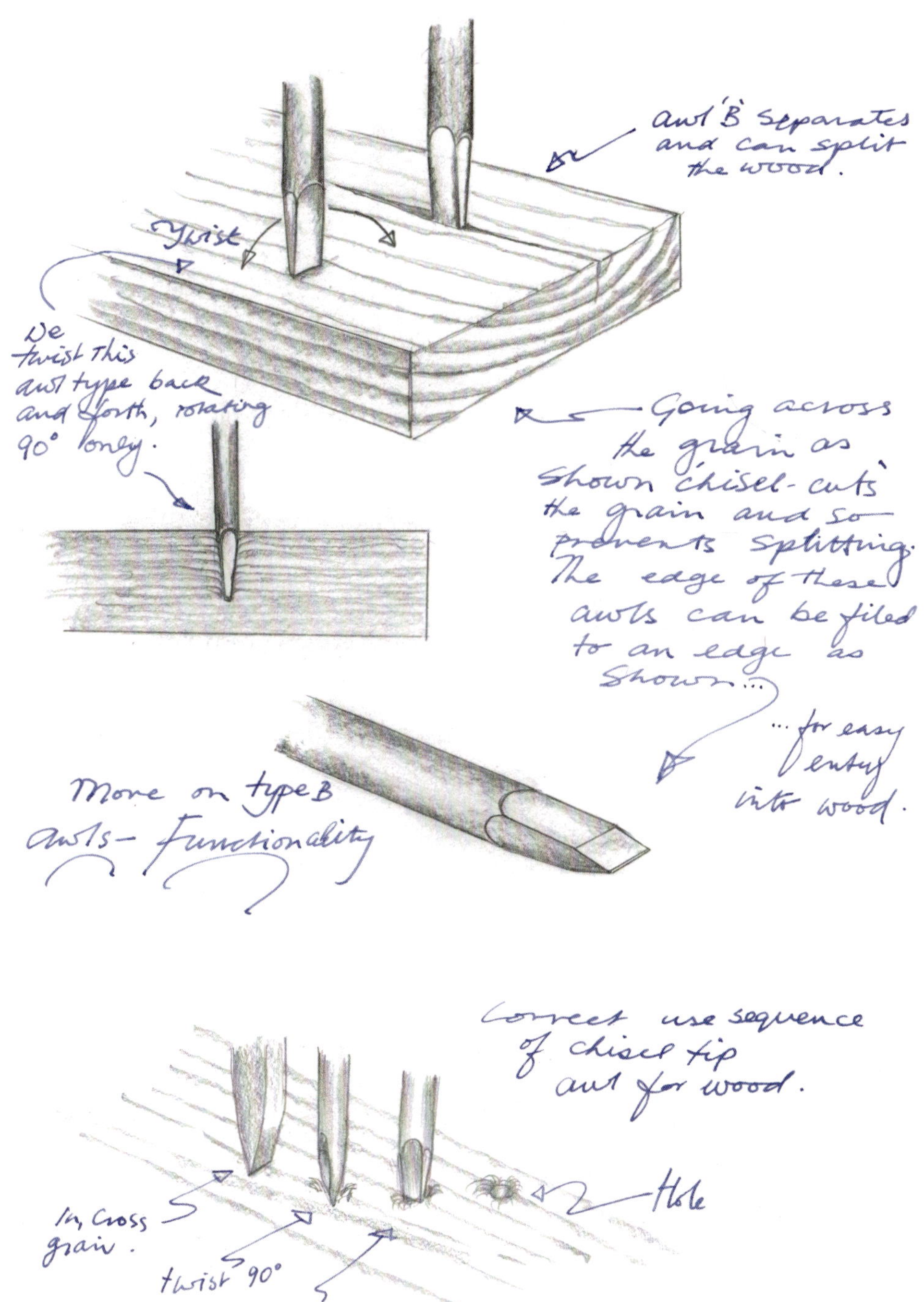
awl 'B' separates and can split the wood.
Twist
We twist this awl type back and forth, rotating 90° only.
Going across the grain as shown 'chisel-cuts' the grain and so prevents splitting. The edge of these awls can be filed to an edge as shown...
...for easy entry into wood.
More on type B awls - Functionality
Correct use sequence of chisel tip awl for wood.
In cross grain.
twist 90°
Back.
Hole

The Scratch Awl

A scratch awl is a long, round, tapered awl and its name is a popular term used mostly by Americans because the pointed tool is used by several different trades and crafts for marking materials including wood, metal, leather, card, plastic, or paper. In most cases these marks preface subsequent work such as cutting, stitching, and painting lines.

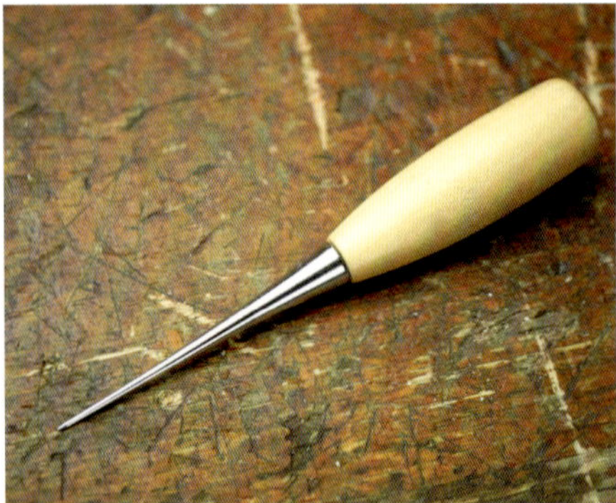

The Birdcage Awl

The square awl is also called the 'birdcage awl'. Historically it was used for making cages to contain birds for transport to and from market or game shooting venues and so on. The square awl was used by agrarians and woodsmen, people whose lives related more to the land and relied on raw wood from the forests, woodlands, and hedgerows of rural life. Perhaps these people could be roughly connected to people who today might be referred to as green or rustic woodworkers because they worked with the raw and uncured wood, straight from the tree. After riving off square splints from smaller sections and branches, these woodsmen created a range of cages by further downsizing the wood using split sections. The square awl capably bored rows of holes, side by side, to receive riven square sections as bars that then formed frames into cages and so we have the term birdcage awl.

“*The square awl capably bored rows of holes, side by side, to receive riven square sections as bars that then formed frames into cages and so we have the term birdcage awl*”

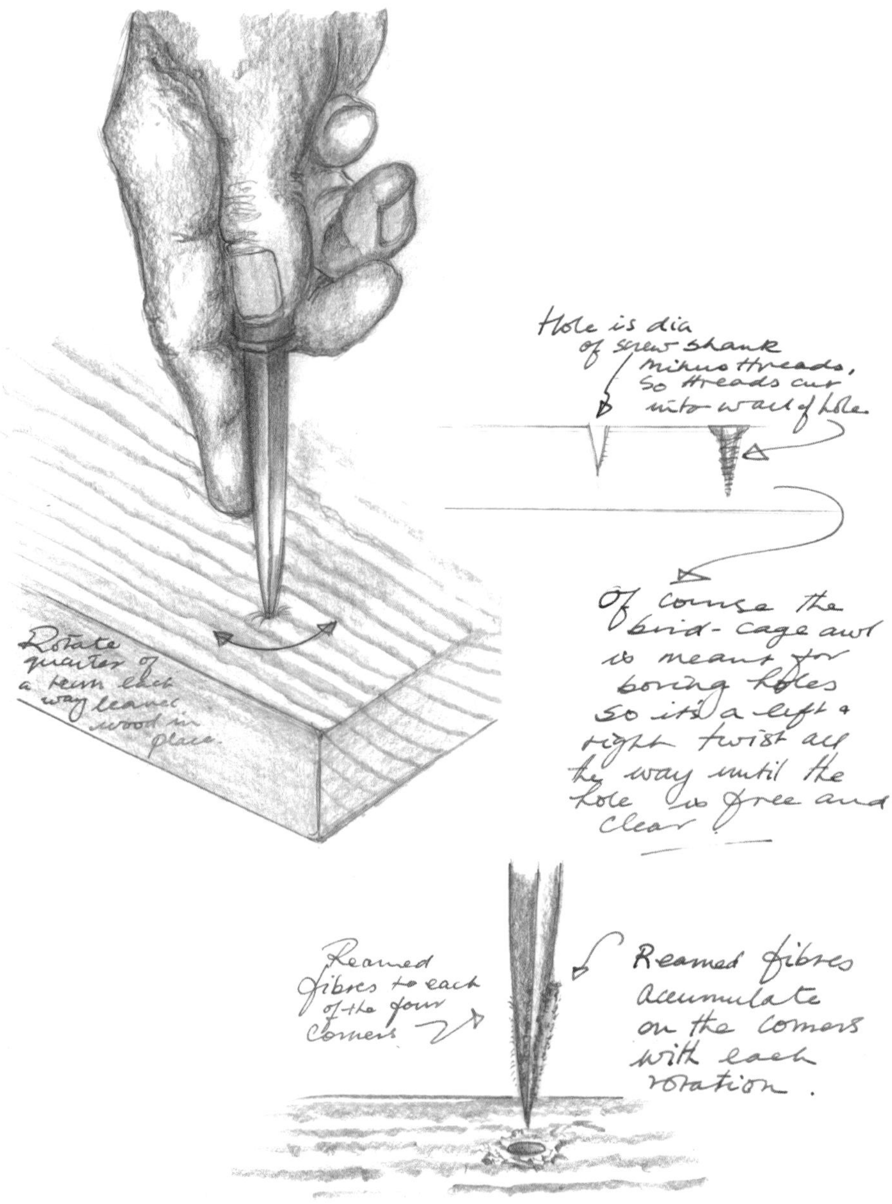

How Different Awls Affect the Wood

It is interesting to explore how the different awl types affect the wood. The round awl quickly splits the wood when you use it near to the end of a section. Soon after applying pressure, the wood starts to split along the grain. Further penetration worsens the condition. This is because the awl has a wedging effect on the wood and when used near the end, as shown (next page), the wood cannot withstand the compression needed to absorb the metal of the blade.

The conical point of a round awl.

The square awl has a squared shank, which is refined to a pyramid shaped tip to further strengthen the point for longevity. Both aspects of the refined blade can ream the walls of the hole in the wood. Even when boring close to the end, the wood shows no sign of splitting; but to fully bore the wood the awl must be continually rotated during the piercing process. Once the full width is reached, further turning refines the wall of the hole and, though not as neat a hole as boring with drill bits, the hole is ideal for much of my work and the awl is a very convenient tool to use.

The bradawl offers yet another awl type that we use for penetrating wood and was perhaps the most commonly used of all during the 1900s. This was the one I was most familiar with growing up. To start the awl, we place it across the grain so that it penetrates the surface fibres crossgrain first. As the awl enters the wood by pressing, we rotate it 90 degrees and press further. This wrist action parts the fibres. By alternate rotations, the awl proceeds ever deeper and, if needed, on through to the other side.

Here you can see the various effects on the outfeed of the different awl types we generally use, side by side.

Making a Round Awl Square

Whereas the chisel-tipped awl is useful for small screw turning, the round awl's usefulness in woodworking is questionable because it will almost always split the wood, rather than just create the desired hole. This happens especially near to end grain. With the square awl a full rotational twist reams the hole wall and reduces the risk of splitting. On round awls, you can take a flat file to form facets to the tip. This then gives the awl this reaming capability and it functions the same as the square awl, even if the remainder of the shaft remains round. Of course, the square awl can also be used for other craft work, such as leather work and paper crafting. If the steel is too hard for filing then heat the tip and let it cool, without quenching, and then file it square.

Hammers

In woodworking, hammers are the drivers behind everything that needs the added force, which the hands alone cannot deliver in such direct and precise amounts. We use them in many different forms, made mostly from wood or a combination of wood and steel; we then discover rubber and plastic versions to add more and less weight when needed. In the hands of an experienced user, hammers seem to somehow exert that certain confidence in the face of resistance. Beyond driving the nail, the wedge, and the stubborn peg, we have joints to seat with certainty, a second before the glue grabs, and chisels and gouges that stop short without them. Hammers and mallets are not heavily driven so much as meted, with sensitivity, to the work by a knowing hand. Woodworking without mallets and hammers would mostly be impossible. They start steel wedges and axes for splitting and riving our rough stock from the tree and also tap together the joints made with the same wood from the same tree. They work between these two extremes when the saws stop and we need an exchange between steel and wood; and now nylon and rubber types too.

As an old woodworker once said to me, "When all else fails, try a more scientific approach – use a bigger hammer."

I have worked with many types of hammers throughout my life and, as a full time woodworker, that has often meant for days and weeks on end. The mallets and chisel hammers I rely on as a furniture maker are different to those today's jobsite carpenter would use to nail studs and build trusses. In my early working life, mallets were always in the joiner's box of tools because they were essential on wooden handled chisels and gouges. I doubt that many carpenters in our western culture would use or perhaps even own a mallet today, yet a century ago they would not have been without one.

Hammers Are Tools of Care and Accuracy

Measured chips, gauged only by eye and hand, fall into piles beneath the workbench and leave only what is

intended in the finished work. Swept up and cast into the fire, these chips reflect the cutting edge of the tool, the intent of the artisan, and the skill of the workmanship. The eye and the hand measure the delivery of every blow to task and direct the exact amount of force and the angle to part the waste from the wanted. Mortised holes and tail and pin recesses receive tenons, pins, and dovetails, cut to exact lines, allowing no air in between the carefully fitted parts. By these things we see that the hammer is indeed tuned to task by the hands of a crafting artisan; not so much as a bludgeoning tool but more a precision instrument, refined and designed to deliver accuracy in every application.

Essential Hammers

I own three hammer types and reach for them or similar versions of them throughout my workday. They mostly rest on the workbench worktop nearby because I use them so much. As with all tools, when you reach for any one of them, usually no other will do. Although these three might be used interchangeably for some tasks, each one of them performs quite differently and often the task is so specific that the others will pale into insignificance by comparison. My three essential hammers are discussed in detail on the following pages:

The Nylon-headed Hammer/Chisel Hammer p. 449
The Steel Hammer p. 457
The Mallet p. 465

The Nylon-headed Hammer/ Chisel Hammer

In my youth I was aware of only two hammer types for the carpenter, the 16 ounce steel claw hammer, with its hickory handle, used for driving nails, and the Warrington hammer, used for driving small panel pins (finish nails USA), installing hardware and, additionally, adjusting wooden planes. For chisel and gouge work we relied on the only tool around, the beechwood wooden mallet. I only bought the ones I could not make for myself. Fashion seemed a very distant thing from the joiner's workshop and little seemed to have changed for a century before. I had never heard the word 'ergonomic' at that time. The term seems to be popular with modern mass-makers of tools today but the tools available then worked well, having been ergonomically tested for centuries in one form or another. It seemed to me then that there really was no need to change anything but, of course, much did change and, in many ways, thankfully so. Without the invention of some new materials, many of the tools we rely on today would not exist. One of the best chisel hammers, as I call them, I have ever used is made mostly from nylon, with a steel head threaded to receive interchangeable faces of plastic, nylon, and rubber. Another has the same head with a wooden handle of ash.

Many changes have redefined the hammers and mallets we woodworkers use in woodworking but, more recently, it has been the materials used in their construction that have changed some of the ones we reach for now. In past eras we had metal and wood alone to make our hammers and mallets from but then the hard plastics like

polyethylene, PVC, and nylon, together with composite materials such as fibreglass, became hybrid materials for moulding and engineering tools. Moulded and milled from different plastics and further shaped by heat, such materials can be formed and set into a rigid or semi hard condition, offering a new generation of hammers to use with chisels and gouges. The same tool is used for much of the assembly work in different trades, including woodworking. Having used wooden mallets for all of my chisel and gouge work over the decades, I felt satisfied that these more compact hammers offered an ideal combination. There are many types to choose from and they are even offered with many choices of head hardness/density.

In working with students, I began looking for alternative chisel hammers to see if there was indeed something better suited to the work; mostly hammers not normally associated with woodworking at all. The most suitable alternatives I found came from an unexpected source in the form of parts assembly hammers, designed for use in factories making plastic and metal goods or auto-body repairs. I was not necessarily looking for a replacement to my mallets but rather for a hammer-type tool with more direct drive. Of the different types I tried over a period of a decade, I adopted one that truly excelled at the workbench for use even possibly in place of the traditional wooden mallet and that would also double for assembly work too. After that prolonged testing, I felt confident that I could indeed introduce it to my students and use it alongside my wooden mallet for any work using chisels. Though I have relied mostly on my wooden mallet through the decades past, today I use this nylon-headed assembly hammer and it really works well. I have found them available with a wooden handle with one side having a hard nylon face and the other a softer face. Others I have come across are fitted with two nylon hammer faces and a nylon handle. This hammer is a little heavier. Apart from melting or burning away, these hammers seem to me to be virtually indestructible. This hammer works better than all of the hammers I have tried, including dead-blow assembly hammers, made from rubber, and other softer, plastic-headed hammers.

In the western world, hammers with steel heads were generally deemed unsuitable for use with chisels. Through the years, chisels made with steel caps and centres emerged, so carpenters could indeed use the steel hammers directly on the chisels; but this was never suited to joinery and finer woodworking. On the other hand, some woodworkers did and do indeed still successfully use steel hammers on their chisels but they do so with chisels that have steel hoops on the end of the handles to prevent both spelching the fibres and the end-grain fracture associated with steel on wood.

Chisel handles bound by hoops prevents splitting.

My preference for the nylon hammer grew through years of use because of its strength and the balance I get in the hand; to the point where every blow I deliver is without any excess energy expended. This becomes important when you work with your hands for long days and, with my students, this is especially so as most of

them are unused to physical work, using their arms and upper body. In terms of the ergonomics, when the head lands there are no awkward twists to create the imbalances that sometimes accompany wooden mallets. Also a decent mallet needs to be fairly sizable to achieve the right weight. The chisel hammers cost very little to buy too and so it gets new woodworkers started with something solid and without compromise. If you are like me, you may want to add other mallet types later. These hammers are also available in different sizes and weights so, again, you can pick heavier- or lighter-weight models to suit your personal strength.

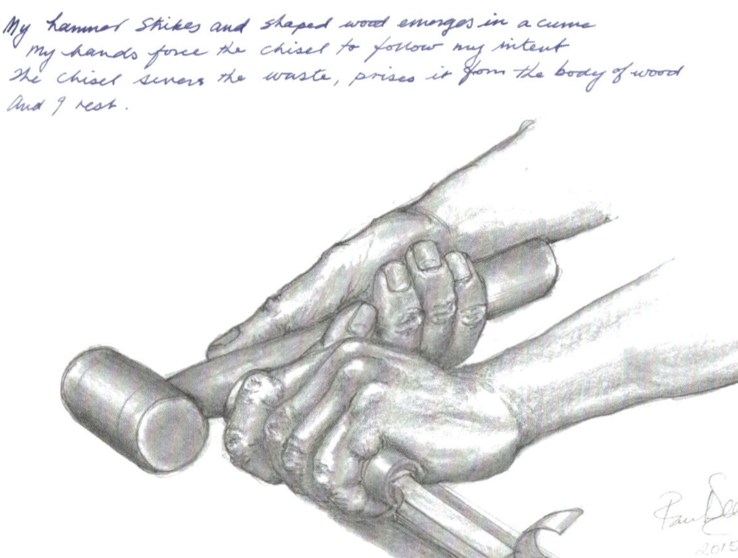

It Is Important to Accept Innovation

Suggesting these hammers for bench work may seem controversial, coming from a woodworker like myself and I admit to struggling with this at first. However, my goal is not just the preservation of traditions so much as the craft. I do find some modern developments to be improvements and they can make woodworking more vibrant, even inspiring. Crafting artisans two and three hundred years ago saw new and innovative ideas come too and they accepted some of them and rejected others, I am sure. My thought is that they would have accepted nylon hammers and liked the combination of the wooden handle as I do.

I Will Always Rely on My All-wooden Mallet

I have used and still use wooden mallets in my work. I like them for some work and find them less suited and less well adapted to others. In a past era there really was no alternative but here we are in a new century. If I am recessing hinges in a tight space inside a cupboard or a box there is no doubt that what seemed free and perfect on a benchtop suddenly becomes cumbersome and awkward. The large mallet head gets in the way and catches on my prized work. The chisel hammer comes into its own here especially. Many new woodworkers, however, will feel daunted by the idea of making their own mallet. The modern day manufactured wooden mallets I have come across are, in general, quite shoddily made and are no comparison to the user-made ones from the era when every craftsman made their own. I discuss making a mallet yourself on page 469 but, in the meantime, alternatives, when necessary, really work well. So, new woodworkers can cut to the chase and avoid a lot of confusion so they can really get on with their new interest, at a low cost and without compromise, by using this simple alternative.

As well as being an alternative to a wooden mallet it is irreplaceable for assembly.

Centre of Percussion

The chisel hammers I have used over the months and years deliver the goods. Weight ratios and balance are critical and so too is something we call the 'centre of percussion' that provides economy of movement and power. I find that, with large-faced mallets, new woodworkers seldom find this centre of percussion, which is often an outer corner and not dead centred in the mallet head. Getting it wrong tilts the mallet, glances the blow and frequently twists the chisel from its course, especially when chopping mortise holes, for instance. On the other hand, the smaller heads hit squarely and directly and with much more accuracy. Most of my students have no difficulty using chisel hammers for chopping and chisel work.

Shaping Nylon-handled Chisel Hammers

I have used a nylon-handled chisel hammer for several years and really like the way that it works with my chisels. The one I have is a 1 ½" (38mm) model. When I bought the hammer it was bright white plastic and had a black plastic grip sleeve that I did not like; nor did I like the shape of the hammer handle. So I removed the plastic sleeve with a knife and shaped the handle to suit my hand, using a spokeshave for most of the shaping work. The nylon peels away like any softwood does and I soon got the oval shape I preferred to fit my hand. The handle, being nylon, felt quite slick so I used a coarse rasp to create a roughened grip and refined it with 180-grit sandpaper. The faces of the hammer were also smooth and slick and tended to slip in use. A quick rub with 180-grit sandpaper on the faces of the hammer did the trick. I used two coats of coloured shellac to reduce the starkness. At first I did not like it too much but after a short time in use it looked fine.

The heads screw into a steel barrel and it is the steel barrel that gives it the weight and easy centre of percussion I need, which is perfect for chopping mortises and other aspects of chopping work.

Balance and Finesse in Hammers

If you use a heavyweight chisel then you must use greater weight in the hammer or mallet. That is fine at the start of the work but, when many mortises are to be cut, the hammer will feel heavier and heavier in use. Wooden mallets tend to be large but not weighty, though they are still usually heavier than the nylon chisel hammer. My chisel hammer delivers the goods in precise measure and unfalteringly. The balance is about as perfect as it gets but it sometimes takes a short time for some people, new to hand work, to master the accuracy. With my chisel hammer, I hit the sweet spot, the centre of percussion, dead centre, almost without fail, every time. That makes for good economy of motion, effort and effectiveness.

Nylon-headed Hammers Are Great for Setting Wooden Planes

I have recommended these hammers as chisel and assembly hammers. Another area I use them is in the shocking and adjusting of wooden hand planes; for loosening cutting iron assemblies and the wedges holding them in place. No matter the plane type, almost all wooden bodied planes rely on wedges to hold the blades in place. A hammer is needed for adjusting the wedges for tightness and then for adjusting the depth of cut. I find these nylon-headed hammers work wonderfully for my wooden planes as they do no damage if used with care. We use hammers to adjust and set the irons by tapping the heel or nose of the plane, which withdraws the cutting iron from the throat. Tapping the iron sets the depth of cut and we also align the cutting edge to the face of the sole by tapping on the top corner. Notice the angled corners at the top end of the plane iron. This angle allows the hammer to hit squarely. I use these wooden planes alongside my steel ones.

This Hammer Type Is Here to Stay

I am not sure whether, reading this, you will feel that wooden mallets are still important. They are. This is another of those issues where it is not really an 'either/or' because they are both quite different. If you have neither and you are learning woodworking, you are best starting out with the nylon hammer and then making your own mallet, using that hammer, when you feel you can tackle the project. I would not give up either of my two types.

I have come across a variety of chisel hammers that work well. I have owned this one for 20 years and it is still going strong though it does show signs of wear now.

The Steel Hammer

For woodworkers, the steel hammer works mostly as steel on steel to drive nails, strike nail punches (called nail sets in the USA), and work metal parts and fittings to fully seat them. Of course, there are many more uses for the hammer in its various forms and beyond woodworking but nailing is its primary purpose. A diverse range of shapes and sizes, developed over centuries, leaves us with many options and here the confusion begins. For the twenty-first century carpenter, it is hard to work well without a claw hammer to both drive and withdraw nails and separate nailed components and so on. However, at the bench, I have little need for a claw hammer and little need for anything more than my 10 ounce (283g) joiner's hammer; a hammer commonly known as the Warrington hammer. It is my favourite hammer to use for most tasks and, though I do indeed use others for some limited work including metal work, the cross-pein Warrington with its worn-in hammer shaft is never far from my right hand. I have not been able to find any authoritative record of why cross-pein joiner's hammers are named after the town of Warrington, in Cheshire, UK, but the name has been in use for a very long time. My own, a Stanley, has been mine from new since 1965. I do own a couple of claw hammers but for general joinery, not for furniture making.

The Joiner's Hammer

With hundreds of hammer types used in woodworking and its related crafts, trades and so on, the woodworker's Warrington joiner's hammer still remains in manufacture today. It did not offer the versatility of the claw hammer but every English woodworker I grew up with and worked alongside owned one. They all found it to be practical and perfectly balanced for finer work. It was once made in a full range of sizes, anywhere from four ounces up to a full two pounds, but joiners rarely used them in weights heavier than 14ozs (397g). Other trades did use them considerably, not the least of which were blacksmiths and other metal workers and upholsterers too.

The hammer head is round-faced and slightly domed to avoid surface damage to the wood; it has a polished bell and hammer face. The part of the hammer called the 'neck' is almost always an eight-sided, chamfered neck, leading to two cheeks, one on each side the of the hammer. From this point the hammer head is symmetrically tapered into two flat faces, culminating in a rounded edge. By holding short panel pins (finish nails) between the fingers, this rounded edge can be used to drive pins, mostly unseen because of length, held between the thumb and forefinger. This rounded edge slips between the finger and thumb holding the nail or pin and makes the first strike to set the pin. From there on the hammer is rotated to the regular flat face that then drives the nail down and flush to the surface of the wood. Small tacks for leatherwork and upholstery can be driven the same way.

"*The hammer head is round-faced and slightly domed to avoid surface damage to the wood; it has a polished bell and hammer face*"

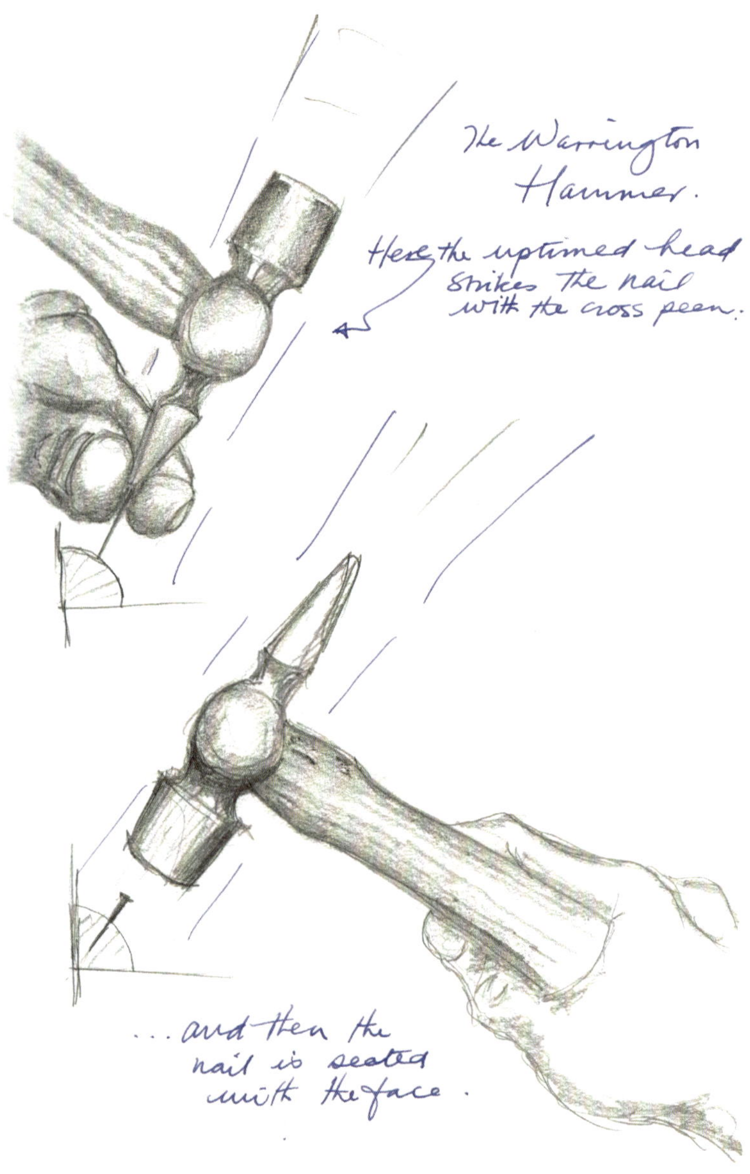

My Daily Hammer

I pick this hammer up several times during any given day. In our present culture, where hammers have become more of a fashion created by designer-makers, looking for new ways to sell what already works well, there still remains something uniquely satisfying in owning a hammer with a wooden shaft, shaped and polished smooth by my own working hands. Many things have reshaped our perceptions of how tools should and should not look; from hi-viz fibreglass shafts, guaranteed never to break, to ripping claws and much more. Looking beyond all of this, there are designs that are indeed irreplaceable and, on the workbench, for me at least, it is the cross-pein Warrington 10 ounce (283g) hammer. I also own 12 ounce (340g) and 14 ounce (397g) versions too but, for driving panel pins (finish nails) and hammer setting and adjusting my small saws, or tapping down a hinge into its recess, the 10 ounce (283g) model works best. Do not go for smaller versions for joinery and furniture making. The 4-8 ounce (113-227g) weights are more for specialised small work such as picture framing, model making and such.

I bought my Stanley 10 ounce (283g) Warrington in 1965 alongside a Stanley 16 ounce (454g) claw hammer, followed by a heavier 20 ounce (567g) one. The claw hammer was used to drive nails larger than 2" (5cm), which I rarely do in making furniture but, in joinery, 4" (10cm) nails are common enough for nailing heads to the stiles of doorframes, alongside the tenons, to fully seat them. This was quicker and easier than using 7 foot (2m) clamps and, of course, meant no waiting for the glue or paint to dry. Some mortise and tenons were glued and some painted prior to assembly - painted ones for outside frames and glued for inside.

We drive wooden wedges in much of our work and steel hammers work best for this, especially the cross-pein hammer. The head is narrow and well centred to the work and it is this that makes it so appropriate.

Re-wedging the Hammer Head

Hammer heads loosen because the wood shrinks inside the 'eye' of the head. In most cases this is because the wood was not as dry as the region in which it might be sold and used. When it goes from one level of humidity, during manufacture, to another region with lower humidity levels, the surrounding atmosphere absorbs moisture from the end-grain fibres and the head becomes loose. There only needs to be a small amount of shrinkage for this to happen. Sometimes the head loosens because of fibre compression too or because of misuse or accidental damage. Also, unlike the claw hammer, which is designed for nail pulling, the cross-pein hammer is not designed to be used for any kind of levering work; inevitably people do use it for this. With these forces exerted the head then loosens even more by continued usage.

This hammer type is not designed for levering work; the eye length is too short and levering with the cross-pein aspect of the head compresses the wood of the shaft inside the eye.

Some hammer heads have two steel wedges that are used to spread the end of the shaft and hold it into the head whereas some have one steel one and then also a wooden one. There are a variety of possible configurations with steel wedges, wooden wedges, or a combination of both. Steel wedges are convenient, especially for mass making hammers, because they do not break. Do not hesitate however to use wooden ones as replacements; steel ones do not hold or spread the fibres any better than wooden wedges. It is often simpler to replace missing steel wedges with wooden ones. I have used simple pine wedges that have held for 20 years to date.

If or when steel wedges have come loose or if the head alone is loose and ill-fitting, you can usually take a nail punch or something similar and drive the wedge (or wedges) deeper and indeed replace any missing wedges with new ones. This almost always works well and the head is then tight and immoveable again. Before tightening the wedges, strike the end of the hammer shaft whilst holding the hammer openly by the shaft without pressing it onto anything. The counterweight of the head will drive the shaft into any loose areas of the eye and close up any gaps inside the eye. It also tightens the shaft in the eye of the hammer head and seats the head to the shaft on the handle side. Once this is done you can drive the wedges deeper or install new ones. The side of a flat-head screwdriver works well for this. If you find the head is not tightening with only one wedge you can use a chisel to start an entry slit in the end of the shaft, inside the eye, then cut a wooden wedge to drive into the opening. This will further split the wood to receive the wedge but will not normally split deeper, beyond the centre of the eye, because the eye of the hammer head will constrain it. Any excess in the wedge length can be cut with a small saw or hacksaw and filed flush as needed.

Treating the Hammer Shaft

Wooden hammer shafts generally do not dry out as we might be led to believe, especially if they are regularly used. However, wooden handles do benefit from a periodic recoat to keep them feeling good and keep them clean and indeed easy to clean too. That is why we wipe them over with a coat of linseed oil by rag now and then. The oil dries overnight and then starts to take on a patina after a period of use.

Treating the Hammer Head

The steel itself needs no treatment, except to keep it free from rust. Few things look worse on tools than rust, I think. Periodic oiling over the whole, except the hammer face, with light machine oil will keep it rust free.

Metal Working Hammer

I frequently need an anvil for metal working and so use a hammer, turned face-up, in the vise. I use these for reducing set on my saws (as discussed on page 305) and also for shaping work. Wear safety glasses in case you miss the work and strike the other hammer. Hammer against hammer can split off a chunk so work carefully. It has never happened to me but the risk is there.

Adjusting Tools

While nylon-headed hammers work great for adjusting wooden-bodied tools, the steel hammer works well too. The steel hammer is especially important for use with the old spokeshaves, which have two tangs protruding through the top for anchoring the blade and for adjusting the depth of cut. Giving a positive tap with the steel hammer sets the irons very precisely, both in and out, and the steel hammer is best for this as the points of the tangs can damage nylon-headed hammers.

The Mallet

When I first started to write about the mallet, my first thoughts were as simple and factual as the mallet itself. From a rectangular stick of wood and a block section, and then some fitting and shaping work, comes a mallet. I used my first mallet for a decade before I sensed there is more to it than that, if the mallet is to work in total alignment with its user for a lifetime. I have made a number of different mallets over my 50 years at the bench. My first one was clunky and angular until, after a few years, I redefined the model, having seen one made by an early craftsman that put mine to shame. The outcome was a mallet pattern I still love and use today. So my writing in this section carries with it the things I see as important.

The mallet's primary function for woodworking is to drive the chisel when chopping and splitting wood. Occasionally we might use it for heavier assembly work too but, with the advent of plastic, rubber, and deadblow hammers, they are seldom used for assembly. Mallets can be bought new and secondhand but it can be difficult to find one that really suits you. However, this is not necessarily a bad thing as you will enjoy making your own but, to do this, you do need something to drive your chisel.

Most of the mallets I have seen are less than adequate in size, shape, and weight and so finding one that is truly fit for purpose often proves difficult.

Picking the Right Wood to Make a Mallet

Making your mallet is a rite of passage for any woodworker and you should take it as early as you feel ready to. It may not be the last mallet you make but the steps are important. Every woodworker at some point, in my view that is, should spend quality time set aside for the task. You start with the search. The right wood may be right there with you or you may start a search that could take a few years. You can still make one to temporarily take care of your needs while you continue your search so grab a hard, dense-grained wood and get started. What you are looking for is a mallet made from dense, hard-grained wood with sizing and proportion that looks and feels balanced in the hand and in action at the bench. This is determined by the wood itself and it is critical to use the appropriate wood. Some woods are indeed dense but so dense they make the mallet too heavy for your preference. Some dense-grained woods split too easily, making them unsuitable too. The harder and denser the wood the better but hard maple, oak, ash, and cherry (as well as several others) will suit for an initial mallet and give you the practice you need before making your ultimate lifelong mallet. Once you find the right wood, most often you must dry it and dry it

A section of Osage orange (bois d'arc) as a mallet blank sent by a friend in the USA.

This image shows a slight hollow of compressed grain that has made the mallet face all the more solid in my cedar elm mallet head. The work it has done has really perfected the mallet.

ever so slowly, away from heat; dry it somewhere in the ambient air of your workshop. Make sure it is cut long enough to dry without end-grain checking affecting the final result. It is best to seal the ends with melted candle wax or use some latex paint. It is best that the blank be about twice as long as the planned mallet head. Also, do not avoid knotty and gnarly wood. This type of wood often makes the stoutest mallet head; the interlocking grain offers much greater resistance to splitting and grain collapse. Both of these deteriorations badly affect the impact of the mallet on the chisel. I waited a few years before cutting into my blanks of Osage orange and cedar elm; two dense-grained North American hardwoods I have found second to none for making mallet heads and all types of handles. Other woods work but these two woods are exceptional and deserve a mention. Once you have made your best mallet, never let it out of your sight for more than a minute and never let anyone else use it if possible.

This is a beech mallet. Beech is one of the most common woods that commercial tool makers use for making mallets.

For good reason, beech has been the preferred wood for mallet makers in Britain for two or three centuries. I have always felt them to be just a little soft and light for delivering the drive I like but do not let that deter you. Many an old and well used mallet still survives to show me a long life at someone else's bench. Common woods that have worked for me are ash, beech, cherry, hard maple, and white and red oak. Lots of choices.

Making a Mallet

My size recommendation would be 2 ¾" (70mm) x 3 ¾" (95mm) x 6 ¾" (171mm) long regardless of the wood type. The handle should be about ¾" (19mm) x 1 ¾" (44mm) x 14" (355mm) long. These sizes offer good weight in the wood types mentioned before and provide an ideal weight-to-strength ratio for most people. Once the mallet is made, it can always be shaved down and reshaped to accommodate personal weight and shape preferences. The weight needs to be sufficient to drive the chisel and the head should be big enough so you do not have to have to look at it to hit the chisel. This means that the face is large enough to strike with and the handle is long enough to feel balanced in the hand. The handle and balance should not force you to hold the handle in an awkward, unwieldy way. Commonly the handle is held quite close to the mallet head; so that the thumb almost touches the head. The opposite end seems to protrude past the hand a lot but this helps give the balance I speak of. This is, of course, a personal choice but it seems best to me; my hand works well from there and it is the least tiring position when I have large amounts of mallet work to pursue.

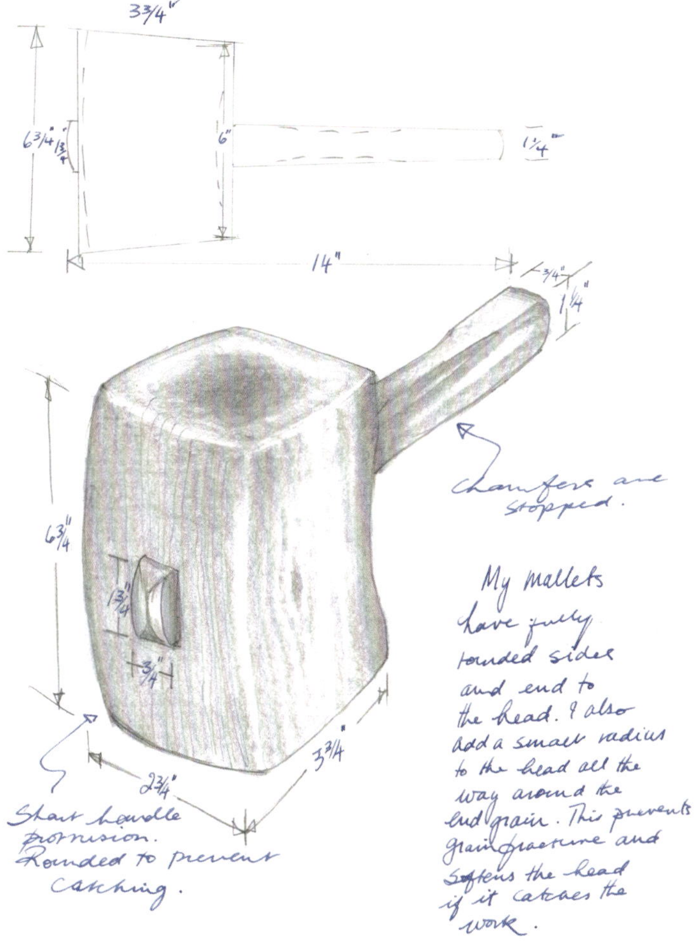

The handle fits perfectly to a tapered mortise hole so that, in the flinging action of work, the head never turns loose from it. I make mine from ¾" (19mm) thick stock and make a long taper along the full length of the shaft. I first make the handle and then cut the mortise to match and not the other way around. The handle wood must be dried down until it loses no more weight on the kitchen scales. Leave an already dry piece of handle wood in a warm spot for a day or two and that will usually take it all the way down. Remember also that certain woods, such as oak, compress within themselves under pressure so you must allow for this also. Considering these things will mean that the handle never shrinks or compresses too much into the mortise hole. The scalloped, stopped chamfers bring great comfort without too much smoothness and this helps present the mallet head squarely to the chisel.

I try to match the shaping of the mallet so that it mirrors my swing, my work, and my strength too. Curving the end of the head and the sides makes my mallet less clunky and it closely follows my swing as I strike. This radius is 17 ½" (445mm). Removing the inside corners with a curved chamfer, paralleling the outer curve, improves comfort as I often work my mallet with my forefinger knuckle nestled there, right by the head. I form the chamfer by eye but if you need a more definitive radius to work to it is 14" (355mm). I added another radius across the top of the mallet head from side to side to remove what is otherwise a harshness and an obstructive area. The remaining shaping is the chamfering to the handle and rounding the ends of the mallet handle. It is a small thing to do but it makes the mallet all the more functional in the hand. The wide sides of my mallet have a wide radius, formed with just a #4 smoothing plane. I found that this radically improves the mallet's overall functionality in use and these added radii reduce the risk of catching and thereby damaging the work. The striking faces of the mallet are, in all cases, the ends and not the sides, although I confess that, in a tight spot, I have used the sides from time to time for light tapping. The last shaping is to the corners. Curve them slightly and they will stay that shape. Keeping square edges usually results in broken corners to the mallet and also the cabinets you work on. It is best to have a ⅛" (3mm) radius all the way round.

This shows the shaping of my personal mallet.

Using the Mallet

I have not met many people who talk much about mallets and the mallets I have seen over the past 40 years or so have not generally been good. Mallets are still essential tools in my view. They work well for heavier joinery work, mostly mortising, and especially for when large and deep mortise holes are needed. They do, of course, work on any size of mortise and for other areas where it is necessary to drive the chisel into the wood, with greater force, to chop and split. They are also indispensable to all carving work too. I use them with the gouge for bowl and spoon carving all the time and also seat carving and shaping too.

Here are some hand positions I use with the mallet. Notice that the thumb generally points and the fingers wrap around the handle.

Here I show the general position of the hand.

This is a mid-point hold for heavier drive.

Then there is the tail-end of the handle for really throwing the head at the work for maximum heavy work.

The weight of a mallet must be lifted and dropped to the chisel with a quick and rhythmic arm and wrist movement. At around 60 mallet strokes per minute, equalling 3,600 strokes in an hour, and with a 2 lb (907g) mallet, that is 7,200 lbs (3266kg) of lifting in an hour, driven with the exact force to deliver each blow to an inch diameter. A momentum grows and the whole dynamic of the shape and size of the mallet needs to match the user. This is why it is so important to marry the mallet to the hand of the person that will use it.

A mallet needs to deliver very direct blows with good weight, power, and accuracy. My mallets weigh in at 2 lbs (907g) and I get them to the same or a similar weight by increasing or decreasing the size of the head. That said, owning two or three of different weights makes sense. To increase the weight of the mallet beyond my preferred weight of 2 lbs, I increase all the dimensions of the mallet head proportionally.

The mallet I developed and continue to use came from an old design I discovered in an elderly man's toolbox back in the late 1970s. The tools no longer worked since the man had passed on and there was no one trained to take them and use them. The situation made me consider the man who thought through the making of his personal mallet. He had been a country furniture maker who spoke to me, through a mallet, and convinced me that everyone should do the same, to make the weight match his arm and the handle his hand. His mallet stood out from any of those I had ever seen before as, I suppose, mine might one day also.

STANLEY
MADE
IN

Notes on Tool Care

Most of the secondhand tools I buy are damaged in different ways and most of the damage could have been avoided. It is a lesson for us to consider the wellbeing of the tools we use and store but the best tool maintenance of all is simply using them regularly. Mostly the damage occurs on the various outside surfaces of the tools. Wood fibres absorb water from spills and drips but mostly from atmospheric moisture and this affects tools more when there is no air circulating. This results in raised grain, staining, and swollen wood fibres, which affects the performance and appearance of the tool. Metal, of course, readily tarnishes and, if left long enough, ends up with surface rusting. If left undetected for too long the rust deepens and forms surface corrosion called pitting. This localized corrosion results in irregular cavities or shallow 'pits' that can affect the performance of the tool in different ways. Tools in constant use need less attention and it is the ones less used that are the ones that will need extra maintenance. Moisture from sweat also causes rust. Prevention in general is simple enough. A light wipe over external metal surfaces with light machine oil or paste wax inhibits rust. Internal surfaces too can be oiled and wiped.

PROTECTING WOOD

Two initial coats of shellac works well to seal any wood on new tools. A periodic follow-up every six months with a wipe of boiled linseed oil keeps the tool handles clean and comfortable to use. Moisture does not just affect the metal parts of tools but the wood as well. Even slight swelling limits or even stops adjustability in tools, such as wooden marking gauges, which lock up when swollen with moisture. Additionally, the tools stick to the surface of the wood being worked.

PROTECTING METAL

Light machine oil gives good lubrication to moving metal parts and also provides a good surface coating to inhibit rust. I have a regular regimen for lubricating any and all mechanisms, whether that be to vise parts, equipment, or tools. Oil remains a favourite without doubt, mostly because of its viscosity. Other options are special water displacement fluids that not only coat surfaces but force out any water residues held in the pores of the metal. These give excellent long term protection and a little research is well worth the effort.

WORKSHOP CONDITIONS

A controlled workshop temperature should be combined with good ventilation, to balance out extremes, and moisture of any kind should be kept to a minimum. Moisture comes from many sources, not the least of which can be the materials we work with. Green wood drying in a workshop is not acceptable at all as it constantly releases moisture into the atmosphere until it reaches equilibrium. Consider heat as the main control element and then periodic airing to remove humidity. Constancy is critical and should be established as a priority; and this goes for the tools I work with too. My daily use tools are mostly on my benchtop somewhere and so air circulates around them and they stay dry. Of course, cupboards, drawers and toolboxes are used to keep tools safe and secure but, left closed, they can hold in moisture. Make certain to allow regular circulation here too.

My tool cabinets are open most of the time because they are in full time daily use.

TOOL STORAGE

All of my case goods have locks, compartments, tills, and so on to keep the tools together or apart, depending on the tool type and what they are used for. My benches hold drawers, shelves, tills, and trays too, and the drawers have dividers mostly to keep the tools aligned in a certain orientation rather than misaligned and crossways to one another. It is important to know your tools are safely stowed, protected where necessary, and secure when needed and this is especially so when the tools must be left for extended periods of time.

Rag-in-a-Can – Surface Treating Tools

My rag-in-a-can causes second looks all the time. There is no mystery about it at all and it came to me as an apprentice when I saw the men I worked with swipe their plane soles to reduce friction during planing or indeed the sides of their saw plates when sawing too. I rely on it because it imparts the perfect amount of oil to the tools without any noticeable trace on the wood when in use. I am regularly asked if this oil affects the surface finishes and the answer is generally no. Usually the first few strokes of the plane remove the oil with the shaving and subsequent strokes leave no trace on the wood. Many woodworkers use candle wax applied to the sole and that works well too. The candle wax is used mainly as an antifriction agent but the rag-in-the-can works both for antifriction and as a protective surface coat as well.

MAKING THE RAG-IN-THE-CAN OILER

Making the oil applicator is simple enough. Use a small tomato can with the lid removed completely and use the side of a screwdriver to press down any protruding metal or rough, sharp edges in and around the rim. Use an old tee shirt or thin towel to stuff the can with. The can I used is a standard can at 2 ¼" (57mm) tall. The cloth needs to stand about half an inch taller than the rim of the can. When the rag is forced into the can it will compress a little and after a year or two of use it will compress and consolidate even more. Therefore I fold the rag to about 2 ¾" (70mm) wide to increase the thickness. I then roll the rag as tightly as possible, adding layers if need be, until I can barely stuff it into the can. I then press it down into the can using a flat head screwdriver to aid it into the wall of the can. Once bottomed out I compress the fabric further into the can using the jaws of the vise. The can is now ready for charging with light machine oil. This can take 50 ml of oil in a first charge. For the first charging, just pour in the oil periodically throughout the day. Then add oil once a day for a few days and leave the can on the benchtop for a day or two; and then start using the can to wipe the plane soles and sides and the saw plates too. Most likely your saws and planes will never rust again and they will function with frictionless ease.

Waxing Tools

You can also use wax on steel surfaces as a lubricant and protectant and then on the wooden parts of tools as well. Wax makes tool handles and wooden plane bodies feel more comfortable. Apply a thin coat of paste wax (furniture wax) with 0000 steel wool. This applies the wax more evenly on the surface. Once applied, leave for 20 minutes or so and then buff out with a soft brush or cloth. I wax my wooden plane soles and sides occasionally to keep them clean and smooth in operation. Any household furniture polish in paste form works well.

Glossary

Arris — The external corner formed by two adjacent faces.

Back spline — Rigid support at the top of some woodworking saw blades.

Bed angle — The incline inside a plane body that supports the blade at a fixed angle.

Bench dog — A round or square peg made from wood or metal and partially inserted into a benchtop that allows the vise to hold wide and/or long boards securely to the top of the bench.

Bevel — In this book the term refers mainly to the angled facet adjacent to a flat face, the intersection of which forms a cutting edge on edge tools.

Bevel heel (or knee) — The point on a cutting edge where the angle changes to create the facet that forms the main face of the bevel.

Bird's-eye figuring — Dormant buds inside wood which results in distinctive markings in certain types of wood, such as maple.

Blank — A piece of wood that is the rough dimensions for a planned project but that has not been started.

Bodger — A type of rural woodworker who generally makes wooden chairs often directly from green wood.

Bridle joint — A type of woodworking joint where one part straddles a narrower part in the adjacent component and shoulders are created to both uniting parts of the joint.

Burnish — In this book this refers to the action of a very hard steel tool called the burnisher (discussed on page 61), which is used to consolidate and turn the edges on scrapers (see page 371).

Burr — There are two types of burr related to metalworking but also sharpening metal tools used in woodworking.

1. The term can refer to the rough edge caused by filing or abrading, where the unsupported metal results in a very small ragged edge on the outstroke.

2. The term can also refer to the highly refined and carefully developed cutting edge used in scrapers for refining the surface of wood (see more details on page 365).

Cap iron — A plane component used to tension a cutting iron and, at the same time, divert a shaving up from the surface of wood during planing.

Chamfer — A bevel formed to relieve a corner (in this context, of a piece of wood).

Cheeks —

1. (of tenons) The wide faces of the tenon in a mortise and tenon joint.

2. (of hammers) The sides of the hammer each side of the eye, where the hammer shaft passes through the hammer head.

Cockbeading — A small bullnose mould recessed into the corners of drawers and doors as a decorative and protective feature.

Coping saw — See section starting page 351.

Countersink — A bevelled edge around the perimeter of a hole to receive the bevelled underside edge of a screw head.

Cross rails — Wooden components that span an opening to connect two opposite parts of, for example, a piece of furniture. They often connect parts such as legs and stiles.

Cross-pein hammer — A type of hammer that has a normal hammer face on one side and on the other side tapers to a narrow flat edge which is used for starting small nails between the fingers (see page 459).

Crotch grain — A unique grain configuration formed at the branching-off area of a tree stem, where branches create two or more stems. This results in highly figured and distinctive grain patterns but they are often difficult to work.

Curly grain — A naturally occurring grain pattern that develops during the growth of a tree and often results in striking visual texture in products made from such wood. This grain can be difficult to work.

Cutting gauge — A woodworking tool with a short, 'V'-pointed blade designed to slice lines parallel to the edge of a piece of wood.

Depth shoe — A section of metal or wood fixed to the body of a plane to control how deep a rebate or groove is cut.

Depth stop — See 'depth shoe'.

Dimensioning The process of cutting and/or planing wood to size prior to developing a project, cutting joints, and fitting parts.

Edge-joint/ edge-jointing Truing the narrow face of a board, usually with the intention of gluing it to another, similarly prepared, piece of wood to create a wider panel.

End-grain checking Cracks that often appear in the surface at the end of a piece of wood, usually caused by the uncontrolled and uneven release of moisture from the section of wood nearest to the ends.

Eye (of a hammer) The hole in a hammer head where the handle passes through the head.

Fence A section of wood or metal attached to a plane to guide the plane in cutting a recess or groove parallel to the edge of a board.

Fence casting A metal-cast plane fence (see 'fence').

Ferrule A short section of metal tubing added to a handle to prevent the wooden handle splitting under pressure.

Fettle To clean, refine or reshape any wood or metal piece. In this book this mainly refers to restoring tools for use in woodworking.

File card A special wire brush with short, closely aligned tines used to remove waste metal from the teeth of files.

Flap sander A series of layered abrasives arranged on a wheel to be used in an electric drill or on a specially devised motor for abrading surfaces.

Frog A part of the plane designed to support and elevate the cutting iron at a specific angle and facilitate the adjustment of the throat opening.

Half-lap joint A joint where two pieces of wood are reduced to receive one another usually in one of three ways: 1. To form a cross over; 2.To form a corner; 3. To join sections end-to-end.

Honing guide An aid to maintaining the correct angle when sharpening a tool. Honing guides usually allow the user to select the desired sharpening angle and, once fixed, maintain that angle throughout sharpening.

Japanning Heavily coated enamel or lacquer as a painted finish.

Kerf The width of a saw's teeth and therefore the distance between the two opposite walls of the saw's cut, once they are used on the wood.

Knifewall A term coined by the author for an age-old method of using a knife to cut a line and using a chisel to emphasise and define that line with an angled cut on the waste-side of the line. A knifewall is used to guide other tools, such as the chisel and saw, in making subsequent cuts directly where they are intended.

Lateral adjustment lever On a plane this is the lever that controls the cutting edge alignment of the plane iron in relation to the sole.

Lever cam In this book this refers to a component of the lever cap (see 'lever cap') that is rigid but that pivots on a pin inside the lever cap, allowing it to lock against a setscrew and hold the lever cap and cutting iron assembly in place.

Lever cap Part of a woodworking plane designed to retain the cutting iron assembly unit within the main body of a plane.

Macro camber In this book this relates to a sharpened tool bevel that is slightly curved across most or all of the bevel.

Micro bevel An additional facet on the edge of a wider bevel on the cutting edge of a tool such as a plane iron or chisel.

Mitre Angles cut at the ends of two sections of wood or moulding at 45 degrees to form, when joined, a right-angled corner.

Mouth (of a plane) The opening in the sole of a plane, through which the cutting edge of the blade passes to plane the surface of wood.

Outcut The far side of any cut made with a tool. Many cuts, with a saw for instance, start on one side of a piece of wood and then go through and come out on the other side. This point where it comes through is the outcut.

Patina A surface texture, which is usually the result of age and use on materials including wood, metal, glass, fabric, leather and many other materials.

Peening Hammering a surface with precise hammer blows.

Plane sole The flat bottom face of a plane that rides on the surface of the wood that is being worked.

Power router A machine developed to hold different bit shapes, which are used for the removal of wood and to define shapes by rotary cuts.

Purfling A border, often referring specifically to an inlaid border used in musical instrument making to bind and strengthen the fragile edges of musical instruments like violins.

Rabbet (also rebate)	A step down to the corner of a section of wood that is parallel to the two original outside surfaces.
Rabbet plane (also rebate plane)	A plane used to form rabbets (see 'rabbet').
Rake	The fixed angle at the fore edge of a cutting blade.
Ream / reaming	To widen or enlarge an opening or hole.
Rear tote	The handle at the back of a plane.
Register	In this book this refers to the act of pressing a tool, often a tool used in laying out parts to projects, against the wood so that marks or cuts can be made parallel to, or at a fixed angle from the original surface.
Reverse grain	A contrary grain running parallel to existing grain but often opposite in direction to the adjacent grain.
Riving	The separation of adjacent sections of wood by controlled splitting.
Scrub iron	A curved plane iron, used in a plane for the roughing down of rough, undulating wood.
Secondary bevel	Similar to a micro bevel (see 'micro bevel') but often larger.
Shooting board	A wooden platform designed to position and hold both the wood and the plane for use in the refinement of square and mitred sections of wood.
Shoulder	The crossgrain cuts on joints that are cut so that they line up with adjacent components when the joint is seated.
Shoulder lines	Lines that are cut to define the shoulders of joints (see 'shoulders').
Sisal	A strong fibrous material used for polishing metals and other resistant materials.
Skate plate	The steel plate used to form the narrow metal soles of plough planes.
Skudding	Intermittent jumps or skips beneath the sole of a plane, resulting in uneven cutting.
Slitting gauge	The same as a cutting gauge (see 'cutting gauge').
Spelching	Broken fibres usually resulting from careless hammer blows on the endgrain of wood and especially chisel handles.
Spindle moulder	A large machine used for profile-cutting wood.
Spiral grain	A grain pattern that occurs around the stem of the tree during growth resulting in a grain configuration that gives the appearance of winding and curving in layers.
Split stick	A sawn kerf in a section of wood used to support a saw blade during saw sharpening and setting.
Spring steel	The name given to special steel alloys processed to retain a tensile condition that resists permanent distortion such as kinking.
Standing grain	Grain that sharply rises amidst straight grain contrary to the normal course of the grain direction.
Stiles	The upright side components forming window frames, door frames, and so on.
Striations	A series of small parallel scratches in the surface of different resistant materials.
Striking knife	A semi-sharp knife, specially shaped for marking wood.
Swarf	Small particles of metal resulting from filing.
Tablesaw	A woodworking machine that houses a circular saw blade that is used for ripping and crosscutting wood.
Thicknessing	The reduction of two parallel faces of a piece of wood to establish a uniform distance between the faces.
Throat	1. (in planes) The opening in the sole of a plane through which the cutting iron protrudes. 2. (in coping saws and other frame saws) The space between the blade and the back of the frame. This is, in other words, the depth that the saw can cut before the back of the frame prevents it from cutting deeper.
Transoms	A crossbar used to divide and/or strengthen larger frames, such as window and door frames.
Wear insert / wear plate	A strip of hard wearing material inserted in wood to reduce and minimise wear.
Winding sticks	Two parallel sections of wood used to exaggerate and gauge the amount of twist in sections of wood.